WHAT PORNOGRAPHY KNOWS

WHAT PORNOGRAPHY KNOWS

Sex and Social Protest since the Eighteenth Century

KATHLEEN LUBEY

STANFORD UNIVERSITY PRESS
Stanford, California

STANFORD UNIVERSITY PRESS
Stanford, California

© 2022 by the Board of Trustees of the Leland Stanford Junior University. All rights reserved.

No part of this book may be reproduced or transmitted in any form or by any means, electronic or mechanical, including photocopying and recording, or in any information storage or retrieval system without the prior written permission of Stanford University Press.

Printed in the United States of America on acid-free, archival-quality paper

Library of Congress Cataloging-in-Publication Data
Names: Lubey, Kathleen, author.
Title: What pornography knows : sex and social protest since the eighteenth century / Kathleen Lubey.
Description: Stanford, California : Stanford University Press, 2022. | Includes bibliographical references and index.
Identifiers: LCCN 2021055926 (print) | LCCN 2021055927 (ebook) | ISBN 9781503611665 (cloth) | ISBN 9781503633117 (paperback) | ISBN 9781503633124 (ebook)
Subjects: LCSH: Erotic literature, English—History and criticism. | Erotic literature, English—Publishing—History. | English fiction—18th century—History and criticism. | Pornography—Social aspects—History. | Feminism and literature—History.
Classification: LCC PR448.E75 L833 2022 (print) | LCC PR448.E75 (ebook) | DDC 823.009/3538—dc23/eng/20220216
LC record available at https://lccn.loc.gov/2021055926
LC ebook record available at https://lccn.loc.gov/2021055927

Cover design: Rob Ehle
Cover image: © The British Library Board. Frontispiece, *The Singular Life, Amatory Adventures, and Extravagant Intrigues of John Wilmot, the Renowned Earl of Rochester* (1860), shelfmark P.C.31.f.24.
Typeset by Motto Publishing Services in 10.5/15 Minion Pro

CONTENTS

List of Illustrations   vii
Preface: Pornography in the Library   ix
Acknowledgments   xv

Introduction: Pornography Without Sex   1

1 Genital Parts: Detachable Properties
   in the Eighteenth Century   28

2 Feminist Speculations: Penetration and Protest
   in Pornographic Fiction   74

3 The Victorian Eighteenth Century:
   Publishing an Erotics of Inequity   123

4 Uncoupling: Pornography and Feminism
   in the Countercultural Era   173

   Coda: A Mindful Pornography   213

   Notes   221
   Bibliography   257
   Index   275

ILLUSTRATIONS

P.1	Title page, *The History of the Human Heart* (1749)	x
1.1	*An Essay on Woman, by the Author of the Essay on Man* (1742)	34
1.2	Isaac Cruikshank, *A Peep at the Parisot!* (1796)	34
1.3	Matthias Darly, *Long Corks, or the Bottle Companions* (1777)	37
1.4	Matthias Darly, *The Siege of Cork* (1777)	38
1.5	Ancient Roman fascinum from Richard Payne Knight, *The Worship of Priapus* (1786)	39
1.6	Frontispiece to Richard Payne Knight, *The Worship of Priapus* (1786)	47
1.7	Reciprocal oral sex depicted in Richard Payne Knight, *The Worship of Priapus* (1786)	49
1.8	Thomas Rowlandson, *A New Cock Wanted* (1810)	66
2.1	Ivory dildo with plunger (1700s)	85
2.2	Footnote detail from *The History of the Human Heart* (1749)	92
2.3	Thomas Rowlandson, *Black Brown and Fair* (1807)	111
2.4	Thomas Rowlandson, *A Milk Sop* (1811)	115
3.1	Title page, *The Child of Nature* (1774)	138
3.2	Title page, *The Philosophy of Pleasure* (c. 1885)	138
3.3	Mrs. Brown and her lover, from Cleland's *Memoirs of the Life of the Celebrated Miss Fanny Hill* (1841)	143
3.4	Mr. Crofts and Fanny, from Cleland's *Memoirs of the Life of the Celebrated Miss Fanny Hill* (1841)	143
3.5	Sex in an alleyway, from *The Singular Life . . . of John Wilmot, the Renowned Earl of Rochester* (c. 1860)	148
3.6	Rochester and a farmer's wife, from *The Singular Life . . . of John Wilmot, the Renowned Earl of Rochester* (c. 1860)	149

3.7 Women with their dildo, from *The Adventures, Intrigues, and Amours, of a Lady's Maid!* (c. 1838) 159

4.1 Cover of the American edition of *Memoirs of a Man of Pleasure* (1968) 176

PREFACE
Pornography in the Library

A single binding at the British Library generated the focus of this book. A duodecimo in brown calf, Cup.702.t.14, holds two titles, *The History of the Human Heart* (1749) and *The Progress of Nature* (1744), anonymous picaresques that narrate the sexual discoveries of adolescent characters. *Human Heart*, longer and less exclusively concerned with genital narration than the more frequently bawdy *Progress*, embodies a model of pornography that I believe has been effaced by historians seeking familiar pornographic conventions in works of the past. Putting it front and center in this book, I argue that it betrays a high level of consciousness about how injustices of gender and sexuality are perpetuated genitally, and that these insights should invigorate our sense of pornography's social meaning. *Human Heart* is held in other rare book archives, but its British Library binding affiliates it with other titles, providing key insights into pornography's diffuse and pervasive history.

Human Heart and *Progress* were bound sometime in the eighteenth century with other "Pamphlets and Poems Gallant," as the binding still reads. It once held five works having to do with sex and marriage, as a manuscript table of contents tells us; two were by Eliza Haywood, known in the eighteenth century for her writings on love and passion. Today, this volume holds only *Human Heart* and *Progress*. At some point, genital content distinguished these two works from the other three, which were removed by a collector who left the original "gallant" designation on the binding. The British Library, probably acquiring the volume in 1982, did not qualify it as pornography. It was therefore never put in the Private Case, a restricted collection of obscene literature established in the mid-nineteenth century. Instead, it was given a "cupboard" shelfmark, designating the texts as more loosely sexological.

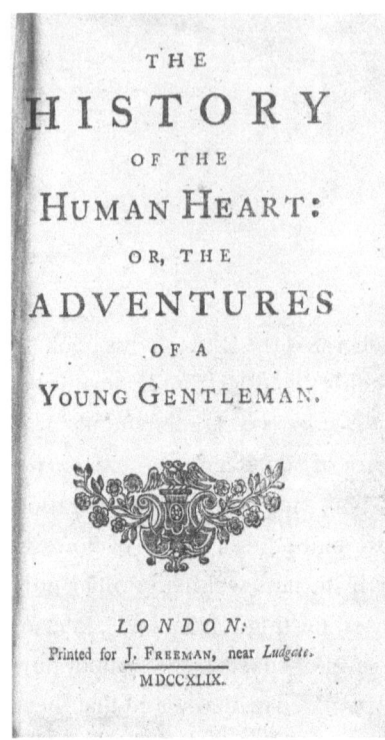

FIGURE P.1. Title page of *The History of the Human Heart; or, The Adventures of a Young Gentleman*. London, 1749. Singer-Mendenhall Collection, Kislak Center for Special Collections, Rare Books and Manuscripts, University of Pennsylvania.

Because of the contingencies of archiving, bibliography, and shelfmarking, *Human Heart* never was counted as pornography, never was held in the Private Case, and therefore it has sat largely unstudied, its highly associative, discursively various structure missed by scholars. Had its acquisition date been earlier, or had it been illustrated, or had its title page alluded to known pornographers, it might have landed in the Private Case, or in the rubbish. What we learn from this binding, as I detail in a 2015 *ELH* article on its publication history, is that in the mid-eighteenth century, a pattern of candid sexual description across a work of prose fiction did not categorically distinguish it from a wider body of literature considering intimate life, nor was such a work expected to deliver sex scenes exclusively. Readers found *Human Heart* meaningful for centuries, and the story of its publication life is told across the chapters of this book. It elicited various attitudes and usages, and its hybrid character made it marginal to bibliographers, malleable to editors, and invisible as pornography to librarians and researchers.

This example shows us that there is, in a sense, no archive of pornography. Ephemeral materials have been destroyed, false imprints defy attribution, digital media and print ephemera evade collection, and changing cataloguing procedures select and deselect material as pornography differently across time. The search terms useful to a researcher of pornography aren't keyed into catalogues, and many materials haven't been read closely enough by archivists to be classified as pornography in the first place. Rather than as an identifiable set of works, "archive" needs to be conceived as a set of practices through which we approach materials relevant to a pornographic history of sexuality. The Private Case, as rich a repository as it is, can obscure the reach and diversity of pornography, implying hard boundaries where there are none. Some researchers limit their pornography research to this collection, reproducing its exclusions; others accept the historical narrative that it separated "secluded print material" into a "closed stack," then grew under increasingly liberated conditions to be fuller and more visible.[1] To the contrary, *Human Heart*—the narrative and the binding—exemplifies pornography as a renegade form, integrated and mobile among a heterogeneous textual culture. It suggests that the genre never was closed, sealed, or secret. Pornography defies parameters—it's what the genre, we'll see, was designed to do.

This kinetic quality makes pornography much like any other object of study—surprising, varied, unpredictable, and defamiliarizing—and it disconfirms Supreme Court Justice Potter Stewart's oft-cited quip about knowing pornography when he sees it. Pornography is often not immediately perceptible as such; and, conversely, its genital spectacles regularly contain discourse and conversations that are easily lost if we dismiss them as mere obscenity or sensationalism. Close reading of rare texts—a slow, decidedly unsexy method—leads us to decadent sexual description but also to all the prose that intervenes: discourse and narrative and paratext that pose questions about social justice, elaborate on gender inequity, and concede that sexual violence is a common form of reining in women's autonomy.

These discoveries refute assumptions that we know what we'll find in pornography. For years, colleagues and friends have joked with me about my research—about suffering the judgment of prudish librarians, or keeping my hands on the table while I read, or asking if what I'm doing with those books really counts as (wink wink) "research." These jokes express some hesitation about taking pornography seriously, but that is precisely what I'm asking readers to do. Careful and dedicated librarians have curated these materials and created conditions hospitable for consulting them with sufficient care that I was able to read, reread, and consider what they actually say, and what they actually say has made me understand pornography as a genre with a unique capacity to envision sexual justice. They contain theories of feminism, statements against sexual violence, and nonbinary alternatives to heteronormativity.

I've been able to arrive at these insights about pornography because libraries make working with pornography feel safe, professional, and serious. Some scholars perpetuate the misconception that such work makes them targets of oppressive regimes of surveillance under which, "monitored by the watchful staff, the sex researcher . . . stages the consumption of pornography," an anecdote commonly circulated about working with Private Case holdings.[2] Legend has it that these materials are stigmatized and their use policed at the British Library, that readers must sit at particular tables in close proximity to the librarian because they are working with obscene materials. What these stories leave out is that a pornography researcher is likely to share a restricted table with a historian studying medieval music manuscripts; or an early modernist working with a Shakespeare quarto; or a specialist examining tiny eighteenth-century children's books; or readers consulting unique letters, maps, contracts, or journals signed, annotated, or written by any number of historical figures—Jacob Tonson, Elizabeth I, James Cook, Samuel Coleridge, or Queen Victoria's amanuensis, to name only a few possibilities.[3] These days, Private Case holdings are restricted not because of a unique obscenity but because they are, like these other varied materials, extraordinarily rare. The librarian supposedly upholding a disciplinary regime is often at work cataloguing, consulting with researchers, or granting photography permissions, of which I've requested many, invariably to have them granted. In the nearly two decades I've been researching pornography in libraries, I've been asked only once—at the Kinsey Institute—to pause a VHS tape of an adult film as a campus tour made its way through the reading room (a reasonable enough request).

Libraries also can't exact surveillance because they don't always know which materials are pornographic. The researcher might just as likely encounter pornography in the unrestricted general area of the rare book room, as I was when I first read *Human Heart* more than a decade ago. I invite readers into the unprepared attitude I had that day, for it is by reading pornography without expectation that we can perceive what it tells us about connections and contests among bodies, people, and institutions.

ACKNOWLEDGMENTS

This book is a love letter to librarians. Their work is to collect and circulate culture, and it is because they define culture inclusively that pornography lives in libraries. They steward the environments where I've been able to read, reread, and compare rare holdings, and they preserve these works so future researchers can ask new questions about them. They've permitted my amateur photography of sensitive materials, handled imaging and permissions with precision, and never once made silly jokes about what I was reading. Working in their orbit has allowed me to take obscene things seriously and to receive the archival gifts that are the rich, complex core of this study. Thank you from the bottom of my nerdy heart to staff at the British Library, New York Public Library, and university libraries at Columbia, Princeton, the University of Pennsylvania, UCLA, and St. John's. Yale's abundant resources and extraordinary librarians especially impacted this book. The Edith and Richard French Fellowship at the Beinecke Rare Book and Manuscript Library and the Lewis Walpole Library/ASECS Fellowship were oases of time, space, and inspiration to read and write deeply, and I made many of my key discoveries in these archives. St. John's University College of Arts and Sciences, Department of English, Office of the Provost, and Summer Support of Research also encouraged research in various ways. I presented early parts of this project at the Columbia University Seminar in European Culture, and I appreciate the Aaron Warner Fund at the University Seminars for its help with publication costs at the finish line.

Speaking of the finish line: thanks to Stanford University Press for getting me there. I have had the wonderful fortune to work with multiple skilled editors who got me writing and kept me at it. Faith Wilson Stein wrote the email that made me decide it was, in fact, a book I was writing, and she projected my timeline to completion with equal parts direction and kindness. Emily-Jane Cohen secured the contract that motivated me, and Erica Wetter helped me understand who might read the book and how to finish it. Caroline McKusick exercised concision and patience in responding to my million questions about manuscript preparation. I am grateful to Emily Smith for shepherding my book through production and to Lizzie Haroldsen for bringing the marketing team's vision to the project. Copyeditor Jennifer Gordon and indexer Kate Mertes saw much that I couldn't see in this book, and their expert work made it more unified and clearer. I could not have asked for more insightful, attentive readers than those SUP chose to review my manuscript, Frances Ferguson and an anonymous reviewer. Their observations and suggestions made this book exponentially stronger. Thanks to this whole team for making me feel smart and cared for, and for believing this work is important.

I am so lucky to know and love people who live in London, and I was only able to work for long stretches at the British Library because they shared their homes with me. It was in 2015 while staying in Tina Lupton's flat that this research really got off the ground. Tanya Canning and Simon Thompson have opened their home to me more times than I can count, and it is no exaggeration to say that this book never would have existed without their generosity. I thank them with love and gratitude for the company, meals, and cheer that make my research trips feel like vacation. Elsa Court is also part of my London family, though our friendship began in New Haven when I was just starting to put this project (and myself) together. She arrived like a miracle into my life, and her compassion and intelligence have sustained me ever since.

Writing this book was a process of asking questions that seemed to make no sense. I simply can't believe—and am grateful beyond measure—that so many people were weird enough to entertain my hypotheses. The earliest of these were Deidre Lynch, who encouraged me to read Richardson alongside the Marquis de Sade in a master's thesis at SUNY Buffalo, and Michael Warner, who agreed to supervise an exam list on pornography during my PhD at Rutgers. Much later, I wrote the very first chunk in a writing group with Joe Drury and Wendy Anne Lee, and I would not have discovered the project's scope without their conviction that I was onto something big. That piece appeared as "Making Pornography, 1749–1968: The History of *The History of the Human Heart*" (Copyright © 2015, Johns Hopkins University Press) in *ELH* 82, no. 3 (2015): 897–935, pieces of which appear throughout this book. A troop of smart and generous colleagues read chapter drafts thereafter, and their suggestions, questions, and encouragement were invaluable: Kasia Bartoszynska, Sarah Bull, Stephanie Hershinow, Amy King, Tricia Matthew, Sal Nicolazzo, Steve Sicari, Lisa Sigel, Chloe Wigston Smith, and Gena Zuroski. Gratitude for the many forms of support lavishly given by others as I wrote: Dohra Ahmad, Kat Alves, Danielle Bobker, Tita Chico, Scott Combs, Al Coppola, Jenny Davidson, Frances Ferguson, Lynn Festa, Kelly Fleming, Devin Garofalo, Kristin Girten, Claire Jarvis, Anjuli Raza Kolb, Jonathan Kramnick, Susan Lanser, Deidre Lynch, Sandra Macpherson, Ramesh Mallipeddi, Melissa Mowry, James Mulholland, Brad Pasanek, Deven Parker, Nicole Rice, John Richetti, Jared Richman, Laura Rosenthal, Courtney Weiss Smith, Erin Spampinato, Rich Squibbs, Dustin Stewart, Elda Tsou, Kathleen Urda, and Abigail Zitin. Zooming into Grace Lavery's trans studies seminar in the fall of 2020 profoundly shaped my understanding of how pornography figures gender, and I thank her for the opportunity to attend. I had two conversations with colleagues—Henry Abelove over Barbuto roast chicken and Suvir Kaul in an Orlando taxi—that crystallized the importance of finishing the book, and I thank them for urging me to keep my foot on the gas. I am indebted to my chairs at St. John's, Steve Sicari and Jen Travis, for the freedom to teach this subject matter; to Lana Umali for adeptly supporting English faculty; and to students in my history of sexuality seminars for thinking with me about perverse old books. Katey Clifford, Kendall Collins, Sarah Guayante, Brian Hicks, and Avey Nelson proved particularly instrumental co-conspirators.

The scholars at work in eighteenth-century studies stun me with their brilliance, creativity, and humor, and if I named each who has impacted me, I'd double my allowed word count. Thanking those who gather at ASECS will have to suffice; most pieces of this project were first iterated to attentive audiences there, and the MLA was my venue for thinking in broader historical strokes. Here in New York, I have the privilege of an intellectual home with the Columbia Seminar in Eighteenth-Century European Culture. Thanks to Al Coppola for inviting me in, and to the scholars whose conversations there continually expand my understanding of the field. Smart and funny academics on Twitter have brainstormed with me and helped me feel connected during the weediest moments. Writing talks played a major role in advancing this project, and I've been honored by invitations to Colorado College, NYU, University of Wisconsin-Madison, Yale, University of York's Centre for Eighteenth Century Studies, University of Colorado-Boulder, Villanova, and UVA. It was especially meaningful to present at two of my alma maters, Ithaca College and Rutgers. Insights from every audience suffuse the finished product.

Now for the mushy bits. I'm blessed with a big and sweet family whose nurturing makes me capable of focusing on my work. My parents, David and Rosemarie Lubey, love me unconditionally, and it's probably because they let me read sexy romance novels as an adolescent that I ended up studying pornography. Each of the twenty-one Lubeys (and Lubey-adjacent persons) that make up my family is a unique and remarkable gift, and my eight nieces and nephews especially fill me with wonder and admiration. The love of my cousin Michelle Ochniak protects and sustains me, as it has since I was a child. I'm grateful to Hassan and Zeinab Abady for giving me a family in Queens. Because they make time, crack jokes, and send me on my way, I thank Heather Connor, Meg Gramins, Lisa Grubka, Susanne Kelly, and Keira Schuler. There are particular women who live in my heart and keep it beating: endless love to Michele Drohan (for pouring the drinks), to Tricia Matthew (for giving the gifts), to Julie Novalle (for keeping me laughing), to Lauren O'Rourke (for sharing a brain), to Aaris Sherin (for telling the truth), and to my best friend Anne Marie Comaratta (for thinking I'm hot shit). How do I even thank my blazing hot chat squad, eighteenth-century extraordinaires Kasia Bartoszynska, Stephanie Hershinow, and Gena Zuroski? (I should start by counting the times they let me text them about this book's title.) They read most chapters, made them better, cheered me on, dissipated my panic, and ensured I never felt lonely during the most isolating times. They are part of my everyday, always on standby. I love them dearly.

Samir Abady and I fell in love in 2015, when this project was starting to gain momentum, and when he was working on a photography project with sex workers as subjects. I learned from him how to look carefully and respectfully at my objects of study and to let them tell their own stories. One of the reasons I've been able to think creatively and write purposefully is because he inspires me and makes me so happy—immeasurably, absurdly happy. Samir is the light in my heart, the breath in my lungs, the spring in my step. I love him with all of me and am grateful every day that he loves me back.

WHAT PORNOGRAPHY KNOWS

INTRODUCTION
Pornography Without Sex

IN THE 1749 BAWDY NOVEL *The History of the Human Heart*, a young Englishman tumbles into a London bagnio with his rambunctious friends. They are entertained by a troupe of female erotic performers who masturbate and ejaculate in spectacular unison:

> Having resumed a proper Posture, with wanton Fingers they entered the mysterious Cave, and heaved, and thrust, and riggled, till they opened the teeming Springs, which shot their volatile Liquids into a Wine Glass, each held in the other Hand. ──But here the Reader will hardly believe me... that what the Glasses received, was mingled with their Wine, and drank off without the least Shock to the Nature of any one present.[1]

A long footnote nearly runs this action off the page, and as I discuss in Chapter 2, it disputes, in inflated philosophical style, the common belief that feminine virtue is part of a natural social order.

This novel was reprinted many times. In 1757, the female ejaculation is deleted from the scene. It reappears in 1844. In 1885, it's gone again and remains omitted in a 1967 anthologized excerpt. But it returns in a 1968 pulp edition. This detail's disappearance and reappearance work as evidence of pornography's uneven relationship to women's bodies, particularly their autonomous and active genitalia. These dancers withhold their bodies from penetrative contact and yet dazzlingly display and arouse their genital parts. At some points in history, it appears, the minute details of women's self-administered sexuality can be countenanced, even enjoyed by pornography's readers. At others, their extreme autoeroticism is incompatible with the genre's sexual representations. Toggling back and forth between exposure and occlusion, the spectacle of the performers' genitalia is not consistent across time, and neither is pornography's attitude toward women's self-governance—the discursive footnote also comes and goes across editions. At times in pornography's history, vaginal and clitoral anatomy is shown to be owned by women; at times it is accompanied by feminist commentary; and at times these elements are absent entirely. In this example from the original *Human Heart*, women's ritualized ejaculation is situated narratively among episodes, discourse, and paratext that qualify, analyze, or delay the penetrative ambitions of men, the very content so often believed to be pornography's *raison d'être*. My research disproves pornography's alleged certainty that heteropenetration is common and pleasurable. Following the three-century timeline of *Human Heart*'s publication history, *What Pornography Knows* looks cumulatively at the contents of narrative pornography from the mid-eighteenth century forward. I argue that *Human Heart*'s complex hybridity—situating dissenting statements beside genital description—makes it uniquely capable of analyzing how genitals and sex acts accrue cultural meaning.

The passage above encapsulates what I mean by "pornography" throughout this study: accounts of genital activity that are embedded within narrative and that connect to a social world beyond the immediate action being described. These episodes are highly specific about genitals, considering, and not always confirming, their capacity to penetrate or be penetrated, their conduciveness to pleasure, and their tenuous attachment to the people in and on whose bodies they reside. I build this study on evidence from several eighteenth-century works virtually unknown to scholars, and use *Human Heart* as a framing case study, given its long publication life. I argue that it and its contemporaries contain a blueprint of pornography long forgotten in modern culture. *Human Heart*'s wayward structure makes it typical of eighteenth-century comic fiction but, it would seem, atypical of pornography. As a specialist in both fields, I'm attuned to the significance of its convergences between sex (pornography's hallmark) and excursus (a habit of eighteenth-century fiction) and find that this one text, perpetually joining sex to discourse, can tell us much about how pornography works as a narrative form—how it wields content beyond ("without") sex.

Human Heart and its contemporaries show genital sexuality to overlap with philosophy, ideology, and culture, and they exemplify pornography as a textual expression of this energetic, frenetic discursive inquiry. They represent what was once pornography's meandering and associative form, a form adept at connecting sex to culture and admitting the infelicities, even violence, of those connections. Penetration sometimes happens, to be sure, but sometimes it does not; and when it does, it is not without questions, refusals, and qualifications. When these narratives do settle into genital detail, they regularly dispute that sexual union is pleasurable, interrupting sex scenes with feminist claims. Genital sexuality fuses with speculation, implying the insoluble bond between a culture's capacity for justice and the ethics of its sexual practices. Such pornographies, representative and consistently present across my three-century chronology, call for a miscellaneous model of reading in which readers balance libidinal curiosity with ethical, social, and philosophical concerns. Not yet pigeonholed as pornography and usually cheaply printed, they invited a wide audience to witness that sex is a significant aspect of social experience.

Combining archival book history with theoretical inquiry, I propose that by reading sex scenes across time, we can grasp their opposition to social hierarchies. Pornography recognizes, I believe, the difference between a body's genital parts and the person believed to be in possession of those parts. The genre remarks upon cultural conditions that designate certain kinds of genitals as receptive and that operationalize their penetration in social institutions like heterosexuality, marriage, and capitalism, and it often registers the injustice of these processes. I locate this pattern of genital criticism across a wide swath of eighteenth-century print (Chapter 1) and track its social concerns into pornographic works of prose fiction, which knit genital action into picaresque coming-of-age narratives (Chapter 2);

then I show the long lives of these texts in re-publication across the nineteenth and twentieth centuries, where they help us understand how pornography continues to circulate skepticism and protest against the way social hierarchies operationalize genital life (Chapters 3 and 4).

This long chain of texts is linked concretely to *Human Heart*, but its discursivity also emanates outward, illuminating the multiple conversations conducted within pornography more broadly. It is this textual ecosystem I invoke through the term "pornography." Rather than attempt an excavation of extant pornographic works—a task that would fly in the face of my sense that pornography is a dispersal of conversations rather than a fixed genre with a definable archive—I have devised a method of focused selection, following the long life of *Human Heart* and the texts with which it was bound, selected, and published in order to highlight its textual complexity and the significance of editorial changes over time. The advantage of this selective method is the focus it affords on patterns of narrative and abridgement across works' publication history, a methodology of close reading not available to studies of pornography with more of a bird's-eye view.[2] My sources contain within themselves a torrent of evidence and self-conscious performance, rewarding close reading and differing from archival projects that contend with absences and gaps. Studying the archive of slavery, for example, requires what Saidiya Hartman calls "critical fabulation" to create history out of elisions and silences.[3] By contrast, my selection of texts abundant with commentary reveals the genre's capacity to relentlessly discuss and prove sexuality's imbrication with social and public life.

Pornography's particular capacity for social insight derives from its insistent foregrounding of genital action. Refusing to occlude genitals, it argues their interactions have social relevance—that the desire for genital access is shaped by a social order and that genitals, subject to social evaluation, confer meaning on the people wearing them. This genital centering, and especially its unsimulated forms in the visual and digital ages, has had a polarizing effect, prompting many feminists to fault it for subjugating women, even as practitioners of pornography declaim its enfranchising potential.[4] I attempt a history of the genre that highlights its political consciousness without taking a pro- or anti-pornography stance. In so doing, I join critics like Frances Ferguson, Jennifer Nash, and Linda Williams, who argue the genre can analyze (respectively) relationality, racial identity, and gender. They converge in the view that pornography articulates social relations beyond the normative and oppressive. (I refer readers to their excellent explanations of anti-pornography feminism's limitations.[5]) I take for granted, as these critics and creators of early pornographic narrative did, that sex thoroughly intersects with social relations, that no account of culture is entire without an acknowledgement of where and how sex happens, and that genital description is a laboratory for studying hierarchies.

Eighteenth-century pornography built in cues that heightened readers' consciousness of what we might call sexual politics—of establishing relationality to another person through penetrative sex that, in the case of both heterosexuality and male homosexuality in the eighteenth century, often entailed hierarchy.[6] Beginning with pornographies that contain social criticism allows me to conjecture that all pornography might contain skeptical attitudes toward the very relations it dramatizes, even, as I suggest in Chapter 4 and the Coda, its modern visual forms that feature real people. If pornography contains this awareness, which I believe it does, the job of the critic needn't be limited to rehearsing what the genre already knew about itself—that sex acts are embroiled with power relations. Instead, I revivify pornography's statements against the hierarchical violence that plays out in sex acts (seductions, rapes, orgies) and cultural institutions (marriage, courtship, family) as well as its speculative reformulations of social structures. Without disregarding the labor of sex workers who appear in modern forms and without assuming they are in every case harmed, I illuminate pornography's three-century capacity to generate resistant social commentary across media shifts, and particularly to clarify how cultures imagine, revise, and normalize their attitudes toward gender through pornography. This analysis aligns with Williams's in *Hard Core*, which finds in pornographic film cultural anxieties about gender, capital, and consumption. Where she turned to film "to ask just what the genre is and why it has been so popular," I turn to pornography's prose-fiction past, tracing how the discourse embedded in and tied to sex acts dissents from the status quo of heterosexuality and heteronormativity, and how we can see that dissent change and condense over time.[7] By focusing on the insights that arise from penetrative action, I take up Williams's provocation that porn-studies scholars confront what they often overlook, "the mainstream heterosexual hard core," that most unredeemable of pornographies.[8] I offer an early history of hard core that highlights penetrative action not as sensationalism but as social contact.

Accounts of pornography that begin in the eighteenth century tend to trace backward to the strict sexual sequencing of the best-known eighteenth-century pornographers, John Cleland and the Marquis de Sade. Contrary to how Fanny Hill has long signified—as "the begetter of the twentieth-century genre," writes Randolph Trumbach, in its tightly sequenced, phallocentric scenes—other eighteenth-century pornographies can be read as both hard core in their genital description and multiple in the topics they engage.[9] Featuring speculation as a primary content around sexual description, the texts that gather around *Human Heart*'s publication history bring into focus an alternate pornographic lineage. To a much higher degree and in a much less organized manner, my examples embed sexuality within a wide array of proximate legal, domestic, and social settings and imagine reform of the inequities they produce, in contrast to the enclosed, doctrinaire libertine spaces of French works. The backward projection of pornography's unceasing imperative to arousal is anachronism, a misreading that has caused scholars to overvalue the genre's sexual content and to submerge the ideas joined to sex acts. This retrospective formation causes Cleland's *Memoirs of a Woman of Pleasure* to look like it has only "a certain blinkered relation to the larger social world," whereas reading this novel alongside its picaresque contemporaries illuminates its worldly engagement.[10] If we approach the genre "without" the imperative to ejaculate, we see that it entertains social possibilities that are shut down by heterosexual mandate.

Reaching this insight requires that we examine pornographic texts with a certain wide-eyed receptiveness, such that we might under-read the content we assume is ubiquitous (penetration, heteronormativity, misogyny) and over-read the content we assume is absent (queerness, feminism, social perceptiveness). Sharon Marcus argues that such an approach reveals queer histories, alternate "social formations [that] swim into focus" when scholars "abandon the preconception of strict divisions" that seem to govern modern sexuality and gender.[11] Approaching eighteenth-century pornography with this attitude, I've discovered social criticism voiced by and around women in patterns that correspond to Susan Lanser's powerful argument that literature "evaded or exploited heteronormative economies" and promised "certain kinds of change" by foregrounding women's attachments to one another.[12] Pornography protests binaries, divisions, and hierarchies, circulating skeptical, anti-heteronormative discourse that we only can perceive if we entertain the possibility that pornography does not endorse the actions it displays. I take pornography at its word, dispensing with what we often assume it will do—arouse, degrade, harm—and listen to what it says about, through, and around genital action. The genre's critical consciousness persists, I argue, through the distilled pornographic fictions of Victorian England; the countercultural era and its cheap pulp fiction; and the digital media of our own time.

What Pornography Is

An ancient term reinvigorated as a curatorial category in the nineteenth century, "pornography" as I use it warrants explanation beyond the *OED*'s typical but insufficient definition as explicit sexual representation "intended to stimulate erotic rather than aesthetic feelings."[13] Commonly, pornography is defined by historians of sexuality precisely this way, as a self-evident category of representation that "aims at an immediate sexual stimulation" and elicits involuntary libidinal effect.[14] The genre, if not the term, developed in conjunction with emerging democratic ideals in early modern Europe, according to Lynn Hunt, a connection pronounced in eighteenth-century works: "If all bodies were interchangeable—a dominant trope in pornographic writing—then social and gender (and perhaps even racial) differences would effectively lose their meaning."[15] Pornography's materialism, it is thought, performs a socially leveling function by presenting bodies as sharing common drives. By such criteria, historians have identified Enlightenment-era France as its key origin point over and above Britain, since French works call repeatedly for narrations of sexual pleasure on philosophical, anti-establishment grounds. French pornography often focuses on the education of an ingénue into libertinage, a conceit that joins elaborate, pristine philosophical explanation with detailed sexual description.[16] Historians of the British book trade reinforce that French titles dominated the market for sexually explicit writing, and they tend to see only Cleland similarly "fus[ing]" sexual description in works that qualify as pornography.[17] English translations of French titles appeared in Britain in the first half of the eighteenth century (prefiguring *Memoirs of a Woman of Pleasure*), and their loose translation anglicizes the originals, bringing them into more proximate relation to British readers and diffusing their highly specific prerevolutionary, republican ethos.[18]

Such diffusion is the hallmark of the British pornographic narratives at the center of this study, which are up to something quite different than their French counterparts. British pornography's arguments are not inherently oriented toward freedom, as Hunt broadly sees European pornography. They are promiscuously associative, finding myriad—even ideologically inconsistent—social and philosophical phenomena to originate in genital encounters. Their topical field is eclectic, opportunistic, far less doctrinaire and specialized than the sustained anti-authoritarianism of French works. British pornography doesn't know its argument in advance; it rather uses the genital scene for narrative improvisation, couching intellectual assertion and cultural analysis in the wide-eyed ingénue rather than the erudite libertine.[19] From her vantage point, we hear that philosophy and materialism do not always serve the purpose of liberation. Where Sade has Dolmancé read a staunch republican tract to the receptive Eugénie in his organized, orgiastic boudoir, Cleland has Fanny Hill fall off a chair in the middle of her condemnation of sodomy, a slapstick move characteristic of mid-eighteenth-century's blithe redirection. Desire arises unpredictably, and ideas occur, shift, drift, disappear, move in impermanent directions. I tease out a persistent, definitive strain of pornography's statements: feminist protests against social practices of heterosexuality and patriarchy. That may strike many readers as surprising, and for good reason, since we often assume pornography and feminism are antithetical. These protests, issued in temporal and spatial proximity to genital description, are given clear voice, then ostentatiously forgotten, overridden, or suppressed by social systems dispassionately invested in imposing gender.

Pornography does not simply describe sex but attends to various elements of sexual interaction, then exposes the processes by which worldly institutions interpret sexual status and affix it to gender or personhood. It regularly objects, often on behalf of women and nonbinary people, to these assignations of social value. It witnesses, that is, the intrusion of culture on the "bodies and pleasures" Michel Foucault believes might stand outside the reach of power.[20] By asking us to conceive of pornography "without sex," I suggest we experiment with the possibility not that it *lacks* sex, but that it contains things *in excess of* sex, outside or beside sex. Ferguson's alignment of pornography with utilitarian social structures in *Pornography, the Theory* similarly understands the genre asking questions about how people are valued within larger groups. I agree with her that pornography is a "performative," a context-laden experiment of genital representation staged in "highly elaborated social fields." While Ferguson focuses on novels deemed pornographic because they assemble persons, evaluate actions, and "carry the process of ranking to an extreme" in the context of utilitarianism, the earlier works I've discovered query the ethics of ranking based on gender, and they make (sometimes futile) statements against it.[21] What we find is a genre indefatigably conversant with its immediate world, a plurality of attitude we miss when we naturalize the genre as merely transgressive, violent, or arousing.

Eighteenth-century pornography makes evident the genre's social consciousness, a point that might seem redundant after work by scholars like Ferguson, Nash, and Williams. But the precise point that pornography knows it is conversing with its world is a strong departure from a key way the genre has been defined since becoming an object of historical inquiry. In his landmark work *The Other Victorians*, Stephen Marcus acknowledged in pornography a social responsiveness—it emerges with modernity, he argues, and reflects attitudes toward Victorian culture, but those attitudes are so repressed within a masculine psyche that they evade clear expression in prose, manifesting as crude fantasies. Pornographic texts want to describe human connection but achieve instead a "detached clarity" under industrialization; they try to dramatize intimacy but stall at "a loose collection of separate organs."[22] The result is a form of privacy so intense that it looks pathological, stunted—an immature withdrawal from a disenchanted world. In this view, texts register the social only unconsciously.[23]

Pornography in general, and eighteenth-century pornography in particular, could not more roundly disprove this characterization of pornography as a site of privacy, masculine dominance, and unconscious expression. To the contrary, it names social problems, their sources, and their perpetrators; it never believes sex is a haven from public life; and it sees genital disconnection as a liberating erotic possibility. Where Marcus faults pornography's objectification of women as an unjust aspect of the psychological needs of Victorian men, I see pornography refusing such objectification, or explicitly registering the process of objectification as one promoted and validated by a world eager to constrain personhood through regulations of sexual life.

This chattiness of pornography, its overt discussions of social relations, might seem a clear instance of sexuality as Foucault defines it in *The History of Sexuality*—as a discourse that fortifies power by spreading commentary on sex. Foucault directly faults Marcus for succumbing to the repressive hypothesis that believes in a nineteenth-century culture with strict sexual boundaries (4). Sex in this era, Foucault famously argues, proliferated as sexuality—that is, as discourse—in social and public contexts. This sexuality comprises not bodily sex acts but endless discussions, regulations, and adjudications circulating around modern subjects and their behavior. (So much for Marcus's belief that pornography reflects a stubborn sexual insularity in Victorian culture.) Sexuality calls on subjects to "speak out against" disciplinary regimes, or to join the "internal ruse" of self-regulation through modern forms of confession (7, 60). They experience sexuality as a truth of identity, a subjective authenticity tied to their desire. This truth production inscribes subjects precisely in the operations of power, since by codifying and categorizing sex in the context of institutions (hospital, school, family), they extend the reach of surveillance. It is in this sense that, for Foucault, sexual subjects are docile, even as they feel empowered. Pornography—its sexual descriptions as well as its social dissent—might appear as one particularly voluminous thread of discourse within this paradigm, a technology of power that "transform[s] desire . . . into discourse" by describing sex, dispersing those descriptions in print, and concentrating them in a genre that conditions subjects' desires (21).

But pornography does not conform wholly or simply to Foucault's definition of power. Indeed, pornography disperses sex as discourse, widely and unapologetically. But read closely, it does not issue or even encourage particular evaluations of or attitudes toward sex. The pornographic moment I foreground, the eighteenth century, is exactly the period leapt over by Foucault, who identifies the seventeenth century as sexually "open" in contrast with a Victorian culture of surveillance (3). Chronologically and dispositionally, eighteenth-century pornography conforms neither to seventeenth-century laxity nor to nineteenth-century regulation, but possesses attributes of both—the irreverence of the former, the self-consciousness of the latter. In contrast with Foucault's highly organized and goal-oriented institutions, this pornography scatters descriptions and statements entropically across genitals, sex acts, and social contexts, offering no synthesis or summary. It does not tidy up the many parts of sex, nor does it situate sex in any one place, nor does it encourage, by my reading, subjective interiority.

While pornography connects sex acts to social contexts and institutions, it does so without making coherent or authoritative claims about those connections. It is happy to participate in the "dispersion of centers" of power Foucault believes sexuality performs, but it refuses to stabilize those centers as sites of knowledge production (37). If modern power is "constant, attentive, and curious," pornography wrests sex from it by being boastfully promiscuous (44). And while I'm referring to an "it" of pornography, it's also important to note that, as I argue in Chapter 1, pornography can itself be apprehended as a dispersed rather than cohesive genre, peppering a wide textual culture with its assertions that sex is not a private pleasure but a social collision. This pornography cannot be said simply to transmit desire, since so often it narrates opposition or disruption. Or, if it does so, that desire is as much social as erotic: a desire for genitals to be recognized as bearing—in the sense of exhibiting and absorbing—social value.

In this disorganized way, pornography hands an agency over to the reader—agency not to masturbate or internalize or arbitrate (for pornography issues no such instruction) but to take note of, wonder at, be confused by, or simply forget the competing realities that collide in sex between people. Pornography resists power without asking to be recognized as resistance, and it does so by dispensing with comprehension or coherence, by asking not to be counted as truth or knowledge. It is as though pornography already knew in the eighteenth century what Foucault knew about nineteenth-century sexuality: that power creates injustice, and so we should aim to disentangle sex from power and the institutions that disseminate it. This dissident attitude, I argue, inheres in pornography well through the Victorian period (and long after), and so differentiates it from Foucauldian sexuality. I invite us to witness pornography, then, not simply transmitting extant attitudes about sex, but inventing, through admixture and apposition, an experimental social vision, one that separates genitals from persons in order to discover how the former are operationalized to produce the latter.

These inventions derive from pornography's literariness, its experimental and elastic capacity to integrate into narrative sex and the many social fields that try to assimilate it—marriage, heterosexuality, rape, labor, commerce, empire. Tirelessly connecting genitals to these domains, pornography is a mode of inquiry that takes for granted the relevance of sex acts to other fields of experience and knowledge. To be sure, this is not the conventional definition, nor was "pornography" used as a descriptor for my early sources in their own time. I use it as a clarifying anachronism, drawing together works that were recognized, as early as the Victorian period, for their insistent conjoining of sex with social criticism. Walter Kendrick, the first to fully historicize the term, writes that "In 1857, 'pornography' meant something very different from what it now means; [and] in 1755, 'pornography' meant nothing at all."[24] *What Pornography Knows* provides a retrospective map across works that were convinced, long before a genre told them so, that no account of social life is complete without narrations of sex. As Robert Darnton writes, just because a "'pure' pornography" would not have been thinkable in the eighteenth-century climate of textual hybridity does not mean the term doesn't apply.[25] It is a useful heuristic for observing the historically contingent ways in which sex acts create meaning in art and literature. Never an end in itself, pornographic sex prompts conversations, discoveries, and questions about how the social constitutes itself by imposing meaning on genital life.

These meanings become evident if we suspend our overdetermined expectations of pornography. I push aside the assumption that pornography will relentlessly arouse its reader and look for different possibilities. I ask, genuinely and with purposeful naiveté, what is in the pornographic text, "without" and beside sex acts; and I suggest the explicitness of the genre resides in its cultural analysis as much as in its sexual description. I also disregard the assumption pornography was designed by men for men. If I am right that British eighteenth-century print culture produced an influential, combative model of narrative pornography, it follows that the genre apprehends its readers as variously gendered, that it promiscuously integrates sex with overlapping discourses, and that it candidly foregrounds women's concerns.[26] To preserve the etymological reminder that the genre "graphs"—represents, draws, invents—sexuality, I choose "pornography" over "porn."[27] My uncommon spin is that pornography isn't consistently erotic—that it does not contain an unwavering imperative to arousal, nor is it monomaniacally focused on penetration for its own gratuitous sake. It is a misunderstanding of the genre, I contend, to find its single ambition to be arousal. To what other genre do we ascribe such uniform power?

It is in fact a misunderstanding of genre altogether to believe any single thing can define it, or that it can be defined by an effect on some abstract reader. Such an attitude simplistically posits that genre issues a "sharp order" to readers (as Derrida writes): the genre of pornography, according to this misunderstanding, would issue a command for erotic affect. But pornography comprises a diverse body of discourse attentive to and candid about sexual materiality, and the attitudes it invites are not uniform. My sense that pornography is a grouping whose parts are dispersed, associative, and agnostic about their effects adheres to Derrida's claims that genre contains a "principle of contamination"—a mark of its own incapacities or undoings—that cause any given work to "participat[e] without belonging" entirely to genre (a formal impossibility).[28] Pornographic narrators and characters develop statements that complicate their forward movement toward what is supposedly erotic—denuded bodies, or genitals, or penetration, or orgasm—and that interfere with assumptions that penetration is inherently pleasurable.

Kendrick sees pornography as "an argument, not a thing," in the sense that it creates cultural debates over categorization.[29] In my analysis, conversely, pornography is an argument because it internally wages contests about sex and acculturation, not because, as it is more commonly treated in feminist analysis, it creates social or legal problems. Focusing on pornography's social effects preoccupies porn-studies scholars who work largely on the genre's visual, digital, and sociological manifestations, and I believe this diversion away from pornographic texts leaves the genre's own commentary undiscovered.[30] While I disagree with critics like Susan Sontag who believe most pornographic writing is "trash," I join her in deriding the attitude that when it comes to pornography "there is no need to examine individual" works.[31] Williams definitively corrected this misapprehension in *Hard Core*, and Laura Kipnis has shown how adult magazines reveal class antagonisms.[32] Joining this company, I double down on the need to read closely, studying texts in reprints across time to show how editors tried to tame their discontents around sex and gender. While some studies of modern pornography acknowledge the genre's "expansionary" character—its practice of "inserting sex" into cultural narratives to generate social criticism—I see it as elastic from its early forms, integrating the many social vectors at work on the body.[33] Scholars regularly point out the genre's paucity of narrative or ideas in the internet age, following the legacy of anti-pornography feminism I address in Chapter 4.[34] I wonder if there are forms of narrative and philosophy that are simply harder to perceive, a possibility I entertain in my Coda.[35] When we allow sex acts to eclipse all else, we abandon a central practice of our discipline—close reading, textual study—and we treat pornography as though it wields metaphysical power to shut down all critical faculties. The model I've found in the eighteenth century refutes such mechanistic understanding.

As must now be clear, I reject on historical and textual grounds Catharine MacKinnon's claim that pornography is mere "masturbation material," but I also part ways with porn-studies scholars who believe the genre "archives pleasure," if by "pleasure" they mean erotic affect only.[36] Libidinal pleasure is shown to serve only some, usually men, while bearing volatile social consequences for others, usually women and nonbinary people, whose protests are clear and pronounced. Its pleasures, though, are prolific if we recognize, as early pornography does, that sexual description arouses intellect, humor, skepticism, and feminist speculation. Such inquisitiveness, highly evident in the eighteenth century, is a feature that comes under editorial fire in later centuries but, I argue, that can never be fully eliminated from a genre defined by its capacity to make sex ask questions of its present.

The Eighteenth Century's Pornographic Conditions

Particular social and literary conditions facilitated the proliferation of writing about sex that began to cohere in mid-eighteenth-century Britain. The narratives I study might at first glance appear to center heterosexuality, but they are deeply uncertain of heterosexuality's capacity to produce equity or safety. They therefore nervously debate its viability. As penetrative heterosex became the normative model of sexual co-mingling in the middle of the eighteenth century, the sites of that co-mingling—the genitals—became especially prominent in printed texts. For instance, Bernard Mandeville, ever attuned to sexuality's relevance to public institutions, writes in parody of eighteenth-century culture's obsession with women's vaginal states and with the social value accorded them: "the least *Breach* in Female Reputation is irreparable; and a *Gap* in Chastity, like a *Chasm* in a young Tree, is every day a *Widening*."[37] Transparently layering cultural identity with its bodily dimension, Mandeville both mocks and confirms the centrality of women's genitals to the social order. These kinds of statements—that women should be chaste, that their genitals are a matter of public interest—are common across eighteenth-century print culture (Chapter 1) and are elaborated and tested in the period's bawdy comic fiction (Chapter 2). There is nothing shy or allusive about these discussions, and they recognize the fragility of women's physical and social states within a heteronormative scheme that fetishizes both their bodies and their chastity. They seem to anticipate Leo Bersani in finding that "[t]he vagina is a logical defect in nature," a genital part that signifies pleasure in the fact of asymmetry and that negates the possibility of "symmetrical partnership" in sexual coupling.[38]

Eighteenth-century pornographers also found the vagina to stand out as a marker of difference, and highlighted, sometimes critically, its overvaluation. They dreamed up alternatives to heterosexual penetration—masturbation, clitoral orgasm, sapphism, polyamory, abstinence—as forms of escape from the impositions of straight culture. In the passage at the start of this Introduction, women self-penetrate, and their ejaculating genitals are held apart from men, who sit on the sidelines. Other scenes show glass dildos, fingers, penises, leather strap-ons, bottle corks, and specula variously doing the penetrating. Scenes that detail penetration give rise to commentary on gender inequity, which in turn gives way to reimaginings of genitals themselves, unfixing anatomy from the subject positions routinely attributed to them. Undifferentiated generically as pornography in its time, eighteenth-century bawdy fiction follows pathways between the genital and the social, alerting us to the situatedness of embodied life within organizations—families, gender, law, labor—that seek to differentiate people. This topic—genital life under modernity—is endemic to a literary, philosophical, and epistemological context that recognized the social shaping of the ostensibly private individual, and it is addressed in descriptions of penetrative sex.

During this period, fiction was a flexible and accommodating form for experimenting with the theory that gender had some basis in genital sexuality. An origin point for imagining the individual, its rights, and its property, narrative fiction famously measured the impact of external material conditions on characters' mental lives.[39] Coincident with dynamic transformations in philosophical conceptions of freedom, kinship, gender, and sexuality, mid-eighteenth-century pornographic prose fiction rethinks which people count as persons, to what degree they can claim property in their own bodies, and the correspondence of those bodies to social identity. These considerations are highly agitated, in the British context, around white women, whom the period's philosophy and literature fantasized might be persons. A conjectural egalitarianism was extended, theoretically, to white women that tested the limits of personhood, making them volatile subjects of pornography, charged with chaperoning their own bodies in a social order unconvinced of their capacity to self-govern. Their conjectural autonomies were regularly thwarted, denied, or punished; women's claims to property were regularly questioned, strained, and disputed.[40]

In eighteenth-century texts, enslaved and colonized women do not signify in the same way, their personhood explicitly refuted by logics of empire. The cultural attention paid to white women's gendering contrasts entirely with the ungendering of Black women under conditions of enslavement, in Hortense Spillers's definitive account; my effort to locate a feminism in this pornography is therefore "necessarily noncomprehensive," as Chandra Talpade Mohanty argues feminist analysis must often be, in its attention to local and historical specificities.[41] When I refer to the British women subjects of pornography, I mean the white women on which it ran its experiments in egalitarianism. In eighteenth-century print culture, British liberalism was testing itself out through figures that could make credible, but usually futile, claims to personhood. These texts, and this history, therefore do not break imperial or racial hierarchies.

White women's bodies were both theirs and not theirs, their chastity both valued and attacked, their personhood temporary and tenuous. I don't mean that this pornography shows sex to shape women's psychology or inner lives (though it might); rather, that social identity is invented and forged through genital action, a sphere over which women did not have full governance. Genital experience, therefore, disproportionately impacted women, and pornography knows this, dramatizes it, and protests it. While texts we now call novels observe the triumph of virtuous women over such conditions, their pornographic counterparts experimented with morally fungible adolescent or women characters. Unguarded by male relations or by social rank, sex workers and laboring women were the conduits through which pornography showed women's bodies in all their genital specificity, depicted clitoral and vaginal self-governance, and laid bare the ways such autonomy is overrun by a culture that condones men's sexual aggression. Because it pairs genitals with explanations of the social forces that co-opt them, and because it knows women's genital experience produced irrevocable social outcomes, eighteenth-century pornography is both feminist and transfeminist, aware of the violence of binarized gender, of the distance between identity and embodiment, and of genitals' potentially impermanent connection to identity.

In this era when possessive individualism was to a high degree defining personhood in philosophy and literature, white British women were a constituency of the many humans not counted as full individuals. C. B. Macpherson long ago noted the exclusionary parameters of this model, particularly as it failed to enfranchise servants. By definition masculine and European, the individual was characterized by his capacity to own and acquire new property through labor. Pornography foregrounds the fallacy of this concept for women, exposing, often sympathetically, that they count not as individuals but as part of the world of property to be claimed by acquisitive men with "the natural right to appropriate something from what was given to mankind in common . . . by a man's mixing his labour with it."[42] While some literature from and scholarship on the period would have us believe women were increasingly treated under heterosexuality as companions and intimates, much writing about sex, from pornography to conduct literature, revealed women to be part of this "common" stock to be claimed by property owners.[43] Under such conditions, I show in Chapter 1, authors imagine women to experience their genitals as alienable and transferrable, available for expropriation by intrusive and often fraudulent means. This pornography circulated volubly and unapologetically among other popular printed works, and across much eighteenth-century print we can see a tethering of cultural criticism to genital parts.

Pornography arises in the period, it seems, to think out loud about the impact of this genital traffic on women. Testing theories of personhood, property, and egalitarianism in episodes of penetrative heterosexuality, pornography asks: If genitals are not the real property of subjects, then what are they? Body parts? Objects? Chattels? Commodities? Things? And if women's ownership of bodily parts can be interrupted, are women individuals? Such questions, applied to the objects in a novel like *Robinson Crusoe*, have occupied scholars for many decades; pornographic fiction asks them of women and their bodies. Vulnerable to having their genital property claimed by others, pornography makes eighteenth-century women an urgent case study for a question Lynn Festa asks about detachable attributes like wigs and hair: "If the individual is composed of removable and attachable layers that it owns, what exactly is doing the owning?"[44] I add: What if those layers are genitalia, and are they traceable to their former owners once they are detached and in use by others? The continual and central narration of genital untethering for women, and particularly virgins, suggests both that invaginated bodies were not fully owned by the people inhabiting them and that women, by virtue of possessing their bodies only partially or temporarily, inhabited a form of personhood marked by interruption and coercion, if not outright violence.

Eighteenth-century pornography clearly argues that sexual hierarchies are artificially produced and aggressively enacted through vaginal traffic, and its candor about this genital contest overlaps with, but also questions, the anatomical discourse that, historians believe, created a gender binary in this period. Thomas Laqueur has influentially posited that a traditional one-sex theory of genitalia, whereby men's and women's bodies manifested complimentary expressions of a shared reproductive anatomy, gave way across the eighteenth century to a two-sex model that rigidly dichotomized biological sex. In this period, "two sexes ... were [being] invented as a new foundation for gender," and this foundation polarized "two incommensurable sexes."[45] This gender binary accrued, in scientific theory, around anatomical structures and relied on social institutions for its reinforcement. I see pornography as another site where the plausibility of this model of gender was explicitly tested. It dramatizes genital life itself, imagining theories of difference in practice, and it bears evidence of Karen Harvey's sense that new gender polarizations generated cultural pushback. The layered conversations in pornography are "rarely univocal" in their assessment of heterosexual co-mingling.[46] If a naturalized, masculinist scheme of difference emerges in the period, so too do disputations of its basis. A conviction in the force of heterosexual, penetrative desire is common in pornography, as is a recognition of that desire as destructive, or fictive, or contingent on conditions that lie beyond men's control.

The persistent strain of feminist protest against the coercions of modern heterosexuality warrants isolation because it tells us a story so contrary to what we assume about pornography: that it is misogynistic, that it aims simply at arousal, that it doesn't tolerate digression from sex scenes, that it advocates masculine dominance.[47] Even as I highlight pornography's discourse on heterosexuality, I wish to distinguish my ambitions from those cultural forces that, in the eighteenth century, naturalized reproductive heterosexuality. Much literature eroticizes same-sex relationships in the period, and I don't want to obscure its role in the history of pornography through my focus on heteropenetration.[48] Pornography, I believe, bears witness to intensifying, and often violent, cultural pressures toward heterosexuality that historians of sexuality have documented. Demographers attribute the rise in population by the end of the eighteenth century to increased incidence of vaginal, seminal intercourse, which suggests, for Henry Abelove, a new cultural ascendancy in the eighteenth century of genitally penetrative activity as "sexual intercourse so-called"—as the particular activity that comes to be defined as sex, consigning the non-penetrative or non-seminal to the auxiliary realm of foreplay and that, Randolph Trumbach argues, stigmatized sodomy.[49] The "changing nature of sex toward penetration," Tim Hitchcock finds, increased pregnancy rates and encouraged marriage while also promoting the penis as the agent of intercourse, pleasure, and reproduction.[50] Pornography, we'll see, disputes this genital hierarchy.

Pornography's Accuracy

Theorists of gender and sexuality recur to a conviction they share, by my reading, with pornography, and by noting the affinity across these discourses, we might become more emboldened to trust pornography's critical insights. Both fields—the gender-theoretical and the pornographic—share a sense that genital relations, with a high degree of accuracy, register dynamics of heteronormativity and misogyny that hierarchize the social world. A recognition of this commonality might make sex in pornography look more like theoretical analysis. We tend, for instance, to associate second-wave feminism with an anti-pornography stance, but writing from this movement shares with pornography a critical take on heterosexuality, a set of insights I discuss in more detail in Chapter 4.

For now, suffice it to say that prior to its anti-pornography outgrowth, feminist theory recognized pornography as a site rich with information about how gender is violently extrapolated from sex. The language they use signals the richness of meaning in sites of genital action. Angela Carter called pornography "art with work to do," a phrase I take as a literal description: it has critical work to do, things to say, points to get across, alternatives to propose for the sexual injustices that impinge on its characters and actors.[51] In most cases, for Carter, intellectual revelation is forestalled by pornography's bad gender politics or its passive readers who are lulled by penetrative scenes. I find this assumption to be what book historian Jonathan Rose calls a "receptive fallacy" about popular literature's "narcotizing effect."[52] Carter believes that some exceptional pornography "form[s] a critique of those relations, even if that is not and never has been the intention of the pornographer";[53] I suggest pornography broadly and definitively protests hierarchical social relations, with special obviousness in its eighteenth-century forms. Through innovations of print and narrative, they brandish an "artificial intelligence" particularly powerful, Christina Lupton argues, in that age of print experimentation.[54] We might see eighteenth-century pornography as art working in the direction of Carter's aspirational pornography. Adrienne Rich conceives of pornography more as a condensed repertoire, an ever-growing collection of sex acts that subjugate women. It entails a predominantly "male, genital fetishist perspective" that "widens the range of behavior considered acceptable from men in heterosexual intercourse."[55] Resisting pornography's own (merely apparent) androcentrism, we might turn the fetishism another way, as pornography's desire to examine the social in the sexual. The "widening" might be perceived, from the historical perspective I offer, as an accumulation of social criticism—accounts not only of inequitable sexual behavior, but of how inequity is produced, and how it might be redressed.

I'm suggesting pornography is not so much a repository for or generator of harm as it is a discussion of what social forces do to people, often women, through penetrative sex. We might see it as a perspectival experiment in cultural criticism, foregrounding the genital as a social field. Sontag argues that exceptional pornographic works distinguish themselves as art by "aiming at disorientation," presenting to readers a furiously pure, and therefore experimental, sexual obsession.[56] I find its strategies of disorientation, rather than in some unrelenting state of arousal and erotic attention, in its undisciplined narrative patterns that hybridize sex with resistance and skepticism. That disorientation aims at an accuracy—what Carter names as pornography's work, what Rich believes is fetishization—on how sex both creates and absorbs social meaning. Pornography, as feminists recognized, insists that genital action is explicitly relational, and as a point of connection across persons, it absorbs and refracts the ways that these persons, in all their differential social value, impact one another.

What I'm calling pornography's accuracy regarding heterosexuality was identified, but I think too quickly vilified, in feminist analysis. Bersani, in surprise agreement with anti-pornography feminists, finds that hard-core images wield "immense power," since their distillations of penetrative action provide the "most accurate" description of "inequality." He takes this pornographic realism to its logical conclusion: if pornography tells a social truth about penetrative sex and the ranking it performs, we must stop having sex altogether until it is "reinvented."[57] Pornography, if its "immense power" yields accuracy, calls for an activist response to the inequities it foregrounds. The sequence is flipped in the historicized account of the genre I provide here: the "most accurate" accounts of sex in early pornographic narrative braid genital action with various and unpredictable spheres of social interaction. Through these experiments, pornography arrived at insights about heterosexuality's inequities. It is from this repeated discovery of the hierarchizing of genitals within social institutions that pornography's "immense power" results. Over time, pornographic scenes and descriptions so tightly condense these contests of meaning that they seem impermeable, void of consciousness, self-evident. My account of the genre reopens them to their miscellaneous history, where we can observe the aired-out, meandering patterns of pornography's connection of the social order to genital life.

For it is by reading those genitals, attending to their cultural situatedness, that we can discern pornography's insistence that sex is a public matter. By believing pornography has something to tell us, we might approach it as the conversation it tries to be. Its widespread availability in the digital age—not unlike its ready inclusion alongside moral fictions, scientific writings, and conduct literature in the eighteenth century—works against the idea that consuming pornography is a private matter or that, more broadly, matters of sex and gender should be relegated to individual privacy. Grace Lavery and Kristin Grogan make a related case in their argument that gender be centered, claimed, and protected in the workplace as a matter of public equity, putting strategically in question any theory that privacy around sex can ensure freedom or thriving. Like their insistence on the activist potential of the workplace, I find that pornography "is a site where gender is performed and made legible," and that can force insistent and uncomfortable recognition of the need for reformulations of how we live and reproduce gender through practices of sexuality, which should be of public and collective concern.[58] Damon R. Young argues that in cinema's publicizing of sex, "women have been made to embody embodiment," a pattern I believe begins during Enlightenment fantasies of the liberal subject.[59] This disproportionate impact on women certainly characterizes sex acts in mid-eighteenth-century print culture, where, Michael Warner and Lauren Berlant note, the construction of privacy had everything to do with publicity and where we can first witness sexuality's counterpublic resistance.[60] Pornography, in the context of the narrative origin point I identify, made sex a common concern and called on readers to perceive it as such, sounding an alarm about heterosexuality particularly.

Trans studies is particularly illuminating to a method of reading for pornography's criticisms of heterosexuality, since it takes as its basis the insight that gender is nonbinary and impermanent, and that it has varying and nonessential connections to genital embodiment. This approach allows us to name and interpret the genitalia pornography displays, having already discredited their status as signifiers of any definitive or permanent gender. In this disputation of genital permanence, trans studies bears an affiliation with the pornography at the heart of this book. Genital scenes in the eighteenth century stage and protest what Julia Serano calls "oppositional sexism," or "the belief that female and male are rigid, mutually exclusive categories, each possessing a unique and nonoverlapping set of attributes, aptitudes, abilities, and desires." Serano believes that left unrefuted, this binarism produces a "male-centered gender hierarchy."[61] Pornographic texts often display and destabilize the genital aspect of this belief in sexual difference, exposing the cultural fiction of oppositional sexism even as they perform it. In penetrative scenes, women and nonbinary people regularly question the sexual advantage that attaches to cis men. They share with these more recent theories of sexuality and gender an accurate, transparent account of genitals and their operations.

If second-wave feminism alerted us to the genital space in which gender hierarchies manifest, trans studies trains our attention to disruptions and discontinuities among embodiment, identity, desire, and society that are possible in that space. Susan Stryker and Paisley Currah argue that "practices of administering gender" can be questioned and resisted by "expressions of gender that vary from expected norms," and pornography is a site rich with these variations in the period where I begin.[62] As women claim knowledge and autonomy over their genital parts, they articulate the difference between their intended disposal of their own bodies and the social positions to which they will be consigned on the basis of genitals regularly under annexation by others. As trans studies foregrounds, gender can be understood as a system of identity connected to but distinct from embodiment. Recognizing that distinction allows for a disarticulation of the heteronormativity that is mystified as natural or uncontested in narratives that elide the body, such as (to give eighteenth-century examples) domestic fiction or conduct literature. Since trans people were not named as such in earlier historical periods, a historicist trans approach, as Lisa Hager writes, can help us "understand the codification of gender as binary for both cisgender and transgender people and characters."[63] As the following chapters show, pornography often redirects heterosexuality by animating nonbinary genital configurations, creating what it sees as a more logical, less harmful system of desire that eschews hierarchy.

Pornography is not sex; it is sex imbricated in a culture's conversation about itself, narrated for an audience, and it therefore takes note of a sex act's impact on the people it involves. To perceive this impact, we need not see women characters as real people, nor treat pornography from a sociological perspective that focuses on its effects, but rather perform the kind of surface reading Heather Love calls "close but not deep," a practice not concerned to bring a humanist imperative to bear on "flatness, objectivity, and literalism" in description.[64] If we read genitals as genitals, and discourse on them as discourse on them, a pornographic environment comes into view that insists on bodies as topics of conversations that explain, explore, and imagine routes between genital contact, personhood, and the social orders that try to streamline them. It might seem that my focus on self-governing women only reinforces categories we should abandon—the individual, personhood, subjectivity—particularly in a historical context that excluded most people from them. But as my source texts make clear, pornography examines dispersed social effects—not individuated, psychological ones—as the outcomes of penetrative sex for women. It shows selfhood as an aspirational category for women, one they lament or reinvent as they variously undergo or evade vaginal penetration. Personhood is at stake in eighteenth-century sex scenes, a revelation pornography stages and restages between gendered persons over the long term. These scenes anticipate Bersani's recommendation of "sex as self-abolition" to divest it of power relations. They know that "[a]s soon as persons are posited, the war begins."[65]

Pornography's social interpretations are less and less apparent as the genre becomes specialized, professionalized, and industrialized. Reprinted over the next two centuries, my source texts have their sexual content increasingly decontextualized by publishers who delete paratext and redact passages that stray too far from sexual matters. At some point between the later eighteenth and early nineteenth centuries, pornographic narrative appears, as I've observed elsewhere, to fall into a streamlining of sexual practice that corresponds to the rise of industrial capitalism. Emphasizing efficiency and productivity, penetration in this historical shift is singularly counted as sex while non-penetrative activities come to be seen as extraneous.[66] The transformations of pornography I document seem on one level to reflect this regimen of productivity. As modern culture became increasingly intolerant of perceived inefficiency, sexual narratives concentrated sexual description, condensing the myriad ways that sexuality previously had entailed critical reflection on diverse aspects of human experience. But as I argue in Chapter 3, this commentary doesn't disappear. It becomes embedded and condensed into increasingly concentrated descriptions, and the machinations required to streamline eighteenth-century sources give the lie to the hermetic Victorian "pornotopia" Stephen Marcus identifies, a conceit of sexual plenitude that "would go on forever," uninterrupted.[67] Attending to editing practices reveals the strenuous and ultimately futile effort of creating this effect.

Eighteenth- and nineteenth-century editors, Leah Price notes, had different notions of "when to skip and where to linger."[68] Where eighteenth-century writers of pornography invited readers into lengthy, rigorous associations between sex and inequitable social institutions, nineteenth-century editors streamlined a focus on penetrative sex acts themselves, cutting out the textual excurses that drew readers' attention away from bodies in motion. By the twentieth century, historians of pornography were reattaching discursive analysis to historical pornography to advance, I argue in Chapter 4, an anti-feminism in pornography that was not originally there, adding to the causes that second-wave feminists had to be suspicious of the genre. Generations of textual "mediators," to adapt Price's observation, "shape[d] a larger generic system" through their editorializing and abridgements of source texts.[69] Their shaping of the genre of pornography made it deceptively plentiful in sex, distracting attention from the concentrated statements it contains about the social conditions under which sex is had, how they pleasure some and disenfranchise others. Editors targeted a feminist contrarianism for deletion; but, ultimately, dissent cannot be fully extracted from narratives that join people to the social through their genital co-mingling. That contrarianism, I maintain, is a constituent of pornography's consciousness over the course of three centuries. By attending more closely to the variegated textual history of pornography, we can recognize the multiple and competing interpretations of sex acts internal to the genre and attune ourselves to how, across time, those contests of meaning became so layered as to be mistaken for neutral descriptions of misogynistic violence.

In writing this book, I've made the decision not to turn away from the sensitive subject matter pornography presents. Readers should know that some quoted passages specifically describe coercion, violence, minors, and racism in sexual contexts. Also, a note on language: I occasionally use "female" and "male" as adjectives, and I do so hesitantly because they risk positing an anatomical sexual binary that I do not want to reinforce. For me, they work as a heuristic for distinguishing among types of genitals. "Female" in particular works as an umbrella term (as in this Introduction's first paragraph) for the genital parts (vulva, vagina, clitoris) typically associated with women in the historical contexts I'm studying. While most of my primary texts assert causality between genitals and gender, it's important to say at the outset that I do not.

GENITAL PARTS
Detachable Properties in the Eighteenth Century

EIGHTEENTH-CENTURY British culture concerned itself centrally with the genital lives of women. Marriageability, bloodlines, inheritance, familial honor, and Christian virtue depended on their chastity, and their chastity required genital vigilance. The earthly rewards for continence were social regard and, often, marriage—a state that, even as it recognized the fulfillment of feminine ideals, erased women as legal persons. This chapter argues that women's specific form of personhood—temporary, limited, revocable, contingent on vaginal status—was perceived as unjust by a wide array of writers in the first half of the century, who noted particularly its evaluation of women's bodies. These writers were aware of the paradox under which women lived: institutions like marriage and courtship demanded chastity, while seduction and prostitution demanded vaginal access. In all of these practices, men, and the institutions that privilege them, overvalued women's genital status; women in turn experienced their bodies as beyond their own command. Literature that touched on British sexual practices, such as popular philosophy, amatory and domestic fictions, and transgender adventure narratives, registers the injustice of simultaneous demands for feminine virtue and for penetrable bodies. While by necessity I engage the period's definition of "women" as people with vaginal anatomy, my analysis reveals that eighteenth-century literature perceived its culture's exertions to build and sustain the often violent link between genitalia and feminine identity, a link that is resisted, we'll see, by gender nonconformers.

This chapter traces genital discussions through the diverse textual environment of eighteenth-century Britain. Manuals and treatises on reproduction, marriage, and prostitution in the century's early decades acknowledge the social forces at work on the sexualized body. They connect women's genital conditions to their cultural and spiritual viability, drawing out different logics of the connection. Writers variously satirize the criteria for social inclusion, support men's penetrative right, and normalize reproductive intercourse. The genital candor established by these texts is expanded in midcentury fiction concerned with British women's sexual experiences. Amatory and domestic fictions dramatize the undue value assigned to their genital parts and the challenges to viable personhood it poses. They, together with transgender picaresques, draw on popular anatomical knowledge to make a case against heterosexuality—or, more precisely, against those institutions that deploy heterosexuality as a strategy for creating and sorting persons based on anatomical sex. We'll see that within pivotal scenes dramatizing intercourse, authors subvert heterosexuality, proposing genital alternatives that eschew cross-sex penetration.

If we look carefully at sexual commentary scattered across the first half of the century, we see that women's genital experiences are palpable and referentially described. Writers trace men's claims to women's bodies in proximate, everyday settings: marital beds, closets, stairways, brothels, taverns, hospitals, anatomy labs. Historians and literary critics are accustomed to locating discussions of sex in genres that concentrate it as a primary content, such as medical writings, prostitute narratives, or Clelandesque pornography.[1] Rather than historicize sexuality as localized in defined genres, I approach pornography in this chapter as a dispersal of genital description across a broad and varied textual culture, and I consider this dispersal evidence of eighteenth-century culture's conviction that sex was imminent in everyday life, embedded in and braided with social institutions and practices. I count this wide web of genital reference as pornography, using that identifier to highlight an explicit genital conversation across texts concerned with other things—public welfare, religion, morality, marriage.

Apprehending pornography as a highly mobile, widespread set of descriptions, references, and speculations brings into view an insistent discourse on sexual injustice and an ongoing objection to the manner in which women's social viability could be so easily transformed by vaginal experience, often over which they had little autonomy. These varied works participate in a common discourse on the uses and design of genitals, and they notice that fictions of social inequity alight on bodies whose parts do not inherently hierarchize them, a discovery we will find is central to pornography as such in the next chapter. Cumulatively, these references articulate how social meaning attaches to genitals and thereby adheres to people, gendering women into peculiar kinds of persons who both do and don't have bodily autonomy. Thomas Laqueur has influentially tracked this gendering process in scientific writing in the period. He argues that anatomical discourse increasingly differentiated and polarized two genders in the eighteenth century, such that "social sex . . . projected downward into biological sex": in other words, a social need for gender hierarchy was made to appear natural and immutable in binarily sexed bodies.[2] This projection, I argue, was known by the wider textual culture to require disproportionate labor and concessions by women and their genitals in everyday practices of heterosexuality like sex work, reproduction, chastity, and conjugality.

Eighteenth-century readers and writers perceived the injustice of mandating women's vaginal integrity in a society that invited men to take possession, lawfully or otherwise, of women's genital parts. Texts uncomfortably count women's genitals among the property that, as marriage law stipulated, transferred to husbands upon marriage, and they often show encroachments on this property to be underway well before marriage. Some literature imagines unauthorized genital traffic to transform women from sexual subjects into atomized ideas and body parts. Their persons are thus fractured and dispersed, their vaginal parts drifting afield of their consciousness. We'll see that this dispersal can also be turned into a fantasy of genital impermanence, where penetrative openings are exchanged for prosthetic dildos. These texts stage ideological disputes around the very claim that pleasure can be a uniform experience for all human subjects, an eighteenth-century skepticism I consider a core attribute of pornography.

Such skepticism is at the surface in scenes of genital penetration. By my reading, these scenes are not irreducibly or even primarily erotic, but in fact tally the human costs of social institutions that organize sexuality. Historians of sexuality recognize pornography as a complex cultural formation but tend not to notice its resistant or critical strains, believing pornography roundly celebrates sexual pleasure. Randolph Trumbach identifies a "religion of libertinism" in British sexual culture, including in its pornographic texts, a belief that "sexual experience was central to human life and that sexual desire and pleasure were good and natural things"; and Hal Gladfelder sees pornography advancing a "porous, transformative relationship between eros and the animal machine" that unites the erotic subject to a community beyond the self, even beyond gender; for both scholars, this pleasure is so profound that it exceeds the physical and enters the philosophical.[3] William Warner has associated sex scenes with the mass entertainment created by popular fiction in this period, and Laqueur sees pornography "linked at all levels" to masturbation in the age of the early novel, solitary pleasures at odds with social concerns.[4]

Across their variations, these accounts of pornography's erotic pleasures fail to heed texts' detailing of feminine experience, which often entails violence and dispossession during sexual encounters. When we presuppose the arousing function of sex scenes, as these historians do, we overread the erotic at the expense of other outcomes—critical, queer, feminist. Women's statements of resistance to penetrative intercourse with men are a common feature in key scenes of midcentury fiction, and they offer two historical discoveries. First, they present penetrative sex as a site of active contestation, and second, they resist the alleged "straight path," Trumbach's history asserts, "of eighteenth-century heterosexuality" and the gender subordination it entailed.[5] It is by anachronism that we smooth this jagged dialogism into an erotics that corresponds with modern pornographic representation.

Eighteenth-century print culture offered readers an attentive, anatomical, pluralistic approach to genital matters. By foregrounding these recurring concerns, my account elucidates print culture's recognition that women's differential personhood was produced in social contexts—courtship, rape, marriage—that linked them to men. The genital activity I trace in this chapter, like these institutions that organize it, is penetrative and heterosexual. Nevertheless, this focus on heterosexuality contains what I consider queer resistances. I find that descriptions of vaginal penetration question its inevitability as well as the justice of institutions that organize and evaluate it. Detailing resistances, refusals, and masculine hubris, texts remark on the absurdity of attaching women's social worth to genital parts that are under the regular appropriation of suitors, husbands, rapists, and johns in all manner of social and domestic settings. Accounts of women's genital experience, we'll see by chapter's end, go so far as to fantasize a penetrative sexuality that excludes men altogether and, with them, the inequitable subject positions that were sustained by eighteenth-century practices of heterosexuality.

Encountering Eighteenth-Century Genitals

Let me demonstrate what I mean by a distributed sexual conversation by first turning to some visual examples that, like genital writing, embed anatomical references into broader cultural commentary. Print satires offer a range of attitudes about the degree to which women might possess their own genitals. Some suggest women don't fully own their bodies, while others imply women are adept and autonomous at managing vaginal penetrations—even to disgraceful ends. Some showcase and satirize men's attempts to appropriate women's genitals as objects of knowledge and curiosity; others eliminate men from their representations of women's pleasurable habits. These prints offer three theories that I'll be tracing through early and midcentury texts. First, women are people who have ideas about what their bodies should do and knowledge about the social consequences of genital activity. Second, masculine efforts to own women's bodies (which men undertake with the support of institutions like marriage, prostitution, science, literature, the arts) can never be complete; prints and texts therefore question if they should be undertaken at all. Third, men's efforts to claim women's genitals often succeed, posing serious material and social consequences for the people to whom those parts are attached.

Even culturally esteemed men are imagined to encroach illicitly on women's genitalia. *An Essay on Woman, by the Author of the Essay on Man* (1742) shows Alexander Pope rescued from an immoral adventure by a solicitous Colley Cibber ("I have sav'd Homer," he rejoices). Pope, horizontal and small, lies before the open legs of a prostitute, his right hand moving toward her genitals, which she covers in response to Cibber's intrusion (Figure 1.1). "Essay" signifies doubly, referring to Pope's venture in sexual commerce, but also, this print imagines, to a sequel to his *Essay on Man* being researched through the woman's body, specifically her vulva. This site, obscured by the prostitute's hand, is redistributed from her body to the foreground of the print. Tossed carelessly aside, the underside of Pope's wig reveals the vulvar and vaginal forms he is attempting to research. The verse lightly admonishes Pope for being "too Bold" in showing his wit; here this boldness overextends into an unorthodox genital content that visually detaches the vulva from the prostitute's body. There is much under examination in this print—prostitution, the feud between Pope and Cibber, the basis for Pope's literary fame, his physical form—but my interest resides with the way Pope's "essay" disperses the prostitute's genitals.[6] She is the center of Pope's study, and the position of his hand suggests that an "essay on woman" must focus on sexual parts. Through purchase, Pope annexes the prostitute's body as literary property, a primary source for the knowledge he'll claim as his own in future publication. While this scrutiny might be edifying for Pope, the location of the prostitute's genitals—not on her person but cast carelessly on the floor—indicates the atomizing effect of this transaction.

Several decades on, Isaac Cruikshank depicts a collective masculine interest in women's genitals in the public venue of a theater. In *A Peep at the Parisot!* (1796), the attention of influential politicians is disproportionately absorbed by the parts of French dancer Mademoiselle Parisot, famous for her balance, flexibility, and revealing costumes (Figure 1.2). Her arabesque opens her skirt fully. From pit, box, and wing, men (among them, Burke, Pitt, Sheridan, and "Old Q," the Duke of Queensberry known for his "lecherous reputation") gape at a full genital prospect, as drawers or pantaloons would not have interposed.[7] Opera glasses, monocles, and

FIGURE 1.1. Pope performs sex research. *An Essay on Woman, by the Author of the Essay on Man.* London, 1742.
Courtesy of the Lewis Walpole Library, Yale University.

FIGURE 1.2. Men peer up a dancer's skirt. Isaac Cruikshank, *A Peep at the Parisot!* London, 1796.
Courtesy of the Lewis Walpole Library, Yale University.

vigilant postures aid their efforts to secure this full view, and at least one woman, espying her companion through her own lens, is skeptical of their interest. Parisot herself faces away from them, her performance unaffected by their intrusive gazes. Unlike Pope's prostitute, her vaginal labor has not been purchased. But like *An Essay on Woman*, this satire displays the encroachment of men's desire as an epistemological claim to women's genital parts; both prints also show these efforts to be frustrated or futile, stalled at a stage prior to possession.

Women's genitals pique but also perplex masculine curiosity. Entitled men in these prints seek access, but forces of cultural propriety hold women's parts at a remove, objects of visual but not tactile possession (though Pope gets close). What were women doing with those parts that men sought but could not fully gain? The gap between men and the parts they seek is pointedly demarcated (we'll see) by midcentury fiction, which fosters diverse statements about penetrative heterosexuality, most provocatively that it be rejected wholesale in favor of sexual practices that do not allocate differential personhood to women. Print satires of fashion offer one answer: women might elect to use sexual prosthetics for genital penetration. The following prints teach us how to see what I'll ask us to observe in fiction: a specific anatomy of penetrative sexuality that, writers and artists imagine, should be located within women's own domain. They imagine women's genital life, like their cosmetic practice, to be autonomous, independent of men's participation.

Print satires of wigs and bustles—rolls of cork used to enlarge women's skirts at the rear—aggregate bottles, corks, curls, and groins into a representation of enclosed feminine practice, one that strongly implies their use of penetrative instruments in the absence of men. *Long Corks, or the Bottle Companions*, for instance, shows two lavishly dressed women seated on corks that serve three functions—to stop the bottles from which they protrude, to extend the women's bustles, and to serve as their seats (Figure 1.3). The corks' functions are non-mimetically represented, occurring simultaneously and connecting the various forms that rely on corks—bottles, and women, specifically the area under their skirts. Pornographically imagined, the corks penetrate these women as they penetrate the bottles, functioning as dildos—another prosthetic among those shown by Chloe

Wigston Smith to cause anxiety around women's fashionably clothed bodies.[8] Their curls—another accessory—float beside their heads, detached shapes with no visual cues beyond color connecting them to the towering wigs. The phallic cylinders imply a shape for the cork (or dildo) that we cannot see and that is available for use alongside the women's other accessories—feathers, silks, fans. These myriad enhancements, also proportionally exaggerated, are semiotically linked to women's autonomous pleasure by the floating curls: like the dildos they invoke, the curls point to the world of material goods that please women in private, through their own use, in the absence of men and their anatomies. The title also invites genital possibilities: Are the women themselves long corks, companions of the bottle? Or does the title refer to the multi-use corks in the print? I read a third possibility in which the title names those shapes that float three-dimensionally apart from the print's other details, striking the eye first and appearing motile and moveable, like the corks that are the print's ostensible topic: they are "long corks"—or, through slant rhyme, long cocks—unattached to men, used to penetrate, plug, prop up, and otherwise tend to the leisured women's desires.[9]

The Siege of Cork makes the association between penetrability and fashion more explicit still. Winged bottles pursue the cork beneath a fleeing woman's skirt, seeking their seals, like the "Maids turn'd bottles [that] call aloud for corks" in Pope's Cave of Spleen (Figure 1.4). The bottles are aggressive, some of them long-necked, and encroach closely. They are at once receptive, lacking their own corks, and penetrative, seeking and threatening to disassemble the woman's figure, their wings evocative of Roman amulets associated with priapic devotion (Figure 1.5). Phallic logs in the foreground amplify the forceful pursuit of her underskirts, a pursuit that manifestly seeks the actual cork rump visible to the viewer, but that implies the presence of other corks, corks of the dimensions that would plug these bottles. Metonymic shapes flank the woman's head, referring to the curls they denote but also redoubling the tumescence of the logs and the long bottlenecks and articulating the shape of a cork/cock that is implied but not etched: a dildo, a luxury item like a pannier or pocket that might be used autonomously by a woman in her intimate spaces without

FIGURE 1.3. Bottle corks and floating cocks. Matthias Darly, *Long Corks, or the Bottle Companions*. London, 1777.
Courtesy of the Lewis Walpole Library, Yale University.

reference to men, their bodies, or their impinging subjectivities. Mine is not a literal interpretation—a dildo, of course, would be made of leather, glass, or ivory, and the woman's fearful countenance suggests not pleasure but alarm.[10]

These prints neither directly tag their objects as dildos nor depict female masturbation; nevertheless their cylindrical shapes and unplugged openings strongly evoke a sphere of vaginal action that, like fashion, is

FIGURE 1.4. A woman pursued by corks. Matthias Darly, *The Siege of Cork*. London, 1777.
Courtesy of the Lewis Walpole Library, Yale University.

FIGURE 1.5. Ancient Roman fascinum from Richard Payne Knight, *The Worship of Priapus*, plate 2. London, 1786.
Courtesy of the Lewis Walpole Library, Yale University.

independently exercised. Genital concerns abound, and the possibility of penis-less penetration imbues the artist's wider consideration of feminine self-fashioning. Their vision of penetration without men is preceded by decades of discourse on the people, places, and things that impose meaning on women's bodies.

Genital Heterosexuality

Visual satires show genitals to be a center of cultural concern. They also show genitals to migrate, untethering orifices and phalluses from bodies and mobilizing them in social settings. The social shaping of genital life had been under discussion in popular writing at least since the late seventeenth and early eighteenth centuries. In social theories, cultural histories, sex manuals, and conduct literature, a candor persists around genital matters. Writers recommend intercourse as central to private happiness and public stability, and they are anatomically specific about the mechanics of penetrative heterosex. Bodies are designed for penetration, sexual literatures contend, and the commonwealth depends on its outcomes—reproduction, national health, empire, domestic stability, masculine sexual right. Leah Benedict observes that "genital descriptions were becoming more elaborate and detailed as the century progressed," attributing the early-century increase to Edmund Curll's publication of impotence trials, which prompted new print conversation about marital sexuality. Through "sexual forensics," trials and sex manuals publicly and medically evaluated acts of coitus, particularly men's capacity to penetrate their wives.[11] Here I locate another outgrowth of this conversation: the resistance to, or at least ambivalence toward, the foregone conclusion of vaginal penetration in heterosexual practices. Laqueur has influentially shown how anatomical writing of this period produces modern sexual difference through its "discovery" of two biological sexes.[12] My sources in this section demonstrate that writers of sexual, social, and cultural theory reflect, unevenly and inconsistently, on the potential injustices of these emerging notions of difference rooted in genital design. The tie between penetrative action and men's initiative is not entire, nor is gender subordination invariably posited as a component of heterosexuality. Women's genitals are imagined as actively receptive and as connected to feminine persons—prostitutes, wives, imperiled virgins—who inhabit identifiable social roles and subject positions. Vaginal parts are often figured as coextensive with women's subjectivity, raising ethical questions about the access that writers at times suggest is men's biological and social right.

Sexual advice literature of this era is both detailed and explicit in its anatomical instruction. *Aristotle's Master-Piece*, the popular 1684 reproductive manual that circulated in variants across the eighteenth century, provides candid instruction to newly married couples on their "Wedlock Actions"—arousal, intercourse, conception, gestation.[13] Its "democratic epistemology" emphasizes pleasure in both partners and seeks to clarify intercourse and anatomy rather than repress the sexual practices of its popular audience.[14] Genitals are not only described, they are characterized as parts connected to integrated persons, warranting individuals' detailed care and understanding. Its anonymous author teaches readers that while "Divine Providence" blesses a couple with desire and progeny, they can manipulate the bodily humors to heighten fertility. The "Genital Humor" (the source "whereof the Yard is erected") and "the Appetite and desire to

Copulation" circulate in both sexes and can be fortified to treat "coldness and dryness of the genital parts" (10–11). Correctively, they might eat "meats of good juice, that nourish well, and makes the body lively and full of sap," a program of self-care that applies to both sexes, since "the Seed of both [is] united in the Matrix by Copulation" (11, 16–17). Undertaken "not too often or yet not too seldom," intercourse should be conducted conscientiously to yield normative fetuses; women are discouraged, for instance, from being "preposterously" on top, a position that risks fetal hermaphroditism (16).

Penetrative sex is often presented in the manual as a collaborative endeavor of two informed, unembarrassed partners. Both will know that for women "the Clytoris...is the Seat of Venereal Pleasure" flanked by "*Nimphe* [labia minora] . . . being of a bloody colour, and shaped like Wings" (105). But a hierarchy emerges. The foreskin, the center of men's sensual pleasure, is sanctified and personified: the "*Præputium* [prepuce] . . . is moveable, for through his consecration the Spermatick matter is the better and sooner gathered together, and sooner cast forth from the Testicles: For by him is had the most delectation in the doing" (184–185). The foreskin is the erotic agent whose sensitivity mobilizes ejaculate, serving the ultimate project of insemination. In this privileged role, the foreskin is figuratively separable from, and elevated within, the larger penetrative act. This passing synecdoche of penile sensation for the apex of sexual pleasure previews an apparent "obsession with the penis" that Tim Hitchcock argues emerges later in the period, an obsession that is disrupted, I'll be suggesting, by counterdiscourses stressing clitoral, labial, and vaginal states.[15]

In the eighteenth century's early decades, discourses on sex within institutions like reproductive marriage and prostitution resisted the overreach of masculine drive. Phallic pleasure was rarely imagined as an uncomplicated, ensured privilege. While *Aristotle's Master-Piece* described sexual pleasure as mutual, Bernard Mandeville's satirical plan for public brothels considers the force of men's heterosexual drive. *A Modest Defence of Publick Stews* satirizes the instrumentalization of women as sexual vessels, proposing that the bodies of some women be deployed as sexual surrogates for all—that a finite number of prostitutes perform the sex work that, left unregulated, would be pursued by men with all women. This measure would preserve the virtue and health of non-prostitutes. Since chaste women's virtue "cannot be effectually secured" in the face of men's rapacious desire, Mandeville proposes brothels as a regulated "common Channel" for their sexual activity.[16] The scheme saves marriageable women from what would otherwise be rape: "the only way to preserve Female Chastity, is to prevent the Men from laying Siege to it: But this Project of the Publick Stews is the only Way to prevent Mens laying Siege to it" (50). For Mandeville, sexual repression is futile, and without the relief afforded by brothels, desire will lead to social and personal disorder. Several negative outcomes await lustful men: they hasten marriages that, in their sexual regularity, reveal sex to be banal and repetitive (35); they overspend grossly on seduction schemes, or are robbed by crafty streetwalkers (25); they mistake lust for love, going all "topsy turvy" (28).

Mandeville's solution calls on prostitutes' genitals to provide public service. Their bodies perform the irreducible vaginal function for which all women are designed, he writes, but from which chaste women must be insulated for reasons of moral and national hygiene. His clinical candor regarding prostitutes ("three Claps shall be reckon'd equivalent to one Pox" [15]) lays bare their social value as quantifiable body parts. But the synecdoche extends to all women, whose bodies are powerfully designed for reproduction and, therefore, for arousal. "Every woman . . . capable of Conception" has sexual parts organized to serve reproduction, and these parts await activation by a penis:

> The whole *Vagina*, as one continu'd *Sphincter*, contracting and embracing the *Penis*, while the *Nymphæ* and adjacent Islands have their particular Emissions at that critical Minute, either as a Vehicle to lubricate the Passage, or else to incorporate with the Masculine Injection: Add to this, that the *Fallopian Tubes* put themselves in a proper Posture to receive the impregnating Fluid, and convey it, as it is suppos'd, to the *Ovaria*. Now it is hard to imagine, that so many alert Members . . . should be at all other Times in a State of perfect Tranquility. (40–41)

Even recent discoveries about the clitoris, Mandeville concludes, find that organ to serve vaginal penetrability, reinforcing—ironically—the stubborn teleology of penetration by men. Designed for reception, women experience a "violent natural Desire" against which their chastity must strive (42). With organs poised not only to be penetrated but to want, seek, and enjoy penetration, women's bodies are part of the modern dilemma: How is this powerful drive, produced cumulatively by so many "members," to be regulated in women who must preserve their continence in order to be marriageable? Their bodies inherently put them at "terrible Risque," and "artificial Chastity," however socially recommended, is insufficient defense (41).

Mandeville's sexual diagnosis parodically naturalizes genital penetration to prove how its imperatives are at odds with cultural expectations around chastity, marriage, and women's conduct. This teleology of sexual difference—women are designed for penetration, men are monomaniacally driven by penetrative desire—uncovers the contradiction posed by women's stipulated modesty and penetrability. His satire asks readers to reverse its claims, suggesting that, for instance, clitoral stimulation might serve a function independent of penetration; that men may manage not to rape even if they are not provided government access to prostitutes; that women's virtue might not be so fragile that it terminates at premarital penetration. He exposes the hypocrisy of men's simultaneous calls for access to permeable "vessels" and for virgins to marry, the sequential use of women's bodies in a culture that grants men the advantage of making sexual demands without social consequence, and the denigration of sex workers who appear, to Laura Rosenthal, as "alienated drones" sorted and counted under government surveillance of their labor.[17] Ironically presented, women's absolute receptivity ridicules a cultural overvaluation of their genitals. Much of Mandeville's purported justification for sexual regulation has to do with preparing men for marriage: the more experienced they become with the ebbing and flowing of desire, the less likely they are to be bored or disappointed with the sexual partnership entailed in the wedded state (33–34). Lying just at the edge of his satirical lens, marriage (unlike prostitution) is not exaggerated or questioned, so much as assumed to be a state that both justifies and privatizes sex acts, and whose lack of variety is likely to erode desire within it.

If Mandeville understates intercourse between spouses, the place of sex in English marriages finds much more notice in Daniel Defoe's Puritan sex manual *Conjugal Lewdness; or, Matrimonial Whoredom* (1727). As its title shouts, the manual affiliates sex traffic with marriage. Specifically, Defoe argues marriage should not be used as a "cover and skreen" for sexual license.[18] Restraint should be extended to the sacred conjugal sphere: "Where Heaven has had the goodness to leave us without a limitation, he expects we should limit our selves with the more exactness," and "matrimonial chastity" consists in the moderation of intercourse that keeps its end of reproduction in view (55). Spouses are to measure their erotic motivations, ensuring their fitness with Christian temperance. In practice, this means marrying not to gratify sexual impulse but to sustain happiness; loving God more than one's spouse; and avoiding the treatment of one's wife as a "Harlot, having no other End but Pleasure" (60).

Defoe's prohibitions are explicitly genital. Good reasons to have sex are: to inseminate, to resolve disagreement, to cultivate intimacy. Sex should likewise be free of persuasions, force, and "sensual Applications" (61). This last category begs for detail Defoe does not provide, but he does suggest that external sexual ideas—fantasies imported from beyond the conjugal context—should be suppressed: "Marriage is a Provision for supply of the natural Necessities of the Body, not for the artificial and procured Appetites of the Mind" (61). Principles internal to the married couple's desire are to be observed; but those too are subject to limitation. Since he's made clear that urgency and force are not to be deployed, rape as well as rough sex are ruled out; and "Bounds and Measures, Times and Seasons always will dictate" certain cessations in sexual activity—a prohibition, it seems, of sex during menses or perhaps late pregnancy (64). The strongest prohibition, though, is placed on sodomy, unnamed but heavily invoked as an "Appetite criminally immoderate," "one of the most notorious Breaches of conjugal Modesty; a thing even Nature abhors," and which leaves "indelible Marks of their Parents unhappy Excesses and Intemperances on [children's] Faces" (64). Defoe's imagining of contaminated offspring merges the new eighteenth-century discourse against sodomy—criminal, unnatural, non-reproductive—with penetrative misconduct in the marriage bed.[19] In short, this text that works to suppress genital detail instead amplifies it, distinguishing licit penetration from illicit and demonstrating that anal and vaginal eroticism can co-mingle, even if, for Defoe, they should not.

Defoe offers, too, a detailed vision of licit conjugal eroticism that contrasts with Mandeville's prediction of marital ennui. Defoe's ideal marriage entails sexual intimacy between husband and wife, an unembarrassed bodily openness in which "modest Reserve and Restraint . . . is taken away" (62). The woman is the agent of this erotic scenario:

> she freely strips off her Cloths in the Room with him . . . she now, without the least Breach of Modesty, goes into what we might call the naked Bed to him, and with him; lies in his arms, and in his Bosom, and sleeps safely, *and with security to her Virtue* with him, all the Night. And this is her Place, her Property, her Privilege, exclusive of all others, for he is her own, and she is his. (62, emphasis in original)

Conjugal possession may be mutual, but the syntax of this passage places the wife in the propertied subject position. Her privileges include her husband's protection, domestic intimacy, and sexual access to his person "all the Night," stripped of social performance. For all Defoe's temperance, he sees in marriage a radical theory of sexual property that privileges women's pleasure and possession—a powerful statement against the hegemony that posits men's wholesale penetrative right as an enduring cultural norm.

Mandeville and Defoe brought detailed anatomical discussions into debates about conjugal propriety and social order. Amatory fiction reverses the structure, presenting vaginal experience as a primary means through which heroines come into contact with the social, for it is through genital activity, these fictions tell us, that women's worldly standing is determined. The genre's coercive dynamics contest Defoe's fleeting vision of propertied libidinal women. His contemporary Eliza Haywood, seeing heterosexuality more as Mandeville does, regularly identifies women within sex scenes as dispossessed, men as enfranchised agents. Unmarried, virginal heroines in particular make pleas for their bodies to remain unpenetrated so that their viability for courtship might stay intact. Haywood packs her seduction scenes with information about the social importance of her heroines' continent bodies and about the methods by which men bypass women's attempts to remain in the realm of the non-penetrative. Non-penetrative sexual activity was common in the period, especially among the middling and laboring classes.[20] Haywood's men, though, seek penetration, and they use force, manipulation, or impassivity to achieve it, repeatedly overriding women's verbalized resistance.[21] Read this way, seduction scenes appear non-erotic or not primarily erotic, despite how many critics have read Haywood; they rather are attentive to disputes over bodily property and the social descent at risk in women's sexual experience.[22]

A brief and well-known example: the heroine of *Fantomina*, disguised as a prostitute, makes a single utterance before her first penetrative sex act—"that she was a Virgin, and had assumed this Manner of Behaviour only to engage" the attractive, charismatic Beauplaisir.[23] He "little regard[s]" the significance of this claim—or even "if he had," it would not have been enough to persuade him to desist. The young woman's declaration baldly states the social value accorded her unpenetrated body and requests it remain unchanged. Beauplaisir bypasses it, indifferent to the feminine "*Dilemma*" that requires her to consider her "Quality" as she exercises passionate "Freedom" (43). Beauplaisir operates according to a different idea of sexual property, believing he has already purchased her favors, and he is "amazed" when she is angered by his payment for what he sees as her sex work (47). His desire and entitlement overrule the heroine's call for her body to remain virginal; and his agenda is aided by the heroine's consciousness, which messily detaches from her ostensible subjectivity. Their penetrative coupling is one clear outcome of an encounter in which thoughts, desires, and actions "tumble," "splatter," and "collapse"—her adventure, after all, was motivated in part by her "extreme Liking" for Beauplaisir (46).[24] Amidst this cognitive chaos, her audible declaration contains a volitional genital statement and a claim to bodily sovereignty, both of which are contravened. Sex plots of the next two decades, and particularly in the decade after Richardson's *Pamela* (1740), centrally feature

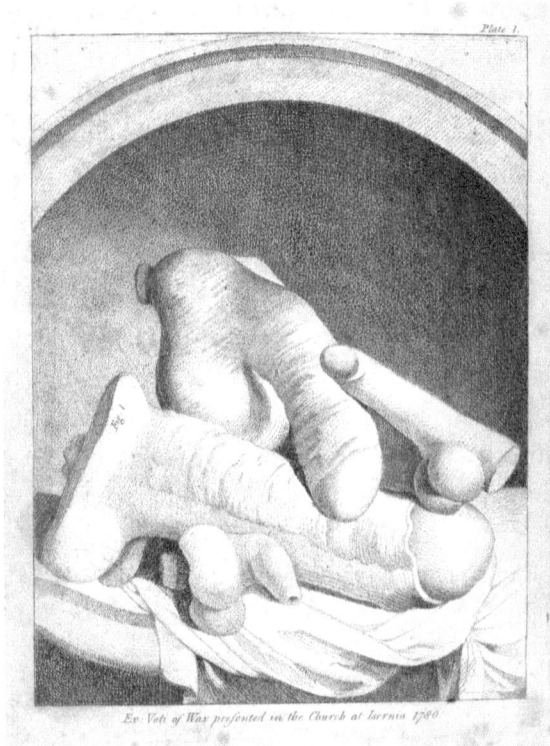

FIGURE 1.6.
Phallic figures adorn the frontispiece of Richard Payne Knight's *The Worship of Priapus*. London, 1786.
Courtesy of the Lewis Walpole Library, Yale University.

this contest over genital property that alights with particular and unjust force on women's bodies in everyday practices of heterosexuality.

By later century, penetrative genitalia are unabashedly celebrated, at least for some, as evidence of masculine cultural and sexual dominance. Richard Payne Knight's *Worship of Priapus* exemplifies such overvaluation. Published privately in 1786, *Priapus* records a cross-cultural, transhistorical devotion to the penis. From ancient Greece to modern Europe, phallic symbols were used to celebrate "the generative or creative attribute" of a divine order.[25] For instance, in a contemporary Neapolitan feast for "the modern Priapus, St Cosmo," waxen phalluses are sold to the faithful, who bear them in church during a ceremonial anointment of afflicted reproductive organs (7). Embodied and prosthetic penises in the form of wax votives abound in this ritual, and they feature prominently in the treatise's frontispiece (Figure 1.6). Payne Knight believes the votives celebrate the masculine role in generation, a reverence that has been distorted by modern religion, which interprets the phallus as an emblem of licentiousness (28).[26] Contrarily, societies of antiquity revered their deity as a "supreme cause of all things" and emphasized its potency through phallic iconography: "The great characteristic attribute was represented by the Organ of Generation in that state of tension and rigidity which is necessary to the due performance of its functions" (46).[27] Chaste women adorned themselves with phallic amulets (see Figure 1.5), suggesting they affiliated procreative power with men's reproductive organs rather than their own. Women's genitals, Payne Knight notes, were represented as *concha veneris*—shells emblematizing the generative powers of non-divine matter, but this artistic tradition does not concern him.

His enthusiasm for the phallic tradition leads him to misread labial or clitoral possibility, even in engravings he commissioned for his treatise. Taken from an ancient temple near Mumbai, one fragment shows an act of reciprocal oral sex (Figure 1.7). A female figure, legs cast over a male figure's shoulders, arches her back acrobatically to place her mouth near her partner's genitals (which are not represented but inferred by the sculpture).[28] Her labia are visible just before her partner's mouth, and the active posture of both figures promises contact. This image shows feminine genital pleasure to be imminent—without penetration by a penis. But Payne Knight cannot articulate this possibility. He sees in the sculpture "an attitude which I shall not venture to describe, but only observe, that the action, which I suppose to be a symbol of refreshment and invigoration, is mutually applied by both to their respective Organs of Generation" (81). Absent any evidence, Payne Knight proposes unfounded meanings to this act: that it must serve a superficial purpose of "refreshment," an ancillary to some (penetrative?) main event, and that the represented action is figurative, a "symbol" of an action other than itself. Shown explicit cunnilingus, this late eighteenth-century historian of sexuality assimilates it to his treatise on phallic worship and orients the sculpture's sexual energy toward the turgid shapes that are in fact missing from the image but that are, for him, omnipresent icons of strength and power. Fictional heroines predating Payne Knight, we'll see, roundly dissented.

FIGURE 1.7.
Reciprocal oral sex in an ancient Indian temple fragment. Richard Payne Knight's *The Worship of Priapus*, plate 10. London, 1786.

Courtesy of the Lewis Walpole Library, Yale University.

Women's Genital Property

In this climate of penetrative right—celebrated by Payne Knight, described by Haywood, diagnosed by Mandeville, restrained by Defoe, and visualized by satirical printmakers—were women experiencing their genital parts as their own, as part of their subjectivity? Were genitals integrated with a body connected to a consciousness and perceived as extensions of personhood or will? The rest of this chapter shows that these questions are posed urgently—and answered in the negative—in fiction of the 1740s, in a hotbed of discussions around women, sex, and marriage that persist between the cultural sensation of *Pamela* and curtailments on marital autonomy imposed by Hardwicke's 1753 Marriage Act.[29] Without attributing absolute causality to these historical events, I suggest they mark a time of discursive agitation around questions of sex and justice—*Pamela* by supporting the sexual sovereignty of a low-born adolescent girl and the Marriage Act by obligating women to greater parental and social control over their spousal (and therefore sexual) choice. Both tried to theorize the status of women's genital parts. To whom did women's parts belong—themselves? employers? suitors? husbands? fathers? families?

Responding to the practices of masculine encroachment described in early-century writings on heterosexuality, midcentury fiction dramatizes the shifting boundaries of bodily self-possession, specifically the question of whether genitals are attached to a self. Together, these texts stage the claiming of women's genital property by rapists, employers, husbands, fathers. Such claims fragment the feminine self, separating the body empirically from the extent of women's self-determination. Women are then socially evaluated as though there were an inviolable link between self and body. If, as Katherine Binhammer has written of seduction narratives, love is an "inquiring subjunctive to be tested and explored," the sexual context of that exploration often entails peril, a woman's good-faith "surrender" to a rakish plot, or her unwitting entry into a contest over her bodily property.[30] Fiction, April London argues, experimented with women's capacity to own property—the marker of Enlightenment selfhood—but ultimately "denied the rewards of coherent selfhood to women" by withholding property from them, reserving that marker for men.[31] Included in this contested category, fiction shows, are genital parts, claimed by women (to whose bodies they are attached) as well as by men (whose rights of sensual, marital, and reproductive possession were backed by institutions and conventions). Melissa Ganz sees early-century fiction making "a powerful argument for legal change" to allow women to divorce and remarry after being abandoned.[32] By my reading, fiction of the 1740s is skeptical that marriage in fact can protect women, since women explicitly seeking a spouse (for mercenary or for virtuous reasons) frequently have their genital parts appropriated by men under coercive or fraudulent conditions. Before Hardwicke's Marriage Act legislated spousal age, parental consent, witnesses, celebrants, banns, and licenses, the path to marriage was shown by fiction to accommodate men's unlawful seizure of property—genitals—that should be differentiated from other kinds of materials involved in courtship or seduction.

The dispute over genital right registers social conflict, specifically the curtailing of women's personhood through the juridical injustices of marriage and property law. These institutions transferred property in women's bodies from women themselves to men, as did sexually coercive, fraudulent imitations of those institutions. While such feminine dispossession has been seen as a "microlevel" of social and economic change, midcentury novelists present the contest over property as a primary sphere of historical experience.[33] They were responding to real conditions. Lawsuits and judicial rulings actively barred women from owning property to which they made compelling claims, claims that were not sufficient, in the words of Hardwicke, "to overturn the general rule" of men's tenancies, ownership, and title-holding in estate transmission.[34] Before marriage, a *feme sole* was a legal person with the right to own and dispose of property, though we know from Clarissa's inheritance of her grandfather's dairy-house such independence could cause high anxiety in a family seeking land and titles.[35] Gillian Skinner considers the *feme sole* a legal theory more than an empirical category, since women were commonly destined for marriage and, if they were not, they lacked the training necessary to understand or assert their property rights.[36] Ruth Perry's account of "the great disinheritance" of daughters illustrates that a midcentury emphasis on conjugal bonds, which replaced consanguineal ties allowing daughters to inherit, actively concentrated property with men: "the daughter's significance as the carrier of a particular bloodline became less important than her instrumental value to her family of destination in aggrandizing their ambition or reproducing their lineage."[37]

After marriage, a woman's personhood, rights, and property were absorbed into those of her husband. A few forms of property, such as pin money or trusts, existed for women within marriage, but they were often badly overseen by male guardians (like Haywood's *Betsy Thoughtless*'s inattentive brothers). Nor did relatives reliably write settlements to secure women's property after marriage. As Susan Staves argues, the shift from dower to jointure meant that widows' property became subject to contingencies. Jointure, unlike dower's default guarantee of one-third of a late husband's property, was settled prior to marriage and could be badly negotiated, canceled by remarriage, or retroactively read into marriage settlements that did not explicitly stipulate it in lieu of dower; it at times guaranteed not real property—land and habitation—but stocks or bonds, and courts "indiscriminately . . . substituted" personal property for the immovable real property jointure was supposed to secure. Courts' interpretations of property law tied land to patriline, manipulating the concept of alienability in particular to enforce men's ownership and to interrupt women's occupancy. Land and estate administrators "exhibited much ingenuity" to "promote alienability" in cases of women's claims.[38]

Midcentury fictions, we'll see, objected to the forcible alienability of women's property, showing that their genitals were counted within this peculiarly transferrable category, and that their separation from women's persons was violently imposed. Often, women characters experience their bodies as unduly atomized by these practices, which proceed without substantial reference to the present or future they envision. Such atomization favors instead men's plans for their genital use.[39] Episodes of genital estrangement mark this peculiar separation of women from their bodies, a process that undermines their autonomy and transforms their social status. Genitals become detached not only from consent but from any degree of subjectivity these characters possess. We know from work by Jonathan Kramnick and Sandra Macpherson that eighteenth-century fiction was invested not singularly in building interiority but in defining persons as sites where worldly conditions congeal.[40] Contingent and unstable, subjectivity, women's in particular, does not assume any one irreducible form or interior content. Frances Ferguson's analysis of the history of rape law shows how misguided an overinvestment in women's interiority can be.[41] Rather, I observe in fiction a sharp attention to the collision of external and internal forces around matters of sexual impingement. Characters articulate hesitancies, resistances, and refusals; they perceive and describe genital encroachment as unwelcome and deeply consequential to their futures. They experience penetration as an unauthorized acquisition of property—a formulation that invokes not only rape, most obviously, but also marriage, itself a practice of property redistribution.

Vaginal genitals present as contested objects within this property transfer. As thing theorists suggest, objects become things when they are disconnected from clearly defined ownership—in Lorraine Daston's words, "concentrat[ing] complex relationships that cohere without being logical" (recall Pope's vaginal wig from Figure 1.1).[42] Jonathan Lamb defines things as objects that have been altered by "[i]nvasions of property from outside, in the form of theft or war," their owners beleaguered subjects "thinned by affliction."[43] Loosed from ownership, things cause anxiety for Enlightenment subjects whose personhood is defined by the striving for property; they force questions, Lynn Festa writes, around who counted as a possessive individual and "which kinds of property are to be deemed essential to personhood."[44] Genitals, fiction shows, were owned by the *feme sole* temporarily but, under persuasions toward heterosexuality and marriage, became untethered from a woman's possession even while housed by her body. Fiction thus presents genitals as such things—claimed by another, detached from the self, lacking a clear domain—and explores the grave ramifications of contested vaginal ownership, the onerous "thinning" of women's self-determination caused by men's claims to their bodies.

I believe that writers were aware of this illogic within feminine personhood—that women could technically own property but didn't, that their genitals were putatively aspects of their subjectivity but were property under dispute—in plots of sexual acquisition. Authors, to dramatize this difficulty, replay moments where women's genitals manage to dispute and disrupt schemes of sexual conquest, and as a result, make plain the social relations that underwrite such efforts. When genitals, becoming things, threaten to "stop working" in expected ways—when their penetrative use is refused, as in fictional representations of virginal sex—vaginal parts tell us stories about their imbrication in social relations.[45] Genitals shift from their place on and in the feminine person to a less proximate, opaque realm of claim and use by another; they are, according to fiction concerned with women's sexual experience, transferrable, their inherent value mutable, their relationship to the subject flexible and mysterious, and their permeability to extra-personal conditions "strange," as we'll hear Clarissa Harlowe remark.

For morally upright heroines, the demarcation of property is apparent, considered, and traumatic when breached. Richardson's Pamela staunchly understands her body, unlike her labor, to be outside of what Mr. B can claim as property, an assertion that earns her a slap from Mrs. Jewkes.[46] Early in the novel, on considering leaving Mr. B's estate, what holds Pamela back is confusion about what she might justly take with her. Distinctions of space, property, and legitimate possession co-mingle for Pamela as she reasons how rightfully to depart, and central to these proprietary questions is her own body. Gifts, clothes, and her body are things that make Pamela vulnerable to either suspicion or rape on the road: "I was at a Loss to resolve whether to take away the Things he had given me or no, and how to take them away: Sometimes I thought to leave them behind me, and only go with the clothes on my back." Her maid's clothing, though, would appear ostentatious outside the estate, leaving her open to sexual assault and to accusations of robbery, in that order: "being pretty well dress'd, I might come to some harm, almost as bad as what I would run away from; and then may-be, thought I, it will be reported, I have stolen something" (24–25). "Some harm" looms at home and outside. Encountering this harm abroad would result in a sequence of problems: first rape, then, Pamela's syntax suggests, an accusation of her thievery against Mr. B. The discovery of her virginal genitals through a penetrative assault, in other words, would lay bare the unpenetrated vaginal property she displaced from Mr. B's estate, the "stolen something." Her genitals, associated with that category of things (gifts, clothes) she's not sure she owns, are contestable property not only within Mr. B's vicious domain, but on the road that unfolds beyond it. Working to adhere to chastity as she understands it, Pamela will struggle indefatigably to keep her genitals under her own possession until they marry. Mr. B's detention of Pamela is, by this reading, a literal "Bondage," an unjust claiming of property in the human person (119).

Richardson ultimately preserves Pamela's virginity until marriage, clearly stating that in the moral world of the novel, her genital property should not, must not, be claimed outside of legal and spiritual institutions.

Clarissa presents a darker, murkier account. Stranded without allies in morally corrupt places, Clarissa's material, spiritual, and bodily property is under steady and violent appropriation by father, brother, uncles, and suitors. It is through Lovelace's assault, of course, that the novel most exhaustively details the violent methods and alienating consequences of vaginal sexual violence. Writing post-rape to her intimates, Clarissa uses the language of alienation—of the "strange"—to relate what has transpired. To Hannah, her former maid: "Strange things have happened to me since you were dismissed my service (so sorely against my will)."[47] Syntactically plastic, this sentence applies "sorely" to the affective impact of Hannah's departure and to the "strange" sexual assault, physicalized through the adverb. Surely Richardson expects his reader to understand the adverb applies to both forms of pain. He also, in using "strange," enriches readers' comprehension of the breadth of ways in which Clarissa has been harmed by Lovelace. What "ha[s] happened" is that Lovelace has assaulted Clarissa and vaginally penetrated her: about this event she is aware and eloquent.[48] What is "strange" exceeds the odd or unfamiliar: her own body has been altered, made foreign, through an act in which she did not participate. His assault is not only conceptually foreign or counterintuitive to her; it is an alteration of her person that has made it alien to her and was effected through fraudulent, coercive power.[49]

"Strange" evokes a breadth of meaning that begins to get at the extent of the violence done to the heroine, since it refers to forces outside of and not known by the self, false or contested claims of ownership, and difference in kind or kinship.[50] "Strange things have happened to me," she repeats in another letter to Mrs. Norton, "very strange things!" (978). Lovelace's coercions make Clarissa's actions external to herself, even before the penetrative assault: "my indiscretion stares me in the face," she writes to Anna of having departed Harlowe Place (380). Lovelace famously truncates the complexity and duration of Clarissa's experiences of alienation, writing of her rape only that "[t]he affair is over. Clarissa lives" (883). Readers apprehended his declaration as a "dreadful sentence too shocking and barbarous . . . for publication," a brutal distillation that ignores the various ways that penetration compromises her personhood.[51] Lovelace's form of heterosexuality cancels all possible life directions for Clarissa but one, in Richardson's view: spiritual resilience on earth and communion with her god in an afterlife. Readers requested a more forgiving future for the heroine, but Richardson adhered to a likely outcome: that a raped woman was ineligible for the socially viable subject positions available in mid-eighteenth-century England.[52] Clarissa's genitals have nothing to do with her consciousness, as proven by her ethically intact emergence from Lovelace's assault;[53] but the world, Richardson implies, evaluates women not on intention or lucidity relative to sex acts, but on the ways their bodies are altered by those acts. Social meaning is assigned not to purity of intention but to vaginal intactness. An impeccable moral interior cannot override, Richardson laments, an illicitly penetrated body in the eyes of the world.

After Richardson, and as she had since her early fiction, Haywood continues to experiment with moral plasticity in her heroines, loosing them serially into sexual encounters not only to track their effects on women (in *Fantomina*, pregnancy; in *The Injur'd Husband*, social ruin; in *Betsy Thoughtless*, an improbably intact but well-tested virtue), but to expose the many environments that enabled men to lay penetrative claim to women's bodies. *Anti-Pamela* emphasizes the tenuousness of women's autonomy in various spaces. Here Haywood tests the possible outcomes for a morally mutable heroine with few spiritual and material resources for shepherding her genital status. Syrena Tricksy's first penetrative intercourse merges genital, possessive, and topographical terms to show the collapse of autonomy under fraudulent, coercive heterosexual pressure. Whereas *Fantomina*'s aristocratic heroine deftly went on to sexualize different meeting places with Beauplaisir, the non-elite Syrena improvises her way through various social, commercial, and domestic spaces in which men design (and succeed) to claim to her body.[54] Syrena's genitals within those spaces cease being her own property. She loses her virginity to the officer Vardine inside a tavern, a space whose threatening resonance is emphasized through its ostentatious repetition. Vardine "attempt[s] to pull [her] into the Tavern" on their second meeting, an attempt that "frighted [her] in good earnest," and that she angrily declines.[55] Mrs. Tricksy concurs, disliking Vardine's "asking [her] to go into the Tavern" (67). The tavern was, for a bachelor like

Vardine, a source of creature comforts in the midcentury city.[56] Hosting gentleman's clubs, sex workers, and couples seeking private rooms, taverns facilitated a spectrum of interactions, from urbane sociability to sexual commerce, and often these aspects overlapped. Samuel Pepys fucked in the main room of a tavern (from behind, a position determined by the room's paucity of furniture); some of Joshua Reynolds's models were sex workers he met around the Turk's Head in Soho.[57] The tavern confirms Vardine as an agent of sexual transaction and Syrena as its commodity—a role she strives against, intent as she is on a profitable marriage.[58] Syrena understands the tavern's implications: it is a place in which she will lack sexual protections, in which her body will be available for sexual use.

On their next meeting, Syrena's anxiety is redoubled by the narrator, who traces with precision the spatial steps that move Syrena from the safety of public view to the tavern's recesses. To escape a storm, Syrena "is obliged to stand up in a Tavern entry" with Vardine, who then reasons he should remove Syrena from "the View of every body" and so coerces her inside to a private room, where he "made her" drink many glasses of wine and try on stockings until "[s]he lost all Memory of the Place, or Danger she was in." The narrator emphasizes Vardine's territorial advances: he "gain'd" "ground," "pursu[ed] the attack," "bombarded her . . . fast" with "Speeches . . . Pressures, Kisses" and wine such that "at length, the Town was wholly his" (75–76). The encounter leaves Syrena weeping. The acquisitive description is familiar. Mandeville wrote in *Publick Stews*, drawing on a long Petrarchan tradition, that virtuous women's defense against seduction "may be compar'd to Towns strongly fortify'd both by Art and Nature, which, without Treachery, are safe from any sudden Attacks, and must be reduc'd by long and regular Sieges," whereas amorous women "may not unjustly be compar'd to a Town well garrison'd, but whose mutinous unruly *Inhabitants* are strongly inclin'd to revolt and *let in* the Enemy" (43).[59] Town and vagina are the substantial properties to be guarded, and once ceded cannot be reclaimed. The following day, Syrena and Vardine go "to the same Tavern they had been in before" (78). Readers know what this means: intercourse happens again, its staging not necessary since Syrena can no longer decline. She ceases to own her body's availability for sex, her genitals now things "freed from the dominion of an owner, moving with varying degrees of impetus toward another."⁶⁰ When Mrs. Tricksy discovers Syrena's ensuing pregnancy, she uses language that fuses her feminine insight with her daughter's genital change: Mrs. Tricksy's "Penetration did not permit her to continue long in the dark as to the Cause [of Syrena's illness]. She soon discover'd that a too near Conversation with a Man had made the Alteration" (83). Proximity and appropriation result in definitive, evident anatomical change.

Spatial references detail Vardine's sexual gains, which begin in a doorway and culminate in vaginal penetration. We are to see, along with Haywood, continuity between masculine right in social domains and the exercise of that right in coercive sexual contexts. While Thomas King believes English "manliness" was in this period "tenuous, limited to certain spaces and times," Haywood shows that in the absence of other men, any man with the real or seeming resources to purchase stockings or ale might also claim sexual access to an unprotected woman (see also *Betsy Thoughtless*'s Fineer, a rogue dressed as an aristocrat who nearly rapes Betsy).⁶¹ Some women may have treated such transactions lightly—*Joseph Andrews*'s chambermaid Betty is unfussed by the groping of travelers, as is *Fantomina*'s heroine, post-penetration—but fictions that stage a woman's attempt to remain unpenetrated highlight the injustice not only of masculine overreach but also of the social and commercial conditions that activate men's privilege.

The pattern is repeated after Vardine has abandoned Syrena. Now employed by an elderly woman in an aristocratic home, Syrena is serially propositioned by her mistress's son and grandson. The former accosts her in all manner of domestic spaces—his study, the lady's chamber, "the Gallery, or the Stairs, or wherever we meet" (111)—the latter repeatedly in her lady's "dangerous Closet," distorting that room's associations with solitude, feminine autonomy, or political enfranchisement (103).⁶² Like the tavern, domestic rooms become a staging ground for successive non-marital claims to Syrena's body by men, suggesting that sites across the spectrum from social to domestic facilitate women's transfiguration from owners of their own bodily property to disenfranchised persons. These sites differ in the sorts of autonomy they theoretically offer Syrena: her domestic service, as Pamela loudly argued, does not entail sex work, her own money should sustain her at the stocking shop, and she should be able to refuse entrance into the tavern. But these features of personhood don't hold up, Haywood suggests, in worldly contexts, all of which facilitate men's pursuits.

Spatial and proprietary terms refer concretely to penetrative sex, signaling women's tenuous claims to property in general, and to genital property in particular, in varied social and domestic contexts. Broadly hermeneutic rather than syntactically local, this "living metaphor" establishes "proximity" between two concepts—tavern and genitalia—that yields "a new way of seeing" the penetration of Syrena: as a fraudulent acquisition of property in her body, and therefore as a rape.[63] Her genitals are made strange, the property of another, in a sex act that—like marriage and prostitution—requires a vaginal person but not her personhood. Syrena—low-born, morally compromised, and mercenary—forges ahead as she must in *Anti-Pamela*, feigning some degree of modesty with succeeding men as she pursues a profitable marriage or settlement.

All of this (Syrena's genital dispossession, Pamela's recognition of property in her body, the "strange" rape of Clarissa) demonstrates an explicit thread of commentary in midcentury fiction about the tenuousness and mutability of genital status. These texts do not sublimate but refer explicitly to the particular genital situations of women characters who seek, in different ways and for different reasons, to be exempt from the sex acts to which they are called. Tapping into a popular sexual discourse I outlined earlier, these texts place genital action at the heart of decisive encounters and diverse spaces. Writers call attention to the specifically genital situation of women who try to exert autonomy over how their bodies are used. These characters are not prudes, not void of desire, not anti-sexual: they are surprised by the genital incursions of men who seek transactions they did not authorize. Routine forms of sexual use alienated genitals from subjects whose personhood was invoked (do you consent to penetrative sex? do you take this man as your husband?) so that it immediately could be erased, through violence or marriage or property law—practices that shared a conceptual basis in eighteenth-century fiction imagining the experiences of women.

Genital Drift

Women in midcentury fiction attempt to decline participation in penetrative heterosexuality, and in so doing they clarify the connection between genital alienation and differential personhood: once their genital parts cease to be their own property, their social viability suffers. Women characters, we've seen, call for other forms of existence, temporarily or permanently, than those that make them vaginally available. Binhammer writes that Clarissa seeks to "disarticulat[e] female knowledge from sexual experience," a formulation that reminds us that some eighteenth-century women tried to claim full personhood by repudiating sexual institutions: they wished to remain outside the tavern, unpenetrated, even (for moneyed women) unmarried.[64] The remainder of this chapter turns to midcentury fictions that imagined how their genital estrangement might be experienced as non-injurious to women. "Sapphic picaresques"—Susan Lanser's term for irreverent adventure fictions featuring "same-sex affiliations" between women—reinvent the forcible alienability of women's property discussed by Staves, imagining the detachment of genital property as nonharmful, pleasurable, and even volitional.[65] These experiments with genital alienability transpire in sex acts involving women or nonbinary people, upholding Lanser's view that a queer countertradition persistently unsettles the heteronormative plots that have been the focus in histories of prose fiction. In the absence of anatomical penises, vaginal parts are imagined as impermanently connected to women as they seek alternatives to penetrative heterosex.

John Cleland's *Memoirs of a Woman of Pleasure*, an effort to encyclopedically record the sex acts of its prostitute heroine and her peers, evaluates the penetrating function of men's organs, those "unwieldy machine[s]" and "splitter[s]" that populate nearly every page (73, 140). In some instances, they traumatize Fanny, as in her first heterosexual encounter, a rape attempt by a man who has purchased her maidenhead. Andrea Haslanger asks us to recognize the novel's first-person "I" as "a vehicle through which women express their adherence to a normative model of sexual function"—penetrability.[66] Same-sex episodes, though, disperse that figure of a unified self, and do so non-injuriously, untethering genital sensation from ostensible centers of subjectivity such as the body, consciousness, and first-person narration. Even this allegedly phallocentric novel "has difficulty leaving the sapphic behind," notes Lanser, presenting genital penetration between women as different in kind from heterosexual intercourse.[67] For Lisa Moore, the "unmooring of the normative codes of heterosexuality seems to cast conventionally gendered bodies adrift," and this drifting, I believe, allows women sensuous experience that does not damage them or change their social standing.[68] This queerness moves past the very notion of a centralized subject, a construct not often available to sexually trafficked women and wives.

Cleland establishes this outcome of sapphic experience early in the novel, immediately upon fifteen-year-old Fanny's arrival in London. Her first encounter with bedfellow Phoebe, a more experienced prostitute in Mrs. Brown's employ, leaves her unharmed, unmarked by the invasive appropriations associated with male partners. The narration separates genital feeling from a coherent, unified subject, fantasizing a sexual experience that insulates the feminine self from consequential changes of social standing. Her "ability to switch between internal and external perspectives," which for Haslanger documents heterosexual harm, here affirms vaginal sensation that arrives without social injury.[69] Fanny is at first "tame and passive," then atomizes when explored by Phoebe during her first night at Mrs. Brown's (11). Sensations disorient Fanny but do not prompt the "terrors" she will soon experience during the rape attempt (19). Here, her genitals stand separate and outward-facing: "every part of me was open" (11). Upon contact with Phoebe, the genitals that are or were Fanny's become things external to her first-person:

> her fingers play'd, and strove to twine in the young tendrils of that moss which nature has contrived at once for use and ornament. But not contented with these outer-posts, she now attempts the main-spot, and began

to twitch, to insinuate, and at length to force an introduction of a finger into the quick itself.... (11)

The sequential checkpoints—tendrils, outer-posts, main-spot, quick—bear no possessive pronouns. When experience surfaces as Fanny's own, it does so conditionally: "had [Phoebe] not proceeded by insensible gradations that enflamed me beyond the power of modesty to oppose its resistance to their progress, I should have jumped out of bed..." (11). Fanny's consciousness, had it been enabled, would have cut the scene, but Phoebe's touch activates her parts rather than her integrated person, disarming her from resistance. Fanny's lack of resistance reads as inconsequential, even safe in the sapphic encounter, in stark contrast to Syrena's attempts to resist Vardine's acquisitive advancements in *Anti-Pamela*.

The "new fire" Fanny feels is the grammatical object to Phoebe's action; Phoebe's "lascivious touches" light it, her hands and Fanny's labia united through their impersonal determiners: "the first strange hands... now busied in feeling, squeezing, compressing the lips, then opening them again, with a finger between, till an Oh! expressed her hurting me" (11). Their body parts mingle without reference to centralized selves, "a" finger and "the" lips signaling increasing indefinition: Which finger, and whose lips, and were those attached to one or more persons? Even the utterance "Oh!" operates as though unowned by Fanny, the fact of its expression anterior to the meaning it bears. This atomization envisions a libidinal plasticity in the sapphic encounter, where sensation circulates among body parts, suspending bodily possession without irrevocably redistributing bodily property. Fanny only provides a coherent statement at scene's end, reminding us of her subjective truancy throughout: "For my part, I was transported, confused, and out of myself" (11). Fanny isn't satiated (unlike Phoebe who is "restor'd to... calm" by a pleasure Fanny "will not say"), but she is unharmed in the sense that her interaction with Phoebe has not culminated in what a heteronormative order would deem a decisive penetration: socially and physically, Fanny has not been altered (she is still marriageable; or her maidenhead will still command a high price).

The sapphic relation has peaceably alienated genitals and their sensations from the subject so imperiled by heterosexual transaction, figuring bodily estrangement as a benefit rather than a cost. Like the speaker of Aphra Behn's "To the Fair Clarinda," Fanny "might love, and yet be innocent" in the absence of the heterosexual order. While her "Oh!" signifies "hurting," it is not the "sharpness of pain" at which she "fainted away" in her first heteropenetration (41). There, the locus of sensation and description is not Fanny but Charles, whose penis is "lip-deep," who "drove [the engine of love-assaults] currently," "resumes his attempts," and "breaks the union of those parts" (40). Fanny's genitals appear only as the objects of Charles's efforts, and her sensation—pain—is not described so much as declared: "he hurt me," "I could have skream'd out" (40, 41). Rather than a circuit of sensations and body parts, this scene delivers a sequential account of action: "I arriv'd at an excess of pleasure, through excess of pain" (42). The doctrine of the heterosexual encounter—its social outcomes, its overdetermination, its movement toward penetrative heterosex, or "intercourse so-called"[70]—streamlines sensation and associates it with a singular narrator whose penetrated genitals become her social identity.

Elective Genitals and Moveable Dildos

The untethering of genitals interrupts the sequence and outcomes of penetrative, embodied heterosexuality that, much midcentury fiction tells us, structured the lives of eighteenth-century women. This section traces in particular the detachable penis—the dildo—as a fantasy of genital activity without conflicts of contested property and personhood. Moveable like Fanny's sensations but prosthetic—and so entirely detachable and exchangeable among persons—the dildo is a kind of wish to alienate genitals, nonviolently, from persons and from the heterosex they are often compelled to perform. Physically and materially, Ula Lukszo Klein argues, the dildo poses "a challenge to heteronormative frameworks for sexual pleasure" and, I add, for personhood.[71] This penetrating instrument, detached from masculine subjects, does not bear the legal and social privilege to rape, marry, or acquire, and it proves vaginal property to be optional, inessential to the feminine person. The dildo suggests that, like Fanny's depersonalized sensations, the setting adrift of genitals needn't always manifest as alienation. This separability manifests in literature as several specific fantasies: that men's penises are dildos, and so separable from masculine subjects and the social institutions that gender them; that dildos float freely into realms of women's use as we saw in the fashion satires, one among other luxury items available for their pleasure; and that dildos are part of a nonbinary economy that eliminates anatomical penises—and with them, the feminine disenfranchisement they enforce—from a penetrative sexual economy altogether.[72]

The threesome among Fanny, fellow sex worker Louisa, and cognitively impaired "Good-Natur'd" Dick is a test case for considering a penis apart from its subject.[73] Dick, a neighborhood flower vendor, is a "boy," "changeling," and "natural" whose subjectivity does not attach him to social or legal masculinity (161). Bereft of normative consciousness and unchecked by socialization, he demonstrates sheer penetrative desire, an unstoppable "butting" and "goring" until orgasm (164). This mechanistic force can seem a symptom of overdetermined phallic sexuality—a drive that prefigures consciousness.[74] But Cleland's description also suggests that Dick's genitals depart his person, that entity endowed with gendered meaning, as they assume penetrative dimension. Louisa, curious to make a "trial of parts," is the scene's agent, "[leading] the ductile youth by that master-tool of his" (163). Dick's penis, once aroused, is organic—a "sensitive plant" that "vegetates" under Fanny's touch—and, once unveiled, a "standard of distinction" that is described as a composite: the "enormous head" tops a long, "broad back of the body" with a "treasure-bag beneath" (162).[75] This object coheres visually not as an anatomical body part but as a dildo—a separable, erect instrument. Its performance overwhelms Louisa, whose sensation gathers in her vulva: "she went wholly out of her mind into that favorite part of her body ... there alone she existed" (164, 165). Louisa's orgasmic pleasure transpires in her genitals "alone" (that is, specifically and only in her genitals); but the sentence also attests to her uninterrupted subjectivity, claiming her as the sole person present in her sexual climax.

Gladfelder reads companionable pleasures in Dick and Louisa, wherein both are "distilled... with no self apart from [their] involuntary responsiveness to physical stimulation."[76] Subtle descriptive cues, though, invite us to see Dick's penis as separable, foremost, and disproportionate, and Louisa as therefore the sole sexual agent. This phallic detachability mobilizes Dick's penis as a dildo, and its penetrative capacity works at a remove from a unified body and from a cohesive masculine subjectivity. His erection is more like an accident, a departure from his person—as Sandra Macpherson reads another eighteenth-century erection[77]—than a statement of its link to an inherent or interior libido. There is, in other words, no man in this encounter, only a detached, unflappable erection, a "transferable thing," as Raymond Stephanson describes the eighteenth-century dildo.[78] Such a reading complicates Scott Juengel's claim that this scene "shores up ... heterosexual imperative."[79] If we consider the genitals in isolation, as the description does, this episode betrays "an inability to maintain a heterosexual point of view" Moore sees suffusing the whole novel, since Louisa does not conjoin with an anatomically unified masculine subject.[80]

Women were imagined to be eager and insatiable enthusiasts of this method of penetration. The bawdy poem *Monsieur Thing's Origin* (1722) figures its dildo hero as a popular socialite: "In little time *Monsieur* came to be known, / Then soon was visited by ev'ry one."[81] *Dildoides* (1706) imagines the objects in various sizes that would satisfy all kinds of women, from "Tender Virgins" to "rank Lady ... so Torn / she hardly feels when Child is born."[82] Some men in that poem praise the dildo as a marital aid; without the sex toy, women might lay with a "'Prentice," or "Foot-Man," and wives of maimed soldiers might commit adultery, driven by their unsatisfied libidos.[83] The lusty maid in *New Cock Wanted* (1810) delights in the tools wielded at groin level by her plumber (Figure 1.8). The length of pipe he grasps implies a vehicle for penetration detachable from his body and therefore from the subjectivity contained there. Through the inscription on the wall—"Anno Domini 1730"—Thomas Rowlandson references this early-century interval that sees so much textual and cultural awareness of dildo circulation.

FIGURE 1.8. A plumber grasps his pipe. Thomas Rowlandson, *A New Cock Wanted. Or Work for the Plumber.* London, 1810.
Courtesy of the Lewis Walpole Library, Yale University.

While Rowlandson's maid seems delighted by the plumber and his tools, the wish for a dildo in the presence of an embodied man can turn into something like rape, as in the Dick episode, since it is wielded by a masculine body in motion that does not hear opposition.[84] In such a usage, it functions like the penis as we've seen it deployed in Haywood and

Richardson but with a key difference. The dildo's separability from the embodied masculine subject undoes, even if incompletely as in Cleland, the imperative that penetrative intercourse curtail women's personhood and alter their capacity to claim property in their bodies. As *Monsieur Thing's Origin* avers, the dildo is "Sex blind."[85] Its prosthetic relationship to masculinity offers the possibility of penetrative sex acts in which masculinity is distant, absent, or non-harmful to women, where it adds to rather than subtracts from feminine personhood.[86] Dildos were understood to work palliatively, too, in the British Atlantic world, as prostheses for injured soldiers.[87] The dildo, associated with reparative potential, signals its inessential connection to the encroaching masculinity to which so many eighteenth-century heroines objected.

A Spy on Mother Midnight (1748) and its sequel, *A Continuation of Mr. F——'s Adventures* (1748), present the dildo in both contexts—it is associated with masculine penetrative right, and it throws into relief the limits and fallibilities of anatomical penises. The epistolary hero cross-dresses in order to deceive women and gain intimate access to their bodies. From the start, his penis asserts its independence from his intentions, "an Enmity to Petticoats . . . *standing up*" and threatening his disguise. He personifies his penis as a "Companion of mine" that must be "persuade[d] . . . to lie down."[88] Cross-dressing reveals the loose connection between man and penis, which stands erect irrespective of its owner's wishes, his peer rather than his subordinate. Reinforcing that erections float freely, the narrator soon encounters a dildo—"an Image of Manhood, an Ivory Substitute of Virility"—in the bedchamber of a beautiful young woman. Still in women's dress, the narrator promises to give Maria "some Kind of Comfort" with it (*Spy* 32). Instead of penetrating Maria with the dildo, and without her consent, he uses his penis. Afterward, in *Continuation*, Maria is so persuaded of penile superiority that she burns her dildo, now seen as the narrator's "inanimate Rival," the next morning.[89] The narrator defensively touts his fleshy organ over its prosthetic substitute; he harangues against "the damn'd Tool," wishing that all dildos in England be collected, burned, and banned by Parliament and sex traffickers alike (*Continuation* 7–8).

But in the midst of his foment, the narrator has a revealing wish to relinquish masculine subjectivity and become a dildo: "that it might be the Fate of my Spirit to inform, in its next Transmigration, the Body of one of these Implements. What a delicious Thought . . . how many Cuckolds should I make in that Figure, more than I'm able to do in my own Proper Person!" (*Continuation* 7). He admits the dildo's greater penetrative power, as well as the greater intimacy women have with it:

> Oh! to be hugg'd, handled, fondled, caress'd, and put——— with their own fair Hands, and to find them yield to the Dictates of glowing Blood and stimulating Nature, without that Reserve and Coyness they sometimes assume . . . when a Man's in the Case! (*Continuation* 7)

A freestanding instrument, the dildo enjoys a privileged form of vaginal penetration: constant, infinite, undeterred by social codes that temper women's sexual enthusiasm. What had been a territorial antagonism with the dildo transforms into the hero's admiration of its supramasculine capabilities. It penetrates more frequently, outperforms men, and immerses its entirety into the bodies of women unrestrained by modesty. He "privilege[s] hard phallus over mundane penis," a distinction that Stephanson argues preoccupied discourses on masculinity.[90] The hero ultimately admits to its superiority, wishing not to use a dildo but to become one.

Through all this hubris we might discern a worry about the stark distinction between dildo and penis. The former possesses a state of constant erection, the latter a variable one. So had the Earl of Rochester's libertine speaker apostrophized to his penis when, "Base Recreant to thy Prince, thou durst not stand"—when, thing-like, the penis stops performing its expected function.[91] Penises can defy the will of their men. So too vaginas that of their women, though for them the separation from will is usually coerced by socio-sexual institutions. Unlike Rochester's libertine, Syrena and Clarissa are not afforded the privilege of psychological distance from their alienated genitals, since their vaginal conditions determine their social position. While my above examples affiliate the dildo with masculine prerogative, it more commonly is imagined as the property of women, and with profound consequences. As Cleland begins to suggest through Dick, penetrative sex might be had without men, their penises, and their rapacious proprietary claims. When the penis is imagined as a dildo, the penetrating object is decoupled from the masculine tasks of amassing property and absorbing women's personhood. Figuring the dildo as penis-alternative is a strategy that places penetrative sex within a domain of feminine autonomy (recall the floating dildos seen in Figure 1.3). This capacity for genital and gendered transformation resists what Jason Farr perceives as the period's efforts "[t]o do heterosexuality correctly" through normative embodiment.[92]

Works centering women and gender-nonconforming characters show that the adoption of masculine dress and genitals is not just a "site of struggle," as Lynne Friedli has claimed, but a practice of transformation and pleasure.[93] Women and nonbinary figures resist the social meaning attached to their genitals by appropriating the dildo, like one enthusiast in *Monsieur Thing's Origin* who "ty'd *Monsieur* to her middle": "She acted Man, being in a merry Mood, / Striving to please her Partner as she cou'd."[94] *A Treatise of Hermaphrodites* (1718) relates the "Female Intrigues" of a same-sex couple who, having sworn off deceitful men, "provided artificial *Penis's* of the largest Dimensions, and with Ribbons they fasten'd the Root of the Instrument, in the same Situation as Nature has plac'd the Substance in Man." They, in fact, use two dildos:

> when their Vigour was so much abated, that they were no longer able to struggle, the Female uppermost withdrew, and taking another Instrument in her Hand, she us'd it on her Companion with an Injection of Moisture, which, with the rubbing, occasion'd such a tickling, as to force a discharge of Matter and facilitate the Pleasure. This was their daily Practice.[95]

Another expert is the protagonist of Fielding's *Female Husband* (1746). The narrative has Mary Hamilton skillfully use a dildo to consummate with three wives. Fielding's prose is equally adept, the dildo referred to allusively as "means" of deception "which decency forbids" the narrator to name; a "*wherewithal*" for performing sex acts; and "something of too vile, wicked, and scandalous a nature . . . produced in evidence against her," the final material proof of Hamilton's serial defrauding of unsuspecting women.⁹⁶ The dildo alights on Hamilton's consciousness as a necessary stratagem for marrying an old widow whose fortune Hamilton is "desirous to possess": "a device entered into her head, as strange and surprizing, as it was wicked and vile" (295). "Device" refers to the duplicitous marriage plan, and it also names the prosthetic with which the sham marriage will be consummated. The "device" is both an aspect of consciousness as well as a material instrument that transforms Hamilton's gender. The narrator registers the impact of this prosthetic and mental "device," shifting pronouns between she/her and he/him and using varying nouns to denote gendered character types—Hamilton is at times "heroine in iniquity" and "female gallant" (289, 295), at others "youth," "adventurer," "bridegroom" (292, 293, 296).⁹⁷

The dildo's signification is so powerful that it dupes three women, shapes the narrator's gender pronouns, and facilitates new forms of desire in Hamilton—for the widow's fortune, to be sure, but also for the "extreamly pretty" young Miss Ivythorn, and finally for Mary Price, with whom Hamilton "was really as much in love, as it was possible for a man ever to be with one of her own sex" (299). As this sentence asserts, the dildo makes the man, and the man is a she/her. The dildo disturbs gender binarism so fully that narrative and character discover new forms of desire, forms that defy discipline. Our parting shot is of Hamilton confined to Bridewell, skin "almost flayed" by whipping, offering to pay a guard "to procure her a young girl to satisfy her most monstrous and unnatural desires" (304). Fielding's narrator may try to condemn Hamilton's queerness, but the narrative associates the dildo with a powerful sexual agency that refuses containment in the heteronormative paradigm—a pornographic expression of what Paula Backscheider sees as "the possibility of a happy life without [heterosexual] marriage" imagined in women's friendship poetry, or of the queer delight Evelina takes, according to Eugenia Zuroski, with the decidedly non-penetrative Mr. Lovel.⁹⁸

Cleland also provides a genital account of sex without cis men through Catharine Vizzani, the cross-dressed "Adventurer" whose history he translates from the original by anatomist Giovanni Bianchi.⁹⁹ This "history" does less to dismiss sapphic sexuality than to detail its successful and volitional execution. Vizzani lives as a man for eight years, seduces women, elopes with one who is pursued by an outraged uncle, and dies of an abscessed gunshot wound "with a fine sound Hymen" intact (38). The scientist-author then dissects Vizzani's body, studying the genitals for signs of aberration before installing them in his own collection. Cleland largely demurs from sexual detail in these adventures, suppressing bits in Bianchi's original, but attends closely to the dildo once Vizzani is ailing in hospital, removed from sexual circulation. We first learn of the dildo when Vizzani removes it: "a leathern Contrivance, of a cilindrical Figure, which was fastened below the Abdomen, and had been the chief Instrument of her detestable Imposture, became so troublesome, that she loosened it, and laid it under her pillow" (34–35). Vizzani promptly feels remorse, partially confirming Cleland's and Bianchi's ostensible sexual normativity.

After so long eschewing genitals, the narrative is very concerned with them after Vizzani's death. And all genitals depart Vizzani—dildo, hymen, clitoris, all "parts of generation"—never to return to the body on which they had been, for a time, fixed (42).[100] Rather, they disperse and circulate among inquisitive men who interpret discrete parts. The dildo is found by surgical assistants on the deathbed; they disassemble it, looking for money inside the leather sheath, but find only rags. The other remaining genitals are distributed to Bianchi. He confirms through dissection that surgeons "had not meddled with the Pudendum Muliebre, nor the Vagina of the Uterus, [and that] the Entireness of the Hymen incontestably proved her being actually a Virgin" (39). He then has the parts delivered to his study, "reposit[ing]" them with those "which [he] found in many Virgins of different Age" (43). He sees in Vizzani's organs a typical set of female parts, including an unremarkable clitoris, "not pendulous, nor of any extraordinary Size"—not the enlarged one attributed to sapphists (43). The typical clitoral size means for Bianchi that Vizzani's gender was not anatomically determined. As Gladfelder has written, the dissection finds that "[t]here is no correspondence between the truth of the body and the identity of the desiring subject."[101] Genitals also offer no explanation for Vizzani's volitional sex acts. In his conclusion, Cleland agrees. Only the mind can be the source of sexual desire, so he urges readers to "acquit Nature" and locate corruption "only in [Vizzani's] Mind" (54). Vizzani's anatomical genitals were attached to a mental state, and Vizzani's will was to refuse penetration, electing a new genital set made of rags and leather. This dildo apparently delighted lovers, leading one close to a marriage based on "Passion" rather than property (22). These adopted genitals, used outside the constraints of state-sanctioned marriage, enacted a penetrative sexuality uninvested in the absorption of another's personhood.

Definitively detachable from masculine persons, the dildo makes possible a penetrative sexuality loosed from heterosexual institutions. As the conclusions of cross-dressing picaresques demonstrate, dildos do not promise a utopian eroticism—the people who wore them dead or incarcerated—but they mark a separation of penetrative sexuality from the institutions that claimed and operationalized it. The fixity of genitals to persons is shown to be temporary and variable, the hymen as inessential as the dildo Vizzani elected as a primary sexual organ. Queer genital sexuality was, of course, not widely embraced in eighteenth-century culture. In *A Treatise of Hermaphrodites*, an astonished seducer severs those "external Members" of one Isabella who possessed along with a vagina "something like the Testicles of a Man." Her partner Diana's nonbinary genitalia is similarly discovered by a cis man, her "masculine Instrument likewise sever'd from her Privities." Afterward, the two "live to be harmless old Women," chastened by the mutilation of genitals they used non-heterosexually.[102]

I've presented a countertradition to such violent consequences in this chapter. The representations of genital sensation as alienated and depersonalized reveal a feminist fantasy that women's bodies—so often trafficked without reference to their owners—might not bear repercussions on their social and legal personhood. The departure of reproductive genitals from the body dreams an impermanent anatomy, a sphere of sexual experience disjoined from social ramification, perhaps a historical preview of the "imperiling [of] static boundaries" Eva Hayward attributes to transsexuality.[103] The dildo yields a twofold revelation: penetrative pleasure might escape the heterosexual institutions that use it as a way to cancel women's personhood, and bodies might opt out of their own permeability in favor of penetrating with a dildo. Such discoveries are particular to the sexual descriptions I'm collecting as pornography; it alone systematically distinguishes between genital states and personal volition. These persistent and candid descriptions constitute a pornography not bound into individual texts but one that reaches across genres and print forms, appearing piecemeal as part of an ongoing consideration of those bodily conditions that defined women's subjectivity but that were not experienced as owned or governed by a self.

These insights are particular to literature about women and nonbinary people because their genitals were the peculiar property under acquisition and inquiry in eighteenth-century society. The texts featured in this chapter knew it was an injustice for genital status to determine social viability when the use of women's bodies so rarely made reference to their preferences. Property so vulnerable to annex, exchange, and appropriation should not, these texts suggest, be a primary criterion for defining a person's social positions and prospects, an insight that strikes me as a kind of genital feminism: a model of personhood that can withstand, even celebrate, bodily transformation and impermanence. We needn't see this revelation as distancing women from sex or upholding a doctrinaire chastity, but as refuting the absurdity of defining social viability based on sexual status, habits, preferences, or practices.

This genital feminism rejects the cultural fiction that would have us believe the bodies that define people's subject positions preexist their interpellation by the institutions that organize society. It is a definitive attribute of eighteenth-century pornographic fiction as well as later pornographies, the topic of succeeding chapters. As I argue in Chapter 2, an explicit strain of feminism is foundational to narratives that take genital action as a main focus. Midcentury pornography takes for granted the consciousness I've documented here: that genital attributes were conceptually and, in many cases, materially separable from the persons whose legal and social status they defined. A set of little-known texts, considered pornographic well into the late nineteenth century, concentrates and foregrounds the broad consciousness that social inequity based on genital difference was an aggressive, pernicious cultural fiction bound to be short-lived. Pornography, we'll see next, explicitly imagines a future without anatomical men and the institutions that secure their privilege.

2 FEMINIST SPECULATIONS
Penetration and Protest in Pornographic Fiction

THIS CHAPTER OFFERS a new way of accessing feminist thought in eighteenth-century fiction, locating it in pornographic narratives that foreground adolescent girls, sex workers, and women of color. It charts this course through little-known fictions that situate genital experience as a key feature of young adulthood. In these sexually candid works, the inexperience of young characters warrants detailed accounts of genitals and their manipulations, accounts that offer commentary on the ways social institutions define embodied persons.[1] Chapter 1 showed the frequency of genital reference in the first half of the eighteenth century, concluding with an account of how literature newly configured genitals as elective and mutable in order to imagine penetrative sexuality without men. This project persists in the texts I introduce here: pornographic picaresques that have a legacy beyond the eighteenth century (as we'll see in Chapter 3) but that have been overlooked by critical accounts of pornography's history.

From 1744 to 1774, three fictional narratives appeared—*The Progress of Nature, The History of the Human Heart,* and *The Child of Nature*—that structure plots around sex and, insistently, explicitly connect genital activity to the spheres of social life that impact it. The first two texts assert continuity between anatomical parts and social categories that fictitiously attach to them, a connection maintained as well in prostitute narratives, where sex work is shown to originate in conditions of social and sexed inequity. Published in the age of *Fanny Hill,* the anonymous pornographers are as unabashed as John Cleland in their detailing of genitals, but they focus with more specificity on labial, clitoral, and vaginal parts, persistently joining young women's genital action with commentary on worldly conventions that misconstrue sexual difference as social hierarchy. They expose the illusory means through which men attribute their social authority to the power of their sexual anatomy, and they recommend alternatives to penetrative heterosex. In *The Progress of Nature* (1744), for instance, young women arrive at political disillusionment rather than erotic discovery during their discussion of a dildo. *The History of the Human Heart* (1749) appends voluminous footnotes to sex scenes in order to elucidate their philosophical and scientific contexts and implications. Sex is often set aside—literally pushed off the page by editorial commentary. *The Child of Nature* (1774)—recognized, like *Human Heart,* as pornography by collectors and bibliographers for the next hundred years, as I show in Chapter 3—demurs from penetrative sex entirely, celebrating the heroine's insulation from those impositions. It imagines her future as a propertied and philosophical individual, equipped financially and intellectually to undertake sex acts irrespective of social institutions, though such action is never detailed. This novel stands as evidence that eighteenth-century pornography developed such a robust feminist voice that its commentary cohered even when genitals dropped out of the narrative. These narratives fuse genital traffic (courtship, rape, seduction, marriage) with commentary on the social and cultural practices that attach value to persons based on their sexual status, and they reveal how women's social value and economic viability are relentlessly traced to their genital conditions. Such commentary is regular, explicit, and feminist, and it is intrinsic to pornographic narrative.

These fictions join sex acts to myriad other topics—science, politics, religion, philosophy—to assert the imbrication of genital life with these related spheres of knowledge and experience. Influential work in social history, such as Lawrence Stone's, and in literary history, such as Nancy Armstrong's, has trained us to see sex and desire in this period increasingly bound up with the married couple, which relied on women's moral attractiveness in a domestic context. But pornography unsettles this historical narrative of feminized sexual privacy, proving repeatedly that bodies issue and absorb social dynamics and that sex signifies and happens primarily outside of private realms (or proves privacy itself to be a fallacy); indeed Stone, even as he charts the tightening of the affectively bonded heterosexual couple in the eighteenth century, notes the period's "unusually relaxed" sexual habits outside marriage.[2] The associative, picaresque qualities of pornography circulate sex beyond conjugality in a social world—usually a disenchanted one—where its costs are weighed against its benefits.[3] The narratives regularly demonstrate that women suffer disproportionate effects of genital activity (their social identity so often determined by vaginal status) and recommend alternative moral systems in which they might exercise sexual, social, and economic freedom.

I contrast these wayward fictions—wandering into and out of sex acts without clearly signaling their return—with Cleland's *Memoirs of a Woman of Pleasure*, whose tempos and descriptions resemble what has come to define modern pornography: namely, an unremitting focus on penetrative action. Providing an overly familiar model of how we think the genre works in its modern forms—relentlessly, seemingly uninhibited by contingency or skepticism—*Woman of Pleasure* has absorbed perhaps too much critical attention, eclipsing the non-penetrative account of sexuality I've found in archival works. Cleland's novel commits fully to the "pleasure" named in its title; the heroine sometimes is unsatisfied by partners, but often her orgasms are minutely documented, and they recur in quick succession.[4] In this, it is more like translations of French libertine fiction, the story goes, than anything being written in England. Judging by this standard of frequency of sexual content, critics regard *Woman of Pleasure* as an outlier in England, where sexual writing has been understood as allusive or metaphorical in its genital treatment until later in the century.[5]

In fact, other early narrative pornographies exist. They are deeply obscene, but not only deeply obscene. They insist on the coexistence of multiple readerly responses at once, drawing on humor, intellectual debate, and cultural critique to emphasize the associative function of sex acts in narrative, and they demand that we recognize pornography as raising plural cognitive responses from readers. Even historians who established the eighteenth century as a pornographically rich period, like Peter Wagner and Julie Peakman, misconstrued the genre as solely eliciting "sexual stimulation," when, as I'll demonstrate, it explicitly asks for plural, complex reactions.[6] I believe it is through selective or partial reading that scholars characterize, as Thomas Laqueur does in his history of masturbation, eighteenth-century pornographic novels as "demand[ing] relatively little work" from readers automated, his account implies, to ejaculate in response to print.[7]

The fiction I've studied embeds sexual descriptions in worlds that exceed the private or the solitary. While Caroline Gonda rightly observes a general "invisibility of women's sexual lives" in the eighteenth-century literary record, pornography provides one significant exception, centering feminine commentary that details how gender inequity is created and sustained in everyday social practices.[8] For Susan Lanser, same-sex relationships between women in literature articulate the injustices of modern culture, and pornography in particular joins women in dialogues that grant them authority on sexual matters and beyond. Pornographic conversations exceed "titillation" and "androcentric imperatives" in Lanser's analysis, and they "outwit" gender hierarchies.[9] It is such resistance I document in eighteenth-century pornographic picaresques. Their accounts of penetrative sexuality recognize its specificity as one kind of sex act with particular social consequences for women. These consequences are explored in pornography's discourse around cultural meanings of vaginal sex and the social institutions that organize heterosexuality. Like sexuality as we have understood it since Foucault, sex acts in these texts constitute a fluid and highly adaptable field of experience that shapes the protagonist's and reader's perceptions of their worlds. This discourse does not operate only in a regulatory fashion, but also imagines how genital parts might escape categorization, surveillance, and gendering. They participate in a history that shows us, as Maia Kostos argues through the longer view of classical history, "[p]enetration is . . . only one way to understand sex/relationality, one that consistently brings traumatic experience with it," and further that heteropenetration was culturally manufactured as a normative ideal, for eighteenth-century people as for the scholars who study them.[10]

The feminist stances activated in these British texts are occasional and piecemeal, uncommitted to any one philosophical tradition but sweeping in their claims about how genitals determine—unjustly—women's social and economic options. This patchwork pornographic genealogy, while persistently philosophical, differs fundamentally from contemporary French works that cohered in a "radical wing of *philosophie*," thoroughbred, so to speak, in their materialist and revolutionary creeds. As James Steintrager notes, the climate of absolutism in France relieved aristocrats of their governing power, creating a particularly fertile environment for libertines to imagine, through literature, a "future of social organization and politics beyond the monarchy," one that celebrated pleasure over productivity. By contrast, "counterfactual alternatives to social and political reality had considerably less purchase" for writers of lewd fiction in England, where constitutional monarchy mitigated the need for radical political opposition.[11] This account is both right—British pornography is not as disciplined or pristine in its philosophical commitments—and partial. Counterfactual futures are regularly imagined for and by women in *Progress*, *Human Heart*, and *Child of Nature*: futures without marriage, without rape, without gender hierarchies, without heterosexuality. The absolutism they resist is not governmental, but social and cultural, calling for a dispersed, hybrid, occasional philosophy. Speculating alternatives to a heteropenetrative sexual order, British works are not bound to "the domain of a physiological responsiveness" that Natania Meeker associates with French pornographic fiction, wherein the lugubrious effects of obscene writing are figured as "proof" that the material body is pleasure-seeking.[12] The feminism in British pornography sometimes evokes sexual pleasure, but it imagines women's pleasures also as cultural, political, and socioeconomic.

These texts joined a British literary marketplace populated with recent translations of French titles that bear out these commentaries on gender. *Venus in the Cloister* (trans. 1725) advocated a sexual practice of spirituality for cloistered women and gave instructions on how to undertake it within church confines, complete with footnotes providing further explication. *Dialogue Between a Married Lady and a Maid* (trans. 1740) prepares virgins for their nuptial beds, extolling men's sexual vigor and depicting consummation as a social concern, attended by family members or wedding guests. Originally published in 1675 and 1659, respectively, they appear in colloquial English translations, I think not coincidentally, in a period of intensified attention not only to the genital experiences of women but to what women have to say about the pain, pleasure, and social outcomes of sex acts.[13] In dialogues between women, these works naturalize sexual desire, asserting it as the domain of women as much as of men. In contrast to the dialogue form, the narrators of British prose fiction expand and complicate this premise, showing sex acts to have grave ramifications for women living in an environment that evaluates their genital condition and assigns their social value accordingly. This specifically feminist, specifically British project is distinct from the political resistance Lynn Hunt locates in early European pornography and predates what Frances Ferguson emphasizes as the utilitarian economy of later pornography, where sexual action is concentrated into the genre's primary focus.[14]

These midcentury texts acquaint us with a miscellaneous model of reading less familiar than the salacious consumption Wagner, Peakman, and Laqueur associated with pornography in the period, and they document a formal complexity in the history of the genre that should, I believe, make us suspicious of characterizations of pornography today as simply or primarily aimed at masturbation. Margret Grebowicz, for instance, delimits "internet porn" to a category of materials designed to "aid in masturbation" and dampen political subjectivity.[15] Tim Dean, introducing an essay collection on a broad range of pornographic texts, sees pornography archiving "heterogeneous feelings and affects"—a pornographic function particularly important for sexual minorities, as he notes—but assimilates those feelings all as "pleasures."[16] If orgasm verifies pornography's insular, irresistible efficiency—its capacity to produce pleasure—these eighteenth-century specimens indicate a countertradition in the genre's history, wherein reading about sex is divorced from a libidinal teleology and joined to the realm of ideas. Such evidence needn't erase the possibility of masturbation, but it controverts the assumption that pornography is designed for a primary purpose or can guarantee a particular response.

The ideas circulated in eighteenth-century pornography show pleasure itself, or personhood, or self-determination to be privileged states inaccessible to many, and these insights do not arrive quickly or easily. Pornographic narrative demands the unpredictable, variable, and meandering habits historians of reading detect in the period. Christina Lupton—in a study showing that eighteenth-century books were made as much for reading as for not-reading, rereading, or selectively reading—finds book use "recalcitrant and resistant to efficiency," a way of spending time rather than a consumption of stipulated content.[17] Deidre Lynch, documenting readers' author-love during the Romantic era, finds less devotion in the earlier eighteenth-century textual culture, which registered "uncertainties about how readers were to comport themselves" in the face of literary objects.[18] The same readers who sought edification through "absorptive or intensive reading" in the eighteenth century delighted in the low humor of ephemera, which they obtained through "more desultory modes of consumption," Simon Dickie argues in a study of unsentimentality.[19] Scholars attribute uncertainty and inefficiency to eighteenth-century readers, states of reading with which pornography is not only comfortable but seems to promote. It figures readers as highly tolerant of, indeed pleased by, multiple registers of meaning unfolding at once and, it would seem, in competing directions, often veering away from genital activity to contemplate the social origins of identities (men, virgins, chaste women) that purport to be rooted in the body. They demand a variety of attitudes in readers. I agree with J. Paul Hunter that modern readers misrecognize the period's popular fictions as "ineffectively focused" when in fact their narrative variations were highly strategic.[20] Through its complex narrative inventions, pornography called on women to display and discuss their bodies, and it circulated the feminist literary project Lanser locates in this period, "an epistemology within which social relations are reimagined in paradigm-shifting horizontal terms."[21] Such speculation is the knowledge pornography generates around women.

By calling these texts pornography, I'm suggesting a definition of the genre as temperamentally inconsistent, discursively hybrid, intermittently erotic, and irreducibly feminist. Defining pornography prior to the genre's establishment is complicated, of course. I argue in *Excitable Imaginations* that sex pervasively informs the instructive aims of eighteenth-century authors and that the arousals elicited by literary sexual representation were believed to facilitate imaginative states of educability idealized in philosophies of the mind.[22] Here, I identify as pornography a denser kind of sexual detail that specifies genital parts and links those parts to hierarchical social formations, fusing the sexual and the discursive, often unevenly but always critically. In his important study of French pornography's philosophical roots, Robert Darnton asserts that while pornography as such "did not exist in the eighteenth century . . . one should not relativize the concept out of existence."[23] The category remains a crucial tool for recognizing how texts share a candid approach to genitals and their actions, sensations, and social meaning. I contend this approach does not stipulate arousal, and may even eschew it, as it loops readers through philosophical speculation and social criticism. Pornography is better understood as a mode of inquiry that takes for granted the relevance of sex acts to other fields of experience and knowledge; and within pornography, descriptions of sex acts constitute a method for engaging or lampooning those other fields.

In this multitasking model of reading we can see pornography as an integration, rather than a separation, of sex acts with a wide array of cultural concerns. What distinguishes these texts as pornographic is their connection of genital detail to explicit statements and reflections on social justice (as well as their visibility as source texts for later generations of pornographers, this book will later show). Readers are expected to shuttle between different registers of literary representation and sexual understanding, and to exercise flexibility of humor and intellect as they do so. Pornography, elastically connecting sex to cultural and political life, not only raises but sustains questions regarding the justice of social status being determined by genital states. It dramatizes the distance between genitals and the persons who are attached to them, and it details how those persons gain or lose social value based on genital traffic. Pornography knows that people with vaginal or non-conforming genitals are most vulnerable to social descent, and it is eager to ask why. It is, therefore, a feminist and transfeminist genre.

Dildo Theory: *The Progress of Nature*

Extant in a single copy, *The Progress of Nature* has evaded the attention of pornography historians, mainly because collectors, reviewers, and bibliographers have not known where to categorize it. It was listed as a "Historical" work in the November 1744 issue of *The London Magazine*, and not under "Poetry and Entertainment," where *The Female Spectator* appeared, or "Miscellaneous," which included midwifery manuals and microscopy texts. Like other salacious texts, it was published anonymously and with a false imprint. An eighteenth-century collector bound it (as I've discussed in the Preface) with *The History of the Human Heart*, short fiction by Haywood, and a courtship manual—grouping it with intimate and amorous, and not necessarily lewd, texts.[24] Today it remains bound only with *Human Heart*, bearing a British Library "Cup." shelfmark that designates it a "cupboard book," indicating some degree of sexual content.[25] The "Cup." holdings range from "sexological works, books on contraception, guides to erotic technique" to books that "embrace sexual questions, or with piquant illustrations."[26] They are distinguished from works held in the Private Case, whose "P.C." shelfmark would seem to indicate a higher degree of sexual content. Because historians of British pornography have focused on the Private Case, and because *Progress* was arbitrarily assigned a less restrictive shelfmark, it (and, as we'll see, *Human Heart*) has slipped under the scholarly radar, perpetuating the misunderstanding that Cleland's *Woman of Pleasure* stands alone as a midcentury work of British prose pornography.[27] *Progress* offers a different logic of sexual display, exhibiting genitals in detail and linking them not to penetration but to social and anatomical analysis. These spectacles function as a prompt for reflection on cultural practices of sex and gender rather than as an overdetermined preamble to penetrative sex.

Progress recounts the sexual curiosities of three adolescent characters who come of age around sexually deviant adults—adulterous parsons, masturbating neighbors, and horny aunties. It establishes and maintains a libidinal atmosphere, where genital activity seems imminent in every encounter but does not deliver heterosexual penetration as a regular, or even frequent outcome. Like so many of the examples in the previous chapter, *Progress* does not accept an unequivocally penetrative account of the penis. In fact, its three protagonists never knowingly enter into heterosexual penetration, even as they are highly responsive to genital sensation. Its catalogue of sexual possibility is thus incomplete, and *Progress* draws attention to its own unfinished status. The prefatorial "advertisement" tells readers it is they who will determine whether successive volumes are published: "in case our first Number be not approv'd of, the other two may be suppress'd," likely a disingenuous claim that promises not future volumes but lurid, controversial content.[28] And it delivers, having the narrators experience masturbation, erotic dreams, dildos, petting, assault, adolescent groping, infantile eroticism, and molestation. Notably absent is penetrative heterosex, of which we receive no complete first-person account. Roger Lovejoy in one instance describes his adoptive mother's penetration by the local parson, which he voyeuristically observes through a hole in the wall; and the narrative closes with a spectacularly penetrative scene. But as we'll see below, the anatomical arrangements of this final genital spectacle are only partially knowable to narrator and reader.

Progress opens by announcing the hero's defunct penis. Roger recounts his early sexual pursuits from a position of castrated reform: "Thrice happy Deprivation of what us'd to be the eternal Object of all my Thoughts! the Spring of my Actions! Thrice welcome enervated Nature! Welcome Amputation!"[29] His narration, though, relays no such remorse, and we never receive an explanation of how or why his genitals have been rendered inoperative. He instead focuses on his sexually eventful childhood, linking his libidinal curiosity to the community of sexual nonconformists that populated it. Roger's unwed parents—a prelate and a singer—were amorous and daring, his adoptive parents non-monogamous, his father largely absent from home and his mother indiscreetly consorting with the local parson (it is by spying on their intercourse that Roger discovers masturbation). Also impactful are the caresses he experiences as an infant, when the women attending his mother's labor celebrate his birthmark as "strong Meaning" that he will be "in almost continual Thraldom" to women (13–14). He traces his fascination with breasts to the pleasure he took in nursing, and his first reciprocal affections are exchanged with a neighboring Mrs. Wilton, who casually masturbates in front of Roger and his sister with "her Hand passing through the Pocket-Hole" of her petticoat (32).[30] Women's environments elicit Roger's preferences and curiosities, and their non-domestic, in most cases non-penetrative sexual proclivities are treated lightly, counted among the pluralities of taste that make up this libidinal, picaresque world. This spectrum of sensuality includes penetrative drive—Roger, after all, attempts to rape his sister (29)—and exalts male ejaculation as the "single One" pleasure that eclipses all others (24). But these sex acts that seem to define modern pornography are not privileged in this early work over vaginal and clitoral experiences.

The narrative's second half comprises a conversation between young women—Roger's sister Polly and her friend Miss Forward. Assuming feminine narrative voice, *Progress* focuses closely on female anatomy, in one case describing Miss Forward's "digitizing." Her discoveries provide a kind of autoerotic manual for people endowed with clitoris and vagina: "My roving Hand a Moment rested on the Part most aggrieved, raging with a violent Inflammation all around . . . I just put the Tip of my Finger upon it, but withdrew it." Her description presents masturbation as anatomically precise, self-governed, and entirely satisfying, an end in itself:

> Then I cautiously cover'd it with the Hollow of my Hand; but by often pressing it, the Sensation at last was too powerful to be restrain'd by Precept: With an Intrepidity, bordering on Rashness, I forc'd myself a Passage, and the Hurt which I did myself was swallow'd up in the Pleasure I felt. (57)

While Cleland will have Fanny Hill "pin[e] for more solid food" as a result of digital penetration, *Progress* offers female masturbation as a skilled and self-contained sexual practice.[31] As we saw in *Aristotle's Master-Piece*,

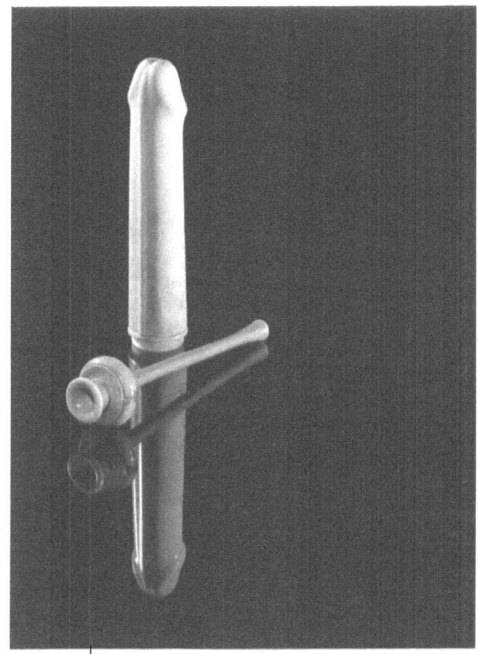

FIGURE 2.1. Ivory dildo with plunger for simulating ejaculation, possibly French, 1700s.
© Science Museum Group.

Mandeville, even Haywood, here women's genitals are considered minutely, and not exclusively for their receptivity. Attention to women's masturbating capacities invites a skepticism in readers: Are penises necessary?

This question expands within the women's conversation. The particular domain of pornography allows them to discuss heterosexual penetration and to distinguish it from the cultural practices—masculine right, secondary feminine personhood—that attempt to operationalize it. Their entry into sexual knowledge entails their examination of a dildo, which in turn entails their discovery of the cultural production of gender inequity. Miss Forward discovers the dildo in her aunt's chamber, first apprehending it as a "misshapen Monster of a thing" (74) but on later inspection perceiving its design and utility: "It is like a long Tube of about two Inches Diameter . . . capable of containing in the Cavity a certain Quantity of any warm Liquid; . . . by touching a little Spring, away goes the Milk, and overflows all the adjacent Parts," simulating "the Transports of the real Blessing," the ejaculation of an embodied penis (82) (Figure 2.1). Miss

Forward shows the dildo to Polly, and together they weigh its similarity to a penis.

As Anjali Arondekar claims of the nineteenth-century dildo, the specimen in *Progress* signifies widely, far beyond a conception of the dildo as "compensatory substitute, or a reminder of a lack."[32] "The Oddness of its Figure" inspires the young women to try to assign it meaning. Miss Forward notes it bears the size and shape of a penis, which she knows is associated with power: "of all the Members of a Man's body, some call it the *Monarch*, others, not improperly, will have it be the *Deity* of Women" (75). Exposing the metaphorical, subjective process of naming, Miss Forward implicitly questions the validity of the associations among penis, king, and god. This challenge is made explicit when ingenue Polly rejects the metonymy: "This Monarch . . . means only something he has about him, that may be equivalent to, tho' different from what we have about us" (75). Binarily sexed persons have different but structurally comparable parts. Genitals are "about," around, near persons, not essentially integrated into personhood, Polly observes, distinguishing legal or philosophical subjectivity from accidental attributes of the body.

Miss Forward explains why authority is so often conferred upon the penis. "This is that arbitrary *he* that enters his Dominions, ravages far and wide . . . in the Gratification of his Pleasures" (think of Vardine's accessions in *Anti-Pamela*, discussed in Chapter 1). But the penis, she concedes, is not always commanding: "This same he that proudly gives Laws to others, is himself subject to the Laws of Sight and Imagination: Without them, he is as mean and pitiful, sneaking and supple, as he is bold and enterprizing" (75–76). This supposedly omnipotent autocrat "contracts himself like a Snail" in the absence of stimulus (76). The phallic man is dialectically constituted, entirely dependent on a feminine figure to "provoke his inclination by her presence [or] . . . by his Ideas [of her] in her absence" (76). Femininity must present itself visually to a man, or he must conjure it in fantasy, in order to activate the penis.

Polly sums up by calling the dildo a "Representative of the Monarch of Man" (81)—a simulacrum (dildo) of a mutable part (penis) of a cultural fiction associated with power and privilege (man). The penis, they find, is not solely driven by its owner's will to pleasure and power but requires external support. Its animus originates not in the mind of its man but depends, outwardly, on feminine parts (feet, stockings, bosoms, the women remark) for action. The conversation exposes penetrative and therefore political power as temporary, fleeting, and environmentally contingent. Cultural practices of masculine authority, the women realize, occlude the fallibility of men's subjectivities and their erections, which are, at best, semi-potent, as dependent on internal will as on external conditions. The dildo's erect supremacy reveals the pernicious fictions that unjustly construct masculine personhood as unvarying. The penis, as likely to be supple as strong, is different but "equivalent" to women's correspondent parts, and it is the sustaining of a series of faulty metaphors that has granted men political, social, and sexual privilege. The permanently erect sex toy is discursively separated from the male body by women characters whose feminist analysis unfolds from their genital knowledge: the takeaway is that there is no sexed basis for political or social privilege. Only pornography can stage women's genital discussion with such candor.

This sapphic conversation refutes the phallocentric logic often attributed to pornography. Stephen Marcus influentially claims that in Victorian pornography the male "organ becomes the person, and woman ceases to be a woman," but here, women not only stay women but become skeptics by recognizing the fallacy exposed by the dildo: always erect, it is not merely but precisely different from the penis, whose capacity to penetrate is as transient as femininity and its parts.[33] And far from joining with unvarying personhood, the "organ" is shown to depend at least as much on "contexts beyond the person," as Jonathan Kramnick emphasizes of eighteenth-century consciousness, as on the will of the subject in the body to which it is joined.[34] Characteristics like ambition and appetite culturally, artificially attach to men. So does the dildo's erect state, and the powerful and territorial acts of which it is thought to be capable. Men's bodies, this scene asserts, are unlike these unchanging aggressive states: the dialogue reveals the illusory process through which phallic genitals are misunderstood and their false associations abstracted into an illegitimate basis for political and legal monopoly. Little wonder then that, as Ula Lukszo

Klein finds, eighteenth-century dildos raised "anxieties about male sexual prowess and fragile masculinity."[35]

The dildo serves a curious purpose in *Progress*. It is mainly a conversation piece, as it had been in the 1706 poem *Dildoides*, where a council of men debates the value of dildos before setting fire to a dozen of them. Some argue that they save women's honor, providing "other Means . . . [f]or Nature to be satisfy'd" than pursuing sex with men, while others believe "Idolatry will fill the Land" if women have easy access to them.[36] Their conversation imagines the orderly and disorderly effects of dildo use. *Progress* implies that the dildo fulfills a demand beyond the vaginal pleasure discussed in *Dildoides*, allowing women to develop expertise on matters of sexual injustice. This knowledge does not cancel their penetrative desire, we'll see, but the narrative cannot imagine a harmonious or sentient heterosexual coupling for these young women. Their analysis of the dildo leads to feminist revelation, and within the temporal frame of the narrative it never is used to penetrate. While it presumably satisfied Miss Forward's aunt, its dimensions are uncompanionable for the desiring virgin's body. Once Miss Forward had examined the dildo's proportions, she determined "to make immediate Trial of its Merit" (83). Her body, though, cannot accommodate it. Despite "various vain attempts . . . laudable Perseverance . . . [and] all the Emolients in the Compass of Pharmacy," Miss Forward is unable to insert the dildo: "The odious Magnitude hinted at, left me no other Consolation than that it was entirely useless" (84). She is dismayed, and yearns for a penis attached to a man, specifically a lusty Irish lord of her acquaintance who, she's certain, would gain vaginal "Admission" (85). But Lord Blessington's penis is absent, and its substitute is the woman's own hand; Miss Forward soon "digitizes," a skill at which, we learned earlier, she is adept.

Miss Forward's wish for Blessington's penis is soon fulfilled when, in the narrative's hasty conclusion, he penetrates her as she sleeps. The closing scene might seem to challenge my claim that *Progress* subordinates penetrative heterosex to other forms of pleasure and knowledge, but it in fact underscores the impossibility of envisioning a socially just heterosexuality. Reading Ovid in a garden temple to Cupid, she drifts off, dreams of

Blessington, and awakes with "Amazement and Confusion" in a "strange Posture," being penetrated from behind by a person she cannot see (93). Seduction, consent, initial penetration are elided. "[T]he vehement agitation of something, that seem'd hot, and very hard" brings on an "Excess of Ecstacy," and a thick brogue—she cannot bring herself to look upon the unknown partner—reveals the aggressor to be Blessington, about whom she'd been dreaming, returned to consummate an earlier flirtation (94–95). The penis is, to be sure, a *deus ex machina* that delivers the ecstasy Miss Forward desired. But the scene does more than confirm the narrator's pleasure. Its physical acrobatics ask us to see consensual intercourse and rape as two sides of the same coin, unfolding as they do simultaneously: in her dream, Miss Forward designates Blessington as her object of desire, but in the waking world, he penetrates an unconscious partner and is unresponsive to her confusion upon waking. This sole instance of penetrative sensation is ostentatiously incomplete, lacking any account of how the coupling comes to be—except, definitively, that Miss Forward is cognitively absent. While *Progress* delivers this penetration as the literal ultimate sex act, the narrative omits any first-person account of volitional vaginal receptivity. Instead, it features penetrable genitals as sites of noncorrespondence with masculinity's signifiers.

Clitoral Spectacle: *The History of the Human Heart*

The single extant copy of *The Progress of Nature* is bound in a volume with the longer pornographic picaresque, *The History of the Human Heart: or, the Adventures of a Young Gentleman*, a novel with a little-known publication history from 1749 to 1968 (see Figure P.1). Its long textual life suggests that its method of featuring sex acts—weaving spectacular genital episodes into a meandering and miscellaneous comic plot—was recognizable to generations of collectors and publishers as pornography. *Human Heart* was first printed in 1749 in London by J. Freeman, publisher of many anonymous texts promising intrigue and topicality to the midcentury reader.[37] It is exactly contemporary with Cleland's *Woman of Pleasure* but is less relentless in its genital focus. In the nineteenth century, it occupied a definitive position in the lineage of texts being assembled by publishers, sellers, and collectors of pornography (see Chapter 3), and it makes a final appearance as a pulp paperback in 1968 (see Chapter 4). It has otherwise been minimally noticed by researchers of pornography's history.[38]

Human Heart deploys many of the characteristics I identified as pornographic in Chapter 1—seduction scenes, genital description, philosophical commentary, failures of vaginal penetration—into a highly performative fictional narrative. It coheres around a hero and his erotic curiosities but does not easily or simply fulfill them; and the narrative often assumes women's critical perspectives on their sexual use. Like *Progress of Nature*, *Human Heart* asks skeptical questions about the origins of gender hierarchy. Genitalia are central and abundant, perhaps stoking erotic interest, but I challenge the knee-jerk conclusion that such a spectacle imperatively aroused readers. Genital activities are not certain or predetermined, and penetrative heterosex is no simple, uninterrupted process. Penetration is, in fact, not the lead story of sexual interaction in eighteenth-century pornography. Sex organs become sites at which the narrative separates bodies from cultural fictions, asking how and why social identities attach to genital parts. I consider this skepticism feminist because it typically concludes in favor of women, making their subordination visible and identifying the conventions through which it is produced and maintained. As we will see in the next section, however, by the time *Human Heart* is first pirated eighteen years later, this feminist project is already being eroded.

Read cursorily, *Human Heart*'s foregrounding of vaginal availability might appear phallocentric, as when the teenage Camillo experiments with his cousin Maria, striving to penetrate her genitally for several nights in a row. They aim at the kind of intercourse argued by Henry Abelove to have become the dominant form by the late eighteenth century: "penis in vagina, vagina around penis, with seminal emission uninterrupted," a form of sex that resulted, Abelove speculates, in a pronounced population increase in this century and that was preceded by a greater plurality of sexual practices not necessarily aimed at seminal penetration.[39] This instance, too, eschews the reproductive model: in the couple's final attempt, Camillo succeeds at the first two stages Abelove describes, but not the last. He "push[es] boldly to pierce the obstructing *Hymen*," staining himself with blood and retreating from action "at a Time, when the ravished Nymph most wanted him to maintain with Vigour that Post she found he had just arrived at, and every Inch of which he had gained with infinite Toil and Labor"—but, it turns out, "he had spent his Fire" during his efforts to penetrate.[40] Maria and her genitals are figured as available, eager, and still desiring ("she asked him why he retired from her Arms" [46]). Camillo is poised in a position of unencumbered access, but his penis does not renew its erection in time to try again. He has so strained himself that he spends the next day in a fever (a giveaway to his disapproving parents). "[T]he hurt he had got" trying to penetrate Maria, who seems to have emerged without injury, reverses the gendered trope of feminine defloration, granting pain instead to the penetrator (46).[41]

Human Heart's plot traces the history of Camillo, a Shropshire boy born to a wealthy family, from conception to marriage. It wends its way through the sexual discoveries of adolescence and the bawdy mischief of his grand tour through London and Holland, during which he seduces women, attends masquerades, patronizes brothels, feigns betrothals, and performs the part of agonized lover until he is tricked into a surprise marriage to the Belgian Angelina. She, having already succumbed to Camillo's "repeated searches" of her body, boldly pursues him from Amsterdam to London (280). An introduction and footnotes frame the main narrative, elaborating on its scientific, cultural, and philosophical assumptions. Their effect is both ponderous and comic, layering the main narrative's sometimes explicit, sometimes allusive descriptions of genital acts with sober reflection and expansive significance. Alternately lusty prose, scientific treatise, and personal history, the narrative features and describes sex acts, but it also does much more. It leads the reader away from local sexual episodes into the discursive nether regions of the footnotes, displaying a confidence that the reader will be attentive and amused as the text meanders. As Figure 2.2 shows, these notes run the main text almost entirely off the page. *Human Heart* advances a historical view of pornography as a disorganized and unplanned field of overlap between narrated sexual

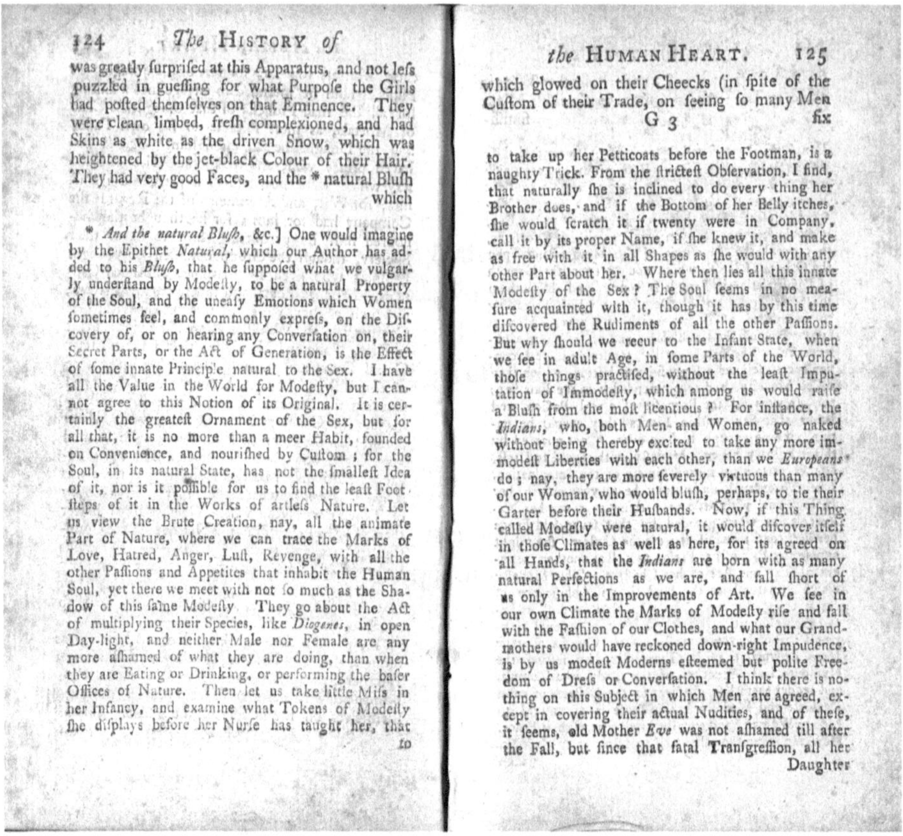

FIGURE 2.2. Speculative footnotes eclipse sexual description in *The History of the Human Heart*. London, 1749.
Singer-Mendenhall Collection, Kislak Center for Special Collections, Rare Books and Manuscripts, University of Pennsylvania.

experience and countless other discourses sexuality engages. It blithely leaves these threads open and unresolved, inviting readers to explore them without a particular endpoint being privileged over any other.[42]

Human Heart's introduction immediately discredits the text's integrity and establishes its comic spirit. The author's lineage, we learn, is a kind of pastiche: he is born in Wales to a father of Scottish Highland descent and a "*Lancashire* Witch" mother whose maternal line extended to Ireland (2). Using his sometimes reliable "Second Sight" (3), the author practices fortune telling, comes under the mentorship of a "*Rosicrucian* Philosopher" (6), and inherits his talisman, which delivers Camillo's story to the author. It is Camillo's "adventures" that constitute the main text. Before publication, the author edits the manuscript with the input of his landlady and appends copious footnotes "moral, historical, and critical" contributed by the landlady's "worthy" gentleman friend (11). These notes divide and defer genital descriptions in the main text. The penetration of Maria's "obstructive *Hymen*," for instance, is dispersed across three printed pages, displaced by a footnote that overviews anatomical debates on the hymen (44–46). (After a lengthy consideration of all sides, the editor concludes that the English overvalue it.)

The accumulation of these various media is the printed text we encounter. The introduction labors to establish that the main text is not to be taken terribly seriously.[43] The story arrives through a dubious medium, the notes are arbitrarily appended, and the author edits the manuscript based on his landlady's level of boredom, cutting until she can "hear it out without once yawning" (11). *Human Heart* offers itself as cumulative labor gathered into print, an example of the mediation Christina Lupton attributes to much midcentury fiction, wherein "a book [is] sentient about its limited conditions of production and reception and resistant to human efforts to usurp its ironic, critical authority."[44] Before the narrative even begins, *Human Heart* resists any singular authority we might grant to the pornographic text, such as the authority to arouse. Sexually excitable reading is not posited as a focused or singular enterprise. Reading is, rather, highly mediated: readers are not positioned to read sex earnestly or transparently, but rather to be part of an extended joke, a comic experiment that episodically offers sexual description. Nor is reading about sex envisioned as a private activity tantamount to masturbation, as Laqueur envisioned; it is instead figured as synchronic exchange among author, landlady, and editor, more closely resembling sociable erotic reading, which Karen Harvey has posited as an eighteenth-century practice.[45] Because of their collective impact on the narrative, the text is positioned as disintegrated, shaped by a motley crew of amateurs and arousing various curiosities among them.

In the main narrative, Camillo's sexual development is not portrayed as a linear, uninterrupted process. Rather, his sexual discoveries constitute an adaptable medium through which his world can be experienced—genitally, yes, but just as often sensibly, affectively, and cognitively. Sexual encounters lead to thinking and speculating, for hero and reader alike. At times, his sexual actions are altogether unwitting, as in his childhood. Readers observe the development of his appetites as he suckles his mother's breast; in the nursery, where he parses the bawdy jokes of nurses; in the family orchard, where he traumatically discovers his sister's "great Wound" as she climbs up a cherry tree (31); in his first circuitous sexual experiments with Maria. In all these early experiences, sex and its bodily effects arrive unannounced to Camillo as points of unsettling confusion. Sex acts are something of a constant in the plot, but their return is not confidently or evenly signaled to the reader, even as Camillo's desires become more conscious and plotted during his grand tour. Camillo's own thoughts reveal uncertainty: until later in the narrative, he is rarely sure how to succeed at courtship and at times appears as flummoxed by the trappings of seduction as are his women partners. He seeks guidance from his tutor Vilario, whose instructions aim at gratifying Camillo's desires above all else. While the plot is largely structured by Camillo's sexual pursuits, the narrator attends commodiously to the thinking, planning, and frustration of those pursuits, unlike Cleland's Fanny Hill, who "slip[s] over matters of no importance" between sexual encounters.[46] In these intervals between sexual events, the text explores other topics: domestic life, education, and maturation.

The footnotes move even further afield of a direct discussion of sexuality. Of the fifteen that are dispersed across the narrative, six describe biological and anatomical concerns, such as fertilization, pregnancy, lust, and the hymen; five weigh in on cultural questions, such as friendship between the sexes and women's education; and four use empiricist epistemology to explain how the mind responds to instances of heightened stimulation. The footnotes impinge on the main narrative. They seem to "block the readers' access to the story," as Darryl Domingo observes typographical design to do in this era of print, "dup[ing] readers into gazing, staring, and gaping at curiosities" other than the ostensible main event.[47]

On the page, footnotes reduce Camillo's sexually eventful history to one or two lines of printed type, and they sometimes run for pages. Thematically, they challenge the easy path to sexual meaning we find in the main narrative. Rhetorically, they are pedantic, and purposefully so, for we are to hear the farcically learned voice as humorously discordant with the main text. The text calls for what Stephen Best and Sharon Marcus call "surface reading," "insist[ing] on being looked *at* rather than . . . see[n] *through*."[48] The notes deflect readers' involvement in any single topic or pursuit, creating a textual surface that invites readers to make connections across its parts. A scene of nuptial passion is paired, for instance, with a footnote on theories of insemination. The notes boast specialized language and training: "This Doctrine [of insemination by the male] was more controverted, and less understood, till the ingenious *Mr. Leewenhoeck*, by his microscopal observations, discovered the Animalculae in the Semen Humanum, which has put the Question beyond all Controversy" (15)—and this is just a way of introducing the larger question of when the soul animates the fetus, which the editor concludes must be when it is yet "in the Loins of the Parent" (16). He also occasionally calls on English history to provide evidence for his claims. He warns women of the impressionability of the fetus, for example, by recalling courtier David Rizzio's murder, a spectacle witnessed by James I's mother during her pregnancy that, he insists, affected the temperament of the king. Scientifically, historically, and rhetorically, the footnotes move away from the personal history being narrated above them.

The comic effect is therefore no quick, slapstick punctuation of the main text's sexual focus; it is comedy hard-won, where readers meander into detailed, lengthy elaborations that tediously debate quick assumptions of the narrator. Further, the authoritative voice lends itself to a skeptical reaction in the reader. The editor espouses modern reproductive knowledge that emphasizes sexual difference between men and women, but he at times sounds antiquated in his beliefs, such as his concern over the fetus's impressionability. The reader is thus called upon periodically to assess the editor's competence—no easy task in an era that, according to Tim Hitchcock, saw the uneven development of an elite medical discourse on reproduction that stood quite apart from an ongoing popular belief in the old humoral model of the body.⁴⁹ *Human Heart* might be seen, in fact, to stage the concurrence of these different registers of sexual understanding. Rather than impart authoritative knowledge, this discussion exercises the flexible attentions of what Natalie Philips calls a "multifocal" reader whose "attention is intrinsically multiple," one willing to follow narrative paths away from an erotic plot and to gauge these dilations' relevance and accuracy.⁵⁰ The text's reprinters in the next century will find them increasingly bothersome and will delete them without ceremony.

Human Heart offers scenes that conform to pornography conventionally defined, but they equally provide philosophical elaboration and feminist commentary on common sexual practice. They feature, as did so much of the literature cited in the last chapter, women whose bodies are transactional—whose genital parts are pursued and overvalued by Camillo, or who are paid for sex work. Their main purpose in the scene is not to be genitally receptive but to prompt discourse on matters of sexual justice. One such episode, which I previewed in my Introduction, involves a performance by posture girls for Camillo and his friends at a London bagnio during a "Town Ramble" (122). This scene is paradigmatic for how I understand pornography to work at this early point in the genre's history as narrative form, interrupting men's pursuit of women's bodies with precise genital description, philosophical paratext, women's statements about the ramifications of sexual labor, and uncertainty about masculine sexual performance. The choreography of the scene is as follows: the posture girls strip "stark naked" and pose on a tabletop, each with a filled wine glass balanced on her pubis from which a man drinks (123).⁵¹ The women then imitate various sexual positions, pay particular attention to Camillo as the novice to their revels, masturbate in unison, and ejaculate into the glasses that are then drunk off by the men. Prostitutes arrive after the posture girls explain they don't offer their bodies for penetrative sex. Thick genital description contends with two other threads: one tracks Camillo's varying affective responses, while the other offers a feminist analysis of the concept of modesty in a footnote so massive it edges the main action off the page.

The focus moves from the women's overall bodies to their faces to their genitals, with Camillo visually arrested by all, and made self-conscious by the novelty with which it strikes him. "They had very good Faces, and the natural Blush which glowed on their Cheeks" (about which the editor will soon have much to say) "rendered them in *Camillo*'s Mind, finished Beauties" (124–127). He is "greatly surprised" (124) at their readiness for genital display, marveling that they blush even though "so many Men fix their Eyes on that Part which all other Women chuse to hide" (125–126). Camillo's visual captivation moves in a clitoral direction:

> From viewing their Faces, he bashfully cast his Eyes on the Altar of Love, which never had so fair a View as at this present time . . . the Parts of the celebrated Posture Girl, had something about them which attracted his attention more than any thing he had either felt or seen. The Throne of Love was thickly covered with jet-black hair, at least a Quarter of a Yard Long, which she artfully spread asunder to display the Entrance to the Magic Grotto. The uncommon Figure of this bushy Spot, afforded a very odd sort of Amusement to *Camillo*, which was more heightened by the rest of the Ceremony which these Wantons went through. (127–128)

The passage alternates between collective genital display of multiple women and a grammatically singular "Throne," "Figure," and "Spot." The "uncommon" "something" that draws his attention implies an enlarged or particularly visible clitoris, an organ by this point associated, as we know from Miss Forward's "digitizing" in *Progress*, with non-penetrative sexual pleasure. By some accounts, the significance of clitoral orgasm was declining in physiological discourses of the moment. As Harvey argues, though, pornography "did not say the same thing" as science, and *Human Heart* showcases women's management of their own sexual climaxes.[52]

The clitoris features as a center of their performance:

> They each filled a Glass of Wine, and laying themselves in an extended Posture placed their Glasses on the Mount of *Venus*, every Man in Company drinking off the Bumper, as it stood on that tempting Protuberance, while the Wenches were not wanting in their lascivious Motions, to heighten the Diversion. Then they went thro' the several Postures and

> Tricks made use of to raise debilitated Lust, when cloyed with natural Enjoyment. (127–128)

The language of fascination merges with terms of disgust as the women more actively display and engage their genitals. Directing the movements of those involved, they next "oblig[e] poor *Camillo*," the initiate to this bawdy ritual, "to shoot the Bridge, and pass under the warm Cataracts"—presumably, positions himself in some way under or between the women's legs—to the amusement of the company (128).[53] Thus far, not only has Camillo's attention been arrested by the "tempting Protuberance" of the clitoris, but he is subordinated to it through the women's direction of the ritual.

The posture girls then masturbate in unison. We've seen this passage in my book's Introduction, but it warrants reiteration here:

> Having resumed a proper Posture, with wanton Fingers they entered the mysterious Cave, and heaved, and thrust, and riggled, till they opened the teeming Springs, which shot their volatile Liquids into a Wine Glass, each held in the other Hand——But here the Reader will hardly believe me, though I assure him on the Credit of my *Talisman*, that what the Glasses received, was mingled with their Wine, and drank off without the least Shock to the Nature of any one present, except *Camillo*. (128–129)

Clitoral display gives way to women's energetic masturbation and simultaneous ejaculation, a climax celebrated by the group's toasting with the discharged liquid. The men then request intercourse, but the posture girls decline, refusing "the Embraces of the Men, for fear of spoiling their Trade," and prostitutes are called (129). Camillo receives two women, and after his hesitation and flaccidity are resolved, manages to satisfy them both.

As the narrator signals, the ceremony around women's ejaculation is spectacular and remarkable. The level of detail is high, and the episode is entirely absorbed with women's genital activity; penises are only inferred at the scene's end, when the men request penetration. The scene is pornographic by any measure, focusing on eroticized bodies, masculine witness, non-reproductive and non-domestic sexuality. It asserts the ejaculative capacity of female genitalia, disputing the belief asserted in other writings of the time, that clitorises "are capable of every Action belonging to a Man, but that of Ejaculation."[54] The pornographic description, it should be noted, is complete without reference to men's bodies or their capacity to penetrate.

In this original edition, the posture-girl episode is textually overrun by a footnote offering feminist speculations on the action in the main text; its beginning is shown in Figure 2.2. In the note, the editor questions a passing remark made by the author that the posture girls possess a natural modesty that causes them to blush. The editor rejects modesty as a natural feminine attribute, defining the concept instead as a longstanding cultural invention. The author assumes, mistakenly in the editor's view, that modesty is

> a natural Property of the Soul, and [that] the uneasy Emotions which Women sometimes feel . . . on hearing any Conversation on their Secret parts, or the Act of Generation, is the effect of some innate Principle natural to the Sex. I have all the Value in the World for Modesty, but I cannot agree to this Notion of its Original. It is certainly the greatest Ornament of the Sex, but for all that, it is no more than a meer Habit, founded on Convenience, and nourished by Custom. (124)

Disputing common consensus, the editor provides evidence that modesty is not instinctual—genital display is practiced by both infants and indigenous people, he points out—and he claims that social fictions are devised to impose strict codes of conduct on English women, curbing their knowledge and ambition. The editor does not disapprove of the result of these strictures. He goes on to imagine the chaos of a culture without modesty in which the sexes encounter each other without cultural interference—that is, without clothing. If women's genitals were exposed, men's "Organs of Sense" would respond with visible erections, "prevent[ing] the Growth of Dissimulation in Female Discourse" (126). These erections would cause heterosexual desire to be made an explicit part of social interaction, either as an embarrassing materiality or a declaration of sexual intention. Sexual possibility would be a manifest content of the social; rituals of politeness would be desublimated. In such a world, chastity would not be a sustainable condition.

The editor recognizes this conjectural world as sexually anarchic:

> The first Moralists, foreseeing these Inconveniences, feigned a supposititious Virtue, which they called Modesty, and recommended it to the Fair Sex; this answers all the Purposes of a real Passion, and keeps that Sex within Limits they would be naturally prone enough to leap over, if not guarded by this imaginary Fence. (126)[55]

Modesty is instrumental, he concludes, a system that maintains the social order. The editor praises this scheme as one that empowers women to determine their social identity and urges parents and educators to impart it as early as possible to girls. Parsed closely, this passage also offers the fleeting insight that women are "naturally prone enough to leap over" impediments to their freedom: modesty is not innate, but liberty is. The note provides a kind of origin story for gendered forms of personhood, moving into realms of conjectural history, social contract theory, and feminist analysis: if we were nudists, we would be heterosexually egalitarian because sexual innocence would be impossible. It follows that the world sustains a custom experienced as natural—in a word, hegemony—that women disavow genital knowledge or feeling, providing an instrumental order to the libidinal underpinnings of heterosociality. Inversely and implicitly, the footnote asserts that genital exposure would establish egalitarianism in the world of heterosexual exchange, reducing men's social primacy.

The footnote departs from the main narrative in many ways. It distracts from the descriptions of sex acts unfolding above it on the page; it strikes a speculative tone that contrasts with the sequential account of Camillo's experience; and it isolates what would seem a minor point ("natural" is a passing adjective) and bloats it into a concept available for deep questioning. Within this questioning, elements of the pornographic topos—genitals and women—are reconfigured and defamiliarized, becoming objects not of erotic fascination but of social interest. The suggestiveness of the editor's insights into sexual injustice may or may not be perceived by the eighteenth-century reader, and there is no way to tell how this discussion would affect the reader's response to the narrative description of sexual performance taking place in the main text. Are readers disgusted by the spectacle? Aroused? Curious? Did readers bother reading the footnote? If they did, did they read carefully, skeptically, dimly, impatiently? Did they detect the feminist implications of the editor's observations? The text is unconcerned with stabilizing these questions, but one fundamental premise is clear: in *Human Heart*, reading about sex is a process of awareness and reflection that exceeds erotic response and that is conducive to associations beyond specifically erotic contexts, leading even, as in this case, to ethical discoveries that might complicate the pleasure of beholding nude women.

This first iteration of *Human Heart*'s posture-girl scene—an episode that will be reprinted and altered through the late twentieth century—is the only version that will pair a complete account of women's genitals with dissenting commentary on their differential personhood. The source text for all later versions, this edition establishes spectacular vaginal and clitoral display as a companion content for feminist theory. The exposure of cultural fictions around women's modesty and sexual capacities was an inception point for modern pornography: at its core, this example suggests, pornographic narrative contains ongoing commentary on the artifice of gender inequity, even as the practices of such inequity make possible the sex acts and desires that motor the narrative. In other words, the very inequities between men and women that eroticize genital scenes are themselves the subject of inquiry and deconstruction in pornographic texts.

As this episode and its footnote make clear, the author of *Human Heart* expects readers to balance multiple demands simultaneously as they move through and around this text, and Chapters 3 and 4 offer further examples of this complexity. Readers and writers seem to have no anxiety about the frequency of erotic episodes, satisfied to read about other forms of mischief between Camillo's first attempts with Maria and his sexual sporting across Europe. The pleasures of reading appear to reside precisely in the multitasking that is required for a full understanding of sexual meaning and the philosophical possibilities that proliferate from it. Through Maria, the author emphasizes the genital vulnerability of the hero and the overvaluation of the hymen; the seduced Saphira condemns sexual violence (a scene I discuss in Chapter 4); and sex workers provide a spectacle of pleasure absent the interventions of men and inviting remarks on the misogynist invention of modesty. At this rich moment in pornography's history, when texts addressing sexual matters were not entirely differentiated from other forms of literature, and long before a distinct market for pornography existed, descriptions of sex acts served as vehicles for discussions of perception, science, ethics, and feminism that unfold instead of—or in competition with, or in service of, or parallel to—erotic satisfaction. There were multiple pleasurable outcomes to reading pornography, and these outcomes did not uniformly serve the body; but they did uniformly theorize sexual justice.

Circumcision: *The Memoirs of B—— Tracey*

In 1757, about two-thirds of *Human Heart* was pirated and retitled *The Memoirs of B—— Tracey*. Its piracy was no secret. A reviewer in Ralph Griffith's *Monthly Review* for 1757 correctly noted that *Tracey* is "stolen from a wretched book, published about seven years ago . . . and now imposed on the Public for a new Work."[56] The dismissive review doesn't convey how the source text was altered: character names are changed, the last third of the novel disappears, the textual apparatus—introduction and footnotes—are omitted, and its descriptions of women's genitals are vastly reduced. Rather than end with the hero's marriage to a resourceful cross-dressed wooer, *Tracey* terminates in the midst of a scene in a Dutch brothel, part of the protagonist's grand tour. With striking precision, the editor of *Tracey* removes not only the assertive Angelina ultimately married by the hero, but also most labial, genital, and clitoral detail, eliding the spectacle and the discourse that had attended women's bodies in the original. What results is a genitally allusive narrative that bypasses opportunities for deliberating over genitalia and their cultural meaning—a narrative that, in other words, wishes to uncomplicate its hero's apprehension of women's sexual availability.

As we saw above, *Human Heart* associated female genital spectacle with masculine adolescent development, and it regularly focused ethical or feminist discussions around the thinking those details prompt in the editor's footnotes. *Tracey* has no concern with developmental narrative or its source text's philosophical debates, eliminating elements the narrator considers "quite immaterial"—twenty-six pages of introduction and early childhood development—to commence the story when the hero, renamed Billario, is twelve and his cousin Lucia (formerly Maria) joins the household.[57] Their initial experiments had featured her genitalia prominently in 1749, from Camillo's initial, non-penetrative "beat[ing] the bush" (42), through several amorous encounters in which Maria pursues genital activity, to Camillo's anti-climactic penetration that leaves him feverish, his antics discovered by his parents, as we saw earlier. These repeated vaginal references are excised by *Tracey*'s editor. In a focused erasure, Billario meets Lucia in bed only once, and their "toy[ing]" is abruptly interrupted by a domestic servant who reports them to his outraged parents. Lucia is locked in for the night, and Billario is punished for indiscretion rather than for the penetrative sex that was revealed in 1749. Five printed pages of the original are suppressed, and along with them, their explication of women's sexual volition.

Accounts of physical contact with women's parts are also suppressed. In the 1749 and 1757 editions, the hero beholds a slumbering nymph, hoping for sexual access. The visual spectacle of her unguarded body delights protagonist and narrator alike. Her face, blush, and smile are

> sufficient to animate the most impotent Mortal; but the lower Region would have given Life to Prometheus's Man of Clay, and saved him the Trouble of stealing Fire from Heaven, for her snowy Bosom appeared in full View; the Bed-cloths . . . left the Nymph quite naked, even her Shift furled itself up above her Middle, and unveiled the sacred Territories of mysterious Love. Her ivory Limbs lay negligently extended, as unwilling to bar the Gates of Bliss. (*H* 188–189; *B* 159–160)[58]

The woman's body lies open and receptive to the hero. *Human Heart* adds a detail: that one hand covers her genitals. This covering invites the hero to imagine the erotic spectacle, which prompts the narrator in the original to assert the superiority of touch over sight:

> ... but, that Imagination might have room to play, and the raptured Swain something more to wish for than what he saw, her Right-Hand was just placed upon the Confines of the Fount of Love, and shrowded that which is better felt than seen. (*H* 188)

In *Tracey*, the encounter is much simpler, with the woman's genitals entirely exposed, skipping straight to the hero arrested by her erotic beauty; he "stopped and gazed, and wished the beauteous Scene might last for ever" (*H* 188; *B* 160). While he watches, she dreams of penetration, miming to grasp a penis (her hands "seemed to hug something between them with extreme Eagerness") and uttering a surrender ("I must,—I must—yield to my Undoing") (*H* 188; *B* 161). The hero interprets her actions as invitation and attempts to rape her, but he is prevented by her "shriek[ing] out loud enough to have awakened those in the next House" (*H* 189; *B* 161). *Human Heart* heightens the complexity of this scene of sexual assault by emphasizing, as *Tracey* did not, that the woman's body is "better felt than seen," a statement by the narrator that previews and rationalizes the hero's sexual aggression. Her hand placed to block her genitals, even as she slumbers, accentuates the hero's breaching of boundaries that he could, the narrative implies, observe. Imaginative complexity, women's genital autonomy, the distinction between unconscious fantasy and conscious will—all are smoothed by the editor of *Tracey*, who directs the hero on a less encumbered path to genital access.

Most significantly, the editor abridges the posture-girl scene. In 1757, clitoral detail is deleted at the sentence level. In *Human Heart*, the hero's attention was absorbed by the beauty of the women overall, then their faces, then the "parts of the celebrated Posture Girl," specifically an "uncommon Figure, this bushy spot." The compressed passage in *Tracey* treats the "uncommon" as though it's the general spectacle of women performing sexual postures.

The uncommon Figure afforded a very odd sort of Amusement to *Camillo*, which was more heightened by the rest of the Ceremony which these Wantons went through. Then they went thro' the several Postures and Tricks made use of to raise debilitated Lust, when cloyed with natural Enjoyment. *Camillo* began now to be disgusted at the prodigious Impudence of the Women; he found in himself no more of that uneasy Emotion he felt at their first setting out, and was desirous of the Company's dismissing them; but his Companions would not part with them, till they had gone through the whole of their Exercise; the Nymphs, who raised a fresh Contribution on every new Discovery of their impudent Inventions, required no Entreaties to gratify the young Rakes, but proceeded, without the least Sense of shame, to shew them how far Human Nature could debase itself. (*B* 93–94)

The entirety of the footnotes excised, no accompanying commentary on modesty unfurls. In 1749, this scene featured labial, clitoral, and vaginal detail within and among the performed actions, and we'll recall Camillo's oscillating affects (admiring, attentive, disgusted, reluctant). It was an eventful, irreverent scene that co-mingled multiple registers of action and meaning. In 1757, we receive distant facts about the sexual performance—*that* it happens, rather than *how*—and, above all, an account of Billario's increasing revulsion and alienation from the action others consider erotic. And readers are not invited, as they were in 1749, to consider the inhibiting effects of customary femininity on women "prone enough" to enlarge their spheres of autonomy.

One other succeeding edition, expensively printed in 1885 and discussed in Chapter 3, removes the coordinated ejaculation and, I think not coincidentally, the footnotes as well. That edition, like *Tracey*, declines to tolerate spectacular evidence of women's bodies being sexually moved by women themselves; it also opts to mute the footnote's argument that artificial constructs of culture are designed to obstruct feminine autonomy. Both editions designated *Human Heart* a source text for producing sensational narrative to engage sexually curious readers; both editions deselect elaborate descriptions of the gendering of women. They represent a thread of pornography's history aimed at reducing sexual content, which in 1749 included clitoral description, ejaculation, and open acknowledgement of the subjugation of women through everyday social operations.

Sex Work, Independence, and Imperial Contexts

Prostitute narratives corroborate the claims made in pornographic fiction about the undue impact on women of the everyday social relations that produce gender. As the young women in *Progress* find phallic power to be illusory, and as *Human Heart*'s posture girls prompt musings on the gender hierarchy sustained by moral philosophy, so narratives of sex work examine how genital traffic creates women's social disadvantage. They do not detail sex acts graphically, but such activity constitutes the very labor of its central characters. And while sex is not portrayed as harmful in every case, the narratives recur to patterns of violence, associating coercion and abuse with women's entry into sex work, but also their entry into marriage, which is shown to be as imperiling as involuntary sex work.[59] Certain episodes show that wives' and prostitutes' privatization by men subjects them to economic vulnerability and physical distress. Disenfranchised by age, poverty, or social invisibility, they are barred from calling for protection or removal. I consider these narratives companion texts to the fictions that form the center of this chapter. Like the picaresque fictions but with a tighter affiliation to the lived world—central characters are often based on historical people—they object to the alienation of women from their own bodies on ethical grounds. The discourse on sex work also registers its global scale, reminding us that British pornography's calls for justice on behalf of white women are insufficient to imagine sexual justice for women in colonial contexts.

Memoirs of the Celebrated Miss Fanny M—— (1758)—a narrative based on the life of the courtesan Fanny Murray—identifies socioeconomic vulnerability as a precondition for the rape and trafficking of young women.[60] By age twelve, Fanny is orphaned and working as a flower vendor in Bath when she is raped and abandoned by the aristocratic Jack Spencer, and by fourteen she is kept by the rake Mr. Easy (based on socialite Beau Nash).

The narrator explains Fanny's constancy to Mr. Easy as rooted in a complex and resilient virtue. When Fanny is courted by the knight Sir Thomas Flighty, she declines his advances by declaring devotion and gratitude to the aging Easy.[61] Flighty abducts her, and Easy manages to reclaim her before Flighty assaults her. The narrator concludes this episode (and prepares readers for the next, which features a sexually inconstant woman) with a discourse on the complexity of feminine virtue in environments that test sexual chastity.

Virtue, the narrator argues, is too often conflated with chastity. Women "are taught to believe all virtue is centered in chastity; and as long as they maintain that unsullied, they think themselves the most virtuous of their sex" (1.20). Chastity is the simpler concept of the two, "a subordinate virtue" requiring defense against myriad petty vices. It can be threatened by a woman's own physical lust as well as other passions: "Vanity, envy, malice, jealousy, revenge, and avarice, are all auxiliaries to incontinence" (1.20). If these fragilities are exposed, women's "small fortress of chastity [might be] taken by surprise or treachery" (1.20). Men may prey on the material and vengeful passions of naive women, using them as points of sexual access. One takeaway is that the young Fanny's refusal of the knight's advances are especially to be admired. More generally, this discursive interval argues that virtue is a larger, more inclusive category than chastity, based on greater criteria than genital continence. As a smaller, more superficial category, chastity is vulnerable to interference by low-order passions. But it has major social implications for women, often mistakenly substituted for virtue, and so requires the most vigilant guarding against a complex array of affective and social forces that might conspire to undo it.

The narrator urges in women a holistic understanding of the means and motivations through which penetrative sex might be accessed by men prepared to exploit their passions. Like *Human Heart*'s "editor," this narrator sees in a sexual subplot an opportunity for exposing the unjust ways women's social identities are conflated with their vaginal conditions, conditions not always under their governance. For both, sex workers have expertise in the disposal of their bodies and therefore merit ethical consideration. *Fanny M*'s narrator wants to count the non-virginal heroine among virtuous women, while *Human Heart*'s footnote exposes the concept of modesty itself as a source of social violence targeting women. Both recommend close analysis of these most crucial states that accrue to women: modesty, chastity, virtue.

Characters of the Present Most Celebrated Courtezans (1780), a collection of biographical sketches, notes the resourcefulness and autonomy of sex workers, often in the face of adversity and abuse. *Celebrated Courtezans* is uneven in its attitude toward prostitutes, at times vilifying their trade as mercenary and immoral. But attention is also paid, consistently, to the difficult physical conditions of their work and to the coercive means through which they enter it. Their labor is sometimes revealed to be genitally harmful, as for Betsy Cox, compelled at age sixteen into "painful and promiscuous prostitution" by a bawd soon after giving birth.[62] Kitty Frederick's labor is likened to that of a horse, "ridden many private matches," by a Duke who, because of physical weakness, "depends on Kit's deep rate and honest bottom to bring him through"; later a captain "rides her hack on the road" and "sometimes takes the liberty to ride her her sweats" (118–119).

Celebrated Courtezans also generates commentary on marriage as a form of sexual exploitation. Some women are coerced into marriage at a very young age, and it is there that their sexual labor begins. Sophia Baddeley becomes wife at fifteen to a man who "availed himself of her extreme youth . . . to prostitute her mind and person by a marriage . . . heterogeneous and unnatural" (30).[63] The narrator details the husband's brutal abuse: "scarcely did a day elapse without her lovely face or tender frame receiving some wound, mark, or contusion from the hand of the tyrant," and these harms excuse her eventual elopement with another (32). For another character compelled into marriage as a teen, her husband's abuse excuses her adultery: "if the most unprovoked ill usage, the most unmerited barbarity can justify or extenuate her indiscretions, these she may with truth offer in excuse" (105). Eventually, the beneficence of a patron allows her to quit her reliance on men, bringing her "domestic independence and comfort, from which she was so early stolen." The narrator asserts such independence is preferable to the company of men: "we are persuaded, that no temptation can ever induce her to commence a new connection, or to renew any former one" (106–107). Given sufficient means, women will refuse heterosexual connection.

This chapter will continue to put great stock in pornography's disentanglement of British women from forms of sexual commerce that subject them to physical, social, and economic disadvantage. An exit from conditions of sexual exploitation is harder to envision for women in colonial contexts. The philosophical skepticism associated with white women in British texts is difficult to mobilize in environments where the sex work of African-descended women intersected with the slave trade, plantation slavery, and modes of racial classification.[64] Accounts of rape, sex work, and reproductive labor by Wendy Warren, Marisa Fuentes, and Brooke Newman show that in colonial environments, women of African descent were sexually exploited more systematically and with fewer, if any, claims to personhood than white women could make. Working from a single reference to a raped and grieving enslaved woman, Warren places sexual violence at the center of commerce, property, and settlement in New England; and Fuentes documents the frequency of Black women's brothel work and enslaved women's sexual hiring-out by plantation owners in Barbados. Newman shows that in Jamaica, mixed-race women descended from slavery were systematically called on to reproduce with British-descended men, an effort to "whiten" the colonial population, typically without the legal affordances of marriage or parental claims to their children.[65] Through violence, enslavement, and hegemonic sexual practices, the bodies of women of color were abused and operationalized in contexts that can't be approximated by the picaresques I examine here, where young people of propertied classes have the free time to explore each other's bodies, or have access to sex toys imported from the continent, or work their way into lucrative marriages.

In England, the sex work of women of color was imagined to be a form of cosmopolitan industry. The print *Black Brown and Fair* (1807) shows mixed-race and Black women at work in a bagnio at the Wapping docks. Solicited by various men at port—a Black dandy, a Chinese traveler, a Dutch tradesman, and a French fop—they represent a range of sexual options enabled by colonial traffic and, apparently, serving the varied tastes of a global clientele (Figure 2.3). The print's title parodies Alexander Pope's three classifications for British women in *Epistle to a Lady*, where he had celebrated feminine beauty as "Matter too soft a lasting mark to bear, / And best distinguish'd by black, brown, or fair." Extending "black, brown, and fair" to encompass complexions of women working the London ports, Thomas Rowlandson acknowledges racial and class differences that would distinguish them from their comparatively privileged white counterparts. The delicacy Pope assumes of women contrasts markedly with the labor of the portside brothel, with customers flocking to the front window and venereal treatments for sale on site—so signaled by the advertisement for "Leake's Pills" to the right of the window. London's sexual revelry called upon the labor of non-white women, and print culture did not generate a discursive apparatus equal to that which attends representations of white women's bodies. The ballad printed beneath the image explicitly makes this differentiation, identifying white women with love and women of color with sexual error. "With Black, Brown, and Fair, I have frolick'd, 'tis true, / but I never lov'd any, dear Mary, but you." The moral disapproval of this "frolick" is conveyed, perhaps, by the dog who breaks the print's frame, locking its sober eyes accusatorily with the viewer.

Such accounts should arm us with a skepticism against narratives that sentimentalize sex for colonial and enslaved women. *The Woman of Colour: A Tale* (1808) asks us to see the virtuous heroine's conception as an act of love between an enslaved woman (Marcia) and a plantation owner (Fairfield), an account the heroine offers in her own epistolary words: "He purchased the youthful Marcia; his kindness, his familiarity, his humanity, soon gained him an interest in her grateful heart! She loved her master!" Unaware of the construct of chastity, Marcia "indulges" her feelings through a sexual consummation: "she yielded herself to her passion, and fell the victim of gratitude!" After learning Christian precept and instructing her "seducer" to see their sex as sinful, Marcia dies in childbirth, a tragic blow to Fairfield, who "loved Marcia with fervour."[66] The conditions of colonial sex work elucidated by historians, or by Rowlandson's frank depiction, resist the agenda of this sentimentality to codify rape as cross-racial love. Historical conditions should make us uncooperative with fictions

FIGURE 2.3. Women of color at work on the docks. Thomas Rowlandson, *Black Brown and Fair*. London, 1807.

Courtesy of the Lewis Walpole Library, Yale University.

portraying sexual happiness in women under forces of colonialism or enslavement. The very Enlightenment concepts that attach to white women's objections to genital traffic (virtue, property, autonomy) were the bases of colonial disenfranchisement, and so excluded a large portion of women performing sexual labor under empire.

Pornography Without Sex: *The Child of Nature*

Accounts of English sex work—in *Human Heart*, *Fanny M*, *Celebrated Courtezans*—assume women will opt for financial or professional independence over genital indebtedness to men. *The Child of Nature* (1774), falsely attributed to materialist Claude Adrien Helvétius, expands this assertion into a remarkable marriage plot—remarkable for insulating its low-born, unprotected heroine from vaginal traffic, against all odds.[67] We saw in the changes made to *Human Heart* by the editor of *B—— Tracey* that at least one bawdy fiction withdrew from women's genital parts. *Child of Nature* retreats further, containing zero episodes of penetrative heterosex. The material presence of women's genital parts we saw in the 1740s begins to recede after 1750. Comprehensive genital knowledge lent itself so completely to an account of women's sexual self-sufficiency that editors and authors may have started to back away from it, finding a gesture toward women's genitals more alluring and less radical than a cartographic account of labia, clitoris, and vagina; these details were only relevant, *Human Heart* and *Progress* imply, in scenes of women's masturbation. We'll see later in the book that some nineteenth-century editors carried on a tradition of subordinating such description. But other eighteenth-century authors, as in *Child of Nature*, pushed penetrative detail entirely out of the pornographic plot, abandoning it in favor of philosophical commentary on the sexual vulnerability of low-born women, women's mistreatment in a culture of marriage, and the ethics of self-determined sexual pleasure free of social evaluation.

I count *Child of Nature* among eighteenth-century feminist pornographies because, firstly, it generates principled statements about women's genital autonomy (and persistent threats to it). I also consider it pornography because, like *Human Heart*, it was categorized as pornography by bibliographers and publishing circles in the following century, as I'll discuss in the next chapter. While it circulates incisive ideas about women's sexual victimization and their empowerment, the novel does not closely describe genital action. In one of the most attentively detailed scenes, a wooer visits the heroine while she is *en deshabille*:

> My dress, which was scarcely decent when I sat down, was no more so when I stood up—the light silk over me concealed hardly the form, and still less the elasticity of my breast—the more lively and rapid, as I attempted, but in vain, to repress it. . . . Mr. R . . . enjoyed my confusion [and . . .] took my hand in his. . . . One part of my gown, being no longer supported, opened—the veil between my bosom and him dropped—his lips telling me the advantages I had given him, I rouzed from my reverie.[68]

She then politely invites him to wait for her in another room, and he obliges. This is as explicit as sexual description gets.

What is pornographic about the novel is not genital description but its ongoing articulation of the social and economic injustices women endure. The novel repeatedly advances a recurring thesis: that, as the heroine is told by her mother, "men and women are in a natural state of war" (1.196). So it seems for Fanny Ramsay, who is dishonorably courted and physically assaulted by various men until she marries a besotted aristocrat on his deathbed. In her account of how eighteenth-century fiction constitutes women's moral authority, Nancy Armstrong claims that heroines "understand social experience as a series of sexual encounters" en route to their ultimate subordination in "legitimate monogamy."[69] *Child of Nature* literalizes this elision of the sexual and social for women and expands it beyond the domestic realm, as Fanny is continually subjected to evaluation and domination by men to whom she has some social tie. The novel approaches sex philosophically, recognizing it as a sphere of experience deeply connected to the social world, of irreversible consequence to women, and not simply aligned with pleasure or happiness—though, ideally, sex would in every case satisfy an individual's desire or "sensibility." What Fanny encounters serially are not sex acts but men's attempts to access her genitals, all of which are thwarted, making way for the ethical questions these actions provoke. Genital traffic, in this case forestalled, prompts social analysis. Katherine Binhammer associates the seduction narrative with women coming to know their own hearts and emotions, as in Clarissa's insistence "that women's knowledge is not always reduced to carnality or absence of it";[70] *Child of Nature* represents a variation on this epistemological project, dramatizing the heroine coming to know her own economic and bodily interests through a pattern of deflected rape attempts.

Fanny works in the inn run by her mother, who has been left in debt by her late husband. Together they try to secure Fanny a lucrative offer of marriage from among their boarders; but their schemes backfire, resulting in little more than near-seductions, extortions, and offers to keep Fanny as a mistress. Fanny's mercenary efforts lead her into various forms of mistreatment, often prompting shrewd realizations. When boarder Sir George Lendal grows intimate with her family, offering to defray their debts and promising marriage to Fanny, he eventually attempts rape. Fanny fends him off but does not sever ties with him as she knows virtuous women would. Her aim is his fortune, so she forgives his violence:

> Should I lose a husband of his rank through a severity which, though right, I might be justified to employ, by singularity of the circumstance, and his passion for me? I was too vain and prudent to be so extremely delicate and severe. (1.71)

Fanny orchestrates a second encounter to test Lendal's intentions, which are revealed to be duplicitous. She grieves the lost opportunity for social ascendancy: "Lady Lendal sunk for ever into Fanny Ramsay!" (1.79). Fanny's desire for material comfort, attainable only through marriage, requires serial trials of men's honor. Through these, she knows she must preserve her virginity, particularly in the face of unsupervised *tête-à-têtes*, where women are "tempted to renounce virtue for pleasure [and] pant secretly after happiness" (1.172).

Fanny and her mother regularly reflect on the gendered inequities of these transactions, through which she is subject to sexual, class, and moral

FIGURE 2.4. Encroachment on the laboring woman's body. Thomas Rowlandson, *A Milk Sop*. London, 1811.
Courtesy of the Lewis Walpole Library, Yale University.

evaluation by privileged men. Rowlandson consolidates the various forms of labor that alight on working women's bodies in *A Milk Sop* (1811), where a young scholar leans out of a university window toward the breasts of a wet nurse transporting two pails, one filled with milk, the other with her infant charges (Figure 2.4). So yoked, the woman cannot actively repel or reciprocate the man's caresses. Rather, her body, "thoroughly soaked" in the demands of bodily work, offers one more form of labor among the others, sexual service now added to the child-minding, nursing, and dairy work already accrued to it.[71] The print isolates the working woman's body as at once domestic, public, commercial, available, and unprotected.

So too Fanny's body, regarded by suitors as theirs to claim and use. Late in the novel, Fanny's wealthy and erudite patron Lady Spelmer argues that this antagonism requires women to arm themselves with reason. "A young woman is [a] soldier—A perpetual exertion of the faculties of her mind, only, can support her against the art of flatterers, and the seductions of her fancy" (2.313). For this reason—the corrupt motivations of seducers and women's own passions—sex is rarely untainted by social factors. Lady Spelmer advocates for reciprocal sexual pleasure between willing lovers, "[b]ut how often does not caprice, pride, envy, curiosity, dispose of women's virtue?" (2.314). Worldly concerns contaminate any ideal plane of bodily pleasure, dispelling a simplistic model of materialism that would isolate bodies from social contingency.

By thoroughly discussing the ways that vaginal status impacts women's happiness, freedom, and social viability, *Child of Nature* offers a different model of what we might consider sexual detail. In lieu of genital description, it articulates the injustices women endure en route to and within the social and economic futures available to them—for Fanny, these include tavern work, courtship, rape, and marriage. By deflecting these states, or dramatizing them through other women characters, the novel sustains a critical distance on vaginal penetration and the end it would put to Fanny's aspiration to a comfortable life. The novel lays bare the difficulty for women to arrest the nuptial attentions of men without being raped. Having only her beauty to attract a husband, Fanny must physically allure and yet repel men's penetrative efforts. Rape and marriage are linked by the novel, each a plausible outcome to the process of courtship, a kind of exposure Fanny must undertake in order to become visible as a possible wife but that also makes her a target of sexual violence. During this stipulated phase of courtship, Fanny gleans dangerous and incisive lessons from various dishonest and inconstant men. After another discovery that a suitor duplicitously sought sex, not marriage, Fanny asks, "[B]y what mark shall I know the man of honour from the knave?" (1.179). The information that she gathers around this question is not genital but social.

So dangerous is the path to marriage for women of the working ranks that Fanny is threatened with rape not only by her own suitors, but also by a man feigning betrothal to her sister. He accosts Fanny on a garden path, and with "uncommon fury" she beats him back. Scared by a shepherd's approach, he leaves, and Fanny knows the proximity of the threat he posed: "A few minutes more in his power, I should have sustained a loss, for which neither Nature, nor love would have given a compensation— though not partaking in the crime, I should have been deemed criminal" (1.292). Fanny is saved from ruin, and so too her sister Betty. A conversation among the sisters and their mother restores Betty's well-being. The women's dialogue is a literal safe space, a form uninterrupted by the persuasions of men and unmediated by male relatives. And Betty rapidly concludes, "I have done with him . . . to your misfortune, Sister, I am indebted for my happiness" (1.301). Even the marriage plots of other women endanger Fanny's genital intactness.

The novel contains radical alternatives to such usage in the form of women's social autonomy. Removed to the country in the second volume, Fanny continues to be ogled and dishonorably courted, but more importantly she interacts with women who articulate a philosophical view of marriage (that it masks adultery) and of widowhood (that it masks sexual license). In this way, the novel bears out the materialism implied by the false attribution to Helvétius, privileging the pursuit of bodily pleasure over civil or religious law. Critics like Margaret C. Jacob have long located pornography's "ethical and philosophical boldness" in its adherence to materialism, a philosophy that justified the elevation of bodily gratification over other forms of order or morality.[72] This philosophical stance had particular advantages for women, allowing women narrators to claim the natural basis of their sexual desire. The "social truthfulness of pornography," for Jacob, consists in women's claiming an active sexual role.[73] The "social truthfulness" I see at work in these British pornographic texts, and particularly this one that subordinates genital detail to the philosophy announced by its title page, entails a criticism of the institutions that try to wrest the material body from a woman's self-determining efforts. In other words, the novel's philosophical commitments are not to a doctrine of sensual pleasure but to exposing social interferences with women's disposal of their bodies. The asserted link to Helvétius establishes a kind of hybrid philosophical commitment in the novel, materialist in showing men regularly attempting libidinal gratification, and feminist in showing the social effects of these attempts on women and, most importantly, in delivering women from them.

Such ideas are most cohesively drawn in Lady B, an aristocratic widow who enters late in the novel and with whom Fanny enjoys long philosophical conversation. In the company of women friends, Lady B defends her sexual liberties and her opposition to marriage:

> "Nature has given me a tender heart—a heart susceptible of pleasure.—I am a widow! Whom can my enjoyments injure or offend? Unknown to society, are they not innocent, since they are productive of no evil? The laws of Nature . . . are before those of Religion . . . by favouring me with the powers of enjoying, [God] has told me to enjoy."

Fanny endorses this perspective and recommends applause in the reader: "Lady B spoke her apology with a grace, an action, a dignity, that would have bribed all the judges in the world" (2.284–2.285). The narrative does not villainize Lady B or punish the utilitarian claims she makes on behalf of women; rather, she joins company with other philosophical women in the text attentive to the social consequence of genital activity. Lady B echoes a precept Fanny's mother had offered her in the first volume, that "men and women of sense" regard virtue as a performative, public quality with no basis in private behavior: "In their discretion consists their honour and modesty—as the world cannot censure the foible, which does not come to their knowledge, they generally take the image of virtue for virtue herself. Hence the usurped reputation most men and women enjoy" (1.270). Echoing *Human Heart*, the novel confirms modesty as cultural invention, here presented as sheer social fabrication and one that can be manipulated by men and women to screen their sexual pleasures.

Sex acts by this logic ideally would be removed from worldly interference and institutions. At one point, Lady B temporarily resigns herself to marry a rich man in response to social pressures. She previews the degradation of her happiness that will ensue:

> "A widow ... can so happily divide her life between love and philosophy, that were it not for the fear of censure and slander, I would despise all the remonstrances [of friends to marry], and follow my own inclinations.... I know too well the human heart, to hope for happiness in a state of slavery. Easy enjoyments ... leave the heart without a desire of them ... A felicity under our hand is bereft of the seductions that make it agreeable." (2.279)

Within marriage, with its waning seductions and plentiful sexual access, desire will flag. Figuring marriage as extreme subjection, Lady B anticipates losing sexual happiness, since monogamy breeds boredom. Later, when she is freed from the betrothal, she celebrates her gains in freedom: "it is still better to be the object of a fortnight's tea-table conversation than to be unhappy all my life" (2.289). Her radical thinking so closely approaches atheism that it is "suppressed" by the ostensible translator, replaced by asterisks and a bracketed redaction of what "Helvétius" must have written "in a fit of the spleen" (2.286–2.287). The novel registers Lady B's speech as a provocation.

Despite its performative suppression of Lady B's stance, her ostentatious philosophy of widows' sexual freedom is relevant to understanding the novel's end. In a rapid conclusion, an enamored suitor lovesick for Fanny proposes marriage on his deathbed, settling his estate of £10,000 a year entirely with her. "Half an hour after" they are wed, he dies, and she chooses not to fake grief for the risk of appearing insincere. "I found myself, before I was yet twenty years old, a maid, wife, and widow! To these characters I may add that of philosopher" (2.350). The novel rewards Fanny's preservation of virginity with copious wealth, and it suggests that a sexless half-hour marriage is the most beneficial sort for women. It is, after all, the conduit through which she exits the laboring class and its economic precarity, and its unconsummated state cancels the possibility of reproductive labor. It is also a safe alternative to the kind of domestic abuse she'd earlier seen afflict Mrs. Lindsey, wife to an abusive drunk: "What maid would think of matrimony, did she fear the chance of having such a husband?" (2.219). In this respect, *Child of Nature* parallels *Betsy Thoughtless* or Bluestocking Sarah Scott's *Millenium Hall* (1762), which free heroines from abusive marriages. It refuses to document sexual pleasures for its heroine and releases her from scenarios that would seem to guarantee impending genital action. Penetrative heterosex is immanent in this pornographic conceit, but it is left unstaged for the heroine, replaced by independence. She has learned to value such autonomy through what Lanser considers "rescue" by other women, a result of "deep attachments between women and [their] strong critiques of patriarchal practices."[74] This lesson can only be offered in a world where most women, in contrast to the heroine, have been sexually privatized.[75]

Child of Nature offers pornography without sex: repeated encounters that articulate the likelihood and the consequences of vaginal penetration but refuse that outcome for the heroine, whose enduring virginity allows her to continue on the path of philosophical learning. The content of her education is a specialized understanding of how to avoid institutions that organize sexual activity and how to separate genital pleasure from social interference. Her closing words confirm that her learning will govern her bodily experience: "What became of my sensibility? Reader! regulated by philosophy, it became the slave of my reason" (2.350). Rather than be subjected within marriage, as Lady B had described it and as Mary Wollstonecraft soon would, Fanny organizes her affect and pleasure within the philosophical frameworks she has learned on her path to economic independence. Reason in this novel has had many voices, some recommending sexual license, some financial gain, some the changing paths of personal happiness. The novel ends before Fanny might practice sexual license, but it accommodates multiple theories of her freedom. Women's insights derive from sexual knowledge in *Child of Nature*. This knowledge makes reference to penetrative sex not to document pleasure but to interrupt its hegemonic practice as seduction or rape (which would ruin economic prospects for Fanny) or as marriage (which would stipulate airless sexual regularity, women's dispossession, and domestic subjugation, even abuse).

Child of Nature shares with *Human Heart* and *Progress of Nature* the explicit awareness that women's subjectivity is artificially produced by a society that calls for their genital, economic, and psychological compliance. At this early moment in its coherence as a genre, pornography included an explicit feminism, a philosophically informed stance favoring women's genital (and therefore social) self-determination and their thriving outside of established sexual institutions. Perhaps such visibility of women's personhood was a precondition for pornography's coagulation: the social relevance of women's sexual exploitation had to be laid bare before it could become a narrative convention available for eroticization. Like Wendy Anne Lee's account of Clarissa making "cheery gossip" of her rape and incarceration, my reading of *Child of Nature* finds a voluble disturbance in the figure of an unwed woman emboldened (albeit through different means) to articulate and sustain a refusal of the feminine subject positions distributed through heterosexual traffic.[76]

Pornography launches a genuinely radical feminism in this period that imagines an outside or an end to dominant social institutions, supplementing eighteenth-century feminisms associated with learning and literary publication. They irreverently dispose of the domestic, intellectual, and Enlightenment—in a word, the liberal—contexts often credited with birthing feminism in this period. In her study of feminist Enlightenment writing, Karen O'Brien finds women imagined their social role as an "energising and conciliatory presence," a civilizing and instructive influence on an unpredictable modernity.[77] The women characters through whom feminist thought takes shape in pornography—tavern girls, sex workers, randy adolescents—would have no access to such polite or public discourse, and their criticisms of gender and its supporting institutions represent an oppositional, unruly strain of resistance. I'm suggesting that this vernacular feminism—one that reimagines women's social roles based on inequities they suffer in genital realms—is taken up in the irreverent sexual attitude of *Child of Nature* and that it represents a central concern of pornography. This novel is an origin point for the genre not because it describes sex, but because it insists on the overlap of society and sexuality and develops a feminist theory within that confluence (as had the dildo scene in *Progress of Nature* and the posture-girl episode in *Human Heart*).

These pornographic fictions—pornographic because they acknowledge perpetual genital traffic and detail its effects on women—experiment on the bodies of British women vulnerable to acquisition by men seeking sexual gratification through various socially sanctioned practices. Unguarded by kin or by social ranks that might screen their bodies from unauthorized masculine reach, adolescent girls, sex workers, and working women are the conduits through which these pornographies show women's bodies in all their genital specificity, depict clitoral and vaginal self-governance, and lay bare the ways such autonomy is overrun by a culture that condones men's sexual aggression. These texts suggest a social function for unmarried women that is disruptive, lewd, and anarchic, featuring their genital availability not for erotic gain but for feminist commentary.

That precise content—not penetrative spectacle—is what makes these texts conspicuous to pornographers over the next century. Their reprinting was not an accident or a misunderstanding of what these texts say about sex; rather, the publication history shows that later publishers wrestled inconclusively with the complexity of pornography that fused radical feminist reflection with gratuitous sexual description. Darnton's term for eighteenth-century French pornographic texts ("philosophical books") has been highly influential on how historians understand the fusion of sex with political and social claims.[78] That phrase also supports the account I'm offering: that pornography is primarily, inherently, inalienably philosophical—that it is a genre for which penetrative content is a contingency, not a hallmark. The next chapter will begin to explain why we've lost sight of pornography's feminist past.

3 THE VICTORIAN EIGHTEENTH CENTURY

Publishing an Erotics of Inequity

IN THE HANDS OF nineteenth-century editors, eighteenth-century pornography was seemingly, but only seemingly, pruned of its feminist content. *The History of the Human Heart* and *The Child of Nature*, which we'll recall from the previous chapter explicitly criticized the traffic in women's bodies, reappear in various nineteenth-century formats that stage penetrative sex in the context of Victorian sensationalism and bibliophilia. Taming the discursive unruliness of the originals, editors recraft these narratives, anticipating audiences eager for sex scenes. But as we saw earlier, *Human Heart* and *Child of Nature* regularly thwart penetrative heterosex, and so despite Victorian editors' strategic abridgements and deletions, eighteenth-century source texts carry questions about the ethics of penetrative sex into the nineteenth century. These sources generate a particularly conflicted account of sex through their literary activity: narratives unstably display and suppress genital penetration, and strategic deletions subdue the social references inherited from eighteenth-century pornography. Reading for those dissenting patterns I identified in texts of the previous century, we'll see them contract, disperse, and hide among the accoutrements of Victorian publishing.

In this period, English pornographic publication resiliently, if evasively, thrived in London, and by century's close was flourishing in the continental print market, where the English trade was driven by tightening obscenity restrictions.[1] Available to English readers were texts of varying cost, length, and genre that were decidedly focused on arousing the sexual curiosity of readers, and a great deal of enterprising went into creating a supply. The little-known texts discussed in Chapter 2 were edited, reprinted, and widely circulated in this environment, showing us that writers, editors, publishers, and booksellers included these hybrid works in a canon of early narrative pornography, one made hard to detect today by the chance and irregularity of collecting practices I described in my Preface. Handling messy, multipurpose narratives from the eighteenth century, editors built strategic deletions and inflations that, even if aiming to simplify sexual content, continue to tell varied and competing stories about the field of sexuality. Abridgements and additions were made to these source texts at all levels—text, sentence, binding—and reveal editors' meticulous recrafting of narrative to create works densely populated by sex scenes. Booksellers' serialization, antiquarianism, and modernization expand sexual description and reduce social reference, creating the kind of specialized narratives we associate with modern pornography by condensing into genital description, I argue, the philosophical speculation, gender critique, and feminist insight that characterized eighteenth-century source texts. Observing what is suppressed and what survives Victorian editing, we can see that pornography's characters, descriptions, producers, and consumers are open and uncertain about what the genre should be doing. Should it be telling stories of sexual justice, or should it eroticize domination? Both strains continue to speak simultaneously "as if they actually hold a conversation with one another," in what M. M. Bakhtin sees as a constitutive structure of the novel.[2]

Nineteenth-century publishers defined the genre inclusively, gathering eighteenth-century materials, editing them at the sentence level to restrain their wayward content, and publishing them as pornographic works. Publishers and collectors were aware, to a greater degree than we are today, that the pornographic tradition included these miscellaneous fictions. *Human Heart* and *Child of Nature* were printed, marketed, and sold as pornography, even as neither one validated the increasingly calcified straight masculinity emerging in much, though not all, Victorian pornography; much of this chapter argues, in fact, that the heteronormativity of the genre has been overstated. To apprehend the genre properly, we must see it as nineteenth-century editors did: variegated, discursive, historical, and improvisational. Tim Dean has suggested pornography is produced and concentrated by "procedures of sequestration" associated with archiving.³ Attentively reading historical texts' contents and observing how they were collected and reprinted, we see a different model of how pornography was apprehended in the era it was defined as a genre. Victorian pornographers see it as an open set of texts that included complex conversations about sex. Lisa Sigel's *Governing Pleasures* inaugurated this approach to Victorian pornography by observing, as I do, its "wide range of foci and uses" that change "as a culture and the symbolic meanings in that culture evolve."⁴ In this view, writers, booksellers, and readers comprehend their world politically, globally, and socioeconomically through depictions of sex. Because the genre is inherently socially responsive, for Sigel, it is open-ended and flexible, adaptable to worldly change.⁵

To be sure, it can be difficult to detect pornography's multiple voices. Nineteenth-century pornography has been seen by others to brandish a decadence of bodily detail and an insularity of erotic fantasy, a precedent set by Stephen Marcus's *The Other Victorians*, the first study of British pornographic writing.⁶ The novels he examines lead Marcus to generalize that pornography documents men's "impotent quest for omnipotence"—impotent not because sex acts are challenged within pornographic texts (as I argue they are) but because the genre's fantasy of endless pleasure can never be fulfilled, rooted as it is for Marcus, psychoanalytically, in lack and loss. This claim—that Victorian pornography is defined by a narrative structure wherein masculine desire repeatedly and ceaselessly pursues its object—is not uncommon; others likewise see it as excessive and tireless, promoting in Anjali Arondekar's words a "rampant heterosexuality" or creating, in William Cohen's terms, "a world in which nothing cannot be said."⁷ To the contrary, the reprinting of eighteenth-century sources shows the critique of heterosexuality to be integral to the genre, and the strategic editing of those texts shows that there was much that

Victorian pornographers wished the texts wouldn't say. Critics' characterization of pornography's straight, patriarchal absolutism is only partial, and pornography's impression of uncontested masculine right had to be consciously built from a model of gender very uncertain of itself. Colette Colligan, whose many articles on nineteenth-century pornography clarify its breadth and variety, explains the narrowness of Marcus's field-defining account. In an analysis of Marcus's source texts and selection methods, she finds he relied on works heralded by Henry Spencer Ashbee's influential erotic bibliography, discussed below, then made sweeping claims based on a narrow sample set. As Colligan writes, "there are many other works we might understand as representative."[8]

This chapter makes a new inroad to Victorian pornography with this project in mind—a pluralizing of what we consider typical to the genre. I chart a path through nineteenth-century pornography that, rather than naturalizing a heteronormative or masculinist sensibility, turns up the volume on the genre's statements against masculine dominance by foregrounding the period's treatment of eighteenth-century texts. Pornographic re-publication shows indecision and conflict about how sex differentiates subjects in social, literary, and exoticized realms, following from eighteenth-century source texts that did not carry forward a monolithic, unified account of sexual pleasure. Publishers reprinted many of them anyway, inflating some narrative aspects while suppressing others. Cohen posits that the period's pornography overdelivers content, "escap[ing] . . . the censoring mechanisms that help to compose sexuality."[9] Far from escaping them, Victorian publishers invented techniques for curtailment and suppression within pornographic texts. This editorializing allows us to see the myriad ingredients the Victorians handled in their building of pornographic narrative, both in reprints and in works original to the period. We'll see that by paring away discourse, Victorians serialized violence, claustrophobically condensing it with reflections on marriage, rape, and genital life we saw aired out in the previous century.

As publishers edited older materials to adapt them to Victorian tastes, they also commissioned and printed new material that moves in a genitally penetrative direction, what will be called "hard core" in the visual era. Situating the modernized editions of older works alongside original Victorian pornography, I argue that hard-core prose learned, as it were, its rapid-fire narrative structure from the laborious editorial exertions on earlier source material. Their preoccupations with masculine dominance contain, like the reprinted works, unsettled debates on gender hierarchies and sexual violence.

Queer and orientalist pornographies shed particularly critical light on the sexual violence harbored within British domesticity. Because this protest is couched within sexually dense narrative, it is simply more difficult to discern than it had been in the previous century. Victorian editors built pornography as a back-formation from materials that were not uniformly concerned with sex. By doing so, they crafted a highly distracting convention—gratuitous genital activity—that has caused centuries of readers, including current scholars, to overlook the genre's other contents. It's my argument that pornography offers something more analytical: not the documentation of pleasure, but of the process by which a culture constructs, sustains, and revises certain fictions *about* pleasure. What Victorian materials show is that pornographers themselves worked according to selective procedures, manufacturing the genre as sexual plenitude by constraining feminist content. From this angle, Victorian pornography looks austere rather than excessive, abundant only in one particular kind of description. Close attention to this description, though, reveals pornography's knowledge that its pleasures are restricted, serving certain actors and readers at the expense of others. The disenfranchisement of disadvantaged sexual subjects, this chapter shows, is as much a primary content of pornography as is the money shot.[10]

My understanding of nineteenth-century pornographic textual history borrows insights from postcolonial scholars who read against the grain of historical materials, finding that the archive tells us much more than is apparent. Anjali Arondekar and Saidiya Hartman demonstrate resistant, interpretive approaches to sources: Arondekar practices "fact-reading rather than fact-finding," analyzing what are posited as facts rather than confirming their status as facts, and Hartman "listen[s] for the unsaid" and "amplif[ies] ... instability and discrepancy" in archival documents.[11] In the face of texts that are written and archived to erase the experience of colonized and enslaved people, we must, in Lisa Lowe's words, "devise other ways of reading so that we might understand the processes through which the forgetting of the violent encounter is naturalized."[12] I likewise believe that sources and their categorization do not tell a straight truth, but reveal processes of assemblage and project a range of cultural effects. My task here is to show how Victorian textual culture discredits its own construction of pornography as a genre unflappably convinced of phallic power and penetrative right. I undertake this resistant reading by paying close attention to ideas brandished, then abandoned by texts themselves, emphasizing deletion and absence rather than the proliferation and abundance we witnessed in the eighteenth century. Victorian pornography documents, through suppression and elision, British culture's deep confusion about how to recognize the impact of penetrative sex on people living in a proximate social world. Discussions about sexual justice, we know from the last chapter, were once an explicit content in pornography. Where did the dissenting voices go?

To attend to the methodical, meticulous distortion of these voices is to discover that modern pornography's seeming indifference to matters of sexual justice had to be conscientiously designed and differentiated from the feminist dissidence of earlier pornographic texts. Pornography's violence isn't simply apparent in the actions it displays. Apprehended as an editorial procedure, pornography shows its violence at the level of form, as a continuous and adaptive displacement of the statements contained in the eighteenth-century pornographic texts I've identified as foundational to the genre. In the Victorian period, such statements become harder to detect. But apprehending historical materials as Hartman instructs—as making apparent a "libidinal investment in violence"—we will see pornography stage its awareness of social disparities endemic to British culture.[13] As feminism is plucked from individual pornographic works, the genre articulates the proximity of sexual violence to power relations that are normalized by heterosexuality and marriage.

Human Heart and *Child of Nature* in the Nineteenth Century

Victorian pornographers' editing of eighteenth-century source texts demonstrates that they were aware of the unruly feminist commentary inherent to pornography, and that they aimed to assimilate that content to pursuits of sex and book collecting associated with a privileged nineteenth-century masculinity. They unevenly grappled with the discursivity of earlier pornographic narrative, sometimes trying to excise it, sometimes selling it as pornography as such. As doggedly as publishers and book collectors pursued their controversial trade, the body of work they produced didn't know if it should register an awareness of sexual injustice or distract readers from it, an indecision that remained unresolved even late in the Victorian period when publishers had been grappling for decades with pornography's unruly textual history.

Some key players carried eighteenth-century works through the Victorian period. William Dugdale, radical publisher and literary pirate, and Henry Spencer Ashbee, still famous today for his bibliography of European pornography, are at the center of two publishing circles that bookend the Victorian pornographic era. Both sets considered *Human Heart* and *Child of Nature* part of their pornographic inheritance, and both made strenuous efforts to tame their wandering, miscellaneous, critical commentary. Dugdale printed, marketed, and sold pornography from the 1820s through his death in 1868, operating in Holywell Street, the commercial center for the obscene book trade.[14] His editions were printed and sold in New York as well. He commissioned original work from inexpensive sources and shamelessly pirated extant bawdy texts, unembarrassed and intrepid in his reliance on existing sources.[15] Dugdale published for wealthy and nonelite customers alike: a single issue of his serial *The Exquisite* cost sixpence (£1.50 presently), whereas his illustrated editions ranged from a half-guinea to three guineas (about £20 and £190 today, respectively), the latter the price of a lavishly illustrated *Fanny Hill*.[16]

A third key figure, James Campbell Reddie, wrote, edited, and translated for Dugdale through the 1860s, and he built an extensive collection of antique pornography that he sold to Ashbee, along with a manuscript bibliography, in 1877. Ashbee, an aristocratic book collector and compiler of a still-authoritative bibliography of erotic literature, owned the majority of Dugdale editions through this purchase of Reddie's collection, and he passed them in his bequest to the British Library, whose trustees appear to have destroyed them against his (literal) will.[17] The transmission and reception of these texts from Dugdale to the British Library allows us to track the continuity of selected works in the pornographic canon as well as their reshaping in different formats and with different publishers. Priced variably across the century, this set of texts disproves what Jonathan Rose calls the "false antithesis" of assuming low- and high-cultural readerships excluded one another.[18] A wide range of readers had access to pornographic texts, and the texts offered themselves without prejudice to whomever was interested.

Ashbee's own copy of his bibliography registers an ongoing, idiosyncratic conception of pornography, doubled in size by interleaved plates, notes, and correspondences.[19] He also exemplifies the most elite late-century pornographic customer, an expert collector whose bibliography represented Europe's erotic literary history. His tastes were shared by a peer group whose interests are exemplified by the Rochester Series of Reprints. A collaboration by publisher Edward Avery and bookseller Arthur Reader in the 1880s, it comprises "works illustrative of Manners and Customs, Public and Private life of the 17th and 18th Centuries."[20] The series is a clear example of how privileged men, as Sarah Bull has documented, invented a "secret museum" out of a "multifarious" pornographic past, setting sexual history apart—in the age of museum collecting—from cultural repositories with broader public appeal.[21] By concentrating works such as they did in Avery's Rochester Series, publishers and booksellers created an aura of forbiddenness around texts that did not originally project such meaning. The series was expensively printed and bound for wealthy collectors.[22] The reprints preserve antique typography and include original publication information, seemingly committed to transmitting eighteenth-century sexual custom to the Victorian reader without editorial interference. The customer for this series was a dedicated collector of erotic books, but also one who valued the trappings of antiquity, who would have read the outmoded narrative style as a quaint aberration from the more focused pornography being written contemporaneously and who would be conversant enough in British literary history to place *Human Heart* among its eighteenth-century textual company—*Woman of Pleasure, Tom Jones, Tristram Shandy*, and the *Essay on Woman* by John Wilkes, the libertine whom Ashbee documents exhaustively in his interleaved copy of the erotic bibliography.

Despite variances in audience and format, the Dugdale and Ashbee/Avery circles confirm the endurance of eighteenth-century texts in the pornographic culture of the nineteenth century. Neither the earlier nor the later publishing activity, though, directly reproduced the source texts. They tailored pornography for contemporary readers through abridgements, alterations, and rebranding to suit niche tastes, rather than to speak broadly, as I've argued the eighteenth-century source texts did, to a less goal-oriented reader of comic fiction. Leah Price has argued that in eighteenth- and nineteenth-century practices of extraction and anthologizing, editors "debated what to do with the non-narrative parts of novels, and both freighted that decision with social consequences."[23] Victorian pornographers knew that social commentary lived within eighteenth-century sources, and they worked to subdue those discursive, critical elements by reducing or eliminating them, and for varying purposes. The ambitions of these publishers were different: Dugdale was concerned with cheap production, fast money, multimodal publication, and sensational content; Ashbee, Reader, and Avery were focused on recirculating rare erotic books and documenting the curiosities of life in the past. Dugdale passed off source texts as original, abbreviated them severely, or invented entirely fictitious ones; Avery curated them as distinctly historical. They meet, though, in their agreement on a spine of eighteenth-century texts as part of their inheritance of British sexual culture. Alterations, both loud and subtle, were made to assimilate texts to the Victorian taste, and significant things were lost in that editorial process.

As early as 1827, Dugdale brought *Human Heart* into the popular market for obscene books, making significant editorial changes. In his hands, *Human Heart* was a malleable source text that could be repackaged for a range of audiences. He gave it a new title that, Cleland-inspired, invoked the eighteenth century: *Memoirs of a Man of Pleasure*. Otherwise Dugdale and his editors erased its antique characteristics, anglicizing stock romance names, modernizing eighteenth-century cultural references, and removing some, but not all, of the footnotes that, as we saw in the last chapter, interrupted sex scenes with philosophical, moral, and ethical musings. These deletions removed the mechanisms that allowed the originals to launch feminist dissent. His editors went in with a scalpel, carving out parts of the narrative that would have seemed historically remote (like eighteenth-century debates around cognition) or irrelevant to erotic interests (how best to choose a private tutor for one's child). He left those notes intact that had to do with sexuality, its science, and its pleasures.

Ashbee's bibliography contains a detailed entry on Dugdale's *Man of Pleasure* editions, and his descriptions indicate how and why *Human Heart* underwent heavy editing. Dugdale's illustrated editions were titled *Memoirs of a Man of Pleasure, or Amours, Intrigues, and Adventures of Sir Charles Manly*. An 1827 edition was priced at a half-guinea (about £30 today), and its title page boasts amorous content and illustrations that are, Ashbee writes, "free" and "suggestive." (Another edition is advertised in Dugdale's 1841 *Fanny Hill* and priced at 7 shillings sixpence, just over £20 in today's currency.) Ashbee's attitude toward the text's discursive material indicates why Dugdale and Reddie would have abridged it: he writes that the footnotes "embrace theories which are at present entirely exploded" and therefore are "worthless"; the comic introduction, which introduced the conceit of editor and footnotes, is "long and irrelevant."[24] Ashbee's impatience suggests that questions of historical contingency and editorial interference either did not occur or did not matter to readers, collectors, and publishers in his time, who instead valued illustration and packaging that highlighted sexual content.

Much of this material was eliminated in another Dugdale edition of *Human Heart/Man of Pleasure*, an 1844 serialization in *The Exquisite*, a miscellany of bawdry, verse, and plates. The copy-text was probably prepared by Reddie (for simplicity I refer only to Dugdale as editor in what follows, despite Reddie's likely involvement in this edition).[25] This serialization, to my knowledge the only extant edition of *Man of Pleasure*, contains significant changes: the introduction gets deleted, and the footnotes are curtailed.[26] In *The Exquisite*, *Man of Pleasure* found a home among other reprinted fictions, erotic oriental tales, bawdy anecdotes, sexological lectures, and nude prints. Available cheaply to a new set of readers, and serving as cost-free material for Dugdale's weekly, *Man of Pleasure* appeared across numbers 120 to 135 in the third and final volume, without illustrations. I take the changes in this edition to reflect many of the changes that Dugdale had already made in 1827, when, as we know from Ashbee's bibliography, he had already modernized character names. They also update the prose, reduce the text's discursive aspects, and accelerate the narrative so that sexual description occurs more frequently. These changes streamline the narrative's sexual focus and radically decrease its level of irony.[27]

Dugdale's *Man of Pleasure* exemplifies Victorian indecision around pornography's historical context. While he modernizes the narrative, he loosely associates *Man of Pleasure* with Restoration-era sexual license, attributing authorship to libertine Charles Sedley, a favorite of Charles II—a preposterous attribution, given the narrative's mid-eighteenth-century style, but one that promises sexual intrigue for the reader prepared to suspend disbelief. This appropriation is one instance of what Sigel identifies in *The Exquisite* as a "truncated form" of libertinism, reduced from a philosophy of pleasure into an emphasis on the "expectation and availability" of women.[28] The 1844 editing bears out an increasing focus on men's heterosexual pleasure. Eager to immerse readers in intrigue, Dugdale deletes the introduction in 1844 and eliminates half of the footnotes, shortening four others. Those retained directly discuss sex, describing fertilization, the hymen, and the role of the imagination in desire. Omitted are footnotes that diverge from the sexual context of the main narrative toward more abstract considerations. The note on modesty glossing the posture-girl episode—which conjectured a world of sexual egalitarianism that relieved women of performing modesty, discussed in Chapter 2—is deleted. This editing creates ostentatious Restoration-era anachronism while skillfully silencing the previous century's radical gender theory.

Philosophical and historical context had not been a distraction in the eighteenth century, whereas nineteenth-century pornography aspires to a ruthless presentism scrubbed of historical references. In addition to pruning the narrative of material seemingly non-erotic, Dugdale strips it of diction, concepts, and historical references that might be unfamiliar to the reader. This edition presents sexual attraction as more automated than his eighteenth-century precursor, carefully updating concepts attached to arousal, desire, and satisfaction to reflect emerging knowledge of species and adaptation. Explaining that animals will mate with one another irrespective of beauty, the eighteenth-century author wrote that a male animal "takes Relief from the next kind She that is disposed for his Use" (*H* 197).[29] Animals are anthropomorphized here, possessing gender and sensibility. Dugdale makes the language more scientific, and decidedly less sociable: the male "takes relief from the first female of its own species that is disposed for its use" (*E* 198). In the same passage, *Human Heart*'s author describes women possessing "Organs fitly disposed to allay the prevailing appetite" of men (*H* 197); Dugdale states they have "organs fitly adapted" to this purpose, stabilizing what once sounded arbitrarily happenstance into an evolutionary premise (*E* 198). References to monarchical history are removed, bygone professions are updated, and old social ranks disappear.[30]

Some of the editorial changes quiet the philosophical musings of the 1749 *Human Heart* in order to streamline explanations of the hero's desire. Enlightenment-era fusions of sex and philosophy of mind are increasingly dissonant with the more direct path toward sexual description Dugdale seeks to craft from his source text. Such revision is evident in a scene involving Camillo, the Quaker virgin Saphira, and her maid Rebecca (for consistency, I'll refer to their 1749 names). With Rebecca's help, Camillo sneaks into Saphira's darkened bedchamber to finish a seduction he attempted the previous day. Unbeknownst to Camillo, Rebecca puts herself in Saphira's bed and "receive[s] his Fire without flinching" (*H* 195). Afterward, he is disgusted to find Rebecca in Saphira's place. The empiricist terms originally used to explain Camillo's desire are replaced with less specialized language by Dugdale. Originally, Camillo is "stung to the quick, that he had been so lavish of himself on such a Creature, whose very Idea chilled his Vigour; (for she had something very forbidding in her Countenance, and nothing but Youth to recommend her)" (*H* 195). "Idea" denotes a specifically empiricist meaning, referring to the visual representation of an object—in this case, Camillo's perception or memory of Rebecca's face. Dugdale carves out this short but significant phrase, making the sentence intellectually less taxing. In 1844, Camillo is "stung to the quick with disappointment, and the thought that he had been so lavish of himself on a creature who had nothing but her youth to recommend her" (*E* 197).

The hero's mind is not the mediating force it was in 1749; gone is the language that reminds us, à la Locke, of the mental faculties involved in perception and desire. Masculine sexual prowess in the 1749 formulation is dependent on cognitive activity, and it is also fallible, subject to diminishments of "vigour." In changes large and small, Dugdale identifies those aspects of *Human Heart* that make the narrative historically remote and that present the desires of the masculine subject as contingent on internal and external factors.[31] These edits show the labor required to present sexual attraction as a seamless response to an alluring object. Such machinations reveal Dugdale constructing pornography as a back-formation, a selection and concentration of salacious content that works on character and reader without interference. Dudgale's changes do not radically alter the plot of *Human Heart*, but they deliberately suppress the textual and stylistic conventions that mark it as a fiction from an earlier era, rendering a relatively presentist text out of the original.

Dugdale treats *Child of Nature* similarly, but with a lighter hand. At least two editions, original title retained, appeared in the 1840s. He serializes it in *The Exquisite* in 1842, suppressing its false attribution and freethinking preface. In 1849 an edition appears whose title page promises "luscious scenes with lovers," and it contains illustrations, repeatedly baring women's breasts, that Ashbee calls "singularly interesting" in his bibliography.[32] In the serialization, *Child of Nature*'s note on translation and a false attribution to materialist philosopher Helvétius disappear from the front matter. But in the main text, the reader is referred to Helvétius's "*L'esprit*" in a fabricated, heavily asterisked redaction. The redaction claims to censor a conversation Fanny has with a philosophical man who debunks virtue as a false category, referring to the French text as a place the reader might find the suppressed content. The nineteenth-century texts flamboyantly draw attention to this taboo freethinking, despite their subduing of eighteenth-century philosophical contexts in their front matter. The materialist philosophy of Fanny's companion is itself the lascivious content: "were I not absolutely in love with his person, I was really so with his wit."³³ As in Dugdale's *Human Heart/Man of Pleasure* editions, other discursive material is eliminated from the narrative, such as a speech against drunkenness and praise for the English book trade.

Dugdale's inclusion of this work in his pornographic canon is peculiar because, as we know from Chapter 2, its heroine is a "maid, wife and widow" at novel's end, having improbably evaded penetrative sex. While *Human Heart* can be mined for its genital action, *Child of Nature* cannot. Its pornography consists in something that is not genital. The persistence of both works belies the claim that by late century, a "formulaic focus on sex acts" characterized print pornography, a development Deana Heath associates with photography.³⁴ Even as a higher-efficiency model of pornography was emerging, these antique works continue to say things about sex, rather than showcase its easily repeatable occurrences. Dugdale's *Human Heart* hero may appear more certain of his exploits, but his sexual freedom is still contained within marriage, and he still faces encumbrances to penetrative acts, as the source text dictated. The heroine in *Child of Nature* practices feminine sexuality as an ongoing rejection of intercourse. Sexual detail in that novel resides in conversations about the institutions and social categories that rank women, not in genital action. Victorian pornographers collect these accounts of sex alongside, as we're about to see, narratives that streamline heroes' paths toward aggressive penetrative action. The editorial procedures we can trace across these sources reveal a waywardness in pornography, a skepticism that direct pursuits of penetrative sex are equitable, and an awareness that the phallocentric hero is one cultural invention among an assortment of sexualized figures, not all of whom desire penetration. Even as individual works might begin to specialize their vision of sexuality, this set of texts tells us this vision is beset by resistances to and questions about heterosexual drive.

The four-volume Rochester Series produced around 1885 by Avery and Reader, to which Ashbee subscribed, reflects a similarly mixed attitude toward its source texts, fetishizing the originals but strategically editing them to assimilate them to their present. The series includes a volume of Rochester's poetry based on a 1757 Curll edition; Cleland's *Memoirs of a Coxcomb*; *Child of Nature* retitled as *The Philosophy of Pleasure*; and *The History of the Human Heart*. True to its mission, the Rochester *Human Heart* seems to restore the antique flair of the original, but, as Crystal Lake finds artifacts so often do, it in fact reveals a "troubling tendency to keep changing [its] story," suppressing key elements of the original.[35] The source text is the original 1749: here appear the Italianate names, the introduction, early modern typography, and continuous quotation marks. A facsimile title page names the original publisher and restores the correct date, features that "reactivate" its connection to a pornographic heritage.[36] But gone are all footnotes as well as the editor figure. He is carefully removed from the introduction, and with him any trace that there were footnotes in the copy-text to begin with. The novel reads, in this form, as a mischievous tale of gallant masculinity, focused on the hero's escapades and unconcerned with the philosophical explanations that had accompanied the narrative previously. As Ashbee had very recently complained in his bibliography, the footnotes—even the abbreviated ones he encountered in the Dugdale editions—too persistently distracted a reader seeking sexual action. Those paratextual outgrowths that had constituted the book's eighteenth-century humor are seen by 1885 as a nuisance even to readers who fashioned themselves genteel antiquarians.

The Rochester Series also reprinted *Child of Nature*. The 1885 title page is much more detailed and suggestive than the original, announcing "luscious scenes with lovers." By contrast, the minimalist title page in 1774 (Figure 3.1) had promised only a "philosophical novel." In 1885, the original title is reduced to a phrase that appears in the subtitling (Figure 3.2). A translator's note mentions only that the author also wrote "De l'Esprit," and Helvétius is not named. Debates around materialism and morality foregrounded in 1774 are thus made more remote by Avery for his bibliophile friends, and the "prurient" and "luxurious" potential of the novel are maximized by this title page rebranding—a curious but significant emphasis, given the narrative's absence of genital detail. The text itself, though, adheres closely to the original typography, down to the number

THE

CHILD

OF

NATURE,

IMPROVED BY CHANCE.

A Philofophical Novel.

By Mr. HELVETIUS, Claude Adrien, pseud.

IN TWO VOLUMES.

VOL. I.

LONDON:

Printed for T. BECKET, Corner of the Adelphi, in the Strand. 1774.

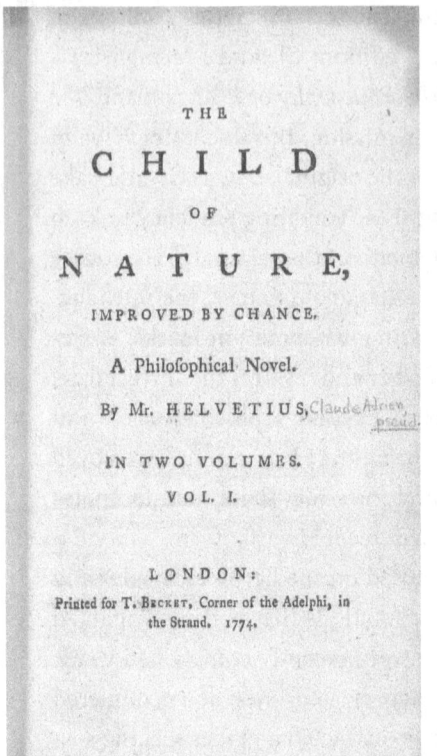

FIGURE 3.1. Title page of *The Child of Nature, Improved by Chance*. London, 1774.

Beinecke Rare Book and Manuscript Library, Yale University.

THE

PHILOSOPHY OF PLEASURE;

OR, THE

History of a Young Lady,

OF

Luxurious Temperament and Prurient Imagination, who experiences repeatedly the

DANGERS OF SEDUCTION,

and whose escapes from the

SNARES OF LOVE

are truly wonderful, depicting many and various Luscious Scenes with her Lovers, and proving herself to be the

CHILD OF NATURE

IMPROVED BY CHANCE.

Freely translated from the original French.

LONDON:

PRINTED FOR T. BECKET, CORNER OF THE ADELPHI, IN THE STRAND, 1774.

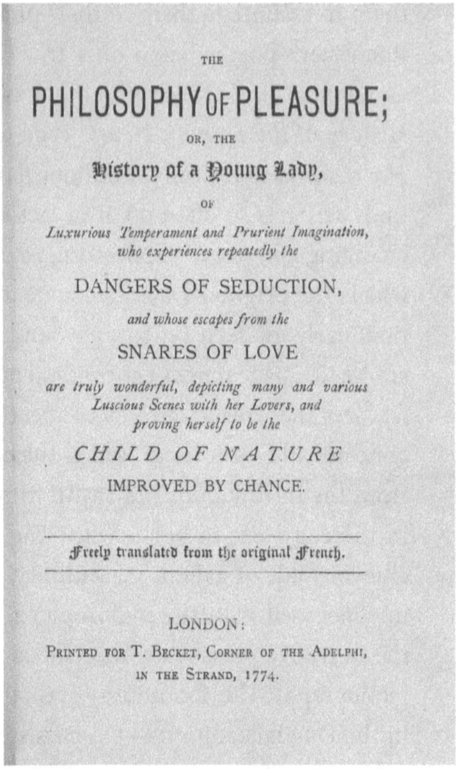

FIGURE 3.2. *The Child of Nature* sensationalized as *The Philosophy of Pleasure; or, The History of a Young Lady*. London, c. 1885.

Library Special Collections, Charles E. Young Research Library, UCLA.

of asterisks used to suppress passages on atheism and libertinism; and eighteenth-century cultural references, such as praise of David Garrick's performances, are preserved.[37]

By counting *Child of Nature* as part of the sexually combative canon they inherited from the eighteenth century, Victorian pornographers see what modern critics miss: such a text is pornographic, but not because it exerts an erotic imperative or shocks us with graphic excess. It is pornographic because in it, genital contact—that zone sought by nearly every man that crosses the heroine's path—is shown to be an imposition, one that Fanny eludes until she is an independent and propertied "philosopher." This novel's claim that a prosperous form of feminine sexuality is virginity—at least until a fortune is secured—dwells archivally among texts that say something altogether different about the use of women's bodies. Differentiated from a marriage plot forerunner like *Pamela* by its varying attitudes toward chastity, this novel shows, on the one hand, eighteenth-century pornography's unique candor about the social meaning of women's genital status and, on the other, the closeness of pornography to mainstream British moralities and marriage plots.

Editorial changes across these reprints reveal an indecision in Victorian culture about how to situate sexual subjects relative to penetrative sex acts: masculinity is fortified and femininity compromised, but editorial traces make this artificial construction so obvious as to expose it as a laborious fiction. Given this evidence, pornography cannot be seen to produce a unified statement for or against phallocentric heterosexuality, nor does it condemn its own violence against women, their genitals, and the social outcomes of penetration, those concerns that had been central in the previous century. In lieu of a singular model of pornographic eroticism, pornography's procedures communicate unsettled sexual debate. Branding assimilates works, but their content betrays variation. These sources refuse to settle on a single pornographic attitude. Through literary interpretation of these texts—an attention to what they say, don't say, suppress, and inflate—we see eighteenth-century debates about sexual justice being sustained across the pornographic field as Victorian culture experimented with the forms of knowledge and imagination that might accompany sex.

As I wrote in this book's Introduction, the editors of the Rochester Series also eliminated a flamboyant description of female ejaculation from *Human Heart*, which also was deselected in the 1757 *B—— Tracey*. So while these late-Victorian erotic bibliophiles decreased textual interference with the gallivanting of their hero, focusing us more exclusively on his sexual mischief, they also subdued a conception of the woman's body as capable of its own orgasmic pleasure. Pornography written across the Victorian era pluralized its catalogue of sex acts, increasingly featuring oral and anal eroticism that had been infrequent in eighteenth-century works. The exclusion of women's self-administered ejaculation therefore must be seen as an aberration from pornography's efforts to catalogue sex exhaustively. The series—on title pages, in editing practices—sensationalizes sex, but eliminates some of its forms. In many cases, as Colligan has written, "pornographic titles told bibliographical lies," suppressing textual provenance or exaggerating scandalous content.[38] It turns out that pornographic prose could lie too, expelling women's masturbation as a self-contained mode of sexual pleasure. Editors create paratext that promises to exhaust sexual possibility, but they remove eroticism that excludes men.

We've inherited many stories about pornography's paucity—its dearth of social consciousness; its thin or veiled presence in libraries; its evacuation of ideas in narrative, actor, and consumer; its unilateral commitment to eliciting pleasure. But the pornographic procedures I've shown here evince a robust field of discussions, and amendments to discussions, about how social institutions interfere with genitals and the people to whom they are attached. This coupling of discourses on penetration and gender is not happenstance: it is an inherent attribute of pornography. The Victorian era was trying to invent a simplified model of sexual writing, but the continuous re-publication of eighteenth-century texts shows that the feminist conversation about genital life remained an ongoing and inconclusive pornographic content. Eighteenth-century dissent, baked into accounts of genital life, could not be fully extracted.

Rochester, Cleland, and Pornographic Deletion

Rochester and Cleland sit alongside the anonymous fictions that the Dugdale and Avery circles considered their eighteenth-century pornographic inheritance. The Rochester Series included a volume of Rochester's poetry and Cleland's *Memoirs of a Coxcomb*, and Dugdale published illustrated editions of *Memoirs of the Life of Miss Fanny Hill* and a spurious autobiography of Rochester. Affiliations with Cleland and Rochester anchor the anonymous *Human Heart* and *Child of Nature* that are today less recognizable as pornography. Publishers' grouping of all these texts together implies, disingenuously, that all share a project of frequent and direct genital reference. But what the grouping actually conveys, if texts are read individually, is a spectrum of perspectives on penetrative sex, including resistant feminist statements against the social inequities it produces.

While Rochester and Cleland are not as susceptible to rebranding as were the anonymous novels discussed in the previous section, Dugdale's and Avery's editions of their works perform their own kind of interpretation, bundling these famous figures into the antique pornographic type being offered to their respective audiences. These interpretations continue to show variation in the ways that Victorian publishers understood eighteenth-century source texts as part of the pornographic canon they were assembling. Their purpose—and by now this should not be surprising—is not solely to produce a static model of phallic masculinity. They also aim to build the genre as multimodal and itself historical—as an adaptable and resilient cultural institution that looks forward and backward at once. Nineteenth-century editing, as Price argues, did not "simply updat[e] inherited texts to match the literary works being currently produced. On the contrary, editing has more often functioned as a conservative counterweight to esthetic change, providing a space in which discarded formal alternatives can be recycled."[39] Editors' efforts to expunge historical context or social commentary leave textual traces in nineteenth-century editions, creating an *oeuvre* that makes multiple, often confusing claims about how sex should happen and for whom. Their editing does not ossify or assimilate all sexuality in the period to a single or straightforward pornographic model. Rather, it begins to gather consensus on some unifying principles (hypermasculinity, misogyny, racism) that one can argue continue to characterize the genre but demonstrates attitudinal and textual variation across publications.

Dugdale's 1841 illustrated *Fanny Hill* uses as its source text the expurgated 1750 *Memoirs of Fanny Hill*, which like all editions through the late twentieth century lacks the infamous sodomy scene.[40] We know from Ashbee's bibliography that some illustrated editions of the novel were "obscene," presumably showing genital action. The engravings in this edition are what he calls merely "free"—no genitals are shown, and characters are almost always fully clothed, even though their accompanying scenes describe penetrative action. Men twice appear shirtless, but bodies are otherwise covered. The engravings point up the episodic structure of the novel, illustrating Fanny's encounters with the rapist Mr. Crofts, the well-endowed Will, and the neurodivergent Dick; as well as her hire by Mr. H. The frontispiece does not clearly depict any particular scene in the novel, and the remaining images don't center Fanny at all, but represent sex scenes involving Mrs. Brown, Harriet, and Emily. They also don't document the main plot of the novel: Fanny's passionate coupling with Charles that culminates in conjugality and family. These illustrations ignore the marriage plot entirely in favor of Fanny's sequential partners and the activities of other characters.

Surprisingly, given the novel's reputation for graphic description, the illustrations do not expose genitalia. In some cases, as with Mrs. Brown and Dick, the illustrations even seem to caricature the sexual encounter, and some emphasize the violent rather than the consensual, as with Mr. Crofts (Figures 3.3 and 3.4). None transparently reproduces the penetration described textually, suggesting that whatever Cleland's significance to Victorian pornographers, it was not based only on the opportunity he afforded for the proliferation of vaginal penetration.

The narrative itself also receives a targeted, attentive makeover. As with his updates in *Human Heart/Man of Pleasure*, Dugdale turns "drawers" into nineteenth-century "waiters," and a "buckle" in a woman's hair into a "ringlet," modernizing material life with extreme precision.[41] The already bowdlerized 1750 source text undergoes further cuts in the Dugdale, and some changes echo *Man of Pleasure*'s simplification of *Human Heart*'s emotional and mental life. When 1750 Fanny narrates Mrs. Brown's fraudulent second selling of her maidenhead, she describes it as a deception that "prevent[s her] going out any where to get better advice," but these coercions are omitted in 1841 (*M* 47).[42] When the parents of fellow prostitute Emily retrieve her late in the novel, the 1750 edition berates them for only caring about their "inhumanly abandon'd" daughter once their better-loved son has died (*M* 244); in 1841, Fanny reports that only "an accident too trivial to detail" brings Emily's parents to find her, subduing the preference for sons in Emily's family (*L* 186). The later edition also omits

FIGURE 3.3. Genitals elided in Mrs. Brown's encounter with the horse grenadier, from John Cleland's *Memoirs of the Life of the Celebrated Miss Fanny Hill*. London, 1841.

© The British Library Board. Shelfmark Cup.805.b.1.

FIGURE 3.4. Mr. Crofts's sexual violence, from John Cleland's *Memoirs of the Life of the Celebrated Miss Fanny Hill*. London, 1841.

© The British Library Board. Shelfmark Cup.805.b.1.

Fanny's substantial commentary on the loss sustained by "our community" upon Emily's departure, so good humored and agreeable was she—"vice, it is probable, had never been her choice, or her fate" but for her desperate "circumstances" (*M* 186). This disposition makes her an excellent wife, a role she soon finds, in 1750, with "a neighbour's son of her own rank . . . who took her as the widow of one lost at sea . . . [in marriage] she naturally struck into all the domestic duties with . . . simplicity of affection . . . constancy and regularity" (*M* 186). The deletions subdue statements about possible alternatives to sex work as well as Emily's poor fit for the trade, quieting too the identity of widow that must be invented in order to reinsert her into a marriage market that would otherwise disqualify her based on her trafficked body. Social complexity and a domestic novel plot—those emerging hallmarks of Victorian fiction—are removed from the pornographic template in 1841. At the level of narrative, we see *Fanny Hill* here becoming pornography, distinct from the novel genre. Hastening to seemingly unstudied genital coupling, it outsources the work of commentary to the social novel and marriage plot.

We'll recall that Dugdale preserved the detail about female ejaculation in his 1844 *Man of Pleasure* (while the Rochester Series excised it), and so seemed willing to preserve all aspects of women's genital experiences. But we see in this 1841 *Fanny Hill* a paring away of some descriptions that feature Fanny's body as open and available. Dugdale eliminates Mr. N's placement of a nude Fanny on the carpet before a fire, "when he would contemplate me almost by the hour, disposing me in all the figures and attitudes of the body" (*M* 207); and Phoebe's sapphic explorations of Fanny's body are in part suppressed (*M* 23). Both examples are absent a penis capable of penetration, perhaps explaining their disposability. Most puzzling is the deletion of a long passage in which Fanny's coworker Louisa describes a consensual, enthusiastic coupling, so moving it gets narrated in the present tense:

> "my youth proceeds to all those extremities, which all my looks, flushings, and palpitations had assur'd him he might attempt without the fear of repulse: those rogues, the men, read us admirably on these occasions." (*M* 176)

Louisa provides affirmative consent, explaining her own bodily symptoms as expressions of desire for the penetrative act that soon ensues. She even—contrary to so many other eighteenth-century scenes documenting virginal experience—claims that men frequently interpret women's bodily signs correctly, providing a particularly felicitous account of heterosexual desire. The 1841 text hastens to penetration itself, discarding this account of active feminine consent.

Dugdale's *Fanny Hill* encapsulates the undecided character of Victorian pornography. Its illustrations don't tease out phallic virility, nor does it exploit every opportunity for overstating vaginal access. He expurgated an already expurgated source text, reducing various complexities from the experience of women sex workers: the conditions that land them in brothels, the manipulations of their traffickers, their baldly stated agency in the face of heterosexual action—all are understated by the deletions I've described, as are moments of transparent display of the unpenetrated woman's body. If we then might guess Dugdale aspires to a phallocentric model of pornography, uninterrupted by non-penetrative material, his illustrations disprove such a theory, clothing characters' bodies, lampooning non-normative subjects, and documenting scenes of monetary rather than bodily transaction. The 1841 edition is a composite text of various pornographic aims: its narrative tries to subdue women's deep subjectivity and sympathetic backstory, perhaps moving toward a phallocentric model of sexuality, but its illustrations don't join the effort.

Fanny Hill, supposedly pornography's ur-text, offers raw materials for crafting an unbridled, sexually enthusiastic text. But, true to what I'm arguing is Victorian pornography's undecided character, this edition is uncertain what it wants to say about women's relation to penetrative sex: Should they want it? Should they enjoy it? Should they pursue it? Should we see their bodies perform it? And so, through different print technologies, it hedges its bets, tamping down opportunities for gratuitous visual titillation and for narrative focus on the worldly conditions that shape women's experience of penetration. Our attention is not simplistically or uniformly fixed on a penetrable feminine figure; rather, Victorian editors heavily mediate what is possible to know about vaginal penetration. This text labors to craft women as simple objects of desire from a source that tells a complicated story about labor and sexual commerce.[43]

Dugdale's editorial interference disgusted Ashbee, who was never able to locate an unexpurgated first edition of *Memoirs of a Woman of Pleasure*. Despite access to extensive collections, the 1749 edition eluded him, preventing direct access to the famed sodomy scene. He expresses frustration with this impediment in his bibliography, and he begins his *Woman of Pleasure* entry by transcribing the scene in full, having obtained it as a fragment from a collaborator.[44] Editorial interference raises his pique: "due to the slovenliness of the irresponsible printers through whose hands [the extant reprints] have passed, it is the more to be regretted that the original reading as approved by the author cannot be established."[45] It is a concern of the highest order to present this scene to the reader of his bibliography, confirming that elite pornographic connoisseurs of the late Victorian period sought to document cultures of sodomy domestically and globally.[46] For Ashbee, deletion is a violence to Cleland's work, censored editions "emasculated" and "castrated." He wishes to hew closely to Cleland's authorial vision. Unable to do so, Ashbee huffily "confine[s] himself" to describing the many bowdlerized editions he has seen, printed mainly in the mid-nineteenth century.[47]

This frustration with violations of textual integrity is paradoxical and contradictory, given the willingness among Ashbee's publishing and bookselling peers to change titles, delete content, and abridge source texts. It seems Ashbee would have wanted his coterie to make editorial decisions based on a verifiably authentic source text, one that reflects authorial intent. Could it be for this reason—the antiquarian fetishizing of textual purity, of a pornographic canon with traceable origins—that *Memoirs of a Woman of Pleasure* is not included in the Rochester Series of Reprints? It's a surprising omission, given the novel's reputation for exhaustive sexual description. Ashbee's extensive bibliographical notes convey that he considered it an essential work of eighteenth-century erotic writing. He must have considered it a real loss that his subscription to the Rochester Series could not, because of Avery's work directly with source texts, include it. But his commitment to textual integrity—or at least to working from a source text with dependable provenance—was sufficiently serious that to reproduce "castrated" *Fanny Hill* editions would be unacceptable, a violation of the series' mission. *Memoirs of a Coxcomb* was easier to access, and perhaps gave Avery and Reader means for connecting Cleland to a late-Victorian readership while maintaining an antiquarian commitment to verifiable sources. This *Coxcomb* adheres closely to the original 1751, preserving continuous quotation marks, capitalization patterns, and narrative division into "parts"; the Rochester edition also makes many corrections based on the 1751 list of errata. In one case, Sir William Delamore's "pleasures" are specified as his "caresses" in 1885, showing, at microlevel, Reader and Avery's eagerness to physicalize *Coxcomb*'s affect.

The first volume published in the Rochester Series in 1884 also streamlines eighteenth-century writing as much as possible to an erotic purpose. *Selected Poetical Works of the Earls of Rochester, Roscommon, and Dorset* is based on a 1757 collection. That source text misattributes dozens of poems to Rochester and includes sexual and nonsexual writings, a centuries-long muddling of his works.[48] Avery and Reader add to the confusion by cutting their source text significantly: gone are dozens of poems on non-sexual topics, producing a volume that is about a quarter the length of its source text. A biographical sketch of Rochester is retained, but other descriptions of "Characters" are eliminated, including an account of Rochester's supposed deathbed repentance for his vicious life. This volume shrinks Rochester's life to his libertinage.

Rochester had also functioned as shorthand for sexual adventure earlier in the century. Around 1830 and again in 1860, Dugdale published a spurious autobiography, *The Singular Life, Amatory Adventures, and Extraordinary Intrigues of John Wilmot, the Renowned Earl of Rochester*, which recounts his gallivanting at court and on the continent.[49] Presenting sometimes as himself and sometimes in disguise, the "brazenly fictitious" Victorian Rochester engages a range of partners, from virgins to farmers' wives to Turkish women to the women claimed by Charles II himself.[50] The narrative exploits Rochester's proximity to the king for its pornographic potential: he fucks Queen Catharine and becomes the "rival of [his] king" by seducing Nell Gwyn "partly by force partly by persuasion"

FIGURE 3.5. Genital penetration, front and center. From *The Singular Life, Amatory Adventures, and Extraordinary Intrigues of John Wilmot, the Renowned Earl of Rochester.* London, c. 1860.
© The British Library Board. Shelfmark P.C.31.f.24.

FIGURE 3.6. Rochester "fucking" a farmer's wife, as a reader annotates. From *The Singular Life, Amatory Adventures, and Extraordinary Intrigues of John Wilmot, the Renowned Earl of Rochester*. London, c. 1860.
© The British Library Board. Shelfmark P.C.31.f.24.

(17). The encounter is typical of the descriptive style, eschewing penetrative detail. But gratuitous illustrations compensate, making genitals their focal point (Figure 3.5 and cover art). The British Library's copy was annotated by a reader (likely Reddie or Ashbee, since the British Library catalogue traces provenance to the latter) who wrote corresponding page numbers to the sex acts being performed in the illustrations—they are not always interleaved with the scene with which they're bound—and who used every opportunity to write "fuck" in the margins. On an illustration facing page 24, the reader provides their own caption: "Rochester fucking the farmer's young wife in bed while he is asleep. (Page 31)" (Figure 3.6). This annotator provides evidence of a particular kind of pleasure being taken in Dugdale's Rochester: the repetition of "fuck" and the tracking of illustrations to their textual descriptions suggest an eagerness to imbue the whole text with a sexual function. Here, a Restoration-era figure meets up with Victorian pornographic style: the rakish and virile Rochester has penetrative sex at a heightened frequency, and all illustrations supplement the narrative account, offering specific genital information—vaginal penetration by a penis—elided in the main text.

Whereas eighteenth-century source texts had forced Victorian pornographers to grapple with (even if they minimized) considerations of sexual injustice, this nineteenth-century invention of Restoration libertinism celebrates masculine aggression. *The Singular Life* shows an uptick in violence and cruelty toward women. We saw that Rochester applied "force" to Nell Gwyn. In another instance, a grandmother invites him to "use force" with her "obstinate" teenage granddaughter (172), who enters the commercial sex trade after being raped by him; this episode is illustrated earlier in the autobiography, where the annotator wrote "p. 172" in the margin to direct the reader to it. Virginal sexuality presented an opportunity for adolescent experimentation in the eighteenth century, but here Rochester's coupling with a young virgin named Cherry shows him to be predatory—he finds her "ripe for the plucking" (32)—and sadistic. Post-coitus, her landlady knocks at the door, at which Cherry hides in "a coal-box which just fitted her size"; Rochester proceeds to fuck the landlady as Cherry "crie[s] for spite" at "the cruel disappointment" of being forced to bear witness (33).

The reader-annotator interprets these actions as proof of sexual power, writing "fucks strong" and "fucks strong again" in the margins of the corresponding descriptions and illustrations, creating a kind of gang rape by text, illustration, and reader. But this coercive masculinity is not simply produced by the narrative and mimicked in illustration and reading. Rather, it is one possible effect of the narrative, achieved cumulatively through various means: the narrative states but does not describe penetrative sex; illustrations graphically render the undescribed genitals; and the annotator interprets narrative and illustration in the crude terminology that suggests a hasty desire for a particular kind of genital action, unencumbered by excess language. If the annotations belong to Reddie or Ashbee as I speculated, they show pornographers at work on a text, consolidating, repeating, and connecting its penetrative actions. This text's situatedness within Victorian pornography promotes this particular sexual meaning but shows it to be an effect of various producers, contributors, and readers.

We must read against the grain of such a work to perceive any statements about sexual justice, and they are only apparent when we situate this work within the procedures of pornographic textual production that contain so much confusion about the ethics of vaginal penetration. Within this diverse environment, even an aggressively phallocentric narrative like *Singular Life* betrays moments of self-consciousness. Before describing one nonconsensual encounter, the narrator shows his awareness that rape is unjust. When the chaste farmer's wife objects "I shall surely be ravished," Rochester provides a sentence of discursive exposition: "It is certain that in committing a rape, two persons must be engaged but if they both agree in the action no rape is effected" (26). Momentarily, the Victorian Rochester introduces a very eighteenth-century convention: candor regarding the ethics of sexual coercion. The hesitation, though, is not whether to pursue penetrative sex—that answer is always affirmative—but whether to bother getting the woman to "agree" or simply proceeding with rape. He concludes in favor of force:

> it is worse than folly to attempt to reason a woman out of her fears, and try to persuade her by honied words to forgive the offence and bless the offender; so [I] instantly proceeded to give her convincing proofs that my passion for her was not governed by reason. (26)

Without conscience, without much of a question, the Victorian pornographic hero proceeds quickly past moments of dialogic reflection, and his enthusiastic reader gallops along beside him, celebrating all the "fucking" this unencumbered attitude permits.

Even as early Victorian pornography speeds up its sequencing of sex scenes, it generates commentary on the the ethics of sexual force, without lingering long enough to resolve the dissonance of that commentary with the cavalier attitude of its heroes. Nineteenth-century editions of eighteenth-century materials work toward this concentration of sex by eliminating discourse seemingly peripheral to a masculine pursuit of penetrative action. As Chapter 2 showed, this omitted content is arguably the most revelatory for understanding eighteenth-century attitudes about not only sexual narrative but sexual justice. The Victorian editors wanted nothing to do with the original feminist content of eighteenth-century pornography; but in their laboring to suppress it, they invented new parameters for discussions of sexual justice. They had less to say about women's personhood as such, and they intensified the ties between sexual violence and conjugal institutions. This chapter will go on to read Victorian pornographic novels produced by affiliates of these mid- and late-Victorian publishers in light of the new, seemingly uncontested predatory masculinity. In narrative that moves rapidly from what Linda Williams calls one hard-core "number" to the next, men mete out force and violence on women who volubly object to penetrative sex.[51] Heterosexual rape becomes a hegemony of pornography, but the genre works to spatially detach it from British culture, distancing sexual violence—disingenuously and incompletely, I argue—from conjugal domesticity.

Pornography, the Novel, and Heterosexuality

The re-publication of eighteenth-century pornographic narrative carried indecision about gender and sexuality into Victorian culture. Specifically, pornography wasn't sure where women's autonomy, or even a full view of their genitals, should feature in the genre. Whether editors knew it or not, their work with pornographic fiction shows that they wrestled with statements and counterstatements about sexual injustice. Editors had to actively, laboriously suppress the mental and social complexity of sex from texts that, in the earlier century, had openly recognized the cultural manufacture of women's sexual disadvantage. The piecemeal, incomplete strategies for quieting pornography's feminist strains reveal that the genre did not know its endgame, had not congealed into an imperative form stipulating orgasmic response; rather it retained statements about women's everyday sexual mistreatment. What does that indecision tell us about pornographic novels original to the nineteenth century?

There is an apparent divergence between pornographic and non-pornographic Victorian novels, the former seeming to present sex in all its excess and irreverence. The latter aligns sexuality with socially sanctioned heterosexual institutions or critiques their misalignment. Since Nancy

Armstrong's *Desire and Domestic Fiction*, the English novel has been credited with assuaging conflicts around sex and gender into chaste, companionate marriage plots. This process was not one of repression, argues Sharon Marcus, but of channeled libidinal desire toward objects that would settle domestic arrangements. Feminized figures consumed by women trained them in a complex dynamic of both desiring and emulating those figures. "Heterosexual women eroticized women" through popular cultural forms, whetting their "appetite for femininity" and preparing them for the gendered subjectivity stipulated by marriage.[52] Claire Jarvis also sees sexuality as a manifest but formally disciplined content of Victorian culture. For Jarvis, desire is lavishly detailed in masochistic scenes of novels where "narrative halts" and readers are suspended in non-genital descriptions that dramatize "ongoing negotiation" of the two-party sexual contract. Such is the novel form's response to cultural demands for chaste plots and characters that also acknowledge the role of eroticism in reproductive marriage: sex is materialized, its inequities displayed, but it is not genitally staged. The masochistic scene pauses action and social realism; it is at the level of plot that "the social order breaks" the sexual formations that were frozen in eroticized tableaux.[53] The novel form organizes sexuality carefully, acknowledging its eroticism, its gender disparities, its contractual codification in decadent instances of aestheticization, then mobilizing plot to support or resist them. These aesthetics prop up companionate British domesticity, allowing pornography to appear as a separate venue for the detailing of heterosexual violence toward women.

On the face of it, pornography might seem the loud, drunk uncle of the highly organized novel form. In pornography, contractual negotiation is hurried or elided so that characters and readers arrive apace to penetration. Action speeds up, goes on, instances of feminine resistance are belligerently handled or entirely ignored. But this haste and silence, I suggest, condenses without erasing the negotiations Jarvis sees being detailed in the "exquisite masochism" of novels. Whereas the novel presents a tableau, then ushers in plot to interfere with its desires, providing an aerated formal terrain for conflicts of sex and gender, pornography claustrophobically layers these negotiations into the very penetrative scenes that are expelled by the Victorian novel. We can only observe these negotiations in all their fullness, I've argued, if we approach texts attuned to what they gain and lose as publishers varnish them for contemporary readers. Victorian pornography and Victorian novels treat sex inversely and complementarily: both extensively connect sexual desire to social realms but do so through different means and to different ends. Like the novelistic marriage plot, pornography offers assessments about justice and equity in its world, but it performs those assessments thickly and rapidly, beside and within moments of genital action, and declines to pass moral or ethical judgments based on those assessments. Further, pornography's analysis expands from questions of heterosexual coupling—the novel's focus—to include an increasingly pluralized sexual world populated by unmarried women, exotic subjects, and nonbinary people. While the Victorian social novel invented forms for balancing and distilling its critical energies, pornographic novels densely and rapidly intermixed their commentaries and skepticisms with sexual description, inverting the proportions of, to invoke Fredric Jameson's formulation, realism's dialectical bond between the "destiny" of gender hierarchy and "the eternal present" of sexual contact.[54] These descriptions, we'll see, often parody marriage, exaggerating and therefore distilling its inequitable gender dynamics.

Victorian pornography often stages marriage as imitation or fraud—as a social form that is useful for non-domestic configurations like sexual trafficking and queer community. The extremities of pornography—Marcus's "pornotopia," "where it is always bedtime"[55]—seem far away from British culture's counter-emphasis on domestic happiness and spousal equity, a cultural ideal that allegedly emerged in the eighteenth century. As my first two chapters argued, an array of sexual writing proclaimed that heterosexuality, as it was practiced in the eighteenth century, held no promise of justice for women. But by the Victorian period, spousal friendship is imagined as a proximate standard, with marriage supposedly purged of the violent associations that attended it in the eighteenth century.[56] Pornography is unconvinced that this cultural change actually took hold. As Victorian realism is depicting marriage chastely as friendship, and channeling its erotic energies into non-genital description, pornography's ties to realism and the British social novel loosen. Its violence, it stands to reason, looks less realist as well, and so can be indulged and repeated with abandon. Within this repetition, marriage is parodied, becoming a site of experimentation for lavish genital interaction, replete with eighteenth-century-style protest against masculine privilege and heteronormativity.

Pornography exploits the divergence between itself and novelistic form to study the heterosexuality being naturalized in literature and culture as companionate British marriage. As the dominant form of heterosexuality, marriage concentrates the gender dynamics under review in the Victorian novel, and it provides an experimental template for pornographic sex scenes, which articulate conjugality's affinity for or even cloaking of sexual violence. Pornography does not simply relish in this content. As Arondekar argues, it both "solidifies and struggles" with aspects of Victorian sexuality, making perceptible, for her, a racist construct of white English masculinity imperiled by colonial sexuality.[57] I find in nineteenth-century pornographic works a commentary that, while exploiting queer and exoticized figures, also directs critical attention at British culture itself. Pornography circulates rape as titillating sexuality but also exposes its likeness to British marriage. From the 1820s through 1880s, a succession of pornographers—including John Benjamin Brookes (d. 1839), William Dugdale (d. 1868) and his brother James (d. 1856), William Lazenby (d. 1880s), and the Ashbee/Avery/Reader circle (1880s), all linked by Reddie's work and collection (d. 1877)—published and re-published narratives that sensationalize sexual violence and show its normalization under heterosexual regimes.[58]

Harmful Heterosexuality: *Lady's Maid* and *Inutility of Virtue*

Pornography expands dynamic and explicit accounts of genital sex that, as Jarvis suggests, Victorian novels formalize into non-genital tableaux or that manifest, as in a novel like *Tess of the D'Urbervilles*, as a set of tragic social effects. Like eighteenth-century fiction as I've accounted for it, pornography written across the nineteenth century highlights and referentially describes quotidian heterosexuality as genital violence. Original nineteenth-century pornographic novels offer a more cavalier attitude toward violence and coercion than earlier ones, making their resistance to heterosexual hierarchies harder to parse. Read closely and in light of the patterns of editorial modifications I've shown were made contemporaneously, they articulate ongoing protests against sexual injustice even as they advance a phallocentric model of pleasure. In this section I focus on two fictions, contemporary with the Dugdale works discussed earlier, that repeat a common pattern, serially submitting their heroines to forced vaginal penetration that invariably gives way to pleasure and doing so without apparent conscience. The publication of *The Adventures of . . . a Lady's Maid* (c. 1838) and *The Inutility of Virtue* (c. 1830) overlaps with the eighteenth-century reprints, their editors and booksellers closely related.[59] These works occasionally reference the reprints, as when the heroine of *Lady's Maid* recalls seeing plates in an edition of *Fanny Hill*—probably a Dugdale, as the plates in *Lady's Maid*, while more explicit, are stylistically similar to those of 1841 and possibly by the same engraver.

Lady's Maid foregrounds its heroine's low birth, her sexual vulnerability as a domestic laborer, and social forces that impinge on her body. The Victorian twist is that the heroine is never able to ward off heteropenetration, and the plot moves so hastily to ensuing sex scenes that social commentary seems muffled. But eighteenth-century discursive patterns loom. They are joined here to new conventions: a vaginal resilience in the heroine, a predisposition to delight in penetrative sex, and a comparatively lax attitude toward devirginization. Despite Louisa's receptivity, the narrative is skeptical about heterosexuality's capacity for justice or safety. Her first penetrative intercourse is nonconsensual, forced by her employer, a reverend who is also revealed to be her father. The novel at once registers the reverend's corrupt sexuality (Louisa regards him with "contempt" and "horror" [18]) and depicts coercion as vaginally pleasurable (she involuntarily feels a "shock of electric and delirious delight" the second time he penetrates her [17]). Indeed, the novel opens chronologically after her employment by the reverend, in the midst of a playful sex act with another employer. The violence of her early nonconsensual, consanguineal experience is prefigured by the reader's certainty that she later enjoys penetrative sex and is thus detoxified.[60]

But the reader is reminded throughout that heterosexuality exerts uncomfortable, even violent pressures on women. *Lady's Maid* sustains its split consciousness about sexual violence through strategies of narrative interruption we'll recognize from eighteenth-century sources, including editorial commentary. Louisa condemns her mother as an "unnatural parent" for selling her (feigned) maidenhead after leaving the reverend's employ. In an eighteenth-century throwback, a footnote appended by a so-called editor joins in the condemnation, declaring parents' entrapment of their daughters a "horrible turpitude," then telling an anecdote of parents locking their daughter Harriet in a chamber to be raped by a captain. However, the footnote does not remain committed to a story of harm: Harriet becomes the "unmarried mistress" of the captain's estate, mother to his children, and "respected by the higher ranks for her exemplary fidelity to the partner of her bed" (33). Rape (a kind of courtship) turns into domestic partnership (a kind of marriage), Harriet's loyalty all the more remarkable because it is not stipulated by church or state. Here, pornography offers a nontraditional domestic arrangement as the lucrative outcome for a woman rendered unmarriageable by a rape orchestrated by at least three other people. Rape's short-term harms reap long-term benefits. Harriet's material fortune is mirrored in the main narrative by Louisa's sexual satisfaction: "ever unable to resist or to delay yielding at once to the impulse of nature," she delights in the physical experience to which she's been sold, even as she continues to condemn her mother's "unnatural avarice" (36). It is the commerce of heterosexual traffic, and not its physical practice, that Louisa finds unethical.[61]

In a refusal of this commerce, the novel for a time suspends its heterosexual plot. When Louisa becomes part of the sapphic household of Madame Fieschi, she routinely remarks on the superiority of women's beauty and gentleness. If Fieschi possessed a penis, Louisa writes, she "should have thought her superior to any man [she] ever beheld" (86). Louisa readily performs and receives vaginal and clitoral pleasure in this long homoerotic episode. The episode and novel end with the arrival of men, Fieschi's death, and the dissolution of the sapphic community—outcomes facilitated by Louisa's conspiring with one of the men to convert the women to the "true religion of nature" (105). But the intervening narrative does not directly pursue this heteronormativity. Louisa enthusiastically reaches orgasm with women, delights in their bodies, and provides anatomical detail. The narrative gives prominence to this sapphic eroticism but also ostentatiously subordinates it. When Louisa addresses "Ye Tribades" as unnatural (despite the pleasure she takes in their company), she incorporates her editor's interjection:

> "But stop! (exclaims my publisher.) Remember, fair Louisa, that my customers don't frequent my shop for the purpose of purchasing dull sermons, or prosing books of moral reflections. Tell them what you did, not what you think, nor fear to o'erstep the modesty of nature." (88)

Emphasizing consumer demand, his shop's specialty, and his censoring of Louisa's ideas ("tell them what did, not what you think"), the publisher draws attention to pornographic narrative as something made for a specific audience through procedures of suppression and redirection, of the heroine's voice in particular. Louisa's convictions arise in speeches and "sermons," but they are silenced. This passage stages the artificial parameters constructed in the creation of pornography, which wants to offer commentary that is summarily rejected by the seller of books.

The novel's curation of "what [she] did" lingers on Louisa's first encounter with a dildo worn by Fieschi. Despite the editor's earlier discouragement of commentary, Louisa qualitatively compares penis to dildo. She will end up concluding that "a prick of real nerve and blood is the thing for me," preferable to "a thing of silk and India rubber" (94).[62] But this preference contradicts the scene and its sumptuous illustration, both of which document the women's delight in their dildo (Figure 3.7). Their conversation acknowledges that the dildo, as Arondekar finds, "bestirs a different level of receptivity" than the penis that is so "unilaterally linked" to masculinity in Victorian pornography.[63] When Louisa complains that her feminine lover lacks a "prick," Fieschi "metamorphoses" by attaching a "godemiche" to her waist (91, 94). Louisa's body is actively receptive:

> the lips of my cunt mechanically swelled forward to meet the object I beheld, like the breast of a pouting pigeon. From the bottom of her belly

FIGURE 3.7. Women delight in their dildo. *The Adventures, Intrigues, and Amours, of a Lady's Maid! Written by Herself.* London, c. 1838.
© The British Library Board. Shelfmark RG.2000.a.2.

protruded a full-grown, proud, and rosy combed priapus, with all its appendages. (92)

The dildo elicits the same reaction Louisa has toward penises. Better still, the woman's body to which it is attached does not cause the abrasions she incurs with men. Louisa pauses a description of Fieschi's penetration—"I snatched her close to my breast, and . . . responded to her vigorous seesaws with pliant loins and bounding buttocks"—to remark on the comparatively injurious feel of a man's body:

> the angular hardness of his bones, the rough harshness of his muscles, . . . in my amorous encounters, had not only sometimes caused me something like pain, but even occasioned erosions of my more delicately textured skin. (92)

By contrast, the feminine body is nonabrasive:

> in Madame Fieschi's embraces, I felt none of these inconveniences. How delightful was the glassy smoothness of her elastic breasts, how inexpressibly soft her plump and rounded limbs, while our bellies resembled two satin cushions of eider down, pressed each to each. (92)

Heterosexual contact is an encounter with a hard, scratchy surface, the harm not rape but a general, uncomfortable friction. Fieschi extols the dildo for "preventing the dangers of maternity"—rather than "the beastly and nauseous seed of man," it is built to ejaculate "an aromatic cream whose odour so agreeably fills the room" (94). Instead of pregnancy, olfactory pleasure.

This episode is the richest example of the indecision around heterosexuality in *Lady's Maid*, constructing a sexual object for Louisa that can penetrate her vaginally—her preferred mode of intercourse—and whose smooth surfaces yield to her own, "each to each." The dialogue between women amounts to a full account of sexual pleasure that eschews the penis-bearing person. Louisa's inchoate refrain of preferring "natural" heterosexuality does not correspond with the specific pleasures she felt in sapphic encounters. These discursive currents circulate competing accounts of sexual pleasure that clash, abut, and yield to one another. *Lady's Maid* tries to valorize phallic dominance and coercive sex. But it does not do so without resistance, which manifests in this text as editorial self-consciousness, mediations of women's sexual expertise, and detailed explanations of the discomforts of heterosexuality.

The skepticisms and alternatives posed in *Lady's Maid* prepare the Victorian reader of pornography to encounter sexual violence as a contested practice, such that when they encounter a serial rape narrative like *The Inutility of Virtue*, whose publication and reprinting closely align with *Lady's Maid*, they will hear its internal protests. Considered a work with "no merit" by Ashbee, *Inutility* subjects its heroine to rape by every man she encounters during travels from Italy to France.[64] She invariably is "rendered . . . subservient" by feelings of enjoyment despite her lack of consent (14). But even this relentless feminine victimization names its violence explicitly. Sexual force is called "rape," and in one instance she recognizes the perpetrator being "like all the others before him" (76). So conditioned is she to violence that she "look[s] upon men as [her] enemies," an entire class of antagonists (80). By late in the novel, she manifests psychological fatigue in the face of rape: "as I could do nothing else, I submitted to my fate, with a comparatively good grace" (111). At length removed to safety by a second husband, she comes into a "princely fortune" from a deceased first husband, despite his family's efforts to "defeat [her] claims and prolong the contest" (114). The property, she tells us, immediately falls into her current husband's possession. *Inutility*, despite its claustrophobic, formulaic eroticization of sexual violence, contains relics of its eighteenth-century forebears, which we saw too, more explicitly untangled, in *Lady's Maid*: commentary on property, pain, masculinity, and the elusiveness of women's sovereignty in a heterosexual economy.

Rape and Marriage in Pornographies of Alterity

Set on the continent, *Inutility* displaces endemic sexual violence to hot, Catholic climes. Ending with the heroine's property absorbed by her husband, it counts marriage as one more conduit for inequity within its serialized rape narrative. Nineteenth-century orientalist and queer pornographies also produce an erotics of rape, and they too layer marriage into it. Pornographers constructing orientalist and queer sexuality transmit confusion about rape's relationship to British marriage: they depict marriage as a site of rape, but they simultaneously contrast conjugal order and temperance with excessive sexual alterities. Orientalist pornography both constructs and blurs the alleged distinction between the two by revealing marriage as particularly hospitable to rape. Queer pornography parodies marital rape to heighten eroticism, and separately constructs instances of earnest sexual violence as inconsequential, their victims lacking subjective or discursive means for resistance. I am treating these two schools of pornography together because they build alterities to British heterosexuality—orientalist texts across spatial and cultural distance, queer texts within the immediate proximity of London. The hegemony of rape and its ties to marriage are ubiquitous across these environments.

Orientalist pornography broadly undertook what Sigel calls a "unidirectional flow of ideas" from metropole to colony, interpreting indigenous sexualities through imperial hegemony.[65] *The Lustful Turk* (1828) and *Seraglio Scenes* (1830s) express this asymmetry in the trope Patrick Brantlinger calls the "terrible Turk," a xenophobic stereotype of despotic masculine sexuality.[66] These novels circulate white virgins around Mediterranean regions, "discursively and literally outside of the realm of the English bourgeois homeplace," as Arondekar describes imperial pornography, where they are abducted, transported, and raped by sultans, deys, and pirates.[67] What Anne McClintock calls the "erotics of imperial conquest," which typically impose the European imagination on colonized people, are here routed homeward, serving an imperial audience hungry for stories of rape but unwilling to count it among its own practices of heterosexuality.[68] These works labor to export violent heterosexuality, and yet to eroticize it, showing that pornographers were producing a sexuality the British audience could enjoy textually while projecting it onto the culture of the harem, an institution long distorted, Danielle Bobker notes, into a site of "sexual subservience."[69] As the British novel is celebrating egalitarian marriage as its domestic product, pornography provides a decadent account of rape that delights in the subjection meted out to women while ensconcing it the sexual traffic of Spanish, Italian, Turkish, and Moorish cultures. The texts' production in Britain gives the lie to their foreign origins and suggests a domestic interest in the methods by which women can be sexually used and subdued, a hypocrisy substantiated by these novels' repeated associations of rape with conjugal sexuality.

An epistolary novel layering multiple women's narration, *The Lustful Turk* implicates Turkish and Italian men as well as English defectors in the abduction and rape of European virgins. It explicitly stages maritime sex traffic as an undoing of Christian marriage. The opening letter from Portsmouth to London expresses a young woman's devotion to her betrothed; the next, from the Dey of Algiers to the Bey of Tunis, extols the trade in sex slaves the woman is soon to enter. This pattern is repeated when a pasha abducts a Greek bride from the altar and installs her as "property of a slave merchant on board a Turkish vessel" bound for Algiers.[70] In both cases, piracy, abduction, and sexual enslavement intervene on marriages motivated by love. This differentiation between European marriage and Turkish enslavement allows an erotics of rape to be developed and repeated under the sign of cultural difference, tethered to the dey and safely detached from British men.

This erotics is presented with particular clarity in *Seraglio Scenes*. Adelaide is a Sicilian abductee from Spain whose maidenhead is preserved by her corsair trafficker on behalf of a Turkish sultan, who deflowers her at the close of that novel. She is prepared for this destiny upon her removal to the Turkish pirate ship, where she is "compelled to witness" the corsair rape a countess.[71] Penetrative logic reigns: Adelaide is made to perceive that the female "sheath" is "destined to receive" the penis (13). The countess's response to being penetrated—she too is a captive—eroticizes rape: "scarlet blushes" appear on her breast, and "in this happy position voluptuous sighs broke forth from [her] half-closed lips" (20). This training in penetrative ideology either works seamlessly or is totally unnecessary because Adelaide responds with automatic vaginal pleasure to penetration. When the corsair minimally penetrates her with a finger, "her alarms became hushed," "her senses seduced" (21). This susceptibility is mirrored by her psychological compliance. Upon being delivered to the sultan, "she felt she was indeed his slave" (55), an outcome of a lengthy grooming process in which she is sexually trained by other women, genitally depilated, and plumped by a rich diet. The elaborate defloration scene emphasizes the sultan's desire to compel her not just physically but verbally. Declaring himself an exception to "Turks [who] do not usually permit love niceties to trouble our pleasures," the sultan debilitates her conscious faculties by freely touching her person while requesting her willing participation (63). She verbally protests, then "at length consented to his happiness" (66). The narrative, for pages, describes her pleasure at being penetrated.

The sultan's idiosyncratic "niceties" aestheticize—they make into narrative—what could easily be an assault bereft of conversation about the woman's penetrative experience. *Seraglio Scenes* prefers to have its heroine submit to what will be done to her anyway. At novel's close, these asymmetrical dynamics seem an approximation of British domesticity. Post-coitally satisfied by the sultan, Adelaide volunteers her subjection: "her submissive caresses extremely gratified him.... Her docility to every thing his desires imposed clearly told how omnipotent were the sacred rights he had obtained in her possession" (79). The logic here is limited: her caresses convey submission, which pleases the sultan, but that submission has been "imposed" by a "possession" of her. The voluntariness of her docility is pleasing but not essential to the sultan's exertion of sexual right. The novel closes with the sultan emphasizing "the necessity of entire submission" to his will, and he installs her in special apartments that signify her preferred status in the harem (85). She is given a degree of domestic power, and she embraces the arrangement.

Exoticized as Turkish and touted as voluntary, Adelaide's sexual, legal, and material inequity characterizes marriage-adjacent plots we've seen in contemporary texts set in England (like the Harriet anecdote in *Lady's Maid*), suggesting that coercive and disenfranchising sex acts can work to women's advantage. But further, these inequities that originate in genital subjection also characterize courtship and marriage, and we know from my first chapter that eighteenth-century texts had deliberated, with more sympathy, over women's genitals, the proprietary claims made to them, and the social and domestic outcomes of those incursions. *Seraglio Scenes* draws on this familiar system of inequity, strips it of its British context, and eroticizes it as an unencumbered penetrative hegemony—a sensuousness that overrides women's political or social desire.

Orientalist pornography, like English domesticity, shows women's voluntary compliance to be commensurate with marriage. Turkish sexual despotism not only interrupts European marriage in *The Lustful Turk*, but parodies it, revealing the structural similarity between the two forms of heterosexuality. Duping another English virgin to his harem, the dey impersonates a Protestant and arranges a sham marriage "to lull her into security" so that he may claim her virginity (135). Enlisting a cast of disguised accomplices, he arranges the trappings of an British marriage: "The ring was ready, the contract made out." He immediately consummates after the mock ceremony, claiming "the absolute authority of a husband" even as she "feebly resisted" (136). Unlike so many stock instances of virgin submission, this woman's body is not quickly receptive, and when the dey, still disguised, penetrates her "to the utmost length," she still "entreated [him] to withdraw the arrow" (141). Even during consummation, she tries to exert autonomy over her genitals. The dey declines, deploying the legal and spiritual logic of marriage: "'No . . . it is now all over; you have nothing further to apprehend; from a pure virgin you have become a chaste wife'" (141). Quickly after ejaculation and despite her grief, he forces penetration again, invoking the proprietary logic of marital authority: "Master of the citadel, I assumed all the conqueror's rights" (141). The dey uses the logic of temperate Protestant marriage against itself, showing serial rape to be a possible version of it—a contract that erases the wife's resistance, assimilates her body to the category of property, and counts as chastity her repeated genital use by a cruel partner. The dey's sexual violence does less to urge the "rescue [of] white women from brown men" than to make British readers desire the forms of subjection into which women can be pressed by heterosexual institutions.[72] Colonial sexuality may threaten to "destroy English masculinity" through its "corrupting influence," as Arondekar writes, but this orientalized version might be more of an analog than an opposite to British heterosexuality, carrying to a logical extreme the masculine right afforded husbands.[73]

Approaching orientalist pornography as a distillation of gender inequities practiced domestically, at home in Britain, allows us to understand how its eroticism works: freed of the implication (unlike their eighteenth-century forebears) that they cannot possibly themselves be rapists, readers can imagine European women as genitally available through persuasion, coercion, or force. Orientalist pornography tells us more than its producers want it to, distilling, clarifying, and exoticizing a violent gender hierarchy that British culture, if the Victorian novel is any indicator, wanted to believe was not its own. *The Lustful Turk* apparently told a compelling story. Editions appeared regularly throughout the nineteenth and early twentieth centuries, its heteroeroticism overlapping with queer pornographies that appear later in the century. These chronologically and thematically different works sustain, despite their seeming alterity from British conjugality, associations of entrenched, harmful gender hierarchy with marital heterosexuality.

If orientalist pornographies conflate rape and marriage at a distance, queer pornographies do so hyperlocally, infusing London with a queer culture that parodies marriage and heterosexuality. *Sins of the Cities of the Plain* (1881) and *Letters from Laura and Eveline* (1883), the latter loosely a sequel of the former, map queer erotic community within the "dominant and widely understood geography" of London, according to Matt Cook.[74] Sex acts in these novels often undo binary identities and embodiments, showing both sex and gender to be highly variant in instances of sexual union. Drawing characters like Jack Saul, John Boulton, and Lord Arthur Somerset from highly publicized sodomy trials of 1870 and 1889, these novels present anal eroticism, drag, nonbinary gender, genital variance, and group sex as norms, immanent in the daily operations of the city.[75] They include heterosexuality and normative gender as modes of pleasure but subordinate them to a dominant focus on sodomy, particularly in *Laura and Eveline*. Acknowledging the power of *Sins*'s "polymorphous pansexuality," Morris Kaplan suggests its queer erotics, transgression of incest taboos, interspecies sex, and class admixture are "unlikely to reflect social practice" but indicate a pervasive non-domestic sexual culture.[76] For Anne Delgado, the fluctuations of bodies and desires in *Sins* evade Foucauldian truth production, "continually resist[ing] . . . the natural order of singular or binary sexual identities."[77]

Doggedly nonbinary, both novels explode any fiction of British sexuality as temperate, domestically organized, or hetero, and they do so in tightly sequenced sex scenes, with little in the way of non-sexual content. When we situate *Sins* and *Laura and Eveline* alongside works that displace heterosexual rape to a distant historical epoch (as in Rochester's biography) or a far-flung exoticized environment (as in *Seraglio Scenes*), we see that it tries to distinguish British sexuality by its enthusiasm and pleasure, populated by ever-consenting subjects engaged in non-monogamous, improvisational sex acts.[78] Lisa Hager argues that coverage of "female husbands" in Victorian periodicals and pamphlets produced gender through social and labor categories.[79] In queer pornographies, sex acts produce gender, linking erotic sensation to malleable aspects of identity—language, clothing, even anatomy. Pornography, the literary construction of genital activity, connects genital sensation and gender identity; queer pornography shows this connection to be highly variable and inventive.

Saul, *Sins*'s narrator, makes his living as a "mary-ann," and he often describes sexual encounters—his own and those he observes—as suspending binary gender and genitals.[80] Patronized by genteel men, he joins in sex parties at elite clubs, often dressing, like other young participants, in "charming female costume" (35). Such costume impacts the morphology of the sex acts and actors that ensue. In one episode, Saul spies on Somerset and Boulton, the latter "superbly got up as a beautiful lady" named Laura. Somerset's "inamorata was not idle, for I could see her unbuttoning his trousers," revealing a sizeable penis. Laura performs fellatio, and when Somerset feels under her clothes, "she gave a very pretty scream and pretended to be shocked at this rudeness." Somerset admires on Laura's body "as manly a weapon as any lady could desire to see," prompting him to ask, "Are you an hermaphrodite, my love?" Saul explains Somerset's pleasure in this encounter deriving specifically from phallic genitalia being joined to a "creature such as an ordinary observer would take for a beautiful lady," tethering the scene's pleasures to a specifically trans eroticism (39).[81]

The pleasure of these erotic inventions is regularly heightened by parody—queer parodies of heterosexuality and marriage. *Sins*'s sequel *Letters from Laura and Eveline* (characters sometimes called Saul and Boulton in *Sins*) has trans characters narrate their erotic pleasure in this context. In two letters, one each by the eponymous protagonists, *Laura and Eveline* describes an elaborate "mock-marriage" ceremony as well as group sex rituals that surround it.[82] Trans women marry cis men, consummate through penetrative sex, and locate intense pleasure in inhabiting femininity. Persuasion, force, and rape, elsewhere harmful to disenfranchised subjects, here heighten erotic affect, their potential to harm removed by the voluntary environment of the sexual performance. Laura writes of consummation with Somerset ("Arthur") in feminine terms: it is

> awfully delicious to be taken for a woman, and addressed as a woman, his manly caresses and terms of endearment, really added to my blushing bashfulness, at the same time perfectly irresistible thrills of desire prevated my person, which seemed to concentrate in my longing arse-quim. (20)

Earlier, her "arse-quim throbbed . . . like a true cunt" (16). Laura's arousal is bound up with being courted "as a woman" by a partner fully sentient of her non-vaginal anatomy, and her arousal "concentrates" in an anatomical site—the anus, experienced as a cunt—that affirms trans embodiment.

A woman without an anatomical vagina and experienced in anal penetration, this bride can delight, without fear of injury, in a husband "sworn to have [her] maidenhead in [her] bridal dress" and thrilled by her "splendid clitoris" (16). Somerset too apprehends and verbalizes Laura's anatomy as variant: "You are like a hermaphrodite; its quite as long as my prick. Is it always excited and stiff like this? . . . Will it spend, dearest Laura?" (17). Laura blushes and resists, affectively experiencing conventional femininity:

> ready to faint with shame, I yet felt how delicious it was to be handled and touched by the man I loved so much, and fancied myself a girl or a real hermaphrodite, and my prick only a big clitoris; how my arse filled with hot lust, and pouted just like a cunt. (17)[83]

Analogy is part of this desire: linguistic reference to nonbinary genitalia and to marriage excites Laura and Somerset. The "as though" and "fancying oneself" within the sexual encounter produces erotic feeling: Somerset desires Laura because she is dressed as a bride, because she deploys feminine modesty, because she has a penis, and because she will be penetrable, while Laura desires Somerset because he desires these aspects of her, and because he, like her, has a "prick . . . so rampant" (13). *Sins* has gendered Laura both masculine and feminine, linking her to the historical Boulton and therefore, in part, to masculinity; *Laura and Eveline* attributes feminine pronouns, genitals that traverse binary sex, and a "fancy" for being lady-like within the erotic context of the "mock-marriage." Bodies, subjects, identities, and expression are produced by the encounter, are irreducible to it. Here, they enter the sex acts voluntarily, and so can parody dynamics of marriage and sexual coercion without incurring its injuries. Unlike cis women's chastity, Laura's guarding of her virginity reads as sexual play rather than susceptibility to rape, an erotics that is recapitulated later by bridesmaids who "shamefacedly, as it were" are "render[ed] powerless to resist" penetration during an orgy (100).[84]

Featuring no cis women, *Laura and Eveline* eschews heterosexual vaginal rape, drawing on it only as a reference point for the feminine virginity parodied by sexually experienced trans women. *Sins*, though, includes hetero acts in its panoply of sexual groupings, the rape of cis women and boys among them. Significantly, the subjective experiences of such violence are not narrated. A Mr. Horner hires Saul to rape an unwilling housemaid as he watches. It is Saul, not she, that narrates her experience: according to him, she is "powerless" under the "humiliating" treatment, "almost dead with shame" at being genitally handled, and at the same time, "excited" with "real erotic emotion" and "carried away by her lubricity" (53–54). The scene incorporates her reluctance into its erotics and shows her body to part ways with her will; to the degree that she possesses interiority, it is speculated by the rapist. Where eighteenth-century texts volubly argued that personhood was elided for victims of sexual violence, Victorian pornography constructs the objects of rape as non-persons.

This technique of eroticizing through depersonalization also structures episodes of pederastic rape in *Sins*. Described as "fair," "olive-tinted," and "black," three adolescent boys are initiated in an orgy attended by cis men and trans women, including Saul/Eveline. They have presumably been trafficked, the first two boys hailing from France and Italy and the third's origins unacknowledged. Eveline's desire for "the little black fellow" is expressed in racist language and racialized, tied specifically to the boy's complexion. The shade of his backside and penis is repeatedly fetishized and his subjectivity effaced. Saul/Eveline is penetrated by another adult while she fellates the boy, and while the penetrator is called Eveline's "partner" (60), the boy's identity is named only in slurs. His "eyes . . . fairly streaming with tears" do not deter the actions meted out to him by Eveline, who is "too excited to feel the least inclined to spare that ebony bum of his" (59).

Eveline and her adult counterparts do to the boy what they themselves enjoy, but without the exchange of conversation or consent. No word is given about the boys' futures after the orgy, but we receive a clue in an ensuing episode narrated by Saul's friend George Brown, who traffics children to supplement his income as a sex worker (69–70). In one instance, he recruits a shoeblack to be his page and forces him to perform sex acts, deploying psychological and physical violence. Brown is initially indifferent to the boy's pain ("I could see he did not like it, but did it to please me"), and it later "add[s] to his lust" (72, 74). Brown is unwilling to tolerate conversation about the boy's experience, gagging him when his protests are too loud and ultimately selling him to "a certain house in Paris" for "a hundred pounds" (70, 74). Saul, the narrator, states but suppresses the knowledge that "there are many more like . . . Brown, who have particular specialties for turning the pederastic vice to account," abandoning this topic to return to his narrative (75).

The erotics of unparodied rape in queer pornography rests on the construction of a receptive character who lacks interiority, or whose subjective expressions are prevented from entering the narrative. These novels distinguish such violence and the empty figures they require from the deeply affective experience of parody, where sexual subjects draw on inequitable social structures like rape and marriage to heighten eroticism.[85] These rituals in *Sins* and *Laura and Eveline*—like the linkage between sexual violence and marriage in orientalist pornographies—show the capacity of heterosexual institutions to convert rape into non-rape, sometimes to forge bonds within sexual minority communities, and to cancel the personhood of the penetrated subject. As we saw in *The Lustful Turk*, the dispassionate parody of marriage generates a logic for discounting the interiority of the rape victim—the protests of the duped Protestant "wife" are inconsequential to the sexual outcomes predetermined by the dey. The overriding of protest, when parodied, functions as eroticism in scenes of orgiastic queer community, and it elsewhere discloses the cultural institutions that support rape.

The few porn-studies scholars who historicize pornography locate the genre's coalescence in the nineteenth century.[86] I've shown that Victorian pornographers crafted old and new works with a high level of self-consciousness regarding a tradition they inherited from a century earlier. The silence in queer pornography around the subjective experience of the non-consenting participant differs profoundly from eighteenth-century texts' elaborations of experiences of sexual violence. *Sins*'s refusal to attend to the subjective experience of rape indicates either an indifference to its violence or, more likely, an exclusion of it from a literary environment actually committed to documenting pleasure—a rare phenomenon in pornography, by my analysis. In other words, *Sins* and *Laura and Eveline* seem committed to building an ecosystem within Victorian London that encloses and sanctifies queer pleasures that, outside of these confines, made sexual subjects vulnerable to stigmatization, arrest, and socioeconomic precarity. The novels are so committed to constructing this world that they marginalize protest, muting dissenting voices but leaving material evidence (pain, tears, social disappearance) of the sexual disadvantage they signify. These figures wield merely erotic power, constructed by the text as transient, interchangeable, receptive.

But, I've argued, Victorian readers of pornography did not encounter these figures naively. Rather, pornographic texts trained them in multiple narrative models, some containing statements against sexual violence, some staging the editorial suppression of those statements, and some inventing voiceless figures, as in queer pornography, that invoke histories of sexual violence even if they don't protest them verbally. Pared-down texts like *Sins* and *Laura and Eveline* retain pornography's social consciousness, condensing it into figures whose appearances and disappearances invoke gendered and imperial power relations. The dispassionate genital use and disposal of persons across the Victorian period shows any differentiation between sensational and domestic sexualities to be incomplete, even contested in the face of pornographic evidence continually joining the familiar (heterosexuality, conjugality) to the exoticized (violence, queerness, alterity). Despite this period's condensation of pornographic description, the genre, inheriting the discursive hybridity of eighteenth-century source texts, sustains utterances on behalf of the persons being swiftly depersonalized and exchanged across tight sexual sequencing. Apprehended as ongoing textual procedures, Victorian pornography keeps us sentient that the disenfranchised persons indifferently operationalized in pornography were invented by editors skilled in manipulating narrative to amplify sexual power and quiet dissent. Its strategies of deletion did not settle British culture's confusion about the ethics of its sexual practices.

4 UNCOUPLING
Pornography and Feminism in the Countercultural Era

> *But what shall I do to get to speak to her? If cold unanimated Writing could banish her Indifference, sure the Eloquence of Words, Lips, Eyes, Prayers, Vows, warm Embraces, and short breathed Sighs, must melt her into Compliance. Oh the nameless transporting Extasy; thus to fold her to my warm Bosom, to see her panting, blushing, sighing, dying! the very Thought transports me beyond mortal Imagination.*
> —THE HISTORY OF THE HUMAN HEART, 1749

> *But what shall I do to get to speak to her? If cold inanimate writing could banish her indifference, surely the eloquence of words, lips, eyes, warm embraces, and short-breathed sighs, must melt her into compliance. Oh, the nameless ecstacy—thus to press her to my heart; to see her blushing, panting, sighing, dying! By heaven, the very thought transports me beyond imagination.*
> —MEMOIRS OF A MAN OF PLEASURE, 1844

> *But what shall I do to get to speak to her? If cold inanimate writing could banish her indifference, surely the eloquence of words, lips, eyes, warm embraces, and short-breathed sighs, must melt her into compliance.*
> —MEMOIRS OF A MAN OF PLEASURE, 1968

MY THREE EPIGRAPHS provide a micro-example of the transformation of pornographic narrative across more than two centuries in a single passage from *The History of the Human Heart*.[1] Originally narrating an amalgam of physical desire, imaginative fantasy, and affective transport, this single passage is pruned to focus on the hoped-for sex act with increasing efficiency. All three versions agree on the essentials of titillation: sighs, lips, a woman's surrender. But the material surrounding the imagined physical union changes, and attention to the mind's role in sexual desire is whittled out. In 1749, the ejaculative, hyperbolic, syntactically fluid passage shows the hero's fantasy to heighten his longing. The erotic wish is trimmed and grammatically tidied in 1844, when an editor finds it more suitable for the masculine protagonist to "press . . . to [his] heart" his beloved than to "fold her to [his] warm Bosom"—presumably too emasculating a term for a man's body—and eliminates the "Prayers, Vows" that would pronounce the spiritual degree of his supplication. By 1968, the passage is halved. It ends with the woman's compliance, doing away with the source text's attention to the power of imagination, to the "transport" that succeeds from purely mental action. By the later twentieth century, pornographic narrative economically focuses on eroticized bodies, masculine prowess, and consummated sex acts, a rather far cry from the eighteenth-century text's equal reliance on the mind to complete the erotic scene.

The previous chapter showed that Victorian editorial interference produced confusion about the sexual attitudes it inherited from the past, circulating dissonant accounts of what counted as pornography, whether its central feature was sex itself or cultural discourse that explains its effects. Eighteenth-century pornography continued to be reprinted in the era of pulp fiction. Rather than dismiss its narrative heterogeneity as a relic of the past, paperback editors and publishers cited it as evidence of historical sexual attitudes and practices, finding transcendent sexual truths in the roving of straight men. The purpose of this final chapter is to sketch some ways we can see eighteenth-century works carrying a concern for sexual justice into the countercultural era. Masculinist print culture, as it claimed to promote sexual liberation through the reprinting of a pornographic archive, in fact continued to pare away women's voices and concerns from historical source texts, enacting (despite explicit claims to the contrary) Victorian editorial habits that normalize women's sexual passivity.

These efforts to subdue feminist dissidence seem particularly pointed in an era during which leftist men claimed solidarity with women under the guise of sexual liberation. Alliance with the women's movement is belied by editing practices that mute feminist and queer discourses within pornographic texts. Such textual interference naturalizes penetrative heterosexuality, the very cultural field that was being exposed by second-wave feminists as perpetuating gendered violence and inequity. Even as it implicated pornography in its critique of heterosexuality, feminist theory took up the discourse on sexual justice that was being carved out of the genre by its modern editors and critics. Refusing to subordinate discussions of genitalia, feminism traced sexual injustice outward from the body, highlighting, as eighteenth-century pornography had done, how women's bodies absorb the violence of social institutions that produce gender through distortions of sexual morphology. Crucially, some writers signaled alternatives to the anti-pornography critique that came to dominate feminism by the late 1970s, imagining genital life as the eighteenth century had—as a site of social and political reform, a possible future for feminism that was foreclosed by the anti-pornography movement.

Pulping Pornography: *History of the Human Heart* in 1968

In 1968, in London and in New York, Tandem Press and Award Books published *Human Heart* under its early Victorian title *Memoirs of a Man of Pleasure* as a mass-market paperback. Priced 95 cents, the American cover boasts it is a reprint of a great archival discovery, "an 18th-century erotic classic ... [d]iscovered in the archives of the British Museum—available in the U.S. for the first time!" (Figure 4.1). The back cover of the UK printing celebrates the novel's "rescu[e] from the obscurity of the British Museum to delight, amuse and instruct the modern reader," previewing such scenes as "the amazing activities of the 'Posture Girls,' the first strip-tease artists." The cover art of nearly nude, contemporarily styled women does not map onto any diegetic moment in the text, but rather sexes up the book to attract attention in a saturated market.² The editor's introduction follows suit, providing a digest of the novel's sexual encounters and emphasizing their "far wider scope" than those of Cleland's *Woman of Pleasure*. He emphasizes the text's historicity as well, considering it documentary evidence of "the amorous life of the period, and the sexological ideas of the day."³

Like the Victorian reprints of *Human Heart* discussed in the previous chapter, these twentieth-century editions sensationalize the novel by emphasizing its raciest scenes and promising exposed bodies, but unlike those earlier reprintings, the pulp editions emphasize the text's archival status, its historical distance from but erotic connection to a countercultural present. This pulping—recrafting, rebranding, and popularizing an original—reflects the character of the pulp medium more broadly, which Paula

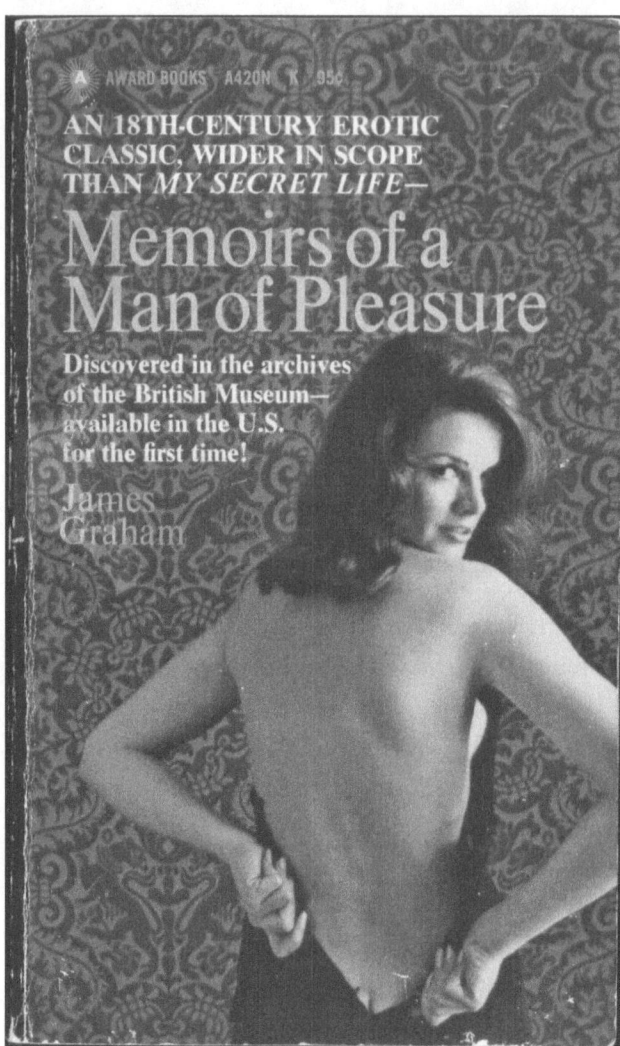

FIGURE 4.1. The pulping of *The History of the Human Heart* as *Memoirs of a Man of Pleasure*. New York, 1968.

Rabinowitz sees as a new, democratic form bridging a popular readership to specialized literature. The 1968 *Human Heart* editions exemplify pulp's "admixture of high and low," and their archival character—"the historiography of the books themselves"—is at the fore of pulp's democratic distribution of literary culture.[4] In this case, the books address a reader ostensibly situated within the rhetoric of sexual liberation, promising to arouse desires that the editions' paratext connects to a historical past authenticated by an archive.

The 1968 edition is a mush of historical references that aims to create an effect of authenticity but, when parsed, reveals the interventions of various editorial actors. Despite claiming transparency on eighteenth-century sexual culture, the edition is based on the 1844 *Exquisite* serialization and so reflects William Dugdale's stripping of social and ethical debate (discussed in the previous chapter). It contains further deletions made by 1968 editor James Graham, a pseudonym based on the eighteenth-century quack sexologist whose lectures are reprinted in *The Exquisite* (and who, I show in the next section, edited several other works of antique pornography for countercultural-era readers). Following Ashbee's famous Victorian bibliography of pornography, Graham misdates *Human Heart*'s publication year as 1769 rather than 1749, a date that would have suggested a more felicitous tie to Cleland. Never working with an earlier copy-text, he uncritically inherits all of Dugdale's accelerations toward sex acts, and creates more paragraph and section breaks to provide a more rapid reading experience. Graham further disencumbers his contemporary reader from contemplative and speculative meditations on sex and its effects. We'll recall that a remarkable 1749 footnote exposing modesty as an oppressive cultural fiction is already gone in 1844; and the 1968 editor continues to remove delays to sexual action. Excessive discussion or reflection around sexual encounters, it seems, were irrelevant or threatening to the pulp reader's enjoyment.

Seeking to deliver erotic adventure to his readers, Graham streamlines the novel's momentum toward sex acts, a trend evident across this chapter's epigraphs. If "sexual content" in the previous two centuries included discussions of heterosexuality's discontents and injustices, by now these elements are seen as tangential and disposable, at odds with the curiosity pulp wants to cultivate. Topics that might distract from a potent masculine heterosexuality are often suppressed, suggesting that the pleasure of pornographic reading by 1968 is not only narrow compared to the miscellaneous pleasures enjoyed by earlier readers, but also that it requires a proud and unfailing hero. Graham eliminates historically contingent associations of sex with other topics, such as medicine, religion, and education, that would be disharmonious and outdated to the pulp reader. He removes some pseudo-medical discussions that are outdated by the late twentieth century, such as a life-threatening episode of hysteria in Camillo's mother (*E* 126; *G* 12) and a description of his infancy that grants him an implausible level of cognition—implausible too in 1749, and funny (*E* 127; *G* 13).[5] A description of the hero's private education, which favored English history over the classics, morality over the "speculative sciences," likewise is deemed irrelevant by Graham (*E* 128; *G* 16), as is the Quaker Saphira's accusation of heresy when Camillo claims that his life depends on her returning his affections (*E* 184; *G* 113). Whereas the 1749 Camillo was at times timid, erring, or ambivalent in his heterosexual pursuits, in 1968 he is self-possessed, his seductive efforts are less frequently interrupted by bouts of uncertainty, and his women partners are quieter, flatter, less condemning of his scheming and duplicity.

This new masculinity calls for the hero to be more regularly in a position of dominance. He, therefore, so unlike his eighteenth-century forebear, falls short of admitting submission to the women he pursues. Graham, for example, eliminates the hyperbole of Camillo's seduction speech to Charlotta, his first successful conquest. In 1749 and 1844 we read, "Those languid Eyes, that heaving panting Bosom, that glowing Blush, all proclaim the God of Love triumphant: Yield my Dearest to his Dictates and make me happy" (*H* 105; *E* 159). Deleting this statement of subjection, Graham has Camillo's conquest succeed from the penultimate line, an imperative that never admits to the triumph of love: "[L]et no childish coyness chill the warm desires that now mutually fire our breasts" (*G* 69). His proclamations to Saphira, whose beauty and virtue particularly pique his desire, are effusive in 1749 but curtailed in 1968. Camillo's poetic *carpe diem* speech to her disappears (*E* 184; *G* 112), as does his abject pledge to banish himself from her sight forever—a sacrifice that would threaten his own life—if she so wishes (*E* 192; *G* 128). It seems the pleasure of the reader in 1968 would be compromised by a pleading and subservient masculinity.

Camillo's authority in sexual encounters, we know from previous chapters, was sometimes challenged by women's protests against penetrative violence and coercion. Graham removes statements by women in which they boldly lament their vulnerability at the hands of predatory men. Camillo accomplishes his goal of penetrative sex with Saphira, which both characters see (he rapturously, she remorsefully) as a seduction. But the 1749 narrative also originally described it as rape, an association that gets both retained and blurred across the publication history. His pursuit of Saphira is homosocially encouraged, fueled by an alderman's suspicion that she is "made up of errant flesh and blood" (*E* 176) and by another Quaker man's scheming to bring Camillo into her company—a feat not easily achieved, as, already betrothed, she is closely policed by her mother and by her own chastity. Predisposed by these men to sexualize Saphira—and with no intention of marrying her (*E* 176)—Camillo watches her closely and decides she "is capable of love, her soul has in it, doubtless, a spark of the social fire that was originally breathed into every creature," despite her many spoken and written statements to him that she wishes to enter her marriage a virgin (*E* 181). His first two attempts at consummation are interrupted, though one comes close: he "overwhelmed" and "stifled" Saphira so that she "had no power to hinder him" (*E* 197). In the third attempt—delayed by a long footnote on heterosexual friendship that is deleted in 1968—Camillo begins by soothing Saphira's anxieties from their previous encounters, then "artfully fanned the virgin's flame," "raised her to the height of expiring extasy," "nimbly sprung upon" and "rushed into her virgin zone, before she could imagine the enemy was so near her quarters" (*E* 199). The narrative is clear that in speech, writing, and action, Saphira declines penetrative sex, and in 1749 and 1844, as in 1968, it recruits readers to observe, blithely, Camillo's dismissal of her will.

Deleted passages in the 1968 edition reduce the narrative's consideration of rape's consequences. This pattern of suppression begins before the rape, minimizing Camillo's attention to Saphira's speech. The original emphasizes Camillo's excitement during conversation with her: "[h]er Words were all Harmony; the Symphony of the Spheres could not be more ravishing to his Ear," a line deleted by 1844, when readers hear only that she speaks "in the language of the angels" (*H* 150; *E* 176). Still, in both cases readers know that Camillo listens to her and finds her capable of meaningful statements, so have more basis for censuring his later disregard for her refusals. Immediately after the rape, she describes her grief to him, and the 1968 edition elides passages that particularly focus on Camillo's culpability, on his purposefulness in exerting force, such as "thou hast now unmasked thyself: the fiend, the lustful ravisher, appears through the disguise, and thy soul stands naked before me, in its natural baseness and deformity." After briefly wishing she might delude herself into trusting his affections, she laments "what a wretch thou hast made me" (*E* 199). Paring out these statements, Graham has Saphira grieve but attenuates her awareness of the hero's cruelty.

Graham also deflects the narrative away from the moral complexity she assigns Camillo, omitting "thy own conscience will be thy tormentor, and I shall be amply revenged by the hourly upbraiding with which it shall embitter all thy pleasure" (*E* 200). The 1968 text relieves itself of such a psychological burden for Camillo (though he does, to be sure, express regret for ruining Saphira's prospects—but never to the extent that he considers marrying her, as she requests). It also suppresses her description of the social descent she will experience: "miserable woman! betrayed, lost, abandoned to the scorn of the wise, the laughter of fools, and without one glimpse of inward peace!" (*E* 200). Adopting an eighteenth-century attitude toward her premarital vaginal penetration, Saphira holds herself responsible for having allowed the transgression to occur; but the narrative provides ample evidence of the clarity of her intention to be chaste for her impending marriage. While the novel circulates a moral debate around Camillo's overreaching, his actions have no consequences (her mother wants to charge him with rape, but Saphira refuses, admits what she sees as her own guilt in the matter, and dies).

What's more—and this is my central point—Graham mutes passages that give particular texture or depth to the consequences of rape for Saphira and, indeed, for Camillo himself. In one case, Graham is helped along in his elision of rape by what appears to be a printing error in the 1844 edition. In 1749, Saphira circulates rape discourse by stating Camillo did *not* rape her, as when she insists on "that Gentleman's Innocence" and instructs her mother "to go and release him," an imperative that floats the possibility of his incarceration but ultimately cancels it (*H* 211). In 1844, this passage is replaced entirely by a block of text identical to one in the adjacent column of print. Whether by accident or design, Dugdale in 1844 jettisoned the figuring of Camillo as a rapist as well as the women's power to clear or not clear his name. In 1968, Graham simply skips the printing error and never recovers the original passage. In this way, Dugdale unwittingly collaborated with Graham across more than a century to quiet a discourse on rape. Passages in which Saphira actively criticizes the hero's actions on moral or religious grounds, describes her grief, or reflects on Camillo's incarceration are subject to removal, reducing the narrative of her voice and its unflattering commentary on masculine power.

Advancing the pornographic hero as unconstrained in his sexual pursuits, the pulp edition also wants to distance itself from marriage and its domestication of heteromasculinity. Conspicuous and stylistically clumsy changes are made to the novel's end to mute its conventional (in eighteenth-century terms) embrace of marriage as a formal means of disciplining the hero's roaming. In a reversal of the novel's established gender dynamics, he is pursued by a cross-dressed woman intent on claiming her sexual right to him. Angelina, having been seduced and abandoned by Camillo in Amsterdam, surprises him in the bedchamber of his London mistress, who has offered to help reunite them. In the comic register of the original, Angelina is a suitable partner for the wayward Camillo, matching him in irreverence and spiritedness—after all, she considers herself marriageable even though he has already seduced her. She has traveled alone, dressed *en cavalier*, and pursued him with loyalty and diligence. Drawing on a familiar means of closure dating at least to Restoration comedy (think of Hellena's masqueraded pursuit of Willmore in Aphra Behn's *The Rover*, or going further back, Rosalind's cross-dressed wooing of Orlando in *As You Like It*), their coupling promises to be lively, even turbulent, the woman already claiming the clothes, actions, and autonomy of another gender.

The 1968 edition is profoundly uninterested in this containment of the hero's serial adventures. Most of Angelina's confrontation of Camillo is deleted by Graham, so in 1968 we do not hear her admonish him, when he renews his pledge of love, to "swear no more! heaven has already witnessed too many of your false oaths; tempt it no more" (*E* 248); or that "nothing is left for [her] but endless misery!" (*E* 248). In 1968, the exclamation is shorter: "[Y]ou cannot give me back my happiness, my peace, my lost innocence" (*G* 222). More abbreviated still is the hero's response, which Graham truncates to a vow passionless even in its punctuation: "Oh, my [Angelina]. Take me back and let my tears heal you" (*G* 222–223). In earlier editions, Camillo's eagerness to reconcile and marry was evident in his emotional response:

> tears started to his eyes, and running to assist her, he exclaimed—Oh! my [Angelina]! thou dear, lovely injured maid! take me to thy lovely bosom, there let me grow, and with my tears heal the wounds my cruelty has given to thee. (*E* 248)

In 1749 and 1844, this proclamation had been a suitably comic conclusion to the hero's picaresque sexual adventures, and the lovers' hyperbolic vows at their reunion animated the impending nuptials. In 1968, the pulp editor seems to view the conclusion as a structural rather than a thematic necessity. The sexual adventures conclude, and masculine desire conforms to monogamy; the reader no longer needs passionate dialogue, or even exclamation points.

Graham quiets discursive aspects of the novel's sexual content, attempting to invent the pornographic hero as one whose sexual roaming meets with no narrative resistance or containment. Graham thus—and unwittingly, not working directly with the 1749 edition—extends Dugdale's editing practices, silently modernizing and abridging the 1844 copytext for the pulp market. Where Victorian texts—even if ambivalently—featured women's awareness of systemic sexual violence, dramatized its impact on victims, and muddled discussions of legal consequences for perpetrators, the pulp edition moves toward the elimination of women's commentary altogether. Graham wants to transmit eighteenth-century sexual culture to a pulp audience, but his editorial hand tells another story, amplifying masculine sexual right at the expense of discourse that, in earlier editions, resisted it. Even as some pulp pornography pushed at social and legal boundaries by foregrounding queer, group, and interracial sexuality,

Graham's sentence-level edits in *Man of Pleasure* rigidify a gender binary, creating a hero without conscience and women characters without persuasive ideas.[6] Content is removed that would have resonated with rising second-wave feminism or that expressed satisfaction with the novel's eventual marriage plot. Abridgements render the hero as self-possessed, his seductive efforts uninterrupted by fewer bouts of uncertainty than in earlier editions, and they quiet and flatten statements of resistance by women. Graham exacts a pseudo-historicism on this text, connecting the frisky candor of antique pornography to the countercultural social movement he inhabits, even as he silently extracts affective and ideological content around scenes of consummation.

By 1968, the pornographic text has been made efficient. Discursive elements remain, but they are trimmed and condensed to be deemed relevant to the sexual concerns of the main narrative. The book's cover may sensationalize the text's historical character, but Graham worked subtly, as had Dugdale, to tame and normalize his copy-text's unruly hybridity. A sexually focused narrative must be artificially curated, this history tells us, imposed through a process of deselection at various levels—sentence, language, text, and title. While Whitney Strub has shown that some pulp reprinting "assert[ed] political significance" through additions of discursive content, *Man of Pleasure*'s editorializing is achieved through suppressions of such content from earlier versions.[7] Across *Human Heart*'s long life, we see pornography narrow into a vision of heteromasculine pleasure imposing itself serially on diminished women; but importantly, we see that this plot was originally conceived as a dubious one, impinged upon by contingencies, internally self-questioning, and speculative about its own hypocrisies. Pornographic narrative transforms across this history from a site of confusion and debate into a stricter, stabler vision of men's unchallenged expression of sexual right—precisely the privilege that was coming under fire in second-wave feminism.

Human Heart and 1960s Pornographic Re-Publication

The architects of this marginalization of feminist discourse in pulp were the very writers, editors, and publishers who claimed to publish pornography in the name of sexual freedom. The countercultural ethos purported women to be among the beneficiaries of the new era of sexual liberation, but the era's pornographic publication worked to conceal its efforts to eliminate feminist objections to heterosexuality as practiced under patriarchy. The local edits to the 1968 *Man of Pleasure* reflect a broader response to the rise of second-wave feminism, one that ignored the limits of sexual liberation for women, who did not simply find themselves empowered or autonomous within the new sexual climate. Counterculture print wanted to act like it served everyone, but it is conspicuously absent the critique of heterosexuality exploding in contemporary feminist writing. The eighteenth century integrated feminist resistance against heterosexual inequity into pornographic narrative, and the nineteenth century tried to overwrite that resistance with descriptions of sexual violence. The final revival of *Human Heart* most strenuously aimed to restrain its narrative hybridity, separating and expelling expressions of women's self-determination. Given the conspicuous presence of the women's movement by 1968, when the *New York Times* coined it as a "second feminist wave,"[8] its purging from pornographic fiction registers not the genre's agnosticism toward sexual justice, but the refusal of editors and publishers to inherit ideas about gender equity as part of the sexual history they claimed to make available to contemporary readers. Consciously and arduously, editors in the age of so-called sexual liberation crafted a pornographic archive as heteronormative and masculinist.

The James Graham of the 1968 pulp *Man of Pleasure* was, I believe, Peter Fryer, the socialist journalist and historian who wrote a 1966 exposé of the British Museum's collection of restricted sexual and pornographic materials, *Private Case—Public Scandal*. An American edition appeared in 1968 as *Secrets of the British Museum*, to which I refer here.[9] Fryer polemically inveighed against restricted access to the Private Case, which had been created around 1857 to designate works unfit for general consultation. Through repeated and tedious bureaucratic processes, Fryer gained access to Private Case materials, and *Secrets* overviews a considerable number of them, describing their purposes, plots, and historical contexts and often providing substantial excerpts.[10] Fryer paid special attention to *Human Heart* in the chapter devoted to the Private Case's eighteenth-century holdings. His three-page synopsis of the novel echoes exact language from the pulp covers and introduction to the 1968 *Man of Pleasure*—it is a "minor masterpiece of the picaresque" that "has been overshadowed by Cleland's novel and is crying out to be reprinted again by some enterprising publisher."[11] "James Graham" also edited a 1968 paperback compendium for Tandem—the UK's publisher of *Man of Pleasure*—called *Gentleman's Relish; or the Buyer's Guide to Young Ladies*. Lacking a table of contents or index, it haphazardly excerpts eighteenth- and nineteenth-century bawdy periodicals, including Dugdale's *Exquisite* (home of the 1968 *Man of Pleasure*'s copy-text), as well as the sexological lectures of the eighteenth-century James Graham and other random erotic narratives.[12] In its introduction, Fryer envisions young men of the earlier centuries navigating an urban landscape full of heterosexual opportunity, the very content he had highlighted in his overview of *Man of Pleasure* in its introduction.

Almost simultaneously, Fryer non-pseudonymously published three hardcover editions rooted in the Private Case: *Venus Unmasked*, a collection of eighteenth-century bawdy verse and prose (which includes the posture-girl episode from *Human Heart*); *The Man of Pleasure's Companion*, an anthology of nineteenth-century pornographic writing; and *The Forbidden Books of the Victorians*, an abridgement of Ashbee's erotic bibliography. Designed for the shelves of a collector or library but also aimed at the curious, non-academic reader, they reside somewhere between pulp sensationalism and archival scholarship. They do little to describe textual provenance or editorial process—"omissions are unrecorded"—instead densely concentrating pithy excerpts of bawdry.[13] Their mission corresponds to Fryer's call for public access in *Secrets*: to bring to light a history of sexuality that had been censored from the historical record. In the introductions to these works, he imagines his task nostalgically, as a restoration of an ancestry interrupted by expurgating mechanisms. He seeks to satisfy readers' curiosity about "the forbidden books of our grandfathers and great-grandfathers," to "reconstruct . . . our great-grandfathers' lives," to provide a "representative picture of the popular sex literature . . . enjoyed by our eighteenth-century ancestors," to imagine the editions' contents being read by "[g]reat-great-great-grandpapa."[14] Across the pulp paperbacks, niche anthologies, and British Library exposé, Fryer dispatches a uniform logic: the "period of outspokenness in literature" of the late 1960s calls for a genealogical treatment of the history of sexual writing, a recognition of an erotic history that was displaced (he believes) during the Victorian period. Within this history, *Human Heart* is acknowledged repeatedly as an overlooked "gem" that deserves recognition.[15]

Fryer saw this archival work as part of a social justice movement that animated his research and writing in general. From early writing on the Hungarian revolution to the book for which he is best known, *Staying Power: The History of Black People in Britain*, his social histories connected macrocosmic superstructures to their impact on specific populations, a concern that can be discerned at the heart of his archival work with pornography: an insistence that sexuality be included as part of public life and knowledge.[16] The eighteenth century figures prominently across these works, too—a site of archival plenitude for pornography as for the "voices" of formerly enslaved Black writers.[17] Of most relevance to his work on pornography is his history of reproductive freedom, *The Birth Controllers* (1965). Resisting repression and shame surrounding discussions of reproductive control, Fryer applauds early advocates of "family limitation" who advanced a "new morality" by bringing matters of sexual health into public discussion and who sought to control population and poverty through pragmatic, secular means. Praising their regard of sex as "health-giving and pleasurable," he hopes this history is moving toward free, NHS-provided contraception with an increased emphasis on reproductive freedom as a matter of social justice for women, rather than as an economic concern for men.[18]

In some ways, Fryer's ambitions in bringing antique pornography to the pulp reader align with the mission of his non-pseudonymous anthologies. In the spirit of the countercultural moment epitomized by 1968, he looks to showcase the unfettered erotic and reading practices of previous generations, naturalizing his era's call for sexual liberation. He deploys the liberal logic of individual rights to make this case. As his exposé of the Private Case argued and as his pulp reprints enact, literary evidence of historical sexuality should be widely, unapologetically available to inquisitive readers, and it's the work of libraries and presses to provide access. The policy of the British Museum to obfuscate the Private Case holdings worked exactly against such transparency. When Fryer began his research, its materials were not listed nor its subject headings indexed in the general catalogue, and access was reserved for "privileged men of letters, rich amateurs, and dilettanti" who were already erotic book collectors in their own right.[19]

The public, and books too, were the victims of these restrictions: "Our national library imprisons books without trial, without a single expert witness from outside the museum being heard in their defence."[20] Fryer frames the sequestering of erotic materials as a violation of habeas corpus, a law he emphasizes repeatedly in *Staying Power* as central to abolitionist efforts to free Black people in Britain from enslavement.[21] In the context of the library, the concept is deracinated, the unlawful detention of books a public disservice that censors a history of sexual culture that should be commonly known. Instead, access is limited to a select readership whose requests are given "special consideration" by the British Museum—including, back in the late nineteenth century, Ashbee, who consulted restricted materials as he compiled his bibliography.[22] Using the logic of liberalism to illuminate sexuality's history (a preview, we'll see in the next section, of some feminist historiography), Fryer situates pornography as an Enlightenment legacy. His hubris—more liberal than socialist, to be sure—made a lasting impact. Patrick Kearney, whose bibliography *The Private Case* encompasses all the items in the collection (a list the British Library itself declined to compile), believes Fryer's "agitation" prompted the Trustees to enter these materials into the General Catalogue, a development that occurred while Fryer was finishing his book.[23] Whereas previously only elite men with pull at the British Museum could access the Private Case, his book airs its contents for the common reader.

Fryer was eager to align his work with the rising tide of feminism. His publications suggest that women are central to the history of sexuality; *Gentleman's Relish*, for instance, excerpts *Harris's List of Covent Garden Ladies*, a well-known eighteenth-century guide to London sex workers. In the introduction to *The Man of Pleasure's Companion*, he apologizes that excerpts reproduce women's "sexual and social servitude," a historical condition that is "against the compiler's will," and that, he warns, persists for his contemporary reader:

> [M]ale attitudes which sustain female servitude . . . are still a prominent feature of sexual and family relationships. Let us by all means congratulate ourselves on having abandoned Victorian prudery and hypocrisy. But these are only part of the twentieth century's heritage from the nineteenth.[24]

A feminist commitment ostensibly suffuses Fryer's transmission of the archive, warning entitled men against perpetuating women's sexual exploitation. Women's liberation—literally, from sexual servitude—is consistent with Fryer's Marxist project, and he knows that liberation is impeded by men's exercise of sexual privilege. He shares with pornography its internal knowledge of how sex disproportionately impacts women at social and economic levels.

But for all his eagerness to align himself with a feminist cause, his writing blames women for the chastening of literature between Cleland and the countercultural era. The prudish "demands" of middle-class women in particular caused a "castration of imaginative literature," purging novels of sexual description and exiling it to pamphlet and sexological ephemera.[25] Fryer's advancement of sexual liberation wants to connect itself to a women's movement, but his historiography naturalizes masculine heterosexuality as a form of freedom threatened by any skeptical discourses about it. His sentence-level editing reflects the limits of his ability to tolerate feminist dissent as it pertains to men's claims to sexual right. Fryer was indignant about the suppression of sexuality's history, but he did not simply reveal the archival text of *Human Heart* to his 1968 reading public. Streamlining his source text as I described above, he tamed what remained in 1844 of this unruly eighteenth-century feminism.

Fryer's countercultural moment tried to idealize its own model of gender-inclusive radicalism by producing an overly simplified version of the eighteenth century, and specifically of eighteenth-century gender. The deletions and abridgements show sexual liberation as masculine practice, one that staunches the skeptical commentary of women. Fryer's pulping of *Human Heart* wants to alleviate sexuality of what he sees as its repressive aspects. But he in turn represses other elements—the hero's sexual uncertainties, women's resistance—censoring pornography of its feminist dissent. Muting history's musings on sexual justice, he delivers a pornographic narrative largely emptied of its thinking.

The year 1968 emblematizes an era of political resistance, of calls for social, racial, and gender equity. For Fryer, it was also a moment to suppress accusations of rape, visions of egalitarian marriage, and statements of feminist resistance. So, why the revival of bawdy works in the name of sexual freedom, only to silently and carefully suppress their expressions of feminist dissent? Fryer undertook this project of re-publication in various formats, from niche, quasi-academic editions for collectors; to polemics against national establishments and their restrictions on public materials; to pseudonymous pulp paperbacks. Across these forms, he constructed his efforts as bringing to light an unjustly secreted history of human sexuality. But there are aspects, feminist ones, he labors to keep secret. The eighteenth century provided a source for a fantasy of uncontested penetrative right—one that only could be invented by deleting women's statements of will. A socialist approach to history in 1968 operated by its own process of selection, and women's freedom was deselected as an integral part of radical politics. Such a claim corresponds to sociologist Lillian B. Rubin's recollection of 1968 as a time when young women in the political movement "were caught between participating in men's vision of female sexual liberation or risk[ing] being seen as retrograde prudes," when there were pressures "to comply or be left out."[26] Nancy Biberman recalls the 1968 Columbia protests—the great signifiers of leftist student resistance—as "profoundly pre-feminist," the contributions of women students "expunged" from the historical record.[27] In this light, we can see Fryer participating in the erasure of dissenting women figures from the socialist climate of the 1960s. The eighteenth century—with its genital candor, wandering picaros, and explicit gender hierarchies—was fertile ground from which to excavate a non-conformist sexual culture, but he did not reckon with the aspects of that irreverence that resist heteromasculinity. Fryer selectively reconstructed the past to support modern masculinity as dominant, unfettered, and rights-bearing.

Fryer was not alone in downplaying pornography's potential relationship to feminism. Stephen Marcus's influential *The Other Victorians*, published in 1966, likewise claimed to uncensor a sexual past, but he inscribed a version of uncontested masculine dominance on historical texts that do not unilaterally support it. The "social character" that Marcus believes pornography explores is solely that of "the class of men to whom it was addressed," and the genre, he argues, assuages a masculine psyche struggling to form attachments in the Victorian world.[28] Such an interpretation depends on partial and selective reading, disregarding, as Chapter 3 showed of the nineteenth century, the ways in which pornography exceeds straight masculinity. Marcus's book has determined to a large extent which works from the Victorian canon get studied as representative of the period and the genre, as Claire Colligan has demonstrated. She sees Marcus's account as a "construction of a particular pornographic canon": it has "enjoyed staying power" as a shaper of pornography studies, even though he never explains his selection process.[29]

This unexplained method should raise our suspicions—particularly when we realize, as Simon Joyce has, Marcus's "apparent repugnance" for queer sex in pornography.[30] Marcus's emphasis on *My Secret Life*'s Walter as representative of the pornographic hero—virile, unflagging, undiscriminating, seeking to "dominate or control his sexual partners"—normalizes a particular kind of masculinity about which pornography had been ambivalent for at least two centuries. He imagines pornography decontextualizing the exploits of such a hero within the "boundless, featureless freedom that most pornographic fantasies require for their action," a depoliticized pornotopia in which the hero "is actually not a man" but "an enormous erect penis." Relieved of thinking and social presence, this hero is not answerable to discourse, a fantasy Marcus believes is uninterrupted in Victorian pornography, a refuge, albeit "infantile," for hero and reader from an alienating world.[31] Given my book's evidence, we should regard this privilege as a strenuous construction, its seamlessness reason for suspicion and an invitation to closer reading.

Under the direction of Barney Rosset, Grove Press also played an influential role in shaping the pornography canon in the late 1960s. After novels like *Memoirs of a Woman of Pleasure* (Putnam 1963), *Lady Chatterley's Lover*, *Tropic of Cancer*, and *Naked Lunch* (Grove 1959, 1961, and 1962, respectively) had been successfully defended again obscenity charges in the first half of the decade, Grove employed anti-censorship rhetoric on its cover copy and editorial matter to categorize pornography with sexual writing whose literary value had been proven, as studies by Amy Wyngaard and Loren Glass show. Even though the pornographic novels Grove published appeared at a time when they were less likely to be targets of censorship, Rosset aimed to attract readers by amplifying their controversial content. His strategy was not to deny sexually explicit material but to declaim its social value, especially by citing academic specialists. The introduction to Grove's *My Secret Life* extensively cites Marcus's *The Other Victorians*, for instance; Sartre is used to introduce Genet, and Beauvoir to preface Sade.[32] Academically distinguishing its publications, Grove disparaged drugstore paperbacks that lacked textual integrity, having been bowdlerized and abridged by modern editors.[33]

At the same time, Grove was trying to profit from the pulping of a pornographic canon for a paperback audience through at least three other imprints. Zebra, Venus, and Black Cat issued editions of eighteenth- and nineteenth-century works that made no claims to the literary but, like the 1968 *Man of Pleasure*, promised to reveal a previously suppressed historical subculture. Whereas Grove's Sade editions boasted textual integrity and scholarly authentication, Zebra's titles include, for instance, a not-very-bawdy eighteenth-century novel misattributed to Cleland and embellished by "pornographically extended scenes" added by the twentieth-century editor.[34] As with Fryer, pornography's various associations were exploited for how they could serve Rosset's own ends. Rosset had his pornography and ate it too, defending its publication by asserting its cultural value while playing fast and loose with pulp editions uncommitted to textual integrity.

Thus Grove moved decidedly into what Wyngaard calls a "less literary" direction.[35] This allegation, though, presupposes that some core of pornography had been literary, or had wanted to be literary, when in fact literariness had always been only an occasional attribute of the genre, as my emphasis on its miscellaneous discourses has shown. More to the point, Grove aggressively marketed the most literary examples of historical pornography to advance its avant-garde brand while, under specialized imprints, providing the broader spectrum of pornographic narrative that included the bawdy, sensational, and sexological. To construct itself as an anti-censorship force, Grove had blurbed scholars on the covers of its first pornographic editions. By the close of the decade, Grove exposed its bad faith in the genre by "openly parodying the paratextual apparatus it had deployed in its earlier campaigns," printing gag blurbs on its covers that mocked any notion of pornography inviting serious engagement, all the while turning a profit from this very material.[36]

The press disavowed pornography as a form of knowledge or inquiry, shedding an unflattering light on its effort to tie pornography to feminism. Earlier, when Grove was identifying itself with radical politics, Rosset tried to knit the 1966 edition of *The Story of O*, the 1954 French novel about sub/dom erotics written by Dominique Aury under the pseudonym Pauline Réage, to the feminist movement. Women's authorship and translation were central to the novel's sensational release and largely positive reception in the US. Grove's American translator Richard Seaver used a feminine pseudonym, Sabine Destré, "redoubling," Wyngaard asserts, "its association with women."[37] In his translator's note, Seaver as Destré promises (in a mode he deems feminine, humble, and non-interfering) to transmit the text transparently and purely. Grove locates pornographic interest, then, in woman-authored erotic candor. The press further affiliated the feminist movement by trying (unsuccessfully) to commission Susan Sontag to write a preface. These efforts to distinguish pornography through its feminization seem to have worked: chief among the virtues of *O*, for critics, was its elevation of what they saw as eroticism above vulgarity. The aura of a feminist commitment to transmitting women's authorship transforms the category of pornography from a phallocentric, patriarchal one into (Grove would have it) an egalitarian erotic field to be engaged by any gender, ending its function as a field in which to debate censorship.[38]

Back at Grove, women experienced none of the feminist sentiment the publisher tried to amass around *O*. Feminists occupied Grove's offices in 1970 to object to its firing of women unionizers and to demand that profits from its pornographic books, magazines, and films go toward bail funds and medical assistance for sex workers, a reparation for what they saw as pornography's harmful impact on women. Grove called in police, and the arrest of the protestors set the press in opposition to the Left and damaged its radical identity.[39] Grove also revealed its antipathy to the feminist movement by siding with Henry Miller against Kate Millett in a copyright dispute. Miller urged Grove to deny Millett permission to quote from his works in her book *Sexual Politics*, which famously rejects the homosocial masculinity of the avant-garde (Grove later relented, heeding legal advice). While Millett's book soared in popularity, Grove's cultural relevance waned until the press was sold in 1985.[40]

Grove's integration of feminist discourse was disingenuous; so, I'm suggesting, was its treatment of pornography. Rosset established and defended pornography as a category wielding historical and cultural power, and of importance to a democratized readership; he then capitalized on a wider pornographic field whose texts were reproduced hastily, cheaply, and without claims to their historical value. Rosset thus distorted the robust and diverse history of sexual writing of which "literary" pornography had been only one part, the part that became overrepresented and overvalued by Grove. Like Fryer and Marcus, Rosset cited pornography as advancing a project of liberation that was not gender exclusive. Also like them, he hierarchized and elided pornography's textual past, obscuring what it might have told us about heterosexuality, women, and feminism by presenting women's relationship to pornography as a novelty, when in fact a discourse on sexual justice had been robustly evident, to anyone handling sources, for two centuries.

As the New Left was crediting itself with advancing sexual liberation, its editors, publishers, and historians buttressed heterosexual masculinity by selectively documenting it in the past. Delivering to readers evidence of a longstanding phallocentric eroticism, purged of counternarratives, they expunged strands of sexuality's textual history containing skepticism, reflections, and resistance. At the same time that Susan Brownmiller was identifying pornography as the "philosophy of rape" in which women's abuse is men's entertainment, the genre's gatekeepers were inventing a masculinist and heteronormative history of the genre (or, when they feminized it, doing so as a marketing ploy).[41] Fryer plucked out the very discourse—a rape critique, a hyperawareness of rape's effects—that formed the backbone of contemporaneous feminist writing. While I'm not arguing a causality, or feminists' awareness of this selective textual history of pornography, I am emphasizing the timeliness of the divergence between pornography and feminism. As the genre was being poorly historicized by men to reflect straight phallocentrism, feminists were carrying the eighteenth-century energy of pornography's discourse and critique into their theoretical writing. Perhaps what feminists rejected wasn't pornography itself, but the version of it crafted by leftist men to reinforce their definition of freedom, intellectualism, and transhistorical veracity. Feminism reattached cultural meaning to genital action, vastly expanding the discourse that was strategically quieted by scholars and editors in their mediation of pornographic textual history. The next section asks what feminist writing gained and lost by taking up this analysis of the ethics of penetrative sex and polarizing it from the genre that had previously been its home.

Feminism's Genital Analysis

I end by thinking about what second-wave feminism had in common, if unwittingly, with pornography as I have situated it historically. It was not inevitable that radical feminists—who were, granted, writing as the rise of film pornography intensified concerns over its impact on real women and their bodies—would narrow into the anti-pornography position made famous by Andrea Dworkin and Catharine MacKinnon. Strands of feminist theory coalesce in what I call a genital analysis that asserts the embodied level at which women experience gendered domination, a cultural process about which pornography had once been eloquent. Second-wave feminists who conducted this genital analysis, studying heterosexuality as the origin of inequity, could have found in pornography not only a similar conviction, but a set of techniques for interpreting genital action as a commentary on social relations—for pornography, as I've argued, is characterized by its capacity simultaneously to delight in genital display, to dissent from the social conditions that restrict this delight only to some and produce it at the disadvantage of many, and to fabricate the effect of exhaustive detail while in fact strategically suppressing certain sex acts and perspectives.

This conglomeration results in pornography's "unparaphrasability," an insight I derive from Frances Ferguson. Pornography, as we've seen in earlier chapters, introduces, articulates, then abandons its statements: "it is an important feature of pornography that it is not particularly committed even to its own ideas . . . it does not aim to reach its audience by getting the members of that audience to agree or disagree."[42] (This attribute is what makes a defense of pornography's ideas wrong-headed, in Ferguson's view.) She favors pornography's definition as action, emphasizing its effects over its messages:

> To ask not what pornography lacks but what it accomplishes is to begin to see that it makes an important contribution, which lies not in its occasional dalliance with ideas but in representing the impact of communication without entirely paraphrasable content, messages that constitute themselves *at least as much as expressions of evaluations as of ideas*.[43]

Entertaining the possibility of "impact of communication without entirely paraphrasable content" is key to a feminist analysis of pornography that is neither pro- nor anti-pornography, but attentive to its fleeting, impermanent "communications" of the process by which persons are impacted and shaped by their interpolation in sexual systems. Pornography shows that persons are implicated in these systems in which they may not have sought participation but which nonetheless delimit the social, sexual, and gendered positions available to them. As I've argued, pornography tracks with particular clarity the routes through which normative institutions confer meaning on genitals, and how, in turn, genitals confer certain kinds of personhood or social value on the persons to whom they are attached. The overt gender hierarchies of the eighteenth and nineteenth centuries incline the periods' narrative pornography to be especially articulate, and sometimes indignant, about the injustices meted out to women and nonbinary people through genital activity over which they often had little autonomy. These insightful objections recede as quickly as they appear, but their temporariness makes them no more trivial than the temporary, fleeting, episodic sex acts that indisputably populate pornographic texts and imbue bodies with meaning. Pornographic effect is cumulative, not atomized; a text's movement past an idea, its making of that idea unparaphrasable, is not the same as negating the idea or denying its existence. Pornography is content to present social problems without solving them.

I don't mean to be willfully simplistic by suggesting second-wave feminists missed an opportunity to engage, even partner with this multivalent pornographic discourse. With the genre increasingly mainstream in the 1970s, emblematized by the blockbuster success of *Deep Throat* and Linda Lovelace's later revelation that she was coerced to perform in the film, it came to be seen by many feminists as a pathogen of women's oppression—dramatizing, normalizing, and dispersing sexual violence as everyday heterosexuality.[44] Pictorial and filmic pornography, contorting women to facilitate men's visual access to their genitals, was not an exaggeration but a commonplace in the radical feminist view, a transparent expression of masculine privilege that structures social relations and endangers women.

The anti-pornography outgrowth famously crafted this causal connection between pornography and rape into a tenet, when feminist theory itself did not stipulate, I suggest, such a conclusion.[45] Like Finn Enke, I see a more "mixed-up sensibility" at work than the historical narrative we currently receive about the second wave. Where Enke revives the strong presence and contributions of trans women, women of color, and sex workers, I emphasize feminism's various accounts of genital life, particularly those conceptions of it that refute heteropenetration as a dominant paradigm. Why, I ask in the context of the feminist analysis of pornography, "are stories of exclusion and abjection so magnetic" that we've received the anti-pornography stance as the inevitable response to women's embodiment in pornography? I offer a path that "highlights feminism's incoherence" on the matter of the genital sex animated in pornography.⁴⁶ Feminism's genital analysis might illuminate pornography's critical voice, its capacity to produce different, competing, irresolvable accounts of sex as we've seen it do since the eighteenth century.

The irreducibility of genital action in second-wave theories of heterosexuality, as in pornography, links the materiality of embodied life to worldly contexts and social institutions that sort and operationalize people. Because of the vocal anti-pornography movement, feminism is understood to have concluded that pornography is coextensive with those institutions rather than critically attuned to them, capable of scrutinizing collisions of world and body. But this stance on pornography is not the sum total of what was happening in the second wave. We tend to remember feminism as anti-pornography or sex-positive. I'm pulling together a different possibility, dispersed and intermittent across feminist theory, that eschewed the binary between these positions. The early second wave didn't envision itself teleologically either as arriving at an anti-pornography platform or at utopian belief in free sexual expression. The well-known anti-pornography genealogy can only be constituted retrospectively (as Carolyn Bronstein has thoroughly done), after that movement's spectacular failure in the courts made feminist critique seem outmoded and discredited. By my reading, feminist texts offered variable concepts for interpreting genital life and resisting its dominant patriarchal practices. Why did feminist discourse come to be understood as reducing sex to heterosexual violence? How did every pornographic text reflect that singular interpretation? Why could pornography not invite the kind of reading—inconclusive, meandering, speculative—that the eighteenth century had initiated? Connecting disparate pieces of feminist commentary on heterosexual pornography, I'll conclude this chapter by imagining a different outcome—maybe a different future—one in which feminism and pornography recouple in their unapologetic habits of genital display.

As Fryer was excising women's protests against sexual injustice from pornographic accounts of heteropenetration—recall his suppression of Saphira's clear statements about Camillo's culpability—feminist writing was identifying genitals as the origin point of women's social oppression.

Radical feminists found heterosex as it is practiced under patriarchy violent at its core, rooted historically in the objectification of women's bodies at the heart of systems of property and exchange. Before it sought to legislate against pornography as the ultimate source and symptom of patriarchal oppression, feminism undertook consciousness raising about the compass of rape, exposing widespread and quotidian violence that structured women's lives.[47] As early as 1969, Kate Millett saw rape as the "particularly sexual" expression of patriarchy's "diffuse and generalized" subjugation, less an aberrant phenomenon than a logical expression of gender inequity.[48] Brownmiller's bestseller *Against Our Will* defined sexual violence as a human abuse of morphology: "man's structural capacity to rape and woman's corresponding structural vulnerability" differentiated the sexes and justified the treatment of women's bodies as violable, valuable, and needing protection by other men, thus women's categorization as property of fathers and husbands.[49] This weaponizing of sexual difference predates accumulation and capitalism and is therefore beyond the reach of Marxist analysis, demanding a theory and revolution of its own, Shulamith Firestone argued in 1970 in *The Dialectic of Sex*. Firestone found anatomical difference so contaminated by patriarchy that she proposed artificial reproduction replace pregnancy, a revolutionary means of detaching women from their anatomy.[50] Radical feminism generated its opposition to dominant culture through an analysis of how women's genitals were violently and coercively operationalized; it did not follow that pornography was destined to be its central point of critique.

What came of this analysis was a generalization, even a misreading: that all women experience patriarchal violence in uniform ways and that pornography is an ur-text for the culture of rape that is baked into heterosexual relations. With the attentiveness to genital life in place, why didn't feminism's reading of pornography differentiate rather than generalize its effects on various women and sexual experiences? It had the interpretive capacity to do so, attending minutely to embodied experience, and pornography for centuries had particularized the voices of women and nonbinary characters in and around sexual description. The countercultural discourse on pornography remained entangled with eighteenth-century thought, but it engaged with the period's dominant narrative—Enlightenment ideology—instead of its miscellaneous and unparaphrasable analysis of heterosexuality. Liberal discourse enabled literary historians to associate a pornographic archive with sexual freedom, even with the freedom of books themselves, as Fryer's appeal to habeas corpus enacted. Debated in the terms of rights and liberty, the circulation of pornographic texts simplified the genre into a vehicle for individual readers' access to and enlightenment through historical sexual activity. This emphasis, so closely kin to mainstream political ideals in its appeal to individual readers and their freedoms, occludes the more radical worlds and interventions pornography imagined—its collective statements against the nonconsensual trafficking of women, its exposures of the fictitiousness of gender binaries and hierarchies, its imagining of sexuality as detached from personhood.

The more limiting liberal legacy of Enlightenment thought was alive and well in feminist theory, for instance in what Ferguson calls Brownmiller's "conjectural history" that locates heterosexual rape at the inception of culture.[51] Energizing that classic Enlightenment genre, Brownmiller imagines how the morphological "accident of biology" became consciously practiced as harm, reanimating the form of the origin story to craft sexual violence as predetermined and inescapable. The speculative mode of Enlightenment historiography allows her to assert rape as an originary and therefore pervasive form of domination inherent to heterosexual society, "a conscious process of intimidation by which *all men* keep *all women* in a state of fear."[52] Figuring violation as an infraction against freedom—as Fryer had imagined the persecution of books—Brownmiller imagines the founding of an inequitable social contract based on genital difference. Uniformly playing and replaying the terms of this contract, men bond with or antagonize one another through the use of women's bodies as property. Codified within familiar liberal concepts, these relations have for Brownmiller one enduring meaning that gets cast across modernity into her patriarchal present, and this dominant narrative, despite its speculative mood, does not allow for the variation a global approach to feminism would entail, in which "male violence must be theorized and interpreted within specific societies," in Chandra Talpade Mohanty's words.[53] Carole Pateman, likewise excavating modernity's "repressed" sexual contract, faults not biology but liberalism's logic of contractual relations with creating fictions of equity that elide women. For Pateman, it is not rape but language—"the way in which contract is presented as freedom"—that undergirds patriarchy, clarifying by contrast the narrow and deterministic character of Brownmiller's identification of rape as the founding sexual differentiation.[54] An irresolvable physical intimidation reduces women's freedom in Brownmiller's account, benefiting all men by centralizing their power—to rape, to not rape, to protect, or to enjoy a homosocial public sphere cleared of fearful women.

Pornography in Brownmiller's view recreated the originary violence of patriarchal culture. Such a reading, unaware of pornography's discursive engagement with its world so evident in early examples, figures the genre and its consumers as transhistorically immune to change. Of course it's not surprising that radical feminism wouldn't share my historical treatment of pornography, not least because they're writing in its visual age of unsimulated sex. But anti-pornography feminists made their claims transhistorical, invoking history to then make an ahistoricist argument. Citing its ancient Greek etymology, Andrea Dworkin assumes pornography has always been depictions of the "lowest class of whore," of "brothel slut[s] available to all male citizens."[55] Indifferent to the term's original function as a curatorial category and dismissive of sex workers, Dworkin grants pornography the power to transform all its content into one uniform function. She shares the indifference to history we see in pornographic re-publication: like Ashbee, Reader, Dugdale, and Fryer, she invokes pornography's history selectively, when it suits her purpose of emphasizing the genre's ubiquity, but generalizes its conventions as transhistorical and unchanging. Within this logic, there is no room to think synchronically about a given pornographic text's conversation with its historical moment. Variations of form and medium, in this approach, make no difference to pornography's transformation of all women into commercialized victims of sexual violence. As Lisa Sigel observes, "pornographic forms have grown while studies of those forms have not."[56] Specifically, anti-pornography feminism treats the genre as "transhistorical" and "transtechnological," which Jennifer Nash argues particularly reduces Black women in pornography to figures of injury.[57]

Insofar as it produced subordination based on sex, rape and its expression as pornography were co-extensive with heterosexuality itself for second-wavers, a point that created the binary thinking about gender that produced trans-exclusionary outbursts in what was, by Enke's considered account, a movement often inclusive of trans women.[58] Decades later, Emi Koyama documented the enduring exclusionary effects of the tenet that sex is the most "pervasive, extreme and fundamental of all social inequalities," a conviction used to justify the racist expulsion of trans women from feminist affiliations.[59] Retrospectively, under the long shadow cast by the legalistic anti-pornography movement, feminism can appear to have determined in advance the privileging of bourgeois white heteronormativity that allowed transphobia and racism to erupt in the movement.[60] But feminism internally resisted movements in this normative direction.

Angela Davis was prescient about feminism's tendency toward hegemony, calling radical feminists' identification of women as a homogeneous class an "unthinking partisanship which borders on racism," since it called on women of color to disavow familial, community, racial, cultural, and socioeconomic ties, including ties with men.[61] Radical feminist accounts of sexual violence ignored Black women's perspectives in two ways: by normalizing white women as rape's primary victims and by insisting Black women adopt a theory of sexual violence that sees all men advantaged by it. As Davis writes, Black women always possessed a more nuanced understanding of the injustices of rape, since they experienced it doubly as their "sexual victimization" and as the "fraudulent rape charge" against Black men that was used to justify lynching. Weaponized as an instrument of white supremacy, "rape was a terribly efficient method of keeping Black women and men alike in check."[62] Rejecting the generalized model of women's oppression, the Combahee River Collective defined its feminism as redressing multiple "interlocking" forms of oppression: "A combined antiracist and antisexist position drew us together initially, and as we developed politically we addressed ourselves to heterosexism and economic oppression under capitalism."[63] Such organizing resisted the doctrine of universality under patriarchal oppression that was so central to a sect of radical feminism with entrenched habits of overgeneralization, and evinces a culture of diversity and healthy dissent within feminism itself.

The anti-pornography direction ultimately assumed by radical feminism did nothing to help failures of intersectionality in the movement. The regulatory approach, which culminated with Dworkin's and MacKinnon's anti-pornography campaigning in the early 1980s, redoubled the marginalization of BIPOC, trans, and working-class women. Rather than cultivating "greater awareness and understanding, not less" of the "different struggles" facing women, as Keeanga-Yamahtta Taylor argues BIPOC feminism did, the anti-pornography contingent, in Bronstein's words, "consciously minimized racial and ethnic differences among women" and "endorsed a narrow range of sexual expression and sexual behavior."[64] This narrowness alienated sex-positive feminists, sex workers, and feminists who formed coalitions with men on the basis of race, class, and ethnicity. To advance their perspective, anti-pornography feminists redirected the movement around their cause and made the Times Square sex industry their target. Women Against Pornography (WAP), which had rent-free office space courtesy of Mayor Ed Koch, began "porn tours," designed by Brownmiller herself, with stops at adult stores, theaters, brothels, and live sex theaters. The tours explained that women's earning power was much higher in sex work than in average jobs available to many of them and so seemed to have some genuinely informative aims; but mainly the tours disrupted the work of women who described their jobs in entirely different terms than the ones radical feminists were imposing on them.[65] WAP's aim ultimately was to interrupt the sex work it saw as exploitative of women, and the tours assumed this aim was in the interest of all women.

Second-wave feminism's well-funded and vocal narrowing into anti-pornography ideology constrained what could have been an open-ended engagement with pornography, a willingness to read and interpret it for a range of what it might say about the bodies and people implicated in its actions. What gets lost in the anti-pornography brouhaha is any sense that pornographic texts can be approached minutely or individually, that they're capable of saying more than one thing, that they share the focus on genitals at the heart of feminism's critique of heterosexuality. As we've seen in earlier chapters, eighteenth and- nineteenth-century pornographic narrative regularly wonders if heterosex is rape instead of arguing that it invariably is: modern pornography might present similar possibilities and confusions. As many feminists devised theory and politics that could account for difference, so the genre's critics might have understood pornographic action as part of a greater culture that privileges heteronormative masculinity without declaring on behalf of characters and performers that the actions of their bodies only can signify one way.

Feminism and Pornography, a Recoupling

Greater attention to the indeterminacy of sexual narratives—a historical feature of pornography—might have led feminism to incorporate rather than expel pornography, to discern how it converses with culture by foregrounding the body's absorption of social relations, and to recognize variation and intersectionality in how that absorption is experienced. To insist, as pornography does, that personhood is established, compromised, and suspended by genital use—that genital action sorts people into different ranks and, as Ferguson puts it, "enables us to raise a question about when a collective action exacts too great a cost for an individual"[66]—is to join with the radical feminist conviction that no account of culture is complete without descriptions of sex and its differential impact on persons. But the feminist genital analysis could have been, like pornography, open-ended, even imaginative in its projection of outcomes. Brownmiller envisioned such a plentiful understanding of sexual activity, counterintuitively, in a speculative definition of rape. She wanted the law to be reformed to define rape as "gender-free, non-activity-specific" so that certain kinds of penetration or assault would not be defined as more harmful than any other. "All acts of sex forced on unwilling victims deserve to be treated in concept as equally grave offenses. . . . Similarly, the gravity of the offense ought not be bound by the victim's gender."[67] A purposeful misreading of Brownmiller sees in her definition of rape a possible nonbinary sexuality whose actions, perpetrators, and victims are not genitally polarized. This kind of redefinition did not have to support carceral systems, nor did it have to abandon its commitment to rectifying sexual injustice. Rather, it might have led to a more curious and open-ended, less suspicious and teleological examination of how sex is practiced, how its violences might be curtailed, and how its capacity to please and enfranchise could become a culture's dominant sexual practice.

It's through such a nondeterministic approach that feminism and pornography might be seen to partner in an analysis of how sex becomes co-opted by society and the state. Read reparatively, pornographic scenes dense with penetrative detail might be seen, like feminism, to issue calls for justice in social realms that unfold from the seeming insularity of genital contact. I draw the potentialities of reparative reading from Eve Sedgwick, following Susanna Paasonen's insight that affect studies reminds us "not to start from fixed assumptions or received knowledge concerning what pornography is, what pornography does, or what it can do."[68] A 180-degree shift from anti-pornography feminist suspicion, such a method calls for the kind of close reading and textual history I've conducted in this book, and it signals other possible entry points through which we might bring questions to pornographic texts rather than predetermined answers and evaluative judgments. These inquiries needn't—indeed, can't, if my readings have been persuasive—result in zero-sum conclusions that pornography is either misogynistically violent or erotically liberating. Rather than yield one kind of payoff, reparative readings of pornography might allow us to appreciate the genre's unparaphrasability as a bombastic refusal to resolve social distortions of genital life.

Paasonen sees analytic potential in the "uncontrollability in our encounters with porn," which might include pleasure but also, if we think back to my central example from the 1749 *Human Heart*, intellectual interventions on and speculative divergences from normative attitudes toward gender as they play out in sex scenes.[69] In the anti-pornography analysis, such scenes invariably are read in state of what Sedgwick calls paranoia, foreclosing surprise, creativity, and alternative ways of knowing. It presumes violence and posits negative affect as truth. An open-ended alternative, reparative reading invites a purposeful naiveté, a wide-eyed optimism that texts, their makers, their actors, and their readers possess capacities for making meaning in excess of what any single content asserts.[70] In the case of pornography, reparative reading would look straight at genital action, whether unsimulated by actors or narrated in a text, and see it holistically, situated within larger narrative frameworks, with reference to the social conditions that imbue them with meaning. We saw in Chapter 2, for instance, that experimentation with a dildo in 1744 leads adolescent girls to discover their culture's elision of dominant masculinity with (mythical) phallic potency; or in Chapter 3, the admission that sexual freedom among a queer Victorian community entails the global trafficking of children. The narratives provide a fuller, variegated, unpredictable account of the world in which sex happens and, if they don't make demands for reform, they signal where a society might be failing many of its members.

Reading feminist theory as we've read pornography—to perceive in genital description protests against normative sexual culture and speculations for alternate realities—shows us its capacity to develop expertise on sexual injustice rather than turn away from dramatizations of it. In what remains, I piece together the genital reimagining offered by the second wave, an aspect of the movement that was drowned out amidst anti-pornography cacophony. What might feminism have made of or done with pornography if genital reinvention had been at the center of its social reforms?

Angela Carter and Audre Lorde show how pornography can be read as a social text, a site where sex reveals what culture does to people. Carter argued in 1979 that pornography can be social criticism, exposing "the real conditions of the world in terms of sexual encounters."[71] The rare "moral pornographer"—like Sade—connects sex acts to their material contexts and refuses to sublimate the ways in which sexual excess makes reference to the very laws, customs, and structures that regulate sexuality. Pornographic sex references the violence not of sex, but of sexual institutions in which people feel free—marriage, specifically. Such a pornographer is the "unconscious ally" of women, forcing readers to connect local instances of sexual violence to the seemingly innocuous institutions that perpetuate them. He (Sade) locates a kind of radical democracy in sexuality, imagining "sexual license for all genders" and "project[ing] a model of the way such a world might work."[72] At its most inventive, this pornography insists on the lateralization of genders and the realization of all sexual claims. Only pornography can imagine such social formations through the co-mingling of genitals, and it can reveal the violent character of "what people do to one another."[73]

Lorde is skeptical of pornography's redeeming potential, but her objection to it is not, as for some of her counterparts, based on its treatment of women. Pornography for Lorde refracts heterosexual relations and forestalls radical politics by devaluing the body, an alienation that works, it seems, across sexes and genders. By contrast, the erotic is a source of "self-connection" and embodied "knowledge," a "sharing of joy [that] forms a bridge between the sharers which can be the basis for understanding much of what is not shared between them, and lessens the threat of their difference."[74] Emphasizing commonly held, sensate experiences of feeling, Lorde's erotic promises a collective politics of care based on dispersed, accessible sexual subjectivity, whereas pornography tries to harness the erotic merely to the sexual, deactivating its capacity to connect the subject to—and recognize the subjectivity of—others in political solidarity. While Lorde objects to what she sees as pornography's interruption of activist politics, she does so not on the basis that it unilaterally harms women, but that it organizes knowledge in a manner that damages all political subjects, alienating them from the possibility of coalition. Such a critique of pornography does not seek censorship as a solution, but rather foregrounds eroticism as a condition for radical collectivity.

Early in the second wave, Anne Koedt likewise worked to establish genital experience as a site of feminist action, specifically by criticizing the naturalization of penetrative heterosex. Her 1970 "Myth of the Vaginal Orgasm" traces the psychological effects of a profound misunderstanding of vaginal and clitoral anatomy. "Women have . . . been defined sexually in terms of what pleases men," and she believes there are "social reasons" why scientific knowledge of clitoral orgasm has been suppressed and transformed into theories of women's frigidity—to maintain heterosexual inequity, a system she believes will expire in a future when women, no longer under the misapprehension that vaginal activity is the primary sexual aim, "will seek the company of other women in a full, human basis."[75]

Koedt—like pornography—conjectures outward from dominant genital practices to their perpetuation through social systems and their imprint on hierarchized people, recommending alternate genital configurations that promise a different future. Firestone shares Koedt's rejection of penetration as a reductive model of feminine sexuality and recommends a "rediffusion" of sexual joy: "Why has all the joy and excitement been concentrated, driven into one narrow, difficult-to-find alley of human experience, and all the rest laid waste?"[76] She imagines a diversified field of acts and sensations that count as erotic, as well as genital possibility beyond the "alley" of heteropenetration. Much later, Tim Dean sees politicized community in acts of penetration, a formation that exceeds the individual, the coupling, and sexual ecstasy itself. Bareback pornography "choreograph[s] a mode of embodied thought" aimed at an ethics of HIV-era queer collectivity, locating in intercourse the potential for social bonds and sexual care that were the aspirations of feminism's genital analysis decades earlier.[77]

Brownmiller's *Against Our Will* fleetingly imagines how heterosexuality's genital dynamics might be reconceived rather than codified and repeated as they are, for her, in pornography. Like Koedt, she faults patriarchal discourse for perpetuating a narrow definition of intercourse as penetration, a model that associates the vaginal body with vulnerability and injury. "If women were in charge of sex," she conjectures, intercourse might be described as "enclosure—a revolutionary concept I'm afraid the world is not yet ready for."[78] The vagina, typically imagined as receptive, here has a capacity for action, expansion, and temporary possession of other organs. Narrative pornography had long linked sex scenes with feminist revelations that sex transforms the personhood of its participants. Its film counterparts delivered such scenes in visual forms, allowing experimentation with morphology and the concepts we attach to it. Pornography's genital candor could explore, visually and narratively, Brownmiller's conception of heterosexual morphology. If feminists had read the genre differently, where might they have found "enclosure" in evidence? What does it look like, and how does it impact gender? What narrative, discursive, or visual elements must attend a genital scene to mobilize this concept against penetration?

Feminist theory continues to reinvent the genital analysis to resist heteronormativity. If we attend to the transfeminist past, Emma Heaney argues, we find genital sexuality to be fundamentally nonbinary, since—when trans women are counted as women—"[a]ll bodies are penetrable and genitals gain sexed meaning through their bearers' experiences of desire and violence."[79] Penetration is not unidirectional, nor is it essentially vaginal, nor is it, as "enclosure" suggests, necessarily passive. Sophie Lewis's vision of gestation as social labor prefers "circlusion" as a description of vaginal action—"the enfolding, sucking, holding, and ... *gestating* component of what is otherwise often referred to as poking, ploughing, seeding..."[80] With its commitment to dramatizing the genital aspect of gender and sexuality, pornography too might be a site for resisting penetration's normalization as sex. Pornography alone depicts the unfolding of this action, and it links such action to characterization, individuation, and plot that examines the social value meted out to sexual participants based on their genital variety—potentially to transformative ends. Partnered with the insights of feminism's genital analysis, pornographic sex might be—and in many of its forms already is—construed as a site of narrative or visual invention for non-normative morphologies, not at odds but partnered with an inclusive feminist ethics.

Feminist readings of Black women in pornography provide instances of such social reimagining through sexual representation. Nash models that, instead of seeing pornography as "doubly dangerous" for women subjugated by both race and gender, racialized pornography offers an opportunity to read the genre as a theory of ecstasy articulated through race. Like Lorde, Nash sees political possibility in the enfleshed experience of imagination and desire: "What if fantasy were articulated as both a right and a freedom, as absolutely central to black feminist political work?"[81] Pornography in this reading creatively aspires to social presence and enfranchisement. Likewise for Mireille Miller-Young: pornography featuring Black women should not be approached uncritically as a site of harm, but as a form of strategic labor. Foregrounding the commercialized consumption of racialized images, Black women's pornographic sexuality might be a method of "disidentification," a manipulation of racialized sexual roles that mobilizes "erotic sovereignty" as "complex subjecthood." Pornography then might mobilize and parody dominant ideas about racialized sexuality while placing value in erotic experience and bodily display, blending viewers' titillation with their awareness of instrumental cultural fictions about race and gender. Such performance needn't take the form of resistance, Miller-Young argues, to exert agency; rather, pornography is equipped to "subver[t] norms, even as it catalyzes and perpetuates them."[82] Again we encounter the unparaphrasable—the contradictory, the forgetful, the inconsistent.

Importantly, reparative reading promises no single model or outcome, and pornography's insights do not uniformly guarantee intervention or critique. In a less sanguine instance of partnership between pornography and feminism's genital analysis, Eugenie Brinkema finds a theory of rape in the repeated, embodied enactments of hard-core film. Brinkema foregrounds harm in a manner altogether different from anti-pornography feminists, suggesting pornography's candor about the mechanics of rape fully admits its violence, refusing to assimilate it to any other kind of relation. Rape manifests in action and narrative but is also a formal property of pornographic film that refuses to resolve rape into some other action (as we saw nineteenth-century pornography try to do, blurring rape with marriage, desire, and pleasure). Rather, pornographic film featuring rape explains it as a violent collapse of signification, an act of force at the level of bodies and of meaning:

> Rape requires an other. There cannot, however, be an irreducible gap between the one and the other; its force requires a point of contact.... Forced entry is the point of intersection of two connected but different terms—it remains necessarily unassimilable to both.[83]

A point of force exterior to both parties, rape remains "perpetually strange," a social pattern visible and proliferated in the pornographic text, but in its force unlike other forms of encounter.[84] Maintaining, reenacting, and specifying rape's points of contact, hard core is capable of delivering transparent insight into the role of force in creating relationality between persons, a roughness repeated in filmic actions, edits, and positions. Concerned with "repetitions of refusal" and their dismissal, such a text offers—brutally and intentionally—no horizon for things to be different.[85]

Pornographic violence offers no conditions for debate, to invoke Ferguson's thinking, and its revelations about force do not deliver paraphrasable insights or action items for addressing the power disparity between the parties involved. But this does not mean we don't see—indeed, in Brinkema's example all we do is see—how force happens, what it does to bodies, and how persons respond to its occurrence. Further, Erin Spampinato argues that to "capaciously" read rape in literary texts is to witness sexual violence always exceeding the particularities of any given scene or instance; scholars should therefore recognize rape as an expansive cultural condition rather than adjudicate it in isolated textual incidents.[86] These formalist analyses of rape offer disillusionment—perhaps a precondition of reparation or reform—as an outcome of feminist interpretation. Hard-core violence, whether visual or narrated, admits and replays power relations that saturate everyday life, confirming the insight that "justice should be rejected as an illusory goal," as Ferguson argues of Sade.[87]

Thinking about how pornography circulates—how it operates within community—is a final way of detaching pornography from a teleology of harm. Anti-pornography feminists analyzed texts, but invariably with a foregone conclusion and often with a slant toward summary. Dworkin provided synopses of pornographic fiction so graphically violent that her book was impounded at the U.S./Canadian border for containing obscenity; Brownmiller summarized the rape fantasies contained in confession magazines; Millett traced pornography's "tendency to hurt or insult" into mainstream modernism.[88] In all cases, pornography's psychological and physical injuriousness was self-evident, unmixed with (in their reading) internal self-questioning. By contrast, Samuel Delany found feminist possibility in the pornographic films he watched in Times Square cinemas in the 1980s. A frequent patron, Delany saw marginalized people—queer, poor, transient—forging community through adult cinemas in Times Square before its redevelopment in the 1990s, and he found WAP's Time Square tours incommensurate with the environment as he experienced it.

After encountering one of the tours, Delany undertook a quantitative comparison of the portrayal of women in pornographic versus mainstream films showing on 42nd Street. He found that pornography dramatized women having careers and same-sex friendships at a decidedly higher incidence.[89] Women's oppression may have been more powerfully normalized in popular culture, Delany's statistics suggest, than in the adult sex industry. The arguably feminist narratives for women in pornographic films and the queer, working-class communities they assembled suggest that pornography hosted forms of safety, inclusion, even flourishing for people left out of WAP's normative purview. For Delany, pornography is—or, more to his point, was—a social context, a space occasioned by films being projected but that exceeds the text, indeed that doesn't matter entirely on its content. Pornography can work as a counterpublic outside of normative regimes that would deem its audiences violent offenders.[90]

Ferguson emphasizes pornography's environments differently, finding pornographic texts potentially harmful in settings where they function as actions by creating differential conditions for the parties who see them. These contexts are highly specific for Ferguson—workplaces or educational institutions whose purpose is to sustain conditions of equity. By creating and enforcing privacy within an institution meant to be public—by "effectively eliminat[ing] the publicness of the public sphere"—pornography violates a society's promise to provide its members equal access to environments where they can "see their value increased," most centrally work or school.[91] This definition narrows what had been an attempt to define all of pornography as hate speech by MacKinnon and Dworkin; instead, Ferguson (like Delany) defines pornography not by its contents but by its context of circulation. They both identify pornography as a site for evaluating the interactions of people, considering the kinds of inclusion or exclusion they create. For Delany, pornography offers voluntary entry into a space conducive to non-normative identities and sexualities with particular forms of care available to those who seek it. These include donations of food or money, safe accommodation, physical intimacy, conversation, anonymity, personalization. In both cases, pornography names a relation rather than a content or an act of violence.

Some critics, I've just shown, situate pornography in social environments, shifting focus away from those features of the genre that so disturbed anti-pornography feminists. I offer this approach to pornographic environments as a way of refreshing our perspective on the pornographic text itself, such that we might return to it, as I modeled in earlier chapters, with the capacity to believe it can do something other than harm or titillate. If it can create environments that make reference to members of a public, pornography must be seen to produce social conditions, or to articulate social conditions in ways that impact the people reading or seeing it. As Nash writes, there are "social and cultural uses to which pornography might be put," the genre capable of complexity and responsive to the social structures within which its actors and consumers exist.[92] Attending to the social components of pornographic sex doesn't guarantee that every text will reveal a feminist meaning, or that any one text will be fully purged of violence (what text, of any genre, is?) but that pornographic texts are always showing us the situatedness of genital action within larger social contexts that, in turn, attach meaning to the persons involved.

Feminism, sharing its insights about the centrality of genital action, can help pornography do this work. It does not necessarily follow that the figures in pornography will be liberated from socio-sexual systems, or that all viewers will become attuned to feminist meaning—though it might, which is perhaps why countercultural leftist men constructed an antique European pornography purged of queerness and feminist dissent, the better to sustain the illusion that modernity had constructed sexuality from the perspective of straight white masculinity. Rather, a feminist genital analysis is equipped to acknowledge complexity in the pornographic text, which interprets social relations and plays them out across genitals, telling us things—various, unparaphrasable, contentious things—about how gender attaches to people through genital use, how labor structures identity, how desire emerges in proximity to available bodies, how bodies are sorted by their capacity to be dispassionately used. Such interpretation was foreclosed by anti-pornography feminism, but I've tried to reconstruct its possibility here and its affinity with the work pornography is equipped to do.

CODA
A Mindful Pornography

TO WRITE OF a mindful pornography in our present is to defy the most entrenched ideas we have about the genre—that it shuts down critical faculties, reproduces violence, creates automated responses in users. I was so determined to highlight pornography's analytic capacities over its sexual content in this book that I long thought its title would be "Pornography Without Sex," an assertion that the genre can be read entirely without reference to its genital descriptions. This idea is so counterintuitive that it turned out, alas, to be wrong as a descriptor of the whole project (but what a title! and one that works for my Introduction, where I insist upon the genre's content "without," outside of, beyond, beside sex). That it lingered as my organizing concept for so long—*What Pornography Knows* didn't stick until very late in the game—shows how energetically I had to insist, even to myself, that pornography could be read as dissident, and often feminist, even in its densest descriptive moments.

I close by suggesting that my detection of the affinity between social criticism and pornography across its long print history should encourage us to seek it in contemporary forms. This book has documented an enduring interest in antique pornography across centuries of print culture, despite editors' uneasy and uneven handling of its feminist content. By the twentieth century, as I've shown, the two discourses seem polarized. I don't conclude any one thing about feminism's apparent separation from the things pornography knows, but I wish to register the ease with which modern culture has come to see the two discourses as incompatible, a result of what I described earlier as feminism's misreading of pornography. I've shown that scholars like Linda Williams, Jennifer Nash, and Tim Dean believe pornography in the age of film "is a form of thinking," that it contains, as its print predecessors did, ideas about sexuality and gender in excess of what its creators and consumers intend;[1] and surely the same is true for the genre in the digital age, despite some scholars' dismissal of it as mentally numbing.

If we accept the allegation of pornography's sheer misogyny (that its "commonplace" violence against women "ruins sex," as Bernadette Barton claims), the genre has had its way with us—burying, deleting, or condensing skepticism so severely that we discern no internal dissent.[2] This book has opened up many avenues for tracing pornography's skepticism about dominant social narratives—about heteronormativity, binary sex, genital permanence, rape culture, gender hierarchy, egalitarian marriage, orientalized sexuality, sexual liberation. My hope is that readers are now attuned to pornography's engagement with such matters and that pornography might be read today for its ongoing intersections of sex and social commentary. I end by turning to yet another matter about which pornography is eloquent: labor.

I suggest—humbly, as a non-expert in digital media—that pornography workers best articulate, in our present, the genre's capacity for resistance and disruption. I trust scholars who point out the complexity of pornography's aesthetics in the digital age, as I noted in my Introduction, and believe it engages users on more than masturbatory levels, as I've shown has always been the case with pornography. There are possibly countless ways we can conceive of pornography making statements in, through, and around sex acts, particularly as consumers can now access cost-free content produced around the globe. As Heather Berg writes in *Porn Work*, such a supply creates an environment in which consumers "feel entitled to free sexual labor."[3] It seems to me that pornography must be conscious of this expectation for free content and that the sex workers who create pornography are best equipped to adapt the genre so that their performance might be perceived as the labor it is.

Current porn-studies scholars like Berg, Sophia Pezzutto, and Mireille Miller-Young turn to performers to understand pornography's working conditions today, in a technological era that has seen the demise of the studio and the rise of the pornography worker herself.[4] Adult performers, for example, often use studio shoot work as an "advertisement for the other things [they] do," performer Korra Del Rio explains to Pezzutto, building an "individual character" as a brand for which users will pay elsewhere, at a personal website or to purchase webcam performances.[5] In this model, individual scenes (like their print forebears) do not exist in isolation, but make reference to other forms of labor and communication. Performers' bodies also signify in ways that can illuminate sexual attitudes and appetites unavailable in mainstream discourse. In Del Rio's experience, "everybody likes trans women" in the production and consumption of pornography, suggesting it might be a site of resistance against transphobia. Further, the performances of trans performers potentially unseat the phallocentrism that allegedly governs pornography: in Del Rio's experience "you don't have to maintain an erection in trans porn to be successful," a change she attributes to testosterone blockers.[6] Pornography's genital candor, in this case, disentangles the penis from its historical affiliation with masculinity and penetration, as threads of feminist commentary did in eighteenth-century narratives.

These insights derived from pornographic labor are uniquely the terrain of sex workers. Focused on uniting sex with broader systems of consumption and capital, they extend the genital analysis made explicit by second-wave feminists, specifying it to the working conditions of a digital, globalized age. This context affords new forms of labor, control, and entrepreneurship to pornography workers, Berg argues, even as the industry "reproduces many of the same harms" as non-pornographic work.[7] Their approach for securing favorable conditions is not collective or organized, and it tends to atomize performers as independent contractors focused on obtaining their own profits and safety. But an attitude that unites sex workers is a firm skepticism that working conditions can be improved by the state, which has historically criminalized sex work and its practitioners. Sex worker activism eschews this stigmatization, Melissa Gira Grant writes, seeking "to reject the systems that use sex to render certain people less valuable" through, for example, policing and carceral practices.[8] The efforts of pornography workers to improve their work conditions and to exert autonomy over them constitute one strategy of resistance against a social, specifically a state, hierarchy that would diminish the knowledge, profits, and self-governance that sex work extends to the sex worker. A primary insight we gain from these accounts is that pornography in the digital age is as much about work as it is about sex—and this content is not invisible or sublimated.

Another way to ask how pornography generates social criticism is to approach it from the perspective of the user. I'll use this angle to conclude, spinning out the possibility that digital pornography is used as a form of resistance against the labor practices of the modern workplace. Berg helps us see how pornography foregrounds labor conditions. Pornography workers today insist "there is something disruptive about getting paid to give and receive pleasure," seeing "porn as an escape from work," and their appearance in videos often diverts the user to paid livestreaming or websites.[9] The user, by extension, watches not only sex in pornography, but labor. The model of labor performed by the sex worker may well be part of the tantalizing invitation extended to pornography's users under late capitalism. They elect into paid services and create profit for a laborer whose on-screen work—linked to pleasure, self-governed—appears so unlike their own. (It's worth noting that pornography workers' foregrounding of sexual pleasure in their labor marks a departure from depictions of sex work from earlier centuries, where the labor was regularly imagined as coerced, fatiguing, and physically perilous.)

Is it possible that digital pornographic consumption is a break from—in the temporal sense, but also as a resistance to—labor as it structures users' daily lives? Melissa Gregg explains that in the knowledge economy, mindfulness—self-care, reflection, meditation—has been increasingly defined against work by management, which devises strategies for encouraging workers to practice mindful self-care while remaining tied to the workplace. The task of designating intervals for mindfulness has migrated from workers themselves to software and prosthetic devices, which "relocate the intentionality of self-reflection from the person"—such is the cyborg laborer of late capitalism, one implicated in "hyperproductive and performative work cultures," ever connected to the workplace but urged by vibrations or notifications to, say, meditate or drink water. If "the pressure of professional performance sometimes shuts down the attentiveness to self and body," mindfulness strategically reinforces worker productivity (by keeping her healthy or safe or creative). If we think of pornography as a form of digital activity that keeps workers harnessed to the technology that structures their labor (internet, device, laptop), we might imagine its short-form videos as intervals of the mindful nature, providing "repair and solace" and attending to the user's person. Still implicated in the "broader logic of productivity governing the workplace," mindfulness (pornography?) extends the opportunity of cognitive respite without disrupting work itself; it gives workers the illusion they are exiting circuits of productivity.[10]

The richness of this possibility—that pornography in the digital age reflects users' labor conditions back to them, and both interrupts and perpetuates their relentless work—is heightened when we consider Sianne Ngai's account of the zany laborer, the Lucy Ricardo of farcical over-performance. In both Gregg's and Ngai's accounts of modern labor, the demands of capitalism erode physical balance and well-being: Gregg's worker numbed by the affective and physical demands of both corporate culture and improvised gig labor, and Ngai's zany worker imperiling herself through an overzealous performance of physical labor. Imagine Ngai's "absolutely elastic subject" as a performer in a pornographic scene:

> [B]y turning the worker's beset, precarious condition into a spectacle for our entertainment, zaniness flatters the spectator's sense of comparative security, thus hailing her as a kind of phantasmagoric manager or implicit owner of the means of production. Yet the experience of zaniness ultimately remains unsettling, since it dramatizes, through the sheer out-of-controlness of the worker/character's performance, the easiness with which these positions of safety and precariousness can be reversed.[11]

An extremely regular feature of digital pornography is its relentless genital penetration, a practice that requires a particular athleticism in performers.[12] Often, the penetrated performer expresses pronounced and seemingly endless enthusiasm, an "out-of-controlness" that offers her body for sustained and repeated use, "too many things coming at her at once."[13] If Ngai's analysis pertains to such a scene, a key element is the user's "comparative security," the sense that the user's labor is so different, it seems, from the kind seen on screen. Might this be a key aspect of the comfort extended to the user of pornography in the digital economy—the reassurance that the user is not the imperiled worker whose body labors zanily on screen? And does the user perceive that, in the quick and easy reversal Ngai imagines, they could be so laboring, and will be, once the "mindful" consumption of pornography is over?

Berg teaches us that pornographic performers know there is a content in their productions about labor that exceeds what is contained in any single video. As they seek scenes of genital action, then, users entertain a fantasy of pornographic labor—it has the potential to be self-directed, pleasurable, and resistant to the regimes of stipulated affect and endless connectivity required by "straight" work. Digital pornography recognizes and thematizes the potential for self-directed sex work, a form of labor we'll recall from Chapter 4 was openly interrupted by anti-pornography, anti-prostitution feminists, as by the WAP tours of Times Square. Could the user be participating, momentarily, in the "life lived otherwise" pornography workers embody?[14] Specifically, might pornography be a mindful rejection of the user's own participation in what Gregg claims is the "belief structure without ethics" that is modern corporate existence?[15] Berg shows that sex workers reject "straight" work on these premises; they reject the complacency and "misery" of such work through pornography's connection to pleasure and autonomy.[16] Pornography insists on at least somewhat resisting productivity—offering pleasure, resisting hyperproductivity, interrupting work, consumed in intimate environments—a temporary escape from the rhythms and boundlessness of work today.

I offer this speculation as a thought experiment in how we might continue, after print, to approach the pornographic text for its social protest, take its content at face value, and be surprised by the sorts of arousal it elicits. The consumption of digital, internet, free, short-form pornography is often vilified as mindless, but I'm suggesting it might be apprehended as a purposeful departure from hyperproductivity—as a momentary labor strike or a fantasy of work that feels good. Gregg believes mindfulness, properly enacted, could provide "a path back to the social" from knowledge-economy insularity.[17] If we sufficiently recognize pornography's centering of labor, might it provide this path? A mindful user will hear, acknowledge, and comprehend the statements of the person who inhabits the performing body, as pornography has for centuries asked its audience to do.

NOTES

Preface

1. Jennifer Burns Bright and Ronan Crowley, "'A Quantity of Offensive Matter': Private Cases in Public Places," in *Porn Archives*, eds. Tim Dean, Steven Ruszczycky, and David Squires (Durham: Duke University Press, 2014), 105, 107.

2. Ibid., 104; see also Anjali Arondekar, *For the Record: On Sexuality and the Colonial Archive in India* (Durham: Duke University Press, 2009), 98. Trade writing perpetuates this mythology; see Louise Levene, "The Naughty Table," *The Bookseller* (29 June 2011): https://www.thebookseller.com/feature/naughty-table-339220.

3. These examples are taken from a Twitter thread, in which I asked about the variety of materials requiring consultation in the restricted area of the British Library reading room. See https://twitter.com/kathylubey/status/1300516739482972160?s=20 Kathy Lubey (31 August 2020). Twitter post. 3:32 p.m.

Introduction

1. *The History of the Human Heart, or the Adventures of a Young Gentleman* (London, 1749), 128–129.

2. These textual changes count as the "living characteristics" of pornography that, David Squires argues, become visible in library archives—though as my Preface suggests, those archives must be conceived as incomplete in order to discover pornography's expansiveness. See Squires, "Pornography in the Library," in *Porn Archives*, eds. Tim Dean, Steven Ruszczycky, and Davis Squires (Durham: Duke University Press, 2014), 91. Examples of the more quantitative approach to pornography's history I mention here include Lisa Sigel, *Governing Pleasures: Pornography and Social Change in England, 1815–1914* (New Brunswick: Rutgers University Press, 2002); Julie Peakman, *Mighty Lewd Books: The Development of Pornography in Eighteenth-Century England* (London: Palgrave Macmillan, 2003); Peter Wagner, *Eros Revived: Erotica of the Enlightenment in England and America* (London: Secker and Warburg, 1988).

3. Saidiya Hartman, "Venus in Two Acts," *Small Axe* 26, no. 2 (2008): 1–14, at 11.

4. To name only a few examples of feminist discussions of pornography's harm: its psychological impact is imagined by Alice Walker in "Porn," in *You Can't Keep a Good Woman Down* (New York: Harcourt Brace, 1981); it is famously defined as harmful action rather than speech by Catharine MacKinnon in *Only Words* (Cambridge,

MA: Harvard University Press, 1993); its shaping of culture and politics is lamented by Bernadette Barton in *The Pornification of America: How Raunch Culture Is Ruining Our Society* (New York: NYU Press, 2021); and its distortion of young people's apprehension of sex, "as something men do *to* rather than *with* women," was the topic of Peggy Orenstein's recent op-ed piece, "If You Ignore Porn, You Aren't Teaching Sex Ed," *New York Times* (14 June 2021). Among those who argue pornography can empower women, see Stormy Daniels, *Full Disclosure* (New York: St. Martin's, 2018); Mireille Miller-Young, "This Is What Porn Can Be Like! A Conversation with Shine Louise Houston," in *Porn Archives*, eds. Tim Dean, Steven Ruszczycky, and David Squires (Durham: Duke University Press, 2014); Candida Royalle, "Porn in the USA," *Social Text* 37 (1993): 23–32; and Linda Williams, "A Provoking Agent: The Pornography and Performance Art of Annie Sprinkle," *Social Text* 37 (1993): 117–133.

5. I discuss these in more detail in Chapter 4. Frances Ferguson, *Pornography, the Theory: What Utilitarianism Did to Action* (Chicago: University of Chicago Press, 2004), 34–55; Jennifer Nash, *The Black Body in Ecstasy: Reading Race, Reading Pornography* (Durham: Duke University Press, 2014), 9–21; and Linda Williams, *Hard Core: Power, Pleasure, and the "Frenzy of the Visible"* (Berkeley: University of California Press, 1989), 16–30.

6. Randolph Trumbach argues a distinction between active and passive roles in sodomy endured in the early eighteenth century. See "The Transformation of Sodomy from the Renaissance to the Modern World and Its General Consequences," *Signs* 37, no. 4 (2012): 832–848.

7. Williams, *Hard Core*, 5.

8. Linda Williams, "Pornography, Porno, Porn: Thoughts on a Weedy Field," *Porn Studies* 1 (2014): 24–40, at 29.

9. Randolph Trumbach, "Erotic Fantasy and Male Libertinism in Enlightenment England," in *The Invention of Pornography: Obscenity and the Origins of Modernity*, ed. Lynn Hunt (New York: Zone, 1996), 259.

10. Scott Juengel, "Doing Things with Fanny Hill," *ELH* 76 (2009): 419–446, at 434.

11. Sharon Marcus, *Between Women: Friendship, Desire, and Marriage in Victorian England* (Princeton: Princeton University Press, 2007), 13.

12. Susan Lanser, *The Sexuality of History: Modernity and the Sapphic, 1565–1830* (Chicago: University of Chicago Press, 2014), 7, 10.

13. See "pornography, n. (1.a)," *OED Online* (March 2020). Oxford University Press (accessed 6 May 2021).

14. Wagner, *Eros Revived*, 246; see also Peakman, *Mighty Lewd Books*, 6; and Michael McKeon, "The Seventeenth- and Eighteenth-Century Sexuality Hypothesis," *Signs* 37 (2012): 791–801, at 795.

15. Lynn Hunt, ed., *The Invention of Pornography: Obscenity and the Origins of Modernity* (New York: Zone, 1996), 43–44.

16. James Steintrager, *The Autonomy of Pleasure: Libertines, License, and Sexual Revolution* (New York: Columbia University Press, 2016), esp. 22–24; see also

Margaret C. Jacob, "The Materialist World of Pornography," in *The Invention of Pornography: Obscenity and the Origins of Modernity*, ed. Lynn Hunt (New York: Zone, 1996). In French works, a feminist voice does not issue from the women protagonists. Robert Darnton notes that these "female narrators," enthusiastically absorbing materialist and freethinking philosophy, "express men's fantasies, not the long-lost voice of early modern feminism" ("Sex for Thought," in *Sexualities in History*, eds. Kim M. Phillips and Barry Reay [New York: Routledge, 2002], 207). Allistaire Tallent provides a counterexample to this absence of feminism in prostitute narratives centering women's experience in "A Space Between: Prostitutes Negotiating the Public and the Private in Memoir Novels of Eighteenth-Century France," in *Everyday Revolutions: Eighteenth-Century Women Transforming Public and Private*, eds. Diane E. Boyd and Marta Kvande (Newark: University of Delaware Press, 2008).

17. Peakman, *Mighty Lewd Books*, 6. On the trade in French works, see James Raven, *The Business of Books: Booksellers and the English Book Trade* (New Haven: Yale University Press, 2007), 111.

18. For example, Edmund Curll published *Venus in the Cloister*, a loose translation of Jean Barrin's 1683 *Venus dans le cloitre*, in 1725; and in 1740, parts of Nicholas Chorier's Latin 1660 *Aloisiae Sigeae Toletanae Satira Sotadica* (*L'Academie des dames* in French) were adapted from the original Latin as *Dialogue Between a Married Lady and a Maid*. Both translations efface their status as translations, seeming to appear as contemporary English works. They appear in Bradford Mudge, ed., *When Flesh Becomes Word: An Anthology of Eighteenth-Century Libertine Literature* (New York: Oxford University Press, 2004).

19. On the particular forms of knowledge possessed by the "novice," see Stephanie Insley Hershinow, *Born Yesterday: Inexperience and the Early Realist Novel* (Baltimore: Johns Hopkins University Press, 2019).

20. Michel Foucault, *The History of Sexuality, Volume 1: An Introduction*, trans. Robert Hurley (New York: Vintage, 1978), 157.

21. Ferguson, *Pornography, the Theory*, 12, 30.

22. Stephen Marcus, *The Other Victorians: A Study of Sexuality and Pornography in Mid-Nineteenth-Century England* (New York: Norton, 1964), 192.

23. Ibid., 247.

24 Walter Kendrick, *The Secret Museum: Pornography in Modern Culture* (Berkeley: University of California Press, 1987), 2; on the history of the term, see 1–32.

25. Robert Darnton, *Forbidden Bestsellers of Pre-Revolutionary France* (New York: Norton, 1995), 87.

26. Susan Lanser illuminates the central and complex influence of "sapphic dialogues" on British novels: they might be written by men and might tell "heterosexual stor[ies]," but they dispatch this content as conversations between women, foregrounding their interests and experiences ("Novel (Sapphic) Subjects: The Sexual History of Form," *Novel: A Forum on Fiction* 42, no. 3 [2010]: 497–503, at 499). They cannot then, in any straightforward sense, be said to serve heteronormative or masculine interests.

For an account that challenges differential reading habits based on gender, see Jan Fergus, "Women Readers: A Case Study," in *Women and Literature in Britain, 1700–1800*, ed. Vivien Jones (Cambridge, UK: Cambridge University Press, 2000).

27. So does Williams; see "Pornography, Porno, Porn," 34.

28. Jacques Derrida, "The Law of Genre," trans. Avital Ronell, *Critical Inquiry* 7 (1980): 55–81, at 56, 59.

29. Kendrick, *The Secret Museum*, 31.

30. Important exceptions are discussed in Chapter 4. Porn studies' contemporary leanings are evident in the journal *Porn Studies* and in *Porn Archives*, edited by Tim Dean, Steven Ruszczycky, and David Squires (Durham: Duke University Press, 2014).

31. Susan Sontag, "The Pornographic Imagination" (1967), in *Styles of Radical Will* (New York: Picador, 1969), 39.

32. Laura Kipnis, *Bound and Gagged: Pornography and the Politics of Fantasy in America* (Durham: Duke University Press, 1997).

33. David Andrews, "Toward a More Valid Definition of 'Pornography,'" *Journal of Popular Culture* 45, no. 3 (2012): 457–477, at 465; Laura Helen Marks, *Alice in Pornoland: Hardcore Encounters with the Victorian* (Urbana: University of Illinois Press, 2018), 20.

34. For Margret Grebowicz, pornography teaches "conformity and subjection" (*Why Internet Porn Matters* [Stanford: Stanford University Press, 2013], 119); in Gail Dines's sociological treatment, it has infiltrated popular consciousness (*Pornland: How Porn Has Hijacked Our Sexuality* [Boston: Beacon, 2010]).

35. On these possibilities, see Sarah Schaschek, *Pornography and Seriality: The Culture of Producing Pleasure* (New York: Palgrave Macmillan, 2014); Helen Hester, *Beyond Explicit: Pornography and the Displacement of Sex* (Albany: SUNY Press, 2014); Susanna Paasonen, *Carnal Resonance: Affect and Online Pornography* (Cambridge, MA: MIT Press, 2011).

36. MacKinnon, *Only Words*, 17; Dean, "Introduction," *Porn Archives*, 9.

37. Bernard Mandeville, *A Modest Defence of Publick Stews* (London, 1724), 44.

38. Leo Bersani, *Receptive Bodies* (Chicago: University of Chicago Press, 2018), 1, 3.

39. The locus classicus of these claims is Ian Watt's *The Rise of the Novel: Studies in Defoe, Richardson, and Fielding* (Berkeley: University of California Press, 1957).

40. Barring women from property ownership was regularly engineered in marriage settlements. And often judicial rulings—case by case, rather than through decisive legislation—interpreted settlements to cancel widows' right to dower or to property guaranteed in marriage settlements (Susan Staves, *Married Women's Separate Property in England* [Cambridge, MA: Harvard University Press, 1990], 32–34, 86, 107).

41. Hortense Spillers, "Mama's Baby, Papa's Maybe: An American Grammar Book," *Diacritics* 17, no. 2 (1987): 64–81; Chandra Talpade Mohanty, *Feminism Without Borders: Decolonizing Theory, Practicing Solidarity* (Durham: Duke University Press, 2003), 45. Pornographic works that thematize colonialism explicitly depersonalize

non-European women; see for instance "Kate's Narrative," "supposed to have been written about A.D. 1797" and published in 1800 in no. 13 of *The Pearl*. White characters narrate, speak, and initiate action; enslaved figures appear only for sexual labor. *The Pearl: Erotica from the Underground Magazine of Victorian England* (New York: Ballantine, 1968), 440–450.

    42. C. B. Macpherson, *The Political Theory of Possessive Individualism, Hobbes to Locke* (Oxford: Oxford University Press, 1962), 215. On the contradiction between Locke's theory of the propertied individual and European practices of enslavement and genocide, see Simon Gikandi, *Slavery and the Culture of Taste* (Princeton: Princeton University Press, 2011), 83–84; and Tiffany Lethabo King, *The Black Shoals: Offshore Formations of Black and Native Studies* (Durham: Duke University Press, 2019), 23, 115.

    43. For his famous account of the rise of companionate marriage, see Lawrence Stone, *The Family, Sex, and Marriage in England, 1500–1800* (New York: Harper, 1979), 217–253. More recently, Melissa Ganz complicates but I think ultimately affirms the period's tendency toward heterosexual egalitarianism in the period's debates on marriage; see *Public Vows: Fictions of Marriage in the English Enlightenment* (Charlottesville: University of Virginia Press, 2019).

    44. Lynn Festa, "Personal Effects: Wigs and Possessive Individualism in the Long Eighteenth Century," *Eighteenth-Century Life* 29, no. 2 (2005): 47–90, at 48.

    45. Thomas Laqueur, *Making Sex: Body and Gender from the Greeks to Freud* (Cambridge, MA: Harvard University Press, 1992), 150, 152.

    46. Karen Harvey, "The Century of Sex? Gender, Bodies, and Sexuality in the Long Eighteenth Century," *Historical Journal* 45 (2002): 899–916, at 913.

    47. This assumption about misogyny falls away in some academic contexts, where a focus on pornography's aesthetics or queerness tends to displace feminist analysis. Heather Love intelligently makes this point in "Pornography Porn," a review essay in *Public Books* (1 October 2015): https://www.publicbooks.org/pornography-porn/. Philosophers, on the other hand, tend to focus on pornography's impact and status (as art or not-art), evading analysis of texts, objects, or films themselves. See for example Nancy Bauer, *How to Do Things with Pornography* (Cambridge, MA: Harvard University Press, 2015); and Andrew Kania, "Concepts of Pornography: Aesthetics, Feminism, and Methodology," in *Art and Pornography*, eds. Hans Maes and Jerrold Levinson (Oxford: Oxford University Press, 2012).

    48. See, for example, David M. Halperin, *How to Do the History of Homosexuality* (Chicago: University of Chicago Press, 2002), esp. chaps. 2 and 4.

    49. Henry Abelove, "Some Speculations on the History of Sexual Intercourse During the Long Eighteenth Century in England," *Genders* 6 (1989): 125–130, at 127, 129; reprinted in his *Deep Gossip* (Minneapolis: University of Minnesota Press, 2005); Randolph Trumbach, *Sex and the Gender Revolution: Heterosexuality and the Third Gender in Enlightenment London* (Chicago: University of Chicago Press, 1998), 9–10.

    50. Tim Hitchcock, "The Reformulation of Sexual Knowledge in Eighteenth-Century England," *Signs* 37 (2012): 823–831, at 826–827.

51. Angela Carter, *The Sadeian Woman: An Exercise in Cultural History* (London: Virago, 1979), 12.

52. Jonathan Rose, "Rereading the English Common Reader," *Journal of the History of Ideas* 53, no. 1 (1992): 47–70, at 64.

53. Carter, *Sadeian Woman*, 20.

54. Christina Lupton, *Knowing Books: The Consciousness of Mediation in Eighteenth-Century Britain* (Philadelphia: University of Pennsylvania Press, 2012), 14.

55. Adrienne Rich, "Compulsory Heterosexuality and Lesbian Existence," *Signs* 5, no. 4 (1980): 631–660, at 640–641.

56. Sontag, "Pornographic Imagination," 47. For a newer version of this philosophical argument, see Petra Van Brabandt and Jesse Prinz, "Why Do Porn Films Suck?" in *Art and Pornography*, eds. Hans Maes and Jerrold Levinson (Oxford: Oxford University Press, 2012).

57. Leo Bersani, "Is the Rectum a Grave?" (1987), in *Is the Rectum a Grave? and Other Essays* (Chicago: University of Chicago Press, 2010), 20–21.

58. Kristin Grogan and Grace Lavery, "Blood Pink," *Social Text Online* (9 July 2020).

59. Damon R. Young, *Making Sex Public and Other Cinematic Fantasies* (Durham: Duke University Press, 2018), 11.

60. Lauren Berlant and Michael Warner, "Sex in Public," in *Publics and Counterpublics*, by Michael Warner (New York: Zone, 2005), 200–201.

61. Julia Serano, *Whipping Girl: A Transsexual Woman on Sexism and the Scapegoating of Femininity* (Emeryville: Seal Press, 2007), 13–14.

62. Susan Stryker and Paisley Currah, "Introduction," *Transgender Studies Quarterly* 1, nos. 1–2 (2014): 1–18, at 5. On modern forms of trans pornography, see Sophie Pezzutto and Lynn Comella, "Trans Pornography: Mapping an Emerging Field," *Transgender Studies Quarterly* 7, no. 2 (2020): 152–171.

63. Lisa Hager, "A Case for a Trans Studies Turn in Victorian Studies: 'Female Husbands' of the Nineteenth Century," *Victorian Review* 44, no.1 (2019): 37–54, at 52.

64. Heather Love, "Close, Not Deep: Literary Ethics and the Descriptive Turn," *New Literary History* 41, no. 2 (2010): 371–391, at 386.

65. Bersani, "Is the Rectum a Grave?," 25.

66. Kathleen Lubey, "Making Pornography, 1749–1968: The History of *The History of the Human Heart*," *ELH* 82, no. 3 (2015): 897–935. My account draws on Abelove's "Some Speculations."

67. Marcus, *The Other Victorians*, 279.

68 Leah Price, *The Anthology and the Rise of the Novel: Richardson to George Eliot* (Cambridge, UK: Cambridge University Press, 2000), 4.

69. Ibid., 10.

Chapter 1

1. For instance, see Roy Porter and Lesley Hall's discussion of sex in eighteenth-century medical literature in *The Facts of Life: The Creation of Sexual Knowledge in*

Britain, 1650–1950 (New Haven: Yale University Press, 1995), 33–121; Laura Rosenthal's study of writing about prostitutes, *Infamous Commerce: Prostitution in Eighteenth-Century British Literature and Culture* (Ithaca: Cornell University Press, 2006); and the sheer volume of scholarship focused on Cleland's *Memoirs of a Woman of Pleasure*, including a recent special journal issue devoted to it: "*Fanny Hill* Now," eds. Clorinda Donato and Nicholas D. Nace, *Eighteenth Century Life* 43, no. 2 (2019).

2. Thomas Laqueur, *Making Sex: Body and Gender from the Greeks to Freud* (Cambridge, MA: Harvard University Press, 1992), 171.

3. Randolph Trumbach, "Erotic Fantasy and Male Libertinism in Enlightenment England," in *The Invention of Pornography: Obscenity and the Origins of Modernity*, ed. Lynn Hunt (New York: Zone, 1996), 254; Hal Gladfelder, "Machines in Love: Bodies, Souls, and Sexes in the Age of La Mettrie," *Eighteenth-Century Fiction* 27 (2014): 55–81, at 78.

4. I depart from the view that reading about sex necessarily entailed entertainment or arousal, such as William Warner's *Licensing Entertainment: The Elevation of Novel Reading in Britain, 1684–1750* (Berkeley: University of California Press, 1998); and Thomas Laqueur's *Solitary Sex: A Cultural History of Masturbation* (New York: Zone, 2003), 330. Symptomatically, Laqueur limits his speculations on the eighteenth-century woman reader of sexual literature to what she was "thought by men" to be—absorbed and ecstatic (340).

5. Randolph Trumbach, *Sex and the Gender Revolution: Heterosexuality and the Third Gender in Enlightenment London* (Chicago: University of Chicago Press, 1998), 63, and on the social and legal enforcement of women's chastity, 23–49. On the socialization of girls for subordination in marriage, see Anthony Fletcher, *Gender, Sex, and Subordination in England, 1500–1800* (New Haven: Yale University Press, 1995), esp. 364–400.

6. The feud is invoked in the print particularly by the painting, top center, that shares a title with the play in which Pope first lampooned Cibber, *Three Hours After Marriage*, as well as by *The Non-Juror* on the floor, in which Cibber retaliated. The year after this print was published, Pope would make Cibber the hero of *The Dunciad*. See William M. Peterson, "Pope and Cibber's *The Non-Juror*," *Modern Language Notes* 70, no. 5 (1955): 332–335. While I emphasize Pope's attempt to make the prostitute his intellectual property, Jason Farr reads a similar print as depicting a sexually passive Pope who figures outside the limits of aggressive libertine masculinity; see "Libertine Sexuality and Queer-Crip Embodiment in Eighteenth-Century Britain," *Journal for Early Modern Cultural Studies* 16, no. 4 (2016): 96–118.

7. William C. Lowe, "Douglas, William, fourth duke of Queensberry (1725–1810, sybarite and politician," *Oxford Dictionary of National Biography* (23 September 2004), Oxford University Press (accessed 16 December 2021). Vic Gatrell identifies the figures in *City of Laughter: Sex and Satire in Eighteenth-Century London* (New York: Walker & Company, 2006), 370. Women only began to wear underpants after 1800, and inseams were not stitched until the later nineteenth century. See Kimberly Chrisman-Campbell, *Fashion Victims: Dress at the Court of Louis XVI and Marie-Antoinette*

(New Haven: Yale University Press, 2015), 42; and Eleri Lynn, *Underwear: Fashion in Detail* (London: V&A Publishing, 2010), 9, 20.

8. Chloe Wigston Smith, *Women, Work, and Clothes in the Eighteenth-Century Novel* (Cambridge, UK: Cambridge University Press, 2013), 188–193.

9. The anatomical meaning was in use by 1618. See "cock, n.1 and int. (A.III.9.a)," *OED Online* (December 2021). Oxford University Press (accessed 3 January 2022).

10. On dildo materials, see Ula Lukszo Klein, "Dildos and Material Sapphism in the Eighteenth Century," *Eighteenth-Century Fiction* 31, no. 2 (2019): 395–412, at 397. Dildos were for sale, "presumably for female customers," alongside sexual paraphernalia like condoms in midcentury London; see Dan Cruickshank, *London's Sinful Secret: The Bawdy History and Very Public Passions of London's Georgian Age* (New York: St. Martin's, 2009), 210.

11. Leah Benedict, "Impotence Made Public: Reading Sex on the Stage and in the Courtroom," *ELH* 85, no. 2 (2018): 441–469, at 448, 450.

12. Laqueur, *Making Sex*, 149–192.

13. *Aristotle's Master-Piece, or the Secrets of Generation Displayed in All the Parts Thereof* (London, 1684), 16.

14. Porter and Hall, *The Facts of Life*, 51.

15. Tim Hitchcock, "The Reformulation of Sexual Knowledge in Eighteenth-Century England," *Signs* 37 (2012): 823–831, at 827.

16. Bernard Mandeville, *A Modest Defence of Publick Stews* (London, 1724), 52, 12.

17. Rosenthal, *Infamous Commerce*, 69.

18. Daniel Defoe, *Conjugal Lewdness; or, Matrimonial Whoredom* in *The Religious and Didactic Writings of Daniel Defoe,* Vol. 5, ed. Liz Bellamy (London: Pickering and Chatto, 2006), 40.

19. Compare Defoe's language with anti-sodomy discourse in *Satan's Harvest Home* (London, 1749); and Ned Ward, "Of the Mollies Club" (London, 1708), in *Homosexuality in Eighteenth-Century England: A Sourcebook,* ed. Rictor Norton (1 December 1999, updated 16 June 2008): http://www.rictornorton.co.uk/eighteen/nedward.htm. On the growing restrictions on sodomy between men in eighteenth century, see Trumbach, *Sex and the Gender Revolution*, 3–8; and Hal Gladfelder on the trial against the publisher of sodomy pamphlet literature in *Fanny Hill in Bombay: The Making and Unmaking of John Cleland* (Baltimore: Johns Hopkins University Press, 2012), chap. 3. On sodomy as "cultural fantasy," see George Haggerty, "Keyhole Testimony: Witnessing Sodomy in the Eighteenth Century," *The Eighteenth Century: Theory and Interpretation* 44, nos. 2–3 (2003): 167–182, at 177.

20. Premarital, non-penetrative sex was "commonplace and practiced by nearly everyone" in rural communities in the first half of the eighteenth century; John Cannon "refuse[d] to penetrate anyone" during courtship, reserving penetrative intercourse for the path toward marriage (Tim Hitchcock, *English Sexualities, 1700–1800* [New York: St. Martin's, 1997], 36, 35). On "intercrural intercourse" in the late seventeenth and early eighteenth centuries, see Will Fisher, "Thigh Sex in England, 1590–1730," *Journal of the History of Sexuality* 24, no. 1 (2015): 1–24.

21. For a different take on Haywood's men that emphasizes their virtue, see Mary Beth Harris, "Upsetting the Balance: Exposing the Myth of Masculine Virtue in Haywood's *Philidore and Placentia*," *The Eighteenth Century: Theory and Interpretation* 58, no. 2 (2017): 195–218.

22. I discuss this critical tradition *Excitable Imaginations: Eroticism and Reading in Britain, 1660–1760* (Lewisburg: Bucknell University Press, 2012), 100, 105.

23. Eliza Haywood, *Fantomina and Other Writings*, eds. Alexander Pettit, Margaret Case Croskery, and Anna C. Patchias (Peterborough: Broadview, 2004), 46.

24. These are Jonathan Kramnick's verbs. See his *Actions and Objects from Hobbes to Richardson* (Stanford: Stanford University Press, 2010), 185, 186.

25. Richard Payne Knight, *An Account of the Remains of the Worship of Priapus* (London, 1786), 27.

26 On its anticlericalism, composition, and reception, see Roy Porter, "The Sorrows of Priapus: Anticlericalism, Homosocial Desire, and Richard Payne Knight," in *Sexual Underworlds of the Enlightenment*, eds. G. S. Rousseau and Roy Porter (Manchester: Manchester University Press, 1987).

27. Despite Payne Knight's emphasis on phallic scale, the dimensions of the votives are at their longest 60 mm and at widest 34 mm, according to the British Museum catalogue notes: https://www.britishmuseum.org/collection/object/H_WITT-319.

28. This piece was "brought from the Island of Elephanta, in the Cumberland man of war, and now belongs to the Museum of Mr. Townley" (Payne Knight, *Priapus*, 81). My reading of the image is indebted to Sarah Carter's "India and the Antiquarian Image: Richard Payne Knight's *A Discourse on the Worship of Priapus*," *RACAR* 45, no. 1 (2020): 49–59.

29. On *Pamela*'s "cross-media" popularity, see James Grantham Turner, "Novel Panic: Picture and Performance in the Reception of *Pamela*," *Representations* 48 (1994): 70–96; on the Marriage Act as "watershed for sexual politics and family life," Eve Tavor Bannet, *The Domestic Revolution: Enlightenment Feminisms and the Novel* (Baltimore: Johns Hopkins University Press, 2000), 94; on fiction's participation in debates about the Act, Melissa J. Ganz, *Public Vows: Fictions of Marriage in Enlightenment England* (Charlottesville: University of Virginia Press, 2019).

30. Katherine Binhammer, *The Seduction Narrative in Britain, 1747–1800* (Cambridge, UK: Cambridge University Press, 2009), 11.

31. April London, *Women and Property in the Eighteenth-Century English Novel* (Cambridge, UK: Cambridge University Press, 1999), 7–8.

32. Melissa J. Ganz, "Moll Flanders and English Marriage Law," *Eighteenth-Century Fiction* 17, no. 2 (2005): 157–182, at 180.

33. "Microlevel" is Michael McKeon's term for marriage as a means of property redistribution from public to private in the domestic realm, of a piece with his larger tracing of the "devolution of absolutism" in the eighteenth century in *The Secret History of Domesticity: Public, Private and the Division of Knowledge* (Baltimore: Johns Hopkins University Press, 2005), 138–140. I'm arguing that literature specifies the

reach of property claims to extend to women's physical persons, an encroachment not generalizable to other historical phenomena.

34. Quoted in Susan Staves, *Married Women's Separate Property in England* (Cambridge, MA: Harvard University Press, 1990), 80.

35. See Christopher Hill, "Clarissa Harlowe and Her Times," *Essays in Criticism* 5, no. 4 (1955): 315–340.

36. Gillian Skinner, "Women's Status as Legal and Civic Subjects: 'A Worse Condition Than Slavery Itself?'" in *Women and Literature, 1700–1800*, ed. Vivien Jones (Cambridge, UK: Cambridge University Press, 2000), 91.

37. Ruth Perry, *Novel Relations: The Transformation of Kinship in England, 1748–1818* (Cambridge, UK: Cambridge University Press, 2006), 50.

38. Staves, *Separate Property*, 102, 76, 79.

39. This pattern of sexual incursions, which I'm suggesting authors saw as explicit and designed, is distinct from the accidental harm, strict liability, and depersonalization Sandra Macpherson sees as central to the novel in *Harm's Way: Tragic Responsibility and the Novel Form* (Baltimore: Johns Hopkins University Press, 2010), 16–24.

40. For Kramnick, characterization "extended outward into external objects and events" (*Actions and Objects*, 5); for Macpherson, plot and accident "mak[e] connections among distant others who do not know and do not care about one another" (*Harm's Way*, 24).

41. Frances Ferguson, "Rape and the Rise of the Novel," *Representations* 20 (1987): 88–112, at 88–98.

42. Lorraine Daston, "Speechless," in *Things That Talk: Object Lessons from Art and Science*, ed. Lorraine Daston (New York: Zone, 2004), 20.

43. Jonathan Lamb, *The Things Things Say* (Princeton: Princeton University Press, 2011), 3, 23. Lamb's chapter on chattel slavery exposes the catastrophic hypocrisies of this affiliation of property with personhood, but he does not consider the limits of this theory for women.

44. Lynn Festa, "Person, Animal, Thing: The 1796 Dog Tax and the Right to Superfluous Things," *Eighteenth-Century Life* 33, no. 2 (2009): 1–44, at 13.

45. For Bill Brown, objects become things when they refuse their usual function; see "Thing Theory," *Critical Inquiry* 28, no. 1 (2001): 1–22, at 4.

46. Samuel Richardson, *Pamela*, eds. Tom Keymer and Alice Wakely (New York: Oxford University Press, 2001), 126.

47. Samuel Richardson, *Clarissa*, ed. Angus Ross (New York: Penguin, 1985), 977.

48. While there is a tradition of reading Lovelace's rape of Clarissa as an unnarrated lacuna, I have made the case elsewhere that the novel represents this rape, and rape more generally, with thoroughness and precision. See Kathleen Lubey, "Sexual Remembrance in *Clarissa*," *Eighteenth-Century Fiction* 29, no. 2 (2016–17): 151–178.

49. On Lovelace's illegitimate authority, see Toni Bowers, *Force or Fraud: British Seduction Stories and the Problem of Resistance, 1660–1760* (Oxford: Oxford University Press, 2011), 263–279.

50. See "strange, adj. and n.," *OED Online* (September 2021). Oxford University Press (accessed 7 October 2021). This entry demonstrates how "strange" applies variously to Clarissa's plight: "belonging to some other place or neighborhood" (A.2), "belonging to others; not of one's own kin" (A.3); "added or introduced from outside" (A.5); "unknown, unfamiliar" (A.7).

51. Janine Barchas, *The Annotations in Lady Bradshaigh's Copy of "Clarissa"* (Victoria: University of Victoria, 1998), 94n1.

52. See Lubey, "Sexual Remembrance," 154–157. Wendy Anne Lee notes the peculiarity of Clarissa's subject position as an unashamed, extroverted "rape victim" whose "disarming" self-identification as such is alien to eighteenth-century sociability in *Failures of Feeling: Insensibility and the Novel* (Stanford: Stanford University Press, 2019), 82.

53. On Clarissa's articulate, continual "negative" to Lovelace after the rape, see Ferguson, "Rape and the Rise of the Novel," 106.

54. Haywood's focus on men's engineering of social spaces coincides with a period in which her politics too became more overt. See Kathryn King, *A Political Biography of Eliza Haywood* (London: Pickering and Chatto, 2012), 95–132.

55. Eliza Haywood, *Anti-Pamela and Shamela*, ed. Catherine Ingrassia (Peterborough: Broadview, 2004), 64.

56. Amanda Vickery, *Behind Closed Doors: At Home in Georgian England* (New Haven: Yale University Press, 2009), 58.

57. The tavern's sordid associations persist in 1741. On sex work in taverns, see Cruickshank, *London's Sinful Secret*, 145, 242, and on Reynolds's club (including Johnson, Goldsmith, and Garrick) and the Turk's Head, 349. On the openness of sex in taverns including Pepys's "backward" position, see Steven Earnshaw, *The Pub in Literature: England's Altered State* (Manchester: Manchester University Press, 2000), 102–107, 117. See also Cleland's *Memoirs of a Woman of Pleasure*, where Fanny spontaneously shags a sailor in a "little room" in a "convenient tavern," ed. Peter Sabor (Oxford: Oxford University Press, 1999), 140. Earnshaw's examples are from the late seventeenth century, and by the 1790s, taverns were thought elegant; see Ian Newman, "Edmund Burke in the Tavern," in *European Romantic Review* 24, no. 2 (2013): 125–148.

58. My reading emphasizes Syrena's hesitancy in her initial experiences of sexual commerce, though she spends much of the novel knowingly scheming. For this emphasis, see Kristina Straub, *Domestic Affairs: Intimacy, Eroticism, and Violence Between Servants and Masters in Eighteenth-Century Britain* (Baltimore: Johns Hopkins University Press, 2009), 61–62.

59. On the influence of Petrarch's martial imagery and its fragmentation of women's subjectivity, see Nancy Vickers, "'The Blazon of Sweet Beauty's Best': Shakespeare's *Lucrece*," in *Shakespeare and the Question of Theory*, eds. Geoffrey Hartmann and Patricia Parker (New York: Routledge, 1985).

60. Lamb, *The Things Things Say*, 3.

61. Thomas A. King, *The Gendering of Men, 1600–1750: Volume 1, The English Phallus* (Madison: University of Wisconsin Press, 2004), 4–5.

62. On these attributes of the closet, see, respectively, Karen Lipsedge, *Domestic Space in Eighteenth-Century British Novels* (Houndsmills: Palgrave Macmillan, 2012), 11, 38; Tita Chico, *Designing Women: The Dressing Room in Eighteenth-Century Literature and Culture* (Lewisburg: Bucknell University Press, 2005); and Danielle Bobker, *The Closet: The Eighteenth-Century Architecture of Intimacy* (Princeton: Princeton University Press, 2020).

63. Paul Ricoeur, *The Rule of Metaphor*, trans. Robert Czerny (Toronto: University of Toronto Press, 1977), 216, 230. "Rape" increasingly in this period referred to forced sexual intercourse, a violation of the woman herself rather than of her male relatives; see Bowers, *Force or Fraud*, 12–17.

64. Binhammer, *Seduction Narrative in Britain*, 31.

65. Susan Lanser, *The Sexuality of History: Modernity and the Sapphic, 1565–1830* (Chicago: University of Chicago Press, 2014), 158.

66. Andrea Haslanger, "What Happens When Pornography Ends in Marriage: The Uniformity of Pleasure in *Fanny Hill*," *ELH* 78, no. 1 (2011): 163–188, at 164. The shorthand title *Fanny Hill* is often used by critics interchangeably to refer to this work. Adhering more closely to Cleland's title, I shorten it to *Woman of Pleasure*. References are to Sabor's edition, whose source text is the 1749 first edition of the novel. One exception is my discussion of the 1841 *Memoirs of the Life of the Celebrated Miss Fanny Hill* in Chapter 3.

67. Lanser, *Sexuality of History*, 171. The reading of the novel as straight and phallocentric was longstanding but has ceded ground in the last decade to queerer readings. See Peter Sabor, "From Sexual Liberation to Gender Trouble: Reading *Memoirs of a Woman of Pleasure* from the 1960s to the 1990s," *Eighteenth-Century Studies* 33, no. 4 (2000): 561–578.

68. Lisa L. Moore, *Dangerous Intimacies: Toward a Sapphic History of the British Novel* (Durham: Duke University Press, 1997), 60. Moore reads a nonbinary gendering in this scene, whereas I'm turning the focus to Fanny's own drifting body parts.

69. Haslanger considers this distance between self and experience evidence of the marriage plot's inability to recompense women for sexual harm; see Haslanger, "What Happens," 166.

70. Henry Abelove, "Some Speculations on the History of Sexual Intercourse During the Long Eighteenth Century in England," *Genders* 6 (1989): 125–130, at 127; on this phrase, see "The Eighteenth Century's Pornographic Conditions" in my Introduction.

71. Klein, "Dildos and Material Sapphism," 399.

72. On the availability of dildos, see Peter Wagner, "The Discourse on Sex—or Sex as Discourse: Eighteenth-Century Medical and Paramedical Erotica," in *Sexual Underworlds of the Enlightenment*, eds. G. S. Rousseau and Roy Porter (Manchester: Manchester University Press, 1987), 52–54.

73. "Dick" did not acquire its modern genital meaning until the late nineteenth century. See "dick, n.1 (4.a)," *OED Online* (December 2021). Oxford University Press (accessed 3 January 2022). On the historical context of Dick's disability, and his presence in the novel as "a bearer of the text's central theme—the superiority of signs and sensation over language and reason," see D. Christopher Gabbard, "From Idiot Beast to Idiot Sublime: Mental Disability in John Cleland's *Fanny Hill*," PMLA 123, no. 2 (2008): 375–389, at 377.

74. Joseph Drury sees Dick as a late instance of the "libertine machine" driven by materialist forces indifferent to morality, law, and convention in *Novel Machines: Technology and Narrative Form in Enlightenment Britain* (Oxford: Oxford University Press, 2017), 63.

75. On anatomical studies that separate and differentiate male genital parts, see Raymond Stephanson, *The Yard of Wit: Male Creativity and Sexuality, 1650–1750* (Philadelphia: University of Pennsylvania Press, 2004), 73–80.

76. Gladfelder, "Machines in Love," 61.

77. Macpherson reads *Memoirs of Miss Sidney Biddulph*'s Faulkland as a male rape victim whose accidental erection leaves him in a state of "human objecthood" with catastrophic consequences (*Harm's Way*, 139).

78. Stephanson, *Yard of Wit*, 82.

79. Scott Juengel, "Doing Things with Fanny Hill," *ELH* 76 (2009): 419–446, at 435. I agree that Cleland seems prescient in articulating pornography's "redeeming social value" (438), but I see that value inhering not in heteronormativity but a queer model of penetration in this scene.

80. Moore, *Dangerous Intimacies*, 56.

81. *Monsieur Thing's Origin* (London, 1722), 12.

82. *Dildoides* was attributed alternately to Samuel Butler and Charles Sedley upon publication, then included and misattributed in the 1707 *Miscellaneous Works of . . . Rochester and Roscommon* and reprinted in *The Cabinet of Love* (1739). It is included in *Eighteenth-Century British Erotica II*, Vol. 2, ed. Deborah Needleman Armintor (Pickering and Chatto, 2004), 3.

83. Ibid., 5.

84. "The torn, split, wounded girl cries, struggles to invoke me to her rescue . . . in vain!" (Cleland, *Woman of Pleasure*, 164).

85 *Monsieur Thing's Origin*, 13.

86. "Prosthesis" retained a grammatical meaning as an additive in this period even as it took on meaning as a supplement for a lack. See Brandon W. Hawk, "*Prosthesis*: From Grammar to Medicine in the Earliest History of the Word," *Journal of Disability Studies* 38, no. 4 (2018): http://dx.doi.org/10.18061/dsq.v38i4.5398.

87. See Jennifer Van Horn, *The Power of Objects in Eighteenth-Century British America* (Chapel Hill: University of North Carolina Press, 2017), 369–374.

88. *A Spy on Mother Midnight: or, the Templar Metamorphos'd* (London, 1748), 8–9.

89. *A Continuation of Mr. F——'s Adventures, Being the Second Part of The Spy on Mother Midnight* (London, 1748), 6. *Spy* and its *Continuation* deploy some conventions around literary representations of dildos. This particular rape strategy, in which a cross-dressed man penetrates a woman with his penis instead of the promised dildo, also appears in *Tractatus de Hermphroditis: or, A Treatise of Hermaphrodites* (London, 1718), reprinted in *Eighteenth-Century British Erotica I*, Vol. 2, eds. Alexander Pettit and Patrick Spedding (London: Pickering and Chatto, 2002), 54–55.

90. Stephanson, *Yard of Wit*, 78.

91. *The Imperfect Enjoyment,* in *The Works of John Wilmot, Earl of Rochester,* ed. Harold Love (Oxford: Oxford University Press, 1999), line 61.

92. Jason Farr, *Novel Bodies: Disability and Heterosexuality in Eighteenth-Century British Literature* (Lewisburg: Bucknell University Press, 2019), 22.

93. Lynne Friedli, "'Passing Women': A Study of Gender Boundaries in the Eighteenth Century," in *Sexual Underworlds of the Enlightenment*, eds. G. S. Rousseau and Roy Porter (Manchester: Manchester University Press, 1987), 240.

94 *Monsieur Thing's Origin*, 18.

95 *Treatise of Hermaphrodites*, 51–52.

96. Henry Fielding, *The Female Husband,* in *When Flesh Becomes Word: An Anthology of Early Eighteenth-Century Libertine Literature*, ed. Bradford Mudge (New York: Oxford University Press, 2004), 295, 296, 303. Sal Nicolazzo reads the dildo as "an instrument of financial fraud" that links Hamilton's sexual transgression with legal violation of the economic order; see "Henry Fielding's *The Female Husband* and the Sexuality of Vagrancy," *The Eighteenth Century: Theory and Interpretation* 55, no. 4 (2014): 335–353, at 341.

97. Pronouns shift throughout but see especially the episode in which Hamilton passes as a doctor (297–299). Like Nicolazzo, I refrain from ascribing a stable gender identity to Hamilton ("Sexuality of Vagrancy," 351n1) and try to track the narrative's own grappling with nonbinary representation. In her trans history podcast ("Female Husband!" *One from the Vaults* [13 November 2016]), Morgan Paige rebuts the efforts of academics to ascribe stable identity to Hamilton, especially as either a protofeminist or an early lesbian:

> In order to believe either of these, you have to believe that internally . . . Hamilton and people like him thought of themselves as women. This is impossible to know for certain, as we have little record . . . of what these people have to say about themselves. . . . What we know for certain is that people who made the decision to live their lives as men went to great lengths to achieve and maintain these lives.

Jen Manion, studying Hamilton as a historical figure beyond Fielding's text, finds that Hamilton had "completely transed gender and was only known by others as a man" (*Female Husbands: A Trans History* [Cambridge, UK: Cambridge University Press, 2020], 36). I find Manion's use of "trans" as a verb helpful for thinking about nonbinary gender identity in the historical past; see 11, 29–43.

98. Paula Backscheider, *Eighteenth-Century Women Poets and Their Poetry: Inventing Agency, Inventing Genre* (Baltimore: Johns Hopkins University Press, 2005), 186; Eugenia Zuroski, "Evelina's Laughter: The Novel's Queerer Theories," *The Eighteenth-Century: Theory and Interpretation* 61, no. 2 (2020): 165–186.

99. John Cleland, trans., *The True History and Adventures of Catharine Vizzani* (London, 1755), 3; reprint, originally published 1751. Major changes Cleland makes in translation are to defer description of the dildo and to make more novelistic and gallant the narration of Vizzani's exploits (Gladfelder, *Fanny Hill in Bombay*, 158, 160–161).

100. The concept of detachable genitals is not as outlandish as it might seem: "representations of genitalia . . . appeared in anatomical treatises, on écorché statues, on wax models, and in glass jars in and around London for viewing by all manner of audiences." See Darren Wagner, "A Bit Exposed: Displays of Male Genitals," in *Secrets of Generation: Reproduction in the Long Eighteenth Century*, eds. Raymond Stephanson and Darren N. Wagner (Toronto: University of Toronto Press, 2015), 394–395.

101. Gladfelder, *Fanny Hill in Bombay*, 165.

102 *Treatise of Hermaphrodites*, 64–65.

103. Eva Hayward, "Lessons from a Starfish" (2008), in *The Transgender Studies Reader 2*, eds. Susan Stryker and Aren Z. Aizura (New York: Routledge, 2013), 184.

Chapter 2

1. On adolescence as a key technique of novelistic representation, see Stephanie Insley Hershinow, *Born Yesterday: Inexperience and the Early Realist Novel* (Baltimore: Johns Hopkins University Press, 2019), where she explains nondevelopmental characters as "requir[ing] explicit and expansive depictions of social life" (3). Substitute "sexual" for "social," and we can see how youthful characters facilitate full descriptions of how bodies work and incisive theories about the ways they are impacted by social practice. While I study pornographic companion texts to the chaster novels that are Hershinow's focus, in both, heroines imagine a future "world without rape" (11).

2. Lawrence Stone, *The Family, Sex, and Marriage in England, 1500–1800* (New York: Harper, 1979), 333. For Armstrong, the sphere privatized by marriage and its related social practices invented feminine subjectivity: "a modern, gendered form of subjectivity developed first as a feminine discourse in certain literature"—eighteenth-century conduct literature and domestic novels—and "it was through this gendered discourse . . . that the discourse of sexuality made its way into common sense and determined how people understood themselves and what they desired in others" (Nancy Armstrong, *Desire and Domestic Fiction: A Political History of the Novel* [New York: Oxford University Press, 1987], 14); and for Stone, "docility and adaptability" were required of women, as they always had been, within the supposedly new, supposedly companionate marriage (249).

3. On picaresque's capacity to remark on "how the world actually works," see Richard Squibbs, "Tobias Smollett's *Ferdinand Count Fathom*: The Purpose of Picaresque," *Eighteenth-Century Fiction* 30, no. 4 (2018): 519–537, at 526.

4. One example of Fanny's sexual dissatisfaction is with the "insufficient" and flaccid Mr. Norbert (John Cleland, *Memoirs of a Woman of Pleasure*, ed. Peter Sabor [Oxford: Oxford University Press, 1999], 139). But his disappointing performance poises her to find pleasure elsewhere. "[R]eturning home from him with a spirit he had rais'd in a circle his wand had prov'd too weak to lay," she runs into a sailor on the street and has sex with him in a tavern, where his "plenteous bedewal of balmy sweets" as well her as her own "effusion . . . drown'd in deluge all [her] raging conflagration of desire" (140–141).

5. Julie Peakman asserts *Woman of Pleasure* is "[t]he only original [i.e., English] fictional obscene book published" in the mid-eighteenth century; *Mighty Lewd Books: The Development of Pornography in Eighteenth-Century England* (London: Palgrave Macmillan, 2003), 188.

6. "Sexual stimulation" is Peter Wagner's phrase in *Eros Revived: Erotica of the Enlightenment in England and America* (London: Secker and Warburg, 1988), 225, and is echoed by Peakman, for whom pornography is "material that contains graphic description of sexual organs and/or action . . . written with the prime intention of sexually exciting the reader" (*Mighty Lewd Books*, 6).

7. Thomas Laqueur, *Solitary Sex: A Cultural History of Masturbation* (New York: Zone, 2003), 334–335; see also Michael McKeon, *The Secret History of Domesticity: Public, Private and the Division of Knowledge* (Baltimore: Johns Hopkins University Press, 2005), 294–301.

8. Caroline Gonda, "Introduction: Friendship and Same-Sex Love," *SEL: Studies in English Literature 1500–1900* 46, no. 3 (2006): 517–521, at 521. I'm emphasizing the conceptual and analytical content of women's same-sex intimacy here. On same-sex erotics between women, see Harriette Andreadis, *Sappho in Early Modern England: Female Same-Sex Literary Erotics, 1550–1714* (Chicago: University of Chicago Press, 2001).

9. Susan Lanser, *The Sexuality of History: Modernity and the Sapphic, 1565–1830* (Chicago: University of Chicago Press, 2014), 155.

10. Maia Kostos, "Penetration and Its Discontents: Greco-Roman Sexuality, the *Acts of Paul and Thecla*, and Theorizing Eros Without the Wound," *Journal of the History of Sexuality* 27, no. 3 (2018): 343–366, at 345.

11. James Steintrager, *The Autonomy of Pleasure: Libertines, License, and Sexual Revolution* (New York: Columbia University Press, 2016), 22, 24. His point is to draw finer distinctions between libertinage and *philosophie* as the century moves forward.

12. Natania Meeker, "'I Resist It No Longer': Enlightened Philosophy and Feminine Compulsion in *Thérèse Philosophe*," *Eighteenth-Century Studies* 39, no. 3 (2006): 363–376, at 365, 364.

13. Fiction in translation was popular at this time, and it was not always done strictly or faithfully. In these instances, setting and custom are anglicized and updated, a practice Leah Orr states is common in the period in *Novel Ventures: Fiction and Print Culture in England, 1690–1730* (Charlottesville: University of Virginia Press, 2017), 144–147, 179.

14. Lynn Hunt, ed., *The Invention of Pornography: Obscenity and the Origins of Modernity* (New York: Zone, 1996), 40. On the narrative economy of pornography after Sade, see Frances Ferguson, *Pornography, the Theory: What Utilitarianism Did to Action* (Chicago: University of Chicago Press, 2004), 13, who emphasizes the "social evaluation" of individual action facilitated by pornography.

15. Margret Grebowicz, *Why Internet Porn Matters* (Stanford: Stanford University Press, 2013), 7.

16. Tim Dean, "Introduction," in *Porn Archives*, eds. Tim Dean, Steven Ruszczycky, and David Squires (Durham: Duke University Press, 2014), 10.

17. Christina Lupton, *Reading and the Making of Time in the Eighteenth Century* (Baltimore: Johns Hopkins University Press, 2018), 8.

18. Deidre Lynch, *Loving Literature: A Cultural History* (Chicago: University of Chicago Press, 2015), 30.

19. Simon Dickie, *Cruelty and Laughter: Forgotten Comic Literature and the Unsentimental Eighteenth Century* (Chicago: University of Chicago Press, 2011), 271. See also Tom Keymer on readers' peaceable synthesis of a wide spectrum of literary conventions in *Sterne, the Moderns, and the Novel* (Oxford: Oxford University Press, 2003), 30–45.

20. J. Paul Hunter, *Before Novels: The Cultural Contexts of Eighteenth-Century English Fiction* (New York: Norton, 1990), 226.

21. Lanser, *Sexuality of History*, 67.

22. Kathleen Lubey, *Excitable Imaginations: Eroticism and Reading in Britain, 1660–1760* (Lewisburg: Bucknell University Press, 2012), 12–24, 75–90.

23. Robert Darnton, *Forbidden Bestsellers of Pre-Revolutionary France* (New York: Norton, 1995), 88.

24. See the Preface and Kathleen Lubey, "Making Pornography, 1749–1968: The History of *The History of the Human Heart*," *ELH* 82, no. 3 (2015): 897–935, at 910–914.

25. British Library, shelfmark Cup.702.5.14. *Progress* has recently been digitized for Google Books; it otherwise appears only in the microform collection *Early British Fiction: Pre 1750* and is not indexed in the *English Short Title Catalogue* or *Eighteenth Century Collections Online* (*ECCO*). To my knowledge this binding contains the only extant copy of *Progress*. The British Library has assigned the 1744 date, which was erased from the title page but is corroborated by the *Gentleman's Magazine*, November 1744. T. Wiltshire, the publisher named on the title page, is most surely an alias, as no other titles with this imprint appear in this volume of the *Gentleman's Magazine* or the British Library catalogue, and Wiltshire has no entry in Henry Plomer's *Dictionary of the Printers and Booksellers in England, 1726–1775* (Oxford: Bibliographical Society at the Oxford University Press, 1932).

26. Peter Fryer, *Secrets of the British Museum* (New York: Citadel, 1968), 22–23.

27. Peakman, Wagner, and Fryer, for example, all use the Private Case as their archive, and so exclude works that broaden the definition of pornography.

28. While this advertisement reads as a tease, it is possible that further volumes would have been published if sales of the first proved profitable, a practice not uncommon in the period (Orr, *Novel Ventures*, 38–39).

29. *The Progress of Nature: Exemplify'd in the Life and Surprizing Adventures of Roger Lovejoy, Esq.* (London, 1744). 2.

30. "[W]hen a woman put her hand through slits in her skirt to access her pockets, she signaled almost directly towards her private parts" (Ariane Fennetaux, "Women's Pockets and the Construction of Privacy in the Long Eighteenth Century," *Eighteenth-Century Studies* 20, no. 3 [2008]: 307–334, at 318).

31. Cleland, *Woman of Pleasure*, 36. This genital detail previews the women's anatomical lessons Diderot would later recommend in France; see Shane Agin, "Sex Education in the Enlightened Nation," *Studies in Eighteenth-Century Culture* 37 (2008): 67–87.

32. Anjali Arondekar, *For the Record: On Sexuality and the Colonial Archive in India* (Durham: Duke University Press, 2009), 123.

33. Stephen Marcus, *The Other Victorians: A Study of Sexuality and Pornography in Mid-Nineteenth-Century England* (New York: Norton, 1964), 213.

34. Jonathan Kramnick, *Actions and Objects from Hobbes to Richardson* (Stanford: Stanford University Press, 2010), 33.

35. Ula Lukszo Klein, "Dildos and Material Sapphism in the Eighteenth Century," *Eighteenth-Century Fiction* 31, no. 2 (2019): 395–412, at 407.

36. *Dildoides*, in *Eighteenth-Century British Erotica II*, Vol. 2, ed. Deborah Needleman Armintor (Pickering and Chatto, 2004).

37. Freeman's midcentury publications include exposés of Henry VIII, the Roman Catholic Church, an "unfortunate young nobleman return'd from thirteen years slavery in America," as well as pamphlets on the hoaxes of street performers and the resignation of Lord Chesterfield. The imprint may be false, according to Plomer's *Dictionary of the Printers and Booksellers*.

38. *Human Heart* is not currently archived in *ECCO* and has only recently been added to Google Books. Previously it was only available in rare book rooms, in the Garland series *The Flowering of the Novel* (1974), and in *The Eighteenth Century* microfilm collection. It is noted briefly in a few studies of eighteenth-century sexual culture, cited for its presentation of sex work as autonomy in Vivien Jones, "Eighteenth-Century Prostitution: Feminist Debates and the Writing of Histories," in *Body Matters: Feminism, Textuality, Corporeality*, eds. Avril Horner and Angela Keane (Manchester: Manchester University Press, 2000), 138–139); in Ruth Perry, *Novel Relations: The Transformation of Kinship in England, 1748–1818* (Cambridge, UK: Cambridge University Press, 2006), in the context of prohibitions on premarital sex (261); in Laura Rosenthal in the bibliography of *Nightwalkers: Prostitute Narratives from the Eighteenth Century* (Peterborough: Broadview Press, 2008); in Raymond Stephanson, *The Yard of Wit: Male Creativity and Sexuality, 1650–1750* (Philadelphia: University of Pennsylvania Press, 2004), for its discussion of "sperm-as-man" (38); and in Randolph Trumbach, "London's Sapphists: From Three Sexes to Four Genders in the Making of Modern Culture," in *Third Sex, Third Gender: Beyond Sexual Dimorphism in Culture and History*, ed. Gilbert Herdt (New York: Zone Books, 1994), for a reference to hermaphroditism in women.

39. Henry Abelove, "Some Speculations on the History of Sexual Intercourse During the Long Eighteenth Century in England," *Genders* 6 (1989): 125–130, at 126.

40. *The History of the Human Heart, or the Adventures of a Young Gentleman* (London, 1749), 46.

41. On the cultural response to non-penetration, see Judith Mueller, "Fallen Men: Representations of Male Impotence in Britain," *Studies in Eighteenth-Century Culture* 28 (1999): 85–102.

42. *Human Heart* might be considered part of the midcentury "male-centered ramble novel" in which the "obligatory romance plot" stands as an organizing principle to various hijinks—fraud, whoring, gambling, drinking, and fighting (Dickie, *Cruelty and Laughter*, 253, 255).

43. I therefore disagree further with Wagner, who claims that "comic effects . . . are detrimental" to pornography's aim of arousal. *History*'s humor may be what causes Wagner to mention it in passing as a "sub-pornographic title" (*Eros Revived*, 225, 246).

44. Christina Lupton, *Knowing Books: The Consciousness of Mediation in Eighteenth-Century Britain* (Philadelphia: University of Pennsylvania Press, 2012), 24.

45. Karen Harvey, *Reading Sex in the Eighteenth Century* (Cambridge, UK: Cambridge University Press, 2004), 61–76.

46. Cleland, *Woman of Pleasure*, 10.

47. Darryl Domingo, *The Rhetoric of Diversion in English Literature and Culture, 1690–1760* (Cambridge, UK: Cambridge University Press, 2016), 169.

48. Stephen Best and Sharon Marcus, "Surface Reading: An Introduction," *Representations* 108, no. 1 (2009): 1–21, at 9.

49. See Tim Hitchcock, *English Sexualities, 1700–1800* (New York: St. Martin's, 1997), 42–57. Roy Porter and Lesley Hall, in *The Facts of Life: The Creation of Sexual Knowledge in Britain, 1650–1950* (New Haven: Yale University Press, 1995), survey the "amalgam of traditional medico-scientific learning with other sorts of information" made available to various strata of eighteenth-century society (65). On gendered forms of knowledge and their impact on women's bodies, see Julie Peakman and Sarah Watkins, "Making Babies: Eighteenth-Century Attitudes Towards Conception, Reproduction, and Childbirth," in *The Secrets of Generation: Reproduction in the Long Eighteenth Century*, eds. Raymond Stephanson and Darren N. Wanger (Toronto: University of Toronto Press, 2015).

50. Natalie Philips, *Distraction: Problems of Attention in Eighteenth-Century Literature* (Baltimore: Johns Hopkins University Press, 2016), 4, 9.

51. By the 1780s, posture-girl performances were advertised as a colonial import from the South Pacific; see Laura Rosenthal, *Infamous Commerce: Prostitution in Eighteenth-Century British Literature and Culture* (Ithaca: Cornell University Press, 2006), 186–187. *Human Heart*'s earlier performers are noted to have "jet-black" hair, but otherwise seem English, as in the personal history one narrates (130–141).

52. Karen Harvey, "The Century of Sex? Gender, Bodies, and Sexuality in the Long Eighteenth Century," *Historical Journal* 45 (2002): 899–916, at 912–913. Harvey points out that sexual writing did not conform to scientific descriptions of the body,

and specifically the subordination of women's sexual pleasure in penetrative intercourse and conception, as other historians have suggested. On the alleged expendability of clitoral orgasm during the eighteenth century, see Thomas Laqueur, *Making Sex: Body and Gender from the Greeks to Freud* (Cambridge, MA: Harvard University Press, 1992), 150–151. Friedli finds, as I do, an enduring awareness of the clitoris's centrality in eighteenth-century writing, particularly its capacity for non-penetrative orgasm (Lynne Friedli, "'Passing Women': A Study of Gender Boundaries in the Eighteenth Century," in *Sexual Underworlds of the Enlightenment*, eds. G. S. Rousseau and Roy Porter [Manchester: Manchester University Press, 1987], 247–248). Popular writings on the body refer to the clitoris as the primary source of women's genital pleasure; see *Aristotle's Master-Piece, or the Secrets of Generation Displayed in All the Parts Thereof* (London, 1684), 105, and *Tractatus de Hermphroditis: or, A Treatise of Hermaphrodites* (London, 1718), reprinted in *Eighteenth-Century British Erotica I*, Vol. 2, eds. Alexander Pettit and Patrick Spedding (London: Pickering and Chatto, 2002), 26. On large clitorises and diagnoses of hermaphroditism, see Courtney E. Thompson, "Questions of *Genre*: Picturing the Hermaphrodite in Eighteenth-Century France and England," *Eighteenth Century Studies* 49, no. 3 (2016): 391–413, at 394–395.

53. "Shooting the bridge" is a nautical reference common in literary accounts of posture girls. "The nature of this routine can only be guessed at, but it alludes to the hazards of negotiating London Bridge by boat," a passageway that was narrow and precarious, water levels being variable on each side of the bridge (Gordon Williams, *A Dictionary of Sexual Language in Shakespearean and Stuart Literature*, 3 vols. [London: Athlone Press, 1994], 3:1077–1078). The "warm cataracts" suggests Camillo is showered by some kind of liquid. Trumbach confirms this phrase was common to some degree in *Sex and the Gender Revolution: Heterosexuality and the Third Gender in Enlightenment London* (Chicago: University of Chicago Press, 1998), 158.

54. *Treatise of Hermaphrodites*, 34.

55. "Supposititious" means something like "supposed," See "supposititious, adj.," *OED Online* (September 2021). Oxford University Press (accessed 7 October 2021). Meanings include both insidiously deceptive and simply imaginary: "Put by devious means in place of another; fraudulently substituted for the genuine thing or person" (1) or "Pretended or imagined to exist; feigned, fictitious" (2). The first definition aligns more fully with the feminist meaning I'm locating in the passage.

56. Reprints constituted a significant portion of the market in fiction, and it was not uncommon for a work to efface its status as a reprint or to abridge original content (Orr, *Novel Ventures*, 71, 105). Surreptitious abridgement sometimes reduced the price of a work (James Raven, *The Business of Books: Booksellers and the English Book Trade* [New Haven: Yale University Press, 2007], 232). But in this case, *Human Heart* and *B—— Tracey* share the same price of three shillings.

57. *Memoirs of B—— Tracey* (London, 1757), 1. The drop-head title reads *The Notorious Libertine; or, the Adventures of B—— Tracey*. The date is provided by British Library catalogue notes for shelfmark 1607.4343, which also notes it is "very rare."

58. When comparing editions, *H* indicates the 1749 *Human Heart*, *B* the 1757 abridged *B—— Tracey*.

59. In noting this pattern, I am not assuming all sex work to disenfranchise women, nor am I limiting sex workers to women. See my Coda to this book.

60. For a biographical note on Murray, see Julie Peakman, ed., *Whore Biographies, 1700–1825*, Vol. 3 (London: Pickering and Chatto, 2006), 1–4.

61. *Memoirs of the Celebrated Miss Fanny M——*, 2nd ed. (London, 1759), 1.9. Parenthetical references are to volume and page number. Manuscript notes in the British Library copy (archived in *ECCO*) fill in the redacted names.

62. *Characters of the Present Most Celebrated Courtezans* (London, 1780), 129.

63. Katherine Binhammer also notes, specifically in narratives of prostitute reform, the common ground between marriage and sexual labor insofar as they create economic dependency for women (*The Seduction Narrative in Britain, 1747–1800* [Cambridge, UK: Cambridge University Press, 2009], 49–52). Conversely, Rosenthal notes that some tradesmen were seen to prostitute their wives by seductively displaying them as means of drawing "legitimate commerce" into their shops (*Infamous Commerce*, 54).

64. On social and legislative practices of racial classification in colonial Jamaica, see Brooke Newman, *A Dark Inheritance: Blood, Race, and Sex in Colonial Jamaica* (New Haven: Yale University Press, 2018), 14–22; in the Pacific Island context and based on scientific writing, see Kathleen Wilson, *The Island Race: Englishness, Empire, and Gender in the Eighteenth Century* (New York: Routledge, 2003), 70–80.

65. Wendy Warren, "'The Cause of Her Grief': The Rape of a Slave in Early New England," *Journal of American History* 93, no. 4 (2007): 1031–1049; Marisa Fuentes, *Dispossessed Lives: Enslaved Women, Violence, and the Archive* (Philadelphia: University of Pennsylvania Press, 2016), 47–52, 61–64; Newman, *Dark Inheritance*, chap. 4.

66. *The Woman of Colour: A Tale*, ed. Lyndon Dominique (Peterborough: Broadview, 2008), 54–55.

67. The Helvétius attribution is false, and beyond invoking an irreverence to law and religion, the novel does not attribute to him a particularly unique materialism. As Steintrager notes, Helvétius was counted among the notorious French philosophers accused of atheism (*Autonomy of Pleasure*, 14). His writings were published regularly in London from 1767 forward, with only two translated into English (*De l'esprit* in 1750; *Treatise of Man* in 1777). On his philosophical impact in England, see Matthias Hoesch, "From Theory to Practice: Bentham's Reception of Helvétius," *Utilitas* 30, no. 3 (2018): 294–316.

68. *The Child of Nature, Improved by Chance. A Philosophical Novel*, 2 vols. (London, 1774), 2.235–2.236. Parenthetical references indicate volume and page number.

69. Armstrong, *Desire and Domestic Fiction*, 29.

70 Binhammer, *Seduction Narrative in Britain*, 26.

71. One particularly apt *OED* definition of "sop" (2d) is "a person or thing thoroughly soaked or steeped in some way." *OED Online* (September 2021). Oxford University Press (accessed 7 October 2021).

72. Margaret C. Jacob, "The Materialist World of Pornography," in *The Invention of Pornography: Obscenity and the Origins of Modernity*, ed. Lynn Hunt (New York: Zone, 1996), 161. Ferguson reveals the staunchest pornographic materialism in her reading of Sade's *Philosophy in the Bedroom* in *Pornography, the Theory*, chap. 3.

73. Jacob, "Materialist World," 165.

74. Susan Lanser, "Second-Sex Economics: Race, Rescue, and the Heroine's Plot," *The Eighteenth Century: Theory and Interpretation* 61, no. 2 (2020): 227–244, at 233.

75. I have in mind Shulamith Firestone's account of "the sex privatization of women" as a class in *The Dialectic of Sex: The Case for Feminist Revolution* (New York: Farrar, Straus, and Giroux, 1970), 133–135.

76. Wendy Anne Lee, *Failures of Feeling: Insensibility and the Novel* (Stanford: Stanford University Press, 2019), 86.

77. Karen O'Brien, *Women and Enlightenment in Eighteenth-Century Britain* (Cambridge, UK: Cambridge University Press, 2009), 11. In *The Domestic Revolution: Enlightenment Feminisms and the Novel* (Baltimore: Johns Hopkins University Press, 2000), 1–21, Eve Tavor Bannet foregrounds women's reform efforts in marriage and the home. And Elizabeth Eger emphasizes women's intellectual "achievement" and print publication in *Bluestockings: Women of Reason from Enlightenment to Romanticism* (Houndsmills: Palgrave Macmillan, 2010), 21. See also Harriet Guest, "Bluestocking Feminism," *Huntington Library Quarterly* 65 (2002): 59–80.

78. Darnton, *Forbidden Bestsellers*, 87.

Chapter 3

1. See Colette Colligan, "Digital Discovery and Fake Imprints: Unmasking Turn-of-the-Century Pornographers in Paris," *Book History* 22 (2019): 249–279; and Peter Mendes, *Clandestine Erotic Fiction in English, 1800–1930* (Aldershot: Scholar Press, 1993), 24–41.

2. M. M. Bakhtin, *The Dialogic Imagination: Four Essays*, trans. Caryl Emerson and Michael Holquist (Austin: University of Texas Press, 1981), 324.

3. Tim Dean, "Introduction," in *Porn Archives*, eds. Tim Dean, Steven Ruszczycky, and David Squires (Durham: Duke University Press, 2014), 1.

4. Lisa Sigel, *Governing Pleasures: Pornography and Social Change in England, 1815–1914* (New Brunswick: Rutgers University Press, 2002), 4. Among those who define pornography as excessive and inherently erotic, see William Cohen, *Sex Scandal: The Private Parts of Victorian Fiction* (Durham: Duke University Press, 1996), 122–123; and Simon Joudrey, whose gratuitous prose style and citations are symptomatic of criticism that reproduces pornography's alleged sensationalism: "Penetrating Boundaries: An Ethics of Anti-Perfectionism in Victorian Pornography," *Victorian Studies* 57, no. 3 (2015): 423–432, at 430.

5 Sigel, *Governing Pleasures*, 14.

6. For this account of Marcus, see "What Pornography Is" in my Introduction.

7. Anjali Arondekar, *For the Record: On Sexuality and the Colonial Archive in India* (Durham: Duke University Press, 2009), 102; Cohen, *Sex Scandal*, 122.

8. Colette Colligan, "Marcus's Sources: Archives, Canons, Texts," *Victorian Studies* 59, no. 3 (2017): 490–505, at 496.

9. Cohen, *Sex Scandal*, 123. He sees pornography's excess—a characterization I contest—as a product of the genre's privacy, in contrast with the novel and scandal sheet.

10. Like Linda Williams, my point about pornographic description is that it can be a "swerving away from . . . 'direct' forms of genital engagement"; see *Hard Core: Power, Pleasure, and the "Frenzy of the Visible"* (Berkeley: University of California Press, 1989), 101.

11. Arondekar, *For the Record*, 4; Saidiya Hartman, "Venus in Two Acts," *Small Axe* 26, no. 2 (2008): 1–14, at 2–3, 12.

12. Lisa Lowe, *The Intimacies of Four Continents* (Durham: Duke University Press, 2015), 2.

13. Hartman, "Venus," 5.

14. Iain McCalman considers Dugdale one of the first "hard-core" specialists; see "Unrespectable Radicalism: Infidels and Pornography in Early Nineteenth-Century London," *Past and Present* 104 (1984): 74–110, at 96. Lynda Nead calls Holywell Street "the single, mythic entity of obscenity" in nineteenth-century London (*Victorian Babylon: People, Streets, and Images in Nineteenth-Century London* [New Haven: Yale University Press, 2000], 164).

15. On Dugdale's use of eighteenth-century sources, see McCalman, *Radical Underworlds: Prophets, Revolutionaries, and Pornographers in London, 1795–1840* (Cambridge, UK: Cambridge University Press, 1988), 206–216; and Sigel, *Governing Pleasures*, 46. While McCalman separates Dugdale's political from his pornographic publication, Sigel sees, as I do, the two participating in potentially radical discourse (46–49). On Dugdale's many arrests, see Sigel (18–23), who suggests legal trouble stemmed from his selling to working-class readers, thought to be more prone to moral corruption than leisured classes. Nead suggests Dugdale's wealthier customers helped with legal problems (*Victorian Babylon*, 180–181).

16. See the third volume of Ashbee's bibliography, *Catena Librorum Tacendorum* (1885) (hereafter *CLT*), 122, 68.

17. Mendes points out in *Clandestine Erotic Fiction* the scarcity of English titles in the British Library's collection from the period 1820 to 1883, suggesting much nineteenth-century material was eliminated. In his bequest, Ashbee allowed for the destruction of duplicates in his collection, but Mendes provides evidence that trustees also permitted the destruction of "offensive" material in his collection (466). Mendes deems Reddie "the pivotal figure in the world of Victorian pornography, as collector, translator, author, and transmitter of texts from authors to publishers," including Ashbee and Dugdale (3.vii).

18. Jonathan Rose, "Rereading the English Common Reader," *Journal of the History of Ideas* 53, no. 1 (1992): 47–70, at 58.

19. British Library shelfmark P.C.14.de.4.

20. Advertisement quoted in Mendes, *Clandestine Erotic Fiction*, 141. For an overview of figures in and connecting these circles, see 3–13.

21. Sarah Bull, "Reading, Writing, and Publishing an Obscene Canon: The Archival Logic of the Secret Museum, c. 1860–c. 1900," *Book History* 20 (2017): 226–257, at 228. See also Sigel's account of literary pornography's increasing exclusivity in the late nineteenth century (*Governing Pleasures*, 55–63).

22. They printed 116 copies of each installment in the series, which were available in two bindings—both very expensive at £1 16s or £2 2s per volume (about £150 to £175 today). On the Rochester Series and the Avery-Reader partnership, see Mendes, *Clandestine Erotic Fiction*, 12–13, 141–142, and 452–453.

23. Leah Price, *The Anthology and the Rise of the Novel: Richardson to George Eliot* (Cambridge, UK: Cambridge University Press, 2000), 7–8.

24. Ashbee, *CLT*, 121–123. As noted in my Preface, Ashbee misdates *Human Heart*'s publication year as 1769, an error that made its way into the twentieth century; see also Chapter 4.

25. See McCalman, "Unrespectable Radicalism," 90. In a few unverified but probably authentic letters, Reddie wrote to Ashbee complaining of the sloppy attributions of Dugdale, to whom he began contributing in 1841. Dugdale's "publication practices I found to be strange and aggravating," and Reddie's work "seldom appeared under the names I . . . gave to them. . . . [Dugdale] seemed puzzled or perhaps amused by my annoyance and I saw that it was useless to protest" (11). Patrick J. Kearney has published these letters as *Five Letters from James Campbell Reddie to Henry Spencer Ashbee* on http://scissors-and-paste.net/pdf/Reddie_Letters.pdf. Thanks to Sarah Bull for bringing them to my attention.

26 *Memoirs of a Man of Pleasure* is contained in *The Exquisite: A Collection of Tales, Histories and Essays, Funny, Fanciful and Facetious, Interspersed with Anecdotes . . . Illustrated with Numerous Engravings*, 3 vols., printed and published by H. Smith [William Dugdale] (London, 1842–1844). "H. Smith" was one of Dugdale's several aliases; see Henry Spencer Ashbee, *Index Librorum Prohibitorum* (1877), 127. On the publication of *The Exquisite*, see Ashbee, *CLT*, 339–343; and Sigel, *Governing Pleasures*, 45. A reproduction of *The Exquisite* is available in the microfilm collection: Bradford Mudge, ed., *Sex and Sexuality, 1640–1940: Literary, Medical, and Sociological Perspectives*, Part 3 (Marlborough: Adam Matthew Publications, 2002).

27. Reddie's letters confirm Dugdale's disregard for source texts. Describing his editing of Edward Sellon's erotic memoir *Ups and Downs of Life* for Dugdale, Reddie writes:

> the MS . . . was twice as long at least as the printed version. . . . [Dugdale] was really only interested in the spicy passages, and I had the unhappy task of reducing the MS down

to its published length. Although much of the book is concerned with army life in India, the MS contained a good deal more which I had to excise. A pity, but D. had little time for Eddie's reflections on the society and religious practices of the Hindoos.... Worse, if possible, I was obliged to insert a few sentences of my own as a bridge.... (*Five Letters,* 19)

28. Sigel, *Governing Pleasures,* 47.

29. Citations are marked *H* to indicate the 1749 *Human Heart, E* to indicate the 1844 *Exquisite* edition.

30. "Wigmakers" (*H* 70) become "hair-cutters" (*E* 144) in 1844. Camillo's tutor is a "worthy Gentleman" (*H* 28) in 1749, later an "excellent man" (*E* 144).

31. For more detailed description of sentence-level textual alterations, see Kathleen Lubey, "Making Pornography, 1749–1968: The History of *The History of the Human Heart,*" *ELH* 82, no. 3 (2015): 897–935, at 918–920.

32. Copy of *The Child of Nature* held in a bound collection at in Princeton's Firestone Library Special Collections, call no. 2010-0007N.

33. *The Exquisite,* 1.357.

34. Deana Heath, *Purifying Empire: Obscenity and the Politics of Moral Regulation in Britain, India, and Australia* (Cambridge, UK: Cambridge University Press, 2010), 45.

35. Crystal Lake, *Artifacts: How We Think and Write About Found Objects* (Baltimore: Johns Hopkins University Press, 2020), 6.

36. Colligan, "Digital Discovery," 266, where she discusses the secret codes pornographers used on title pages. Three copies of the Rochester Series *Human Heart* are held at the British Library; one of these was probably Ashbee's, held in the Private Case until at least the late 1960s before being assigned its current shelfmark, Cup.805.d.3. Fryer quotes from this edition in *Secrets of the British Museum,* indicating it was held in the Private Case (P.C.27.a.19) in the 1960s, but it does not appear in Kearney's bibliography so had been reassigned by 1980. The two other copies (Cup.804.p.41 and 43) bear the bookplate of J. B. Rund, a collector who made a donation of erotic books in the later twentieth century (Patrick J. Kearney, *The Private Case: An Annotated Bibliography of the Private Case Erotica Collection in the British (Museum) Library* [London: Jay Landesman Limited, 1981], 65).

37. Examples of suppressed passages appear in *Philosophy of Pleasure* (1885), 275, 278; on Garrick, 214, 231–232.

38. Colligan, "Marcus's Sources," 494.

39. Price, *Anthology,* 11.

40. Hal Gladfelder, *Fanny Hill in Bombay: The Making and Unmaking of John Cleland* (Baltimore: Johns Hopkins University Press, 2012), 80–82. To attest to the difficulty of studying these rare editions: today the 1749 edition is held at only four research libraries, the illustrated 1766 at two. In the copy of the 1766 edition held at the BL, an apparent error in binding interrupts the sodomy scene (116–117) with illustrations

from another scene (Louisa and Dick, 125–126). It's unclear whether this was done on purpose, to disperse the objectional sodomitical content, or was a coincidental error.

41. "Waiter" refers to a dumbwaiter when Dugdale is updating the prose, and "buckle" was by then an antiquated term for curled hair. See "waiter, n. (IV.10)" and "buckle, n. (3)," *OED Online* (December 2021). Oxford University Press (accessed 3 January 2022).

42. John Cleland, *Memoirs of Fanny Hill* (London, 1750), 47, BL shelfmark C.133.a.9; and John Cleland, *Memoirs of the Life of the Celebrated Miss Fanny Hill*, ed. William Dugdale (H. Smith pseudonym) (London, 1841), BL shelfmark Cup.805.b.1. Hereafter parenthetical citations are marked *M* for the 1750 edition and *L* for the 1841.

43. The tradition of seeing women as objects of an ostensible masculine gaze originates with Laura Mulvey's "Visual Pleasure and Narrative Cinema," *Screen* 16 (1975): 6–18, which informs the critique of pornography's objectification of women made famous by Andrea Dworkin; see *Pornography: Men Possessing Women* (New York: E.P. Dutton, 1989).

44. Ashbee, *CLT*, 60–61. Ashbee worked from Reddie's manuscript notes, especially eighteenth-century editions, which is how the erroneous 1769 date for *Human Heart* originates.

45. Ashbee, *CLT*, 64.

46. Colette Colligan, "'A Race of Born Pederasts': Sir Richard Burton, Homosexuality, and the Arabs," *Nineteenth-Century Contexts* 25, no. 1 (2003): 1–20; Bull, "Reading, Writing," 240–241.

47. Ashbee, *CLT*, 62, 69–70, 64.

48. Attributions to Rochester have been studied and corrected by David Vieth, *Attribution in Restoration Poetry: A Study of Rochester's Poems of 1680* (New Haven: Yale University Press, 1963) and Harold Love, ed., *The Works of John Wilmot, Earl of Rochester* (Oxford: Oxford University Press, 1999).

49. *The Singular Life, Amatory Adventures, and Extraordinary Intrigues of John Wilmot, Earl of Rochester*, ed. H. Smith [William Dugdale] (London, 1860). BL shelfmark P.C.31.f.24.

50. Nicholas Fisher, "A Surprise Appearance by the Earl of Rochester in Nineteenth-Century New York," *Princeton University Library Chronicle* 72, no. 2 (2011): 569–573, at 571. Fisher located an 1831 New York imprint of Dugdale's text, less obscenely illustrated, in Princeton's collection and notes that it "marks the low watermark of Rochester's reputation" (572).

51. Williams, *Hard Core*, 72, 133–132.

52. Sharon Marcus, *Between Women: Friendship, Desire, and Marriage in Victorian England* (Princeton: Princeton University Press, 2007), 112.

53. Claire Jarvis, *Exquisite Masochism: Marriage, Sex, and the Novel Form* (Baltimore: Johns Hopkins University Press, 2016), 7, 11, 95.

54. Fredric Jameson, *The Antinomies of Realism* (London: Verso, 2013), 26.

55. Stephen Marcus, *The Other Victorians*, 268, 269.

56. Sharon Marcus, *Between Women*, 66–68.

57. Arondekar, *For the Record*, 102.

58. See Mendes, *Clandestine Erotic Fiction*, 3–4.

59. *The Adventures of . . . a Lady's Maid!* (London, c. 1838), British Library shelfmark RG.2000.a.2, bears a false imprint of 1822 and was published by Dugdale's brother John Dugdale (J. Ryder pseudonym) (Ashbee, *CLT,* 279). *The Inutility of Virtue* (London, c. 1830) was published by John Benjamin Brookes, again in 1860 by William Dugdale (Ashbee, *CLT,* 132), and in 1880 by the "Society of Vice," probably William Lazenby (British Library P.C.17.b29). Hereafter parenthetical references are to the 1838 *Lady's Maid* and the 1880 *Inutility*.

60. For another example of incestuous rape tied to a young woman's voraciousness, see *My Grandmother's Tale*, serialized in *The Pearl* (London, 1879–1881), issues 11 to 18. Partially set on a West Indian plantation, this narrative contrasts the heroine's sexual subjectivity with the forced sexual labor of enslaved women.

61. See also *Lady's Maid*, 74–76, where Louisa declines a financial arrangement that strikes her as prostitution but enjoys sexual intercourse itself.

62. On the India rubber dildo as a barometer of modernity and globalization in pornography, see Arondekar, *For the Record*, chap. 3. For my purposes here, it's worth noting that, unlike its glass or ivory counterparts, it "sets forth a different order of mimesis. . . . Its resemblance to a penis lies not in that it *looks* like a 'prick,' but in that it *feels* like one" (ibid., 100).

63. Ibid.

64. Ashbee, *CLT,* 179.

65. Sigel, *Governing Pleasures*, 68.

66. Patrick Brantlinger, "Terrible Turks: Victorian Xenophobia and the Ottoman Empire," in *Fear, Loathing, and Victorian Xenophobia*, eds. Marlene Tromp, Maria K. Bachman, and Heidi Kaufman (Columbus: Ohio State University Press, 2013), 208–230. Brantlinger points out this xenophobia overlaps with increasing British support of Ottoman imperial interests in the period.

67. Arondekar, *For the Record*, 105–106. An inverse of this imperial pornography is exemplified by the photographs of half-clothed Algerian women that circulated among European men in this period; see Malek Alloula, *The Colonial Harem*, trans. Myrna Godzich and Wlad Godzich (Minneapolis: University of Minnesota Press, 1986).

68. Anne McClintock, *Imperial Leather: Race, Gender, and Sexuality in the Colonial Conquest* (New York: Routledge, 1995), 23.

69. Danielle Bobker, *The Closet: The Eighteenth-Century Architecture of Intimacy* (Princeton: Princeton University Press, 2020), 68.

70. *The Lustful Turk* (Ware: Wordsworth Classic Erotica, 1997), 70; originally published by Brookes in 1828, again by Dugdale in the 1860s, and regularly throughout the early twentieth century (*CLT,* 134–136). Hereafter parenthetical references are to the 1997 edition.

71. *Seraglio Scenes* (London, 1841), 15. Hereafter parenthetical references are to this edition by Dugdale (British Library shelfmark RG.2013.a.5), a reprint of the 1830s original published by Brookes (Mendes, *Clandestine Erotic Fiction*, 429).

72. Brantlinger, "Terrible Turks," 213.

73. Arondekar, *For the Record*, 111.

74. Matt Cook, *London and the Culture of Homosexuality, 1885–1914* (Cambridge, UK: Cambridge University Press, 2003), 20. Both novels were originally published by Lazenby.

75. "Introduction," in *Sins of the Cities of the Plain*, ed. Wolfram Setz (Kansas City: Valancourt, 2013), viii–ix. On the sodomy trials, see Cook, *Culture of Homosexuality*; and Morris B. Kaplan, *Sodom on the Thames: Sex, Love, and Scandal in Wilde Times* (Ithaca: Cornell University Press, 2005).

76. Kaplan, *Sodom on Thames*, 223, 100.

77. Anne Delgado, "Scandals in Sodom: The Victorian City's Queer Streets," *Studies in the Literary Imagination* 40, no. 1 (2007): 21–34, at 27.

78. For another account that emphasizes the continuity of queer and straight Victorian pornography—or, that more to the point argues the distinction is a false one—see Simon Joyce, "Past, Present, and Pornography," *Victorian Studies* 50, no. 3 (2017): 466–476, at 472–474.

79. Lisa Hager, "A Case for a Trans Studies Turn in Victorian Studies: 'Female Husbands' of the Nineteenth Century," *Victorian Review* 44, no.1 (2019): 37–54. Hager warns against effacing the specificity of transgender by subsuming it under the rubric of queerness (40). Still, I call this pornography "queer" because it does not exclusively focus on experience we today we would call trans—rather, I see *Cities of the Plain* and *Laura and Eveline* attempting to catalogue as many non-normative sex acts as they can. "Queer" reflects this variety.

80. These suspensions seem to enact "transing" as a verb, as Jen Manion in *Female Husbands: A Trans History* (Cambridge, UK: Cambridge University Press, 2020), 11.

81. Emma Heaney shows, in the historical documents on Boulton and Park, a "vernacular trans femininity" that affiliated trans and cis women; see *The New Woman: Literary Modernism, Queer Theory, and the Trans Feminine Allegory* (Evanston: Northwestern University Press, 2017), 164.

82. *Letters from Laura and Eveline, Giving an Account of their Mock-Marriage, Wedding Trip, Etc.* (1883) (London: Privately Printed, 1903). I reference the later "privately printed" edition held at the British Library (P.C.13.c.11). Recently Valancourt published an edition by Justin O'Hearn.

83. For other conflations of penis and clitoris, anus and vagina, see *Laura and Eveline*, 72, 82, 97, 117, 119; the character Eveline also describes the body in these terms.

84. See also *Laura and Eveline*, 91–94.

85. For Judith Butler's famous account of parody's capacity to destabilize gender, see *Gender Trouble: Feminism and the Subversion of Identity* (New York: Routledge, 1990), 181–190.

86. Laura Helen Marks, *Alice in Pornoland: Hardcore Encounters with the Victorian* (Urbana: University of Illinois Press, 2018), 19–22.

Chapter 4

1. Compare *The History of the Human Heart* (London, 1749), 182–183; *Memoirs of a Man of Pleasure* in *The Exquisite*, ed. William Dugdale, Vol. 3 (London, 1844), 190; and *The History of the Human Heart*, ed. James Graham (New York: Award Books, 1968), 121.

2. Cover art was sensationalized post-war when changes in the market for pulp led to declining sales. See Lisa K. Speer, "Paperback Pornography: Mass Market Novels and Censorship in Post-War America," *Journal of American and Comparative Cultures* 24, nos. 3–4 (2001): 153–160, at 154.

3. "Editor's Foreword," in *Memoirs of a Man of Pleasure* (London: Tandem, 1968), 5–6. These editions, other than cover art, are identical. By the 1960s, some publishers were trying to chasten their books through text-only covers, so the choice to feature racy photographs was a conscious one designed to draw an erotically curious, probably heteromasculine, reader (Paula Rabinowitz, *American Pulp: How Paperbacks Brought Modernism to Main Street* [Princeton: Princeton University Press, 2014], on covers 275–276, on heteronormative cover art, 191–194).

4. Rabinowitz, *American Pulp*, 46, 81.

5. Parenthetical references compare the American version of *Memoirs of a Man of Pleasure*, ed. James Graham (pseudonym) (New York: Award Books, 1968), abbreviated *G*, with this edition's source text, Dugdale's 1844 *Exquisite*, abbreviated *E*, and occasionally the original 1749 edition, abbreviated *H*.

6. On pornographic pulp that resists conventional heterosexuality, see Whitney Strub, "Lavender, Menaced: Lesbianism, Obscenity Law, and the Feminist Antipornography Movement," *Journal of Women's History* 22, no. 2 (2010): 83–107; Rabinowitz, chap. 7 of *American Pulp* on "Uncovering Lesbian Pulp"; B. Astrid Daley and Adam Parfrey, eds., *Sin-a-Rama: Sleaze Sex Paperbacks of the Sixties*, expanded edition (Port Townsend: Feral House, 2016).

7. Whitney Strub, "Historicizing Pulp: Gay Male Pulp and the Narrativization of Queer Cultural History," in *1960s Gay Pulp Fiction: The Misplaced Heritage*, eds. Drewey Wayne Gunn and Jaime Harker (Amherst: University of Massachusetts Press, 2013), 62–63.

8. Martha Weinman Lear, "What Do These Women Want? The Second Feminist Wave," *New York Times Magazine* (10 March 1968).

9. I speculate on Fryer's authorship advisedly, keeping in mind Vareschi's argument that anonymity and pseudonymity can wield meaning and action of their own. Mark Vareschi, *Everywhere and Nowhere: Anonymity and Mediation in Eighteenth-Century Britain* (Minneapolis: University of Minnesota Press, 2018), 14–19. Fryer presents a special case where his political rhetoric is so pointedly at odds with his editorial practice—unconsciously so—that it bears identifying him as a single actor.

10. For Fryer's account of requesting and accessing materials, see *Secrets of the British Museum* (New York: Citadel, 1968), 29–33, 125–138.

11. Ibid., 80.

12. Graham's other Tandem titles include *The Homosexual Kings of England* (1968) and *A History of Morals* (1966). The British Library catalogue identifies him as James Kenneth Graham-Murray.

13. Peter Fryer, "Introduction," *Venus Unmasked, or an Inquiry into the Nature and Origin of the Passion of Love*, eds. Leonard de Vries and Peter Fryer (New York: Stein and Day, 1967), 13.

14. Peter Fryer, *Forbidden Books of the Victorians: Henry Spencer Ashbee's Bibliographies* (London: Odyssey Press, 1970), 15; *Man of Pleasure's Companion: A Nineteenth Century Anthology of Amorous Entertainment* (London: Arthur Barker Limited, 1968), 13; *Venus Unmasked*, 7; *The Gentleman's Relish; or the Buyer's Guide to Young Ladies* (London: Tandem, 1968), 6. Patrick Kearney's bibliography of Fryer's work shows an abiding interest in historical sexual writing; see *A Catalogue of the Books and Journalism of Peter Fryer* (Santa Rosa: Scissors and Paste Bibliographies, 2019): http://www.scissors-and-paste.net/pdf/Peter_Fryer.pdf.

15. Fryer, *Venus Unmasked*, 12.

16. Peter Fryer, *Hungarian Tragedy* (London: Dennis Dobson, 1956) and *Staying Power: The History of Black People in Britain* (London: Pluto, 1984).

17. Fryer, *Staying Power*, 172–210.

18. Peter Fryer, *The Birth Controllers* (London: Secker and Warburg, 1965), 11, 12, 269.

19 Fryer, *Secrets*, 41.

20. Ibid., 71.

21. Fryer, *Staying Power*, 215, 221–225.

22. Fryer, *Secrets*, 46.

23. Patrick J. Kearney, *The Private Case: An Annotated Bibliography of the Private Case Erotica Collection in the British (Museum) Library* (London: Jay Landesman Limited, 1981), 61.

24. Fryer, *Man of Pleasure's Companion*, 14.

25. Fryer, *Venus Unmasked*, 7–8.

26. Lillian B. Rubin, contribution to "1968: Lessons Learned," *Dissent* 55, no. 2 (2008): 5–25, at 21.

27. Nancy Biberman, "Children of the New Age," in *A Time to Stir: Columbia '68*, ed. Paul Cronin (New York: Columbia University Press, 2018), 2–3.

28. Stephen Marcus, *The Other Victorians: A Study of Sexuality and Pornography in Mid-Nineteenth-Century England* (New York: Norton, 1964), 263.

29. Colette Colligan, "Marcus's Sources: Archives, Canons, Texts," *Victorian Studies* 59, no. 3 (2017): 490–505, at 490, 496.

30. Simon Joyce, "Past, Present, and Pornography," *Victorian Studies* 50, no. 3 (2017): 466–476, at 472.

31. Marcus, *The Other Victorians*, 160, 269, 272, 286.

32. Loren Glass, *Rebel Publisher: Grove Press and the Revolution of the Word* (New York: Penguin, 2018), 139-140, 123; Amy Wyngaard, "Translating Sade: The Grove Press Editions, 1953-1968," *Romanic Review* 104, nos. 3-4 (2013): 313-331, at 314.

33. Wyngaard, "Translating Sade," 323.

34. Hal Gladfelder, "'By the Author of Fanny Hill': Selling John Cleland," *Eighteenth-Century Life* 43, no. 2 (2019): 46-47.

35. Wyngaard, "Translating Sade," 328.

36. Glass, *Rebel Publisher*, 142-143; on profits, 193.

37. Wyngaard, "The End of Pornography: The Story of *Story of O*," *MLN* 130, no. 4 (2015): 980-997, at 986.

38. Ibid., 990.

39. Glass, *Rebel Publisher*, 195-207; Carolyn Bronstein, *Battling Pornography: The American Feminist Anti-Pornography Movement, 1976-1986* (Cambridge, UK: Cambridge University Press, 2011), 78.

40. Glass, *Rebel Publisher*, 209-215.

41. Susan Brownmiller, *Against Our Will: Men, Women, and Rape* (New York: Simon & Schuster, 1975), 394.

42 Frances Ferguson, *Pornography, the Theory: What Utilitarianism Did to Action* (Chicago: University of Chicago Press, 2004), 11.

43. Ibid. Emphasis in original.

44. Linda Lovelace, *Ordeal* (Secaucus: Citadel Press, 1980). On pornography within 1970s popular culture, see Whitney Strub and Carolyn Bronstein, "Introduction," in *Porno Chic and the Sex Wars: American Sexual Representation in the 1970s*, eds. Carolyn Bronstein and Whitney Strub (Amherst: University of Massachusetts Press, 2016), 1-23.

45 See Bronstein, *Battling Pornography*, esp. 6-11, 62.

46. Finn Enke, "Collective Memory and the Transfeminist 1970s: Toward a Less Plausible History," *Transgender Studies Quarterly* 5, no. 1 (2018): 9-29, at 10, 12.

47. Bronstein, *Battling Pornography*, 44-47.

48. Kate Millett, *Sexual Politics* (New York: Avon Books, 1969), 44.

49. Brownmiller, *Against Our Will*, 13.

50. Shulamith Firestone, *The Dialectic of Sex: The Case for Feminist Revolution* (New York: Farrar, Straus, and Giroux, 1970), 179-182.

51. Frances Ferguson, "Rape and the Rise of the Novel," *Representations* 20 (1987): 88-112, at 93.

52. Brownmiller, *Against Our Will*, 15. Emphasis in original. On eighteenth-century conjectural history's intersection with sexual violence, see Stephanie Insley Hershinow, *Born Yesterday: Inexperience and the Early Realist Novel* (Baltimore: Johns Hopkins University Press, 2019), 33-58. On the long reach of conjectural history, see Frank Palmieri, *State of Nature, Stages of Society: Enlightenment Conjectural History and Modern Social Discourse* (New York: Columbia University Press, 2016).

53. Chandra Talpade Mohanty, *Feminism Without Borders: Decolonizing Theory, Practicing Solidarity* (Durham: Duke University Press, 2003), 24.

54. Carole Pateman, *The Sexual Contract* (Stanford: Stanford University Press, 1988), 15.

55. Andrea Dworkin, *Pornography: Men Possessing Women* (New York: E.P. Dutton, 1989), 199.

56. Lisa Sigel, "Looking at Sex: Pornography and Erotica Since 1750," in *The Routledge History of Sex and the Body, 1500 to the Present*, eds. Sarah Toulalan and Kate Fisher (London: Routledge, 2013), 233.

57. Jennifer Nash, *The Black Body in Ecstasy: Reading Race, Reading Pornography* (Durham: Duke University Press, 2014), 7.

58. See Enke, "Collective Memory," 11–24; also C. Riley Snorton, *Black on Both Sides: A Racial History of Trans Identity* (Minneapolis: University of Minnesota Press, 2017), 5–11.

59. Emi Koyama, "Whose Feminism Is It Anyway? The Unspoken Racism of the Trans Inclusion Debate," *Sociological Review Monographs* 68, no. 4 (2020): 735–744, at 738.

60. See Emma Heaney, "Women-Identified Women," *Transgender Studies Quarterly* 3, nos. 1–2 (2016): 137–145.

61. Angela Y. Davis, *Women, Race, and Class* (New York: Vintage, 1981), 198; see also Bronstein, *Battling Pornography*, 56. Examples of the subordination of race to gender include Millett's claim that "sexism may be more endemic in our society than racism" (*Sexual Politics*, 39); Firestone's statement that "racism is sexism extended" (*Dialectic of Sex*, 97); and Brownmiller's belief that the discrediting of white women's rape accusations against Black men was a strategy through which the New Left distanced itself from the history of lynching (*Against Our Will*, 228–238, 253–254).

62. Davis, *Women, Race, and Class*, 183.

63. "The Combahee River Collective Statement," in *How We Get Free: Black Feminism and the Combahee River Collective*, ed. Keeanga-Yamahtta Taylor (Chicago: Haymarket Books, 2017), 18. As Taylor writes, "Black women could not quantify their oppression only in terms of sexism or racism, or of homophobia experienced by Black lesbians. They were not ever a single category" (4). On trans women's work toward this end, see *Screaming Queens: The Riot at Compton's Cafeteria*, directed by Susan Stryker and Victor Silverman (San Francisco: Frameline, 2005).

64. Keeanga-Yamahtta Taylor, "Black Feminism and the Combahee River Collective," *Monthly Review* 7, no. 8 (1 January 2019): https://monthlyreview.org/2019/01/01/black-feminism-and-the-combahee-river-collective/; Bronstein, *Battling Pornography*, 228–229, 236.

65. Bronstein, *Battling Pornography*, 220–224.

66. Ferguson, *Pornography, the Theory*, 14.

67. Brownmiller, *Against Our Will*, 378.

68. Susanna Paasonen, "Between Meaning and Mattering: On Affect and Porn Studies," *Porn Studies* 1, nos. 1–2 (2014): 136–142, at 140.

69. Ibid., 138.

70. Eve Sedgwick, *Touching Feeling: Affect, Pedagogy, Performativity* (Durham: Duke University Press, 2003), 130–150.

71 Angela Carter, *The Sadeian Woman: An Exercise in Cultural History* (London: Virago, 1979), 21.

72. Ibid., 19–22.

73. Ibid., 17.

74. Audre Lorde, "Uses of the Erotic" (1978), in *Sister Outsider* (Berkeley: Crossing Press, 2007), 57, 56.

75. Anne Koedt, "The Myth of the Vaginal Orgasm," in *"Takin' It to the Streets": A Sixties Reader*, eds. Alexander Bloom and Wini Breines (New York: Oxford University Press, 2003), 423, 424, 428.

76. Firestone, *Dialectic of Sex*, 139.

77. Tim Dean, *Unlimited Intimacy: Reflections on the Subculture of Barebacking* (Chicago: University of Chicago Press, 2009), 105.

78. Brownmiller attributes this term to Barbara Mehrhof; *Against Our Will*, 334.

79. Emma Heaney, *The New Woman: Literary Modernism, Queer Theory, and the Trans Feminine Allegory* (Evanston: Northwestern University Press, 2017), 196.

80. Sophie Lewis, *Full Surrogacy Now: Feminism Against Family* (London: Verso, 2019), 81.

81. Nash, *Black Body*, 11, 10, 151.

82. Mireille Miller-Young, *A Taste for Brown Sugar: Black Woman in Pornography* (Durham: Duke University Press, 2014), 15–16, 8.

83 Eugenie Brinkema, "Rough Archive," in *Porn Archives*, eds. Tim Dean, Steven Ruszczycky, and David Squires (Durham: Duke University Press, 2014), 279.

84. Ibid.

85. Ibid., 278.

86. Erin Spampinato, "Rereading Rape in the Critical Canon: Adjudicative Criticism and the Capacious Conception of Rape," *Differences* 32, no. 2 (2021): 122–160, at 142.

87. Ferguson, *Pornography, the Theory*, 25–26.

88. Dworkin, *Pornography*, 30–47 (on her book's impounding, see Bronstein, *Battling Pornography*, 330); Brownmiller, *Against Our Will*, 343–346; Millett, *Sexual Politics*, 46.

89. Samuel Delany, *Times Square Red, Times Square Blue* (New York: NYU Press, 1999), 79.

90. A "counterpublic maintains ... an awareness of its subordinate status.... The discourse that constitutes it is not merely a different or alternative idiom but one that in other contexts would be regarded with hostility or with a sense of indecorousness" (Michael Warner, *Publics and Counterpublics* [New York: Zone, 2005], 119).

91. Ferguson, *Pornography, the Theory*, 55, 35.
92. Nash, *Black Body*, 23.

Coda

1. Tim Dean, *Unlimited Intimacy: Reflections on the Subculture of Barebacking* (Chicago: University of Chicago Press, 2009), 105.
2. Bernadette Barton, *The Pornification of America: How Raunch Culture Is Ruining Our Society* (New York: NYU Press, 2021), 59.
3. Heather Berg, *Porn Work: Sex, Labor, and Late Capitalism* (Chapel Hill: University of North Carolina Press, 2021), 16. This vast supply entails risk: The free site Pornhub recently restricted its uploading feature to curb content containing minors. See Nicholas Kristof, "The Children of Pornhub," *New York Times* (4 December 2020): https://www.nytimes.com/2020/12/04/opinion/sunday/pornhub-rape-trafficking.html; and Jacob Kastrenakes, "Pornhub Just Removed Most of Its Videos," *The Verge* (14 December 2020): https://www.theverge.com/2020/12/14/22173858/pornhub-videos-removed-user-uploaded-visa-mastercard-verified.
4. Mireille Miller-Young, *A Taste for Brown Sugar: Black Woman in Pornography* (Durham: Duke University Press, 2014), chap. 5; see also Mireille Miller-Young, "This Is What Porn Can Be Like! A Conversation with Shine Louise Houston," in *Porn Archives*, eds. Tim Dean, Steven Ruszczycky, and David Squires (Durham: Duke University Press, 2014).
5. Korra Del Rio as told to Sophie Pezzutto, "Professionalism, Pay, and the Production of Pleasure in Trans Porn," *Transgender Studies Quarterly* 7, no. 2 (2020): 262–267, at 263; see also Berg, *Porn Work*, 15–16.
6. Del Rio and Pezzutto, "Professionalism," 262, 264. On the need for continued resistance against transmisogyny in the pornography industry, see Angela Jones, "Cumming to a Screen Near You: Transmasculine and Non-Binary People in the Camming Industry," *Porn Studies* 8 no. 2 (2021): 239–254: https://doi.org/10.1080/23268743.2020.1757498. Jones argues, "The invisibility of sex-positive trans and non-binary sexualities in the mainstream means that, for now, porn industries can often be the only place where trans and non-binary folks can find empowering and ethical representations of their sexual desires, fantasies, and sex lives."
7. Berg, *Porn Work*, 8.
8. Melissa Gira Grant, *Playing the Whore: The Work of Sex Work* (London: Verso, 2014), 124. See also Melinda Chateauvert, *Sex Workers Unite: A History of the Movement from Stonewall to SlutWalk* (Boston: Beacon, 2013).
9. Berg, *Porn Work*, 184.
10. Melissa Gregg, *Counterproductive: Time Management in the Knowledge Economy* (Durham: Duke University Press, 2018), 116, 120, 109, 110, 122.
11. Sianne Ngai, *Our Aesthetic Categories: Zany, Cute, Interesting* (Cambridge, MA: Harvard University Press, 2012), 11.

12. Del Rio and Pezzutto, "Professionalism," 264.
13. Ngai, *Our Aesthetic Categories*, 183.
14. Berg, *Porn Work*, 184.
15. Gregg, *Counterproductive*, 99.
16. Berg, *Porn Work*, 29.
17. Gregg, *Counterproductive*, 126.

BIBLIOGRAPHY

Primary
Unless noted by a call number or shelfmark, seventeenth-century works were consulted through *Early English Books Online* (ProQuest) and eighteenth-century works through *Eighteenth Century Collections Online* (Gale).

The Adventures, Intrigues, and Amours, of a Lady's Maid! Written by Herself. Edited by John Dugdale (J. Ryder, pseudonym). London, c. 1838. British Library shelfmark RG.2000.a.2.
Aristotle's Master-Piece, or the Secrets of Generation Displayed. London, 1684.
Ashbee, Henry Spencer (Pisanus Fraxi, pseudonym). *Centuria Librorum Absconditorum: being notes bio-biblio-icono-graphical and critical, on curious and uncommon books.* London, 1879. British Library shelfmark P.C.14.de.4.
Ashbee, Henry Spencer. *The Encyclopedia of Erotic Literature.* 3 vols. New York: Documentary Books, 1962. Reprint of (Pisanus Fraxi, pseudonym) *Index Librorum Prohibitorum* (1877), *Centuria Librorum Absconditorum* (1879), and *Catena Librorum Tacendorum* (1885).
Barchas, Janine, ed. *The Annotations in Lady Bradshaigh's Copy of "Clarissa."* Victoria: University of Victoria, 1998.
Characters of the Present Most Celebrated Courtezans. London, 1780.
The Child of Nature, Improved by Chance. A Philosophical Novel. London, 1774. Beinecke Library call number Im H369 774.
Cleland, John. *Memoirs of a Coxcomb.* London, 1751. British Library shelfmark 12611.e.13.
———. *Memoirs of a Coxcomb* (Rochester Series of Reprints). London, 1885. British Library shelfmark 12611.b.28.
———. *Memoirs of Fanny Hill.* London, 1750. British Library shelfmark C.133.a.9.
———. *Memoirs of the Life of the Celebrated Miss Fanny Hill.* Edited by William Dugdale (H. Smith, pseudonym). London, 1841. British Library shelfmark Cup.805.b.1.
———. *Memoirs of a Woman of Pleasure.* Edited by Peter Sabor. Oxford: Oxford University Press, 1999.
———, trans. *The True History and Adventures of Catharine Vizzani.* London, 1755.
A Continuation of Mr. F———'s Adventures, Being the Second Part of The Spy on Mother Midnight. London, 1748.

Defoe, Daniel. *Conjugal Lewdness; or, Matrimonial Whoredom* in *The Religious and Didactic Writings of Daniel Defoe*, Vol. 5. Edited by Liz Bellamy. London: Pickering and Chatto, 2006.

Dildoides. In *Eighteenth-Century British Erotica II*, Vol. 2. Edited by Deborah Needleman Armintor. London: Pickering and Chatto, 2004.

Dugdale, William, ed. *The Child of Nature, Improved by Chance, or, The History of a Young Lady of Luxurious Temperament and Prurient Imagination, Who Experiences Repeatedly the Dangers of Seduction*. New York, 1849. Princeton University Library Special Collections call no. 2010-0007N.

——— (H. Smith, pseudonym), ed. *The Exquisite: A Collection of Tales, Histories and Essays, Funny, Fanciful and Facetious, Interspersed with Anecdotes ... Illustrated with Numerous Engravings*. 3 vols. London, 1842–1844. Volume 1 Beinecke Library call number 2007 +14; Volumes 1–3 British Library shelfmark P.C.20.b.1-3.

——— (H. Smith, pseudonym), ed. *Memoirs of the Life of the Celebrated Miss Fanny Hill*. London, 1841. British Library shelfmark Cup.805.b.1.

——— (H. Smith, pseudonym), ed. *The Singular Life, Amatory Adventures, and Extraordinary Intrigues of John Wilmot, Earl of Rochester*. London, 1860. British Library shelfmark P.C.31.f.24.

Fielding, Henry. *The Female Husband*. In *When Flesh Becomes Word: An Anthology of Eighteenth-Century Libertine Literature*. Edited by Bradford Mudge. New York: Oxford University Press, 2004.

Fryer, Peter. *The Birth Controllers*. London: Secker and Warburg, 1965.

———. *Forbidden Books of the Victorians: Henry Spencer Ashbee's Bibliographies*. London: Odyssey Press, 1970.

———. *Hungarian Tragedy*. London: Dennis Dobson, 1956.

———. *The Man of Pleasure's Companion: A Nineteenth Century Anthology of Amorous Entertainment*. London: Arthur Barker Limited, 1968.

———. *Secrets of the British Museum*. New York: Citadel, 1968.

———. *Staying Power: The History of Black People in Britain*. London: Pluto, 1984.

Fryer, Peter (James Graham, pseudonym). *The Gentleman's Relish; or the Buyer's Guide to Young Ladies*. London: Tandem, 1968.

———. *A History of Morals*. London: Tandem, 1966.

———. *The Homosexual Kings of England*. London: Tandem, 1968.

———. *Memoirs of a Man of Pleasure*. New York: Award Books, 1968.

———. *Memoirs of a Man of Pleasure*. London: Tandem, 1968. British Library shelfmark H.68/795.

Fryer, Peter, and Leonard de Vries, eds. *Venus Unmasked, or an Inquiry into the Nature and Origin of the Passion of Love*. New York: Stein and Day, 1967.

Haywood, Eliza. *Anti-Pamela and Shamela*. Edited by Catherine Ingrassia. Peterborough: Broadview, 2004.

———. *Fantomina and Other Writings*. Edited by Alexander Pettit, Margaret Case Croskery, and Anna C. Patchias. Peterborough: Broadview, 2004.

The History of the Human Heart. London, 1749. British Library shelfmark Cup.702 .t.14.(1.).
The History of the Human Heart (Rochester Series of Reprints). London, 1885. British Library Shelfmark Cup.804.p.41.
The Inutility of Virtue (c. 1830). Edited by William Lazenby ("Society of Vice"). London, 1880. British Library shelfmark P.C.17.b29.
Letters from Laura and Eveline, Giving an Account of their Mock-Marriage, Wedding Trip, Etc. (1883). London: Privately Printed, 1903. British Library shelfmark P.C.13.c.11.
Letters from Laura and Eveline. Edited by Justin O'Hearn. Kansas City: Valancourt, 2015.
The Lustful Turk (1828). Ware: Wordsworth Classic Erotica, 1997.
Mandeville, Bernard. *A Modest Defence of Publick Stews*. London, 1724.
Memoirs of B—— Tracey. London, 1757. British Library shelfmark 1607.4343.
Memoirs of the Celebrated Miss Fanny M——. 2nd edition. London, 1759.
Monsieur Thing's Origin. London, 1722.
Mudge, Bradford, ed. *Sex and Sexuality, 1640–1940: Literary, Medical, and Sociological Perspectives*, Part 3. Marlborough: Adam Matthew Publications, 2002.
———, ed. *When Flesh Becomes Word: An Anthology of Eighteenth-Century Libertine Literature*. New York: Oxford University Press, 2004.
Payne Knight, Richard. *An Account of the Remains of the Worship of Priapus*. London, 1786. Lewis Walpole Library call number 49 2404.
The Pearl: Erotica from the Underground Magazine of Victorian England. New York: Ballantine, 1968.
The Philosophy of Pleasure; or, The History of a Young Lady (Rochester Series of Reprints). London, 1885. British Library shelfmark X.907/7532.
The Progress of Nature: Exemplify'd in the Life and Surprizing Adventures of Roger Lovejoy, Esq. London, 1744. British Library shelfmark Cup.702.t.14.(2.).
Reddie, James Campbell. *Five Letters from James Campbell Reddie to Henry Spencer Ashbee*. Edited by Patrick J. Kearney. Santa Rosa: Scissors and Paste Bibliographies, 2019. http://scissors-and-paste.net/pdf/Reddie_Letters.pdf.
Richardson, Samuel. *Clarissa*. Edited by Angus Ross. New York: Penguin, 1985.
———. *Pamela*. Edited by Tom Keymer and Alice Wakely. New York: Oxford University Press, 2001.
Satan's Harvest Home. London, 1749.
Seraglio Scenes; or Such Things Are. An Amorous Tale (1830). London, 1841. British Library shelfmark RG.2013.a.5.
Sins of the Cities of the Plain (1881). Edited by Wolfram Setz. Kansas City: Valancourt, 2013.
A Spy on Mother Midnight: or, the Templar Metamorphos'd. London, 1748.
Tractatus de Hermaphroditis: or, A Treatise of Hermaphrodites (1718). Reprinted in *Eighteenth-Century British Erotica I*, Vol. 2. Edited by Alexander Pettit and Patrick Spedding. London: Pickering and Chatto, 2002.

Ward, Ned. "Of the Mollies Club" (1708). In *Homosexuality in Eighteenth-Century England: A Sourcebook*. Edited by Rictor Norton. http://www.rictornorton.co.uk/eighteen/nedward.htm.

Wilmot, John. *The Poetical Works of the Earls of Rochester, Roscommon, and Dorset*. London, 1757. British Library shelfmark 1508/1661.

———. *Selected Poetical Works of the Earls of Rochester, Roscommon, and Dorset* (Rochester Series of Reprints). London, 1884. British Library shelfmark Cup .800.i.3.

———. *The Works of John Wilmot, Earl of Rochester*. Edited by Harold Love. Oxford: Oxford University Press, 1999.

The Woman of Colour: A Tale (1808). Edited by Lyndon Dominique. Peterborough: Broadview, 2008.

Secondary

Abelove, Henry. *Deep Gossip*. Minneapolis: University of Minnesota Press, 2005.

———. "Some Speculations on the History of Sexual Intercourse During the Long Eighteenth Century in England," *Genders* 6 (1989): 125–130.

Agin, Shane. "Sex Education in the Enlightened Nation." *Studies in Eighteenth-Century Culture* 37 (2008): 67–87.

Alloula, Malek. *The Colonial Harem*. Translated by Myrna Godzich and Wlad Godzich. Minneapolis: University of Minnesota Press, 1986.

Andreadis, Harriette. *Sappho in Early Modern England: Female Same-Sex Literary Erotics, 1550–1714*. Chicago: University of Chicago Press, 2001.

Andrews, David. "Toward a More Valid Definition of 'Pornography.'" *Journal of Popular Culture* 45, no. 3 (2012): 457–477.

Armstrong, Nancy. *Desire and Domestic Fiction: A Political History of the Novel*. New York: Oxford University Press, 1987.

Arondekar, Anjali. *For the Record: On Sexuality and the Colonial Archive in India*. Durham: Duke University Press, 2009.

Backscheider, Paula. *Eighteenth-Century Women Poets and Their Poetry: Inventing Agency, Inventing Genre*. Baltimore: Johns Hopkins University Press, 2005.

Bakhtin, M.M. *The Dialogic Imagination: Four Essays*. Translated by Caryl Emerson and Michael Holquist. Austin: University of Texas Press, 1981.

Bannet, Eve Tavor. *The Domestic Revolution: Enlightenment Feminisms and the Novel*. Baltimore: Johns Hopkins University Press, 2000.

Barton, Bernadette. *The Pornification of America: How Raunch Culture Is Ruining Our Society*. New York: NYU Press, 2021.

Bauer, Nancy. *How to Do Things with Pornography*. Cambridge, MA: Harvard University Press, 2015.

Benedict, Leah. "Impotence Made Public: Reading Sex on the Stage and in the Courtroom." *ELH* 85, no. 2 (2018): 441–469.

Berg, Heather. *Porn Work: Sex, Labor, and Late Capitalism.* Chapel Hill: University of North Carolina Press, 2021.
Berlant, Lauren, and Michael Warner. "Sex in Public." In *Publics and Counterpublics.* By Michael Warner. New York: Zone, 2005.
Bersani, Leo. *Is the Rectum a Grave? and Other Essays.* Chicago: University of Chicago Press, 2010.
———. *Receptive Bodies.* Chicago: University of Chicago Press, 2018.
Best, Stephen and Sharon Marcus. "Surface Reading: An Introduction." *Representations* 108, no. 1 (2009): 1–21.
Biberman, Nancy. "Children of the New Age." In *A Time to Stir: Columbia '68.* Edited by Paul Cronin. New York: Columbia University Press, 2018.
Binhammer, Katherine. *The Seduction Narrative in Britain, 1747–1800.* Cambridge, UK: Cambridge University Press, 2009.
Bobker, Danielle. *The Closet: The Eighteenth-Century Architecture of Intimacy.* Princeton: Princeton University Press, 2020.
Bowers, Toni. *Force or Fraud: British Seduction Stories and the Problem of Resistance, 1660–1760.* Oxford: Oxford University Press, 2011.
Brantlinger, Patrick. "Terrible Turks: Victorian Xenophobia and the Ottoman Empire." In *Fear, Loathing, and Victorian Xenophobia.* Edited by Marlene Tromp, Maria K. Bachman, and Heidi Kaufman. Columbus: Ohio State University Press, 2013.
Bright, Jennifer Burns, and Ronan Crowley, "'A Quantity of Offensive Matter': Private Cases in Public Places." In *Porn Archives.* Edited by Tim Dean, Steven Ruszczycky, and David Squires. Durham: Duke University Press, 2014.
Brinkema, Eugenie. "Rough Archive." In *Porn Archives.* Edited by Tim Dean, Steven Ruszczycky, and David Squires. Durham: Duke University Press, 2014.
Bronstein, Carolyn. *Battling Pornography: The American Feminist Anti-Pornography Movement, 1976–1986.* Cambridge, UK: Cambridge University Press, 2011.
Bronstein, Carolyn, and Whitney Strub, eds. *Porno Chic and the Sex Wars: American Sexual Representation in the 1970s.* Amherst: University of Massachusetts Press, 2016.
Brown, Bill. "Thing Theory." *Critical Inquiry* 28, no. 1 (2001): 1–22.
Brownmiller, Susan. *Against Our Will: Men, Women, and Rape.* New York: Simon & Schuster, 1975.
Bull, Sarah. "Reading, Writing, and Publishing an Obscene Canon: The Archival Logic of the Secret Museum, c. 1860–c. 1900." *Book History* 20 (2017): 226–257.
Butler, Judith. *Gender Trouble: Feminism and the Subversion of Identity.* New York: Routledge, 1990.
Carter, Angela. *The Sadeian Woman: An Exercise in Cultural History.* London: Virago, 1979.
Carter, Sarah. "India and the Antiquarian Image: Richard Payne Knight's *A Discourse on the Worship of Priapus.*" *RACAR* 45, no. 1 (2020): 49–59.

Chateauvert, Melinda. *Sex Workers Unite: A History of the Movement from Stonewall to SlutWalk*. Boston: Beacon, 2013.
Chico, Tita. *Designing Women: The Dressing Room in Eighteenth-Century Literature and Culture*. Lewisburg: Bucknell University Press, 2005.
Chrisman-Campbell, Kimberly. *Fashion Victims: Dress at the Court of Louis XVI and Marie-Antoinette*. New Haven: Yale University Press, 2015.
Cohen, William. *Sex Scandal: The Private Parts of Victorian Fiction*. Durham: Duke University Press, 1996.
Colligan, Colette. "Digital Discovery and Fake Imprints: Unmasking Turn-of-the-Century Pornographers in Paris." *Book History* 22 (2019): 249–279.
———. "Marcus's Sources: Archives, Canons, Texts." *Victorian Studies* 59, no. 3 (2017): 490–505.
———. "'A Race of Born Pederasts': Sir Richard Burton, Homosexuality, and the Arabs." *Nineteenth-Century Contexts* 25, no. 1 (2003): 1–20.
Combahee River Collective. "The Combahee River Collective Statement." In *How We Get Free: Black Feminism and the Combahee River Collective*. Edited by Keeanga-Yamahtta Taylor. Chicago: Haymarket, 2017.
Cook, Matt. *London and the Culture of Homosexuality, 1885–1914*. Cambridge, UK: Cambridge University Press, 2003.
Cruickshank, Dan. *London's Sinful Secret: The Bawdy History and Very Public Passions of London's Georgian Age*. New York: St. Martin's, 2009.
Daley, B. Astrid, and Adam Parfrey, eds. *Sin-a-Rama: Sleaze Sex Paperbacks of the Sixties*, expanded edition. Port Townsend: Feral House, 2016.
Daniels, Stormy. *Full Disclosure*. New York: St. Martin's, 2018.
Darnton, Robert. *Forbidden Bestsellers of Pre-Revolutionary France*. New York: Norton, 1995.
———. "Sex for Thought." In *Sexualities in History*. Edited by Kim M. Phillips and Barry Reay. New York: Routledge, 2002.
Daston, Lorraine. "Speechless." In *Things That Talk: Object Lessons from Art and Science*. Edited by Lorraine Daston. New York: Zone, 2004.
Davis, Angela Y. *Women, Race, and Class*. New York: Vintage, 1981.
Dean, Tim. *Unlimited Intimacy: Reflections on the Subculture of Barebacking*. Chicago: University of Chicago Press, 2009.
Dean, Tim, Steven Ruszczycky, and David Squires, eds. *Porn Archives*. Durham: Duke University Press, 2014.
Delany, Samuel. *Times Square Red, Times Square Blue*. New York: NYU Press, 1999.
Delgado, Anne. "Scandals in Sodom: The Victorian City's Queer Streets." *Studies in the Literary Imagination* 40, no. 1 (2007): 21–34.
Del Rio, Korra, as told to Sophie Pezzutto. "Professionalism, Pay, and the Production of Pleasure in Trans Porn." *Transgender Studies Quarterly* 7, no. 2 (2020): 262–267.
Derrida, Jacques. "The Law of Genre." Translated by Avital Ronell. *Critical Inquiry* 7 (1980): 55–81.

Dickie, Simon. *Cruelty and Laughter: Forgotten Comic Literature and the Unsentimental Eighteenth Century*. Chicago: University of Chicago Press, 2011.
Dines, Gail. *Pornland: How Porn Has Hijacked Our Sexuality*. Boston: Beacon, 2010.
Domingo, Darryl. *The Rhetoric of Diversion in English Literature and Culture, 1690–1760*. Cambridge, UK: Cambridge University Press, 2016.
Donato, Clorinda, and Nicholas D. Nace, eds. "*Fanny Hill* Now." Special issue. *Eighteenth Century Life* 43, no. 2 (2019).
Drury, Joseph. *Novel Machines: Technology and Narrative Form in Enlightenment Britain*. Oxford: Oxford University Press, 2017.
Dworkin, Andrea. *Pornography: Men Possessing Women*. New York: E.P. Dutton, 1989.
Earnshaw, Steven. *The Pub in Literature: England's Altered State*. Manchester: Manchester University Press, 2000.
Eger, Elizabeth. *Bluestockings: Women of Reason from Enlightenment to Romanticism*. Houndsmills: Palgrave Macmillan, 2010.
Enke, Finn. "Collective Memory and the Transfeminist 1970s: Toward a Less Plausible History." *Transgender Studies Quarterly* 5, no. 1 (2018): 9–29.
Farr, Jason. "Libertine Sexuality and Queer-Crip Embodiment in Eighteenth-Century Britain." *Journal for Early Modern Cultural Studies* 16, no. 4 (2016): 96–118.
———. *Novel Bodies: Disability and Heterosexuality in Eighteenth-Century British Literature*. Lewisburg: Bucknell University Press, 2019.
Fennetaux, Ariane. "Women's Pockets and the Construction of Privacy in the Long Eighteenth Century." *Eighteenth-Century Studies* 20, no. 3 (2008): 307–334.
Fergus, Jan. "Women Readers: A Case Study." In *Women and Literature in Britain, 1700–1800*. Edited by Vivien Jones. Cambridge, UK: Cambridge University Press, 2000.
Ferguson, Frances. *Pornography, the Theory: What Utilitarianism Did to Action*. Chicago: University of Chicago Press, 2004.
———. "Rape and the Rise of the Novel." *Representations* 20 (1987): 88–112.
Festa, Lynn. "Person, Animal, Thing: The 1796 Dog Tax and the Right to Superfluous Things." *Eighteenth-Century Life* 33, no. 2 (2009): 1–44.
———. "Personal Effects: Wigs and Possessive Individualism in the Long Eighteenth Century." *Eighteenth-Century Life* 29, no. 2 (2005): 47–90.
Firestone, Shulamith. *The Dialectic of Sex: The Case for Feminist Revolution*. New York: Farrar, Straus, and Giroux, 1970.
Fisher, Nicholas. "A Surprise Appearance by the Earl of Rochester in Nineteenth-Century New York." *Princeton University Library Chronicle* 72, no. 2 (2011): 569–573.
Fisher, Will. "Thigh Sex in England, 1590–1730." *Journal of the History of Sexuality* 24, no. 1 (2015): 1–24.
Fletcher, Anthony. *Gender, Sex, and Subordination in England, 1500–1800*. New Haven: Yale University Press, 1995.
Foucault, Michel. *The History of Sexuality, Volume 1: An Introduction*. Translated by Robert Hurley. New York: Vintage, 1978.

Friedli, Lynne. "'Passing Women': A Study of Gender Boundaries in the Eighteenth Century." In *Sexual Underworlds of the Enlightenment*. Edited by G. S. Rousseau and Roy Porter. Manchester: Manchester University Press, 1987.

Fryer, Peter. *Secrets of the British Museum*. New York: Citadel, 1968.

Fuentes, Marisa. *Dispossessed Lives: Enslaved Women, Violence, and the Archive*. Philadelphia: University of Pennsylvania Press, 2016.

Gabbard, D. Christopher. "From Idiot Beast to Idiot Sublime: Mental Disability in John Cleland's *Fanny Hill*." *PMLA* 123, no. 2 (2008): 375–389.

Ganz, Melissa J. "Moll Flanders and English Marriage Law." *Eighteenth-Century Fiction* 17, no. 2 (2005): 157–182.

———. *Public Vows: Fictions of Marriage in Enlightenment England*. Charlottesville: University of Virginia Press, 2019.

Gatrell, Vic. *City of Laughter: Sex and Satire in Eighteenth-Century London*. New York: Walker & Company, 2006.

Gikandi, Simon. *Slavery and the Culture of Taste*. Princeton: Princeton University Press, 2011.

Gladfelder, Hal. "'By the Author of Fanny Hill': Selling John Cleland." *Eighteenth-Century Life* 43, no. 2 (2019): 38–57.

———. *Fanny Hill in Bombay: The Making and Unmaking of John Cleland*. Baltimore: Johns Hopkins University Press, 2012.

———. "Machines in Love: Bodies, Souls, and Sexes in the Age of La Mettrie." *Eighteenth-Century Fiction* 27, no. 1 (2014): 55–81.

Glass, Loren. *Rebel Publisher: Grove Press and the Revolution of the Word*. New York: Penguin, 2018.

Gonda, Caroline. "Introduction: Friendship and Same-Sex Love." *SEL: Studies in English Literature 1500–1900* 46, no. 3 (2006): 517–521.

Grant, Melissa Giro. *Playing the Whore: The Work of Sex Work*. London: Verso, 2014.

Grebowicz, Margret. *Why Internet Porn Matters*. Stanford: Stanford University Press, 2013.

Gregg, Melissa. *Counterproductive: Time Management in the Knowledge Economy*. Durham: Duke University Press, 2018.

Grogan, Kristin, and Grace Lavery. "Blood Pink." *Social Text Online*. 9 July 2020.

Guest, Harriet. "Bluestocking Feminism." *Huntington Library Quarterly* 65 (2002): 59–80.

Hager, Lisa. "A Case for a Trans Studies Turn in Victorian Studies: 'Female Husbands' of the Nineteenth Century." *Victorian Review* 44, no. 1 (2019): 37–54.

Haggerty, George. "Keyhole Testimony: Witnessing Sodomy in the Eighteenth Century." *The Eighteenth Century: Theory and Interpretation* 44, nos. 2–3 (2003): 167–182.

Halperin, David M. *How to Do the History of Homosexuality*. Chicago: University of Chicago Press, 2002.

Harris, Mary Beth. "Upsetting the Balance: Exposing the Myth of Masculine Virtue in Haywood's *Philidore and Placentia*." *The Eighteenth Century: Theory and Interpretation* 58, no. 2 (2017): 195–218.

Hartman, Saidiya. "Venus in Two Acts." *Small Axe* 26, no. 2 (2008): 1–14.

Harvey, Karen. "The Century of Sex? Gender, Bodies, and Sexuality in the Long Eighteenth Century." *Historical Journal* 45 (2002): 899–916.

———. *Reading Sex in the Eighteenth Century*. Cambridge, UK: Cambridge University Press, 2004.

Haslanger, Andrea. "What Happens When Pornography Ends in Marriage: The Uniformity of Pleasure in *Fanny Hill*." *ELH* 78, no. 1 (2011): 163–188.

Hawk, Brandon W. "*Prosthesis*: From Grammar to Medicine in the Earliest History of the Word." *Journal of Disability Studies* 38, no. 4 (2018). http://dx.doi.org/10.18061/dsq.v38i4.5398.

Hayward, Eva. "Lessons from a Starfish" (2008). In *The Transgender Studies Reader 2*. Edited by Susan Stryker and Aren Z. Aizura. New York: Routledge, 2013.

Heaney, Emma. *The New Woman: Literary Modernism, Queer Theory, and the Trans Feminine Allegory*. Evanston: Northwestern University Press, 2017.

———. "Women-Identified Women." *Transgender Studies Quarterly* 3, nos. 1–2 (2016): 137–145.

Heath, Deana. *Purifying Empire: Obscenity and the Politics of Moral Regulation in Britain, India, and Australia*. Cambridge, UK: Cambridge University Press, 2010.

Hershinow, Stephanie Insley. *Born Yesterday: Inexperience and the Early Realist Novel*. Baltimore: Johns Hopkins University Press, 2019.

Hester, Helen. *Beyond Explicit: Pornography and the Displacement of Sex*. Albany: SUNY Press, 2014.

Hill, Christopher. "Clarissa Harlowe and Her Times." *Essays in Criticism* 5, no. 4 (1955): 315–340.

Hitchcock, Tim. *English Sexualities, 1700–1800*. New York: St. Martin's, 1997.

———. "The Reformulation of Sexual Knowledge in Eighteenth-Century England." *Signs* 37 (2012): 823–831.

Hoesch, Matthias. "From Theory to Practice: Bentham's Reception of Helvétius." *Utilitas* 30, no. 3 (2018): 294–316.

Hunt, Lynn, ed. *The Invention of Pornography: Obscenity and the Origins of Modernity*. New York: Zone, 1996.

Hunter, J. Paul. *Before Novels: The Cultural Contexts of Eighteenth-Century English Fiction*. New York: Norton, 1990.

Jacob, Margaret C. "The Materialist World of Pornography." In *The Invention of Pornography: Obscenity and the Origins of Modernity*. Edited by Lynn Hunt. New York: Zone, 1996.

Jameson, Fredric. *The Antinomies of Realism*. London: Verso, 2013.

Jarvis, Claire. *Exquisite Masochism: Marriage, Sex, and the Novel Form*. Baltimore: Johns Hopkins University Press, 2016.

Jones, Angela. "Cumming to a Screen Near You: Transmasculine and Non-Binary People in the Camming Industry." *Porn Studies* 8, no. 2 (2021): 239–254.

Jones, Vivien. "Eighteenth-Century Prostitution: Feminist Debates and the Writing of Histories." In *Body Matters: Feminism, Textuality, Corporeality*. Edited by Avril Horner and Angela Keane. Manchester: Manchester University Press, 2000.

Joudrey, Simon. "Penetrating Boundaries: An Ethics of Anti-Perfectionism in Victorian Pornography." *Victorian Studies* 57, no. 3 (2015): 423–432.

Joyce, Simon. "Past, Present, and Pornography." *Victorian Studies* 50, no. 3 (2017): 466–476.

Juengel, Scott. "Doing Things with Fanny Hill." *ELH* 76, no. 2 (2009): 419–446.

Kania, Andrew. "Concepts of Pornography: Aesthetics, Feminism, and Methodology." In *Art and Pornography*. Edited by Hans Maes and Jerrold Levinson. Oxford: Oxford University Press, 2012.

Kaplan, Morris B. *Sodom on the Thames: Sex, Love, and Scandal in Wilde Times*. Ithaca: Cornell University Press, 2005.

Kastrenakes, Jacob. "Pornhub Just Removed Most of Its Videos." *The Verge*. 14 December 2020. https://www.theverge.com/2020/12/14/22173858/pornhub-videos-removed-user-uploaded-visa-mastercard-verified.

Kearney, Patrick. *A Catalogue of the Books and Journalism of Peter Fryer*. Santa Rosa: Scissors and Paste Bibliographies, 2019. http://www.scissors-and-paste.net/pdf/Peter_Fryer.pdf.

———. *The Private Case: An Annotated Bibliography of the Private Case Erotica Collection in the British (Museum) Library*. London: Jay Landesman Limited, 1981.

———. Scissors and Paste Bibliographies. http://www.scissors-and-paste.net.

Kendrick, Walter. *The Secret Museum: Pornography in Modern Culture*. Berkeley: University of California Press, 1987.

Keymer, Tom. *Sterne, the Moderns, and the Novel*. Oxford: Oxford University Press, 2003.

King, Kathryn. *A Political Biography of Eliza Haywood*. London: Pickering and Chatto, 2012.

King, Thomas A. *The Gendering of Men, 1600–1750: Volume 1, The English Phallus*. Madison: University of Wisconsin Press, 2004.

King, Tiffany Lethabo. *The Black Shoals: Offshore Formations of Black and Native Studies*. Durham: Duke University Press, 2019.

Kipnis, Laura. *Bound and Gagged: Pornography and the Politics of Fantasy in America*. Durham: Duke University Press, 1997.

Klein, Ula Lukszo. "Dildos and Material Sapphism in the Eighteenth Century." *Eighteenth-Century Fiction* 31, no. 2 (2019): 395–412.

Koedt, Anne. "The Myth of the Vaginal Orgasm." In *"Takin' It to the Streets": A Sixties Reader*. Edited by Alexander Bloom and Wini Breines. New York: Oxford University Press, 2003.

Kostos, Maia. "Penetration and Its Discontents: Greco-Roman Sexuality, the *Acts of Paul and Thecla*, and Theorizing Eros Without the Wound." *Journal of the History of Sexuality* 27, no. 3 (2018): 343–366.

Koyama, Emi. "Whose Feminism Is It Anyway? The Unspoken Racism of the Trans Inclusion Debate" (2000). *Sociological Review Monographs* 68, no. 4 (2020): 735–744.

Kramnick, Jonathan. *Actions and Objects from Hobbes to Richardson*. Stanford: Stanford University Press, 2010.

Kristof, Nicholas. "The Children of Pornhub." *New York Times*. 4 December 2020. https://www.nytimes.com/2020/12/04/opinion/sunday/pornhub-rape-trafficking.html.

Lake, Crystal. *Artifacts: How We Think and Write About Found Objects*. Baltimore: Johns Hopkins University Press, 2020.

Lamb, Jonathan. *The Things Things Say*. Princeton: Princeton University Press, 2011.

Lanser, Susan. "Novel (Sapphic) Subjects: The Sexual History of Form." *Novel: A Forum on Fiction* 42, no. 3 (2010): 497–503.

———. "Second-Sex Economics: Race, Rescue, and the Heroine's Plot." *The Eighteenth Century: Theory and Interpretation* 61, no. 2 (2020): 227–244.

———. *The Sexuality of History: Modernity and the Sapphic, 1565–1830*. Chicago: University of Chicago Press, 2014.

Laqueur, Thomas. *Making Sex: Body and Gender from the Greeks to Freud*. Cambridge, MA: Harvard University Press, 1992.

———. *Solitary Sex: A Cultural History of Masturbation*. New York: Zone, 2003.

Lear, Martha Weinman. "What Do These Women Want? The Second Feminist Wave." *New York Times Magazine*. 10 March 1968.

Lee, Wendy Anne. *Failures of Feeling: Insensibility and the Novel*. Stanford: Stanford University Press, 2019.

Levene, Louise. "The Naughty Table." *The Bookseller*. 29 June 2011. https://www.thebookseller.com/feature/naughty-table-339220.

Lewis, Sophie. *Full Surrogacy Now: Feminism Against Family*. London: Verso, 2019.

Lipsedge, Karen. *Domestic Space in Eighteenth-Century British Novels*. Houndsmills: Palgrave Macmillan, 2012.

London, April. *Women and Property in the Eighteenth-Century English Novel*. Cambridge, UK: Cambridge University Press, 1999.

Lorde, Audre. *Sister Outsider*. Berkeley: Crossing Press, 2007.

Love, Harold, ed. *The Works of John Wilmot, Earl of Rochester*. Oxford: Oxford University Press, 1999.

Love, Heather. "Close, Not Deep: Literary Ethics and the Descriptive Turn." *New Literary History* 41, no. 2 (2010): 371–391.

———. "Pornography Porn." *Public Books*. 1 October 2015. https://www.publicbooks.org/pornography-porn/.

Lovelace, Linda. *Ordeal*. Secaucus: Citadel Press, 1980.

Lowe, Lisa. *The Intimacies of Four Continents*. Durham: Duke University Press, 2015.
Lubey, Kathleen. *Excitable Imaginations: Eroticism and Reading in Britain, 1660–1760*. Lewisburg: Bucknell University Press, 2012.
———. "Making Pornography, 1749–1968: The History of *The History of the Human Heart*." *ELH* 82, no. 3 (2015): 897–935.
———. "Sexual Remembrance in *Clarissa*." *Eighteenth-Century Fiction* 29, no. 2 (2016–17): 151–178.
Lubey, Kathleen, et al. Twitter post and thread. 31 August 2020. https://twitter.com/kathylubey/status/1300516739482972160?s=20.
Lupton, Christina. *Knowing Books: The Consciousness of Mediation in Eighteenth-Century Britain*. Philadelphia: University of Pennsylvania Press, 2012.
———. *Reading and the Making of Time in the Eighteenth Century*. Baltimore: Johns Hopkins University Press, 2018.
Lynch, Deidre. *Loving Literature: A Cultural History*. Chicago: University of Chicago Press, 2015.
Lynn, Eleri. *Underwear: Fashion in Detail*. London: V&A Publishing, 2010.
MacKinnon, Catharine. *Only Words*. Cambridge, MA: Harvard University Press, 1993.
Macpherson, C. B. *The Political Theory of Possessive Individualism, Hobbes to Locke*. Oxford: Oxford University Press, 1962.
Macpherson, Sandra. *Harm's Way: Tragic Responsibility and the Novel Form*. Baltimore: Johns Hopkins University Press, 2010.
Manion, Jen. *Female Husbands: A Trans History*. Cambridge, UK: Cambridge University Press, 2020.
Marcus, Sharon. *Between Women: Friendship, Desire, and Marriage in Victorian England*. Princeton: Princeton University Press, 2007.
Marcus, Stephen. *The Other Victorians: A Study of Sexuality and Pornography in Mid-Nineteenth-Century England*. New York: Norton, 1964.
Marks, Laura Helen. *Alice in Pornoland: Hardcore Encounters with the Victorian*. Urbana: University of Illinois Press, 2018.
McCalman, Iain. *Radical Underworlds: Prophets, Revolutionaries, and Pornographers in London, 1795–1840*. Cambridge, UK: Cambridge University Press, 1988.
———. "Unrespectable Radicalism: Infidels and Pornography in Early Nineteenth-Century London." *Past and Present* 104 (1984): 74–110.
McClintock, Anne. *Imperial Leather: Race, Gender, and Sexuality in the Colonial Conquest*. New York: Routledge, 1995.
McKeon, Michael. *The Secret History of Domesticity: Public, Private and the Division of Knowledge*. Baltimore: Johns Hopkins University Press, 2005.
———. "The Seventeenth- and Eighteenth-Century Sexuality Hypothesis." *Signs* 37, no. 4 (2012): 791–801.
Meeker, Natania. "'I Resist It No Longer': Enlightened Philosophy and Feminine Compulsion in *Thérèse Philosophe*." *Eighteenth-Century Studies* 39, no. 3 (2006): 363–376.

Mendes, Peter. *Clandestine Erotic Fiction in English, 1800–1930*. Aldershot: Scholar Press, 1993.
Miller-Young, Mireille. *A Taste for Brown Sugar: Black Woman in Pornography*. Durham: Duke University Press, 2014.
———. "This Is What Porn Can Be Like! A Conversation with Shine Louise Houston." In *Porn Archives*. Edited by Tim Dean, Steven Ruszczycky, and David Squires. Durham: Duke University Press, 2014.
Millett, Kate. *Sexual Politics*. New York: Avon Books, 1969.
Mohanty, Chandra Talpade. *Feminism Without Borders: Decolonizing Theory, Practicing Solidarity*. Durham: Duke University Press, 2003.
Moore, Lisa L. *Dangerous Intimacies: Toward a Sapphic History of the British Novel*. Durham: Duke University Press, 1997.
Mueller, Judith. "Fallen Men: Representations of Male Impotence in Britain." *Studies in Eighteenth-Century Culture* 28 (1999): 85–102.
Mulvey, Laura. "Visual Pleasure and Narrative Cinema." *Screen* 16 (1975): 6–18.
Nash, Jennifer. *The Black Body in Ecstasy: Reading Race, Reading Pornography*. Durham: Duke University Press, 2014.
Nead, Lynda. *Victorian Babylon: People, Streets, and Images in Nineteenth-Century London*. New Haven: Yale University Press, 2000.
Newman, Brooke. *A Dark Inheritance: Blood, Race, and Sex in Colonial Jamaica*. New Haven: Yale University Press, 2018.
Newman, Ian. "Edmund Burke in the Tavern." *European Romantic Review* 24, no. (2013): 125–148.
Ngai, Sianne. *Our Aesthetic Categories: Zany, Cute, Interesting*. Cambridge, MA: Harvard University Press, 2012.
Nicolazzo, Sal. "Henry Fielding's *The Female Husband* and the Sexuality of Vagrancy." *The Eighteenth Century: Theory and Interpretation* 55, no. 4 (2014): 335–353.
O'Brien, Karen. *Women and Enlightenment in Eighteenth-Century Britain*. Cambridge, UK: Cambridge University Press, 2009.
Orenstein, Peggy. "If You Ignore Porn, You Aren't Teaching Sex Ed." *New York Times*. 14 June 2021.
Orr, Leah. *Novel Ventures: Fiction and Print Culture in England, 1690–1730*. Charlottesville: University of Virginia Press, 2017.
Paasonen, Susanna. "Between Meaning and Mattering: On Affect and Porn Studies." *Porn Studies* 1, nos. 1–2 (2014): 136–142.
———. *Carnal Resonance: Affect and Online Pornography*. Cambridge, MA: MIT Press, 2011.
Paige, Morgan. "Female Husband!" Podcast. *One from the Vaults*. 13 November 2016.
Palmieri, Frank. *State of Nature, Stages of Society: Enlightenment Conjectural History and Modern Social Discourse*. New York: Columbia University Press, 2016.
Pateman, Carole. *The Sexual Contract*. Stanford: Stanford University Press, 1988.

Peakman, Julie. *Mighty Lewd Books: The Development of Pornography in Eighteenth-Century England*. London: Palgrave Macmillan, 2003.

———, ed. *Whore Biographies, 1700–1825*. Vol. 3. London: Pickering and Chatto, 2006.

Peakman, Julie, and Sarah Watkins. "Making Babies: Eighteenth-Century Attitudes Towards Conception, Reproduction, and Childbirth." In *The Secrets of Generation: Reproduction in the Long Eighteenth Century*. Edited by Raymond Stephanson and Darren N. Wagner. Toronto: University of Toronto Press, 2015.

Perry, Ruth. *Novel Relations: The Transformation of Kinship in England, 1748–1818*. Cambridge, UK: Cambridge University Press, 2006.

Peterson, William M. "Pope and Cibber's *The Non-Juror*." *Modern Language Notes* 70, no. 5 (1955): 332–335.

Pezzutto, Sophie, and Lynn Comella. "Trans Pornography: Mapping an Emerging Field." *Transgender Studies Quarterly* 7, no. 2 (2020): 152–171.

Philips, Natalie. *Distraction: Problems of Attention in Eighteenth-Century Literature*. Baltimore: Johns Hopkins University Press, 2016.

Plomer, Henry. *Dictionary of the Printers and Booksellers in England, 1726–1775*. Oxford: Bibliographical Society at the Oxford University Press, 1932.

Porter, Roy. "The Sorrows of Priapus: Anticlericalism, Homosocial Desire, and Richard Payne Night." In *Sexual Underworlds of the Enlightenment*. Edited by G. S. Rousseau and Roy Porter. Manchester: Manchester University Press, 1987.

Porter, Roy, and Lesley Hall. *The Facts of Life: The Creation of Sexual Knowledge in Britain, 1650–1950*. New Haven: Yale University Press, 1995.

Price, Leah. *The Anthology and the Rise of the Novel: Richardson to George Eliot*. Cambridge, UK: Cambridge University Press, 2000.

Rabinowitz, Paula. *American Pulp: How Paperbacks Brought Modernism to Main Street*. Princeton: Princeton University Press, 2014.

Raven, James. *The Business of Books: Booksellers and the English Book Trade*. New Haven: Yale University Press, 2007.

Rich, Adrienne. "Compulsory Heterosexuality and Lesbian Existence." *Signs* 5, no. 4 (1980): 631–660.

Ricoeur, Paul. *The Rule of Metaphor*. Translated by Robert Czerny. Toronto: University of Toronto Press, 1977.

Rose, Jonathan. "Rereading the English Common Reader." *Journal of the History of Ideas* 53, no. (1992): 47–70.

Rosenthal, Laura. *Infamous Commerce: Prostitution in Eighteenth-Century British Literature and Culture*. Ithaca: Cornell University Press, 2006.

———, ed. *Nightwalkers: Prostitute Narratives from the Eighteenth Century*. Peterborough: Broadview Press, 2008.

Rousseau, G. S., and Roy Porter, eds. *Sexual Underworlds of the Enlightenment*. Manchester: Manchester University Press, 1987.

Royalle, Candida. "Porn in the USA." *Social Text* 37 (1993): 23–32.
Rubin, Lillian B., et al. "1968: Lessons Learned." *Dissent* 55, no. 2 (2008): 5–25.
Sabor, Peter. "From Sexual Liberation to Gender Trouble: Reading *Memoirs of a Woman of Pleasure* from the 1960s to the 1990s." *Eighteenth-Century Studies* 33, no. 4 (2000): 561–578.
Schaschek, Sarah. *Pornography and Seriality: The Culture of Producing Pleasure*. New York: Palgrave Macmillan, 2014.
Screaming Queens: The Riot at Compton's Cafeteria. Directed by Susan Stryker and Victor Silverman. San Francisco: Frameline, 2005.
Sedgwick, Eve. *Touching Feeling: Affect, Pedagogy, Performativity*. Durham: Duke University Press, 2003.
Serano, Julia. *Whipping Girl: A Transsexual Woman on Sexism and the Scapegoating of Femininity*. Emeryville: Seal Press, 2007.
Sigel, Lisa. *Governing Pleasures: Pornography and Social Change in England, 1815–1914*. New Brunswick: Rutgers University Press, 2002.
———. "Looking at Sex: Pornography and Erotica since 1750." In *The Routledge History of Sex and the Body, 1500 to the Present*. Edited by Sarah Toulalan and Kate Fisher. London: Routledge, 2013.
Skinner, Gillian. "Women's Status as Legal and Civic Subjects: 'A Worse Condition Than Slavery Itself?'" In *Women and Literature, 1700–1800*. Edited by Vivien Jones. Cambridge, UK: Cambridge University Press, 2000.
Smith, Chloe Wigston. *Women, Work, and Clothes in the Eighteenth-Century Novel*. Cambridge, UK: Cambridge University Press, 2013.
Snorton, C. Riley. *Black on Both Sides: A Racial History of Trans Identity*. Minneapolis: University of Minnesota Press, 2017.
Sontag, Susan. *Styles of Radical Will*. New York: Picador, 1969.
Spampinato, Erin. "Rereading Rape in the Critical Canon: Adjudicative Criticism and the Capacious Conception of Rape." *Differences* 32, no. 2 (2021): 122–160.
Speer, Lisa K. "Paperback Pornography: Mass Market Novels and Censorship in Post-War America." *Journal of American and Comparative Cultures* 24, nos. 3–4 (2001): 153–160.
Spillers, Hortense. "Mama's Baby, Papa's Maybe: An American Grammar Book." *Diacritics* 17, no. 2 (1987): 64–81.
Squibbs, Richard. "Tobias Smollett's *Ferdinand Count Fathom*: The Purpose of Picaresque." *Eighteenth-Century Fiction* 30, no. 4 (2018): 519–537.
Squires, David. "Pornography in the Library." In *Porn Archives*. Edited by Tim Dean, Steven Ruszczycky, and David Squires. Durham: Duke University Press, 2014.
Staves, Susan. *Married Women's Separate Property in England*. Cambridge, MA: Harvard University Press, 1990.
Steintrager, James. *The Autonomy of Pleasure: Libertines, License, and Sexual Revolution*. New York: Columbia University Press, 2016.

Stephanson, Raymond. *The Yard of Wit: Male Creativity and Sexuality, 1650–1750*. Philadelphia: University of Pennsylvania Press, 2004.

Stone, Lawrence. *The Family, Sex, and Marriage in England, 1500–1800*. New York: Harper, 1979.

Straub, Kristina. *Domestic Affairs: Intimacy, Eroticism, and Violence Between Servants and Masters in Eighteenth-Century Britain*. Baltimore: Johns Hopkins University Press, 2009.

Strub, Whitney. "Historicizing Pulp: Gay Male Pulp and the Narrativization of Queer Cultural History." In *1960s Gay Pulp Fiction: The Misplaced Heritage*. Edited by Drewey Wayne Gunn and Jaime Harker. Amherst: University of Massachusetts Press, 2013.

———. "Lavender, Menaced: Lesbianism, Obscenity Law, and the Feminist Anti-pornography Movement." *Journal of Women's History* 22, no. 2 (2010): 83–107.

Strub, Whitney, and Carolyn Bronstein. "Introduction." In *Porno Chic and the Sex Wars: American Sexual Representation in the 1970s*. Edited by Carolyn Bronstein and Whitney Strub. Amherst: University of Massachusetts Press, 2016.

Stryker, Susan, and Paisley Currah. "Introduction." *Transgender Studies Quarterly* 1, nos. 1–2 (2014): 1–18.

Tallent, Allistaire. "A Space Between: Prostitutes Negotiating the Public and the Private in Memoir Novels of Eighteenth-Century France." In *Everyday Revolutions: Eighteenth-Century Women Transforming Public and Private*, eds. Diane E. Boyd and Marta Kvande. Newark: University of Delaware Press, 2008.

Taylor, Keeanga-Yamahtta. "Black Feminism and the Combahee River Collective." *Monthly Review* 70, no. 8 (1 January 2019). https://monthlyreview.org/2019/01/01/black-feminism-and-the-combahee-river-collective/.

———. *How We Get Free: Black Feminism and the Combahee River Collective*. Chicago: Haymarket, 2017.

Thompson, Courtney E. "Questions of *Genre*: Picturing the Hermaphrodite in Eighteenth-Century France and England." *Eighteenth Century Studies* 49, no. 3 (2016): 391–413.

Trumbach, Randolph. "Erotic Fantasy and Male Libertinism in Enlightenment England." In *The Invention of Pornography: Obscenity and the Origins of Modernity*. Edited by Lynn Hunt. New York: Zone, 1996.

———. "London's Sapphists: From Three Sexes to Four Genders in the Making of Modern Culture." In *Third Sex, Third Gender: Beyond Sexual Dimorphism in Culture and History*. Edited by Gilbert Herdt. New York: Zone Books, 1994.

———. *Sex and the Gender Revolution: Heterosexuality and the Third Gender in Enlightenment London*. Chicago: University of Chicago Press, 1998.

———. "The Transformation of Sodomy from the Renaissance to the Modern World and Its General Consequences." *Signs* 37, no. 4 (2012): 832–848.

Turner, James Grantham. "Novel Panic: Picture and Performance in the Reception of *Pamela*." *Representations* 48 (1994): 70–96.

Van Brabandt, Petra, and Jesse Prinz. "Why Do Porn Films Suck?" In *Art and Pornography*. Edited by Hans Maes and Jerrold Levinson. Oxford: Oxford University Press, 2012.

Van Horn, Jennifer. *The Power of Objects in Eighteenth-Century British America*. Chapel Hill: University of North Carolina Press, 2017.

Vareschi, Mark. *Everywhere and Nowhere: Anonymity and Mediation in Eighteenth-Century Britain*. Minneapolis: University of Minnesota Press, 2018.

Vickers, Nancy. "'The Blazon of Sweet Beauty's Best': Shakespeare's *Lucrece*." In *Shakespeare and the Question of Theory*. Edited by Geoffrey Hartmann and Patricia Parker. New York: Routledge, 1985.

Vickery, Amanda. *Behind Closed Doors: At Home in Georgian England*. New Haven: Yale University Press, 2009.

Vieth, David. *Attribution in Restoration Poetry: A Study of Rochester's Poems of 1680*. New Haven: Yale University Press, 1963.

Wagner, Darren. "A Bit Exposed: Displays of Male Genitals." In *Secrets of Generation: Reproduction in the Long Eighteenth Century*. Edited by Raymond Stephanson and Darren N. Wagner. Toronto: University of Toronto Press, 2015.

Wagner, Peter. "The Discourse on Sex—or Sex as Discourse: Eighteenth-Century Medical and Paramedical Erotica." In *Sexual Underworlds of the Enlightenment*. Edited by G. S. Rousseau and Roy Porter. Manchester: Manchester University Press, 1987.

———. *Eros Revived: Erotica of the Enlightenment in England and America*. London: Secker and Warburg, 1988.

Walker, Alice. *You Can't Keep a Good Woman Down*: New York: Harcourt Brace, 1981.

Warner, Michael. *Publics and Counterpublics*. New York: Zone, 2005.

Warner, William. *Licensing Entertainment: The Elevation of Novel Reading in Britain, 1684–1750*. Berkeley: University of California Press, 1998.

Warren, Wendy. "'The Cause of Her Grief': The Rape of a Slave in Early New England," *Journal of American History* 93, no. 4 (2007): 1031–1049.

Watt, Ian. *The Rise of the Novel: Studies in Defoe, Richardson, and Fielding*. Berkeley: University of California Press, 1957.

Williams, Gordon. *A Dictionary of Sexual Language in Shakespearean and Stuart Literature*. London: Athlone Press, 1994.

Williams, Linda. *Hard Core: Power, Pleasure, and the "Frenzy of the Visible."* Berkeley: University of California Press, 1989.

———. "Pornography, Porno, Porn: Thoughts on a Weedy Field." *Porn Studies* 1 (2014): 24–40.

———. "A Provoking Agent: The Pornography and Performance Art of Annie Sprinkle." *Social Text* 37 (1993): 117–133.

Wilson, Kathleen. *The Island Race: Englishness, Empire, and Gender in the Eighteenth Century*. New York: Routledge, 2003.

Wyngaard, Amy. "The End of Pornography: The Story of *Story of O*," *MLN* 130, no. 4 (2015): 980–997.

———. "Translating Sade: The Grove Press Editions, 1953–1968." *Romanic Review* 104, nos. 3–4 (2013): 313–331.

Young, Damon R. *Making Sex Public and Other Cinematic Fantasies*. Durham: Duke University Press, 2018.

Zuroski, Eugenia. "Evelina's Laughter: The Novel's Queerer Theories." *The Eighteenth-Century: Theory and Interpretation* 61, no. 2 (2020): 165–186.

INDEX

Page numbers in *italics* indicate illustrations.

Abelove, Henry, 20, 90
abuse of women: in marriage, 108, 119–20; race and, 109; sex workers, 106, 108. *See also* rape; sexual violence
accuracy of pornography, 20–25
adolescence, 74–75, 83, 235n1
The Adventures of . . . a Lady's Maid (c. 1838), 156–61, *159*, 247n59, 247n61
Against Our Will (Brownmiller), 198, 207
Anti-Pamela (Haywood, 1741), 56–59, 62, 68, 86, 231n58
anti-pornography feminism, 5, 14, 21–22, 175, 194–97, 200–202, 204, 210, 218
archive: libraries, pornography in, xi, 221n2, 237n27; pornographic, countercultural-era construction of, 174, 177, 184, 188, 199; of pornography, defined, 4, 127–28
Aristotle's Master-Piece (1684), 40–41, 85
Armstrong, Nancy, 75, 113, 151–52, 235n2
Arondekar, Anjali, 86, 125, 127–28, 155, 158, 162, 165
Ashbee, Henry Spencer: British Library and, 187, 243n17; on Cleland and Rochester, 141, 146–47, 149, 150; erotic bibliography of, 126, 129–31, 185; on *Human Heart* and *Child of Nature*, 131–33, 135–37, 177, 244n24, 245n36, 246n44, 249n3; on *Inutility of Virtue*, 161

Avery, Edward, 130, 136, 140, 141, 147, 155
Award Books, 175

Backscheider, Paula, 70
Baddeley, Sophia, 108
Bakhtin, M. M., 124
Bannet, Eve Tavor, 229n29, 242n77
Barrin, Jean, 223n18
Barton, Bernadette, 214, 222n4
Beauvoir, Simone de, 191
Behn, Aphra, 181
Benedict, Leah, 40
Berg, Heather, 214–16, 218
Berlant, Lauren, 23
Bersani, Leo, 16, 22, 25
Best, Stephen, 95
Betsy Thoughtless (Haywood, 1751), 51, 56, 58, 120
Bianchi, Giovanni, 70, 71
Biberman, Nancy, 189
binary gender. *See* gender
Binhammer, Katherine, 50, 60, 114, 241n63
The Birth Controllers (Fryer, 1965), 186
Black Brown and Fair (Rowlandson print, 1807), 109–10, *111*
Black Cat (publishing imprint), 191
Bobker, Danielle, 162
Brantlinger, Patrick, 162, 247n66

Brinkema, Eugenie, 209
British Library/Museum: Ashbee's bequest to, 130; "cupboard books" in, 82; destruction of material by, 130, 243n17; and pulp reprinting, 175; Private Case, ix–xii, 82, 184–87
Bronstein, Carolyn, 197, 202, 251n44
Brookes, John Benjamin, 155, 247n59
Brown, Bill, 230n45
Brownmiller, Susan, 194, 198–200, 202, 203, 207, 210, 252n61, 253n78
Bull, Sarah, 130, 244n25
Burke, Edmund, 33
Butler, Judith, 248n85
Butler, Samuel, 233n82

Cannon, John, 228n20
Carter, Angela, 21, 22, 205
Catharine of Braganza, (queen consort of Charles II of England), 147
Characters of the Present Most Celebrated Courtezans (1780), 108–9
Charles II (king of England), 133, 147
chastity, women's: cultural importance, 28, 57; *Child of Nature* on, 113–21; Mandeville on, 15, 41–42, 57; pornography's insights on, 15–16; virtue versus, 107
The Child of Nature (1774), 74, 112–21; on elision of sexual and social, 113–21; as feminist text, 78, 112–13, 118, 121; Helvétius, false attribution to, 112, 117–18, 119, 135, 137, 241n67; materialist philosophy in, 116–18, 241n67, 242n72; as pornography, 75, 112–13, 118–21; publication history, 123; title pages for, 137, *138*; Victorian editions of, 123, 124, 135–40, *138*; women's dialogue in, 117–18
child pornography, 169–70, 205, 254n3
Chorier, Nicholas, 223n18
Cibber, Colley, 33, *34*, 227n6

Clarissa (Richardson, 1748), 51, 54, 55–56, 59, 60, 68, 114, 121, 230n48, 231n50, 231nn52–53
Cleland, John: *Memoirs of a Coxcomb* (1751), Victorian edition of, 137, 140, 147; modern misattributions to, 191; *The True History and Adventures of Catharine Vizzani* (1755), 70–72, 235n99. See also *Memoirs of a Woman of Pleasure*
clitoris: 18th-century awareness of, 240n52; in *History of the Human Heart,* 97–99; in Knight's *Worship of Priapus,* 48, *49*; Koedt, Anne, "Myth of the Vaginal Orgasm" (1970), 206–7; orgasms, clitoral, 16, 97, 206, 240n52; penis as, 168, 248n83; in *Progress of Nature,* 84; sex manuals on, 41, 43; of Vizzani, 71
Cohen, William, 125, 126, 242n4, 243n9
Colligan, Colette, 126, 140, 190, 245n36
colonialism/imperialism: masculinity imperiled by, 155, 165; orientalist pornography, 127, 162–66, 247n60, 247n67; pederastic rape as, 169–70
Combahee River Collective, 201
community/social environments, operation of pornography within, 210–12
companionate marriage, 18, 154, 225n43
Conjugal Lewdness (Defoe, 1727), 44–45, 49, 228n19
A Continuation of Mr. F———'s Adventures (1748), 67–68
Cook, Matt, 166
countercultural era, pornography in, 173–202; claims of solidarity with feminism, 174, 183–94; cover art, 175, *176*, 249nn2–3; feminist approaches to, 174–75, 193–203; Fryer's editions, 184–91, 193–94, 197, 199, 200; Grove Press, 191–93; marriage, distancing

from, 181–82, 189; masculinity in, 174, 177–79, 182, 183–94; *Memoirs of a Man of Pleasure* (1968 edition of *Human Heart*), 173–74, 175–83, *176*, 184, 185, 191, 249n3; narrative efficiency in, 173–74, 177–78, 183; sexual subcultures in, 182; rape, treatment of, 179–81, 194, 196; social consciousness and, 174, 186, 189, 191; student protests, women in, 189
counterpublic, 23, 211, 253n90
Cox, Betsy, 108
cross-dressing, 67, 70, 72, 102, 181, 234
Cruikshank, Isaac, 33–35, *34*
"cupboard books," British Library, 82
Curll, Edmund, 40, 136, 223n18
Currah, Paisley, 24

Darly, Matthias, 35–38, *37*, *38*
Darnton, Robert, 13, 81, 122, 223n16
Daston, Lorraine, 53
Davis, Angela, 201
Dean, Tim, 79, 125, 207, 214
Deep Throat (film), 196
Defoe, Daniel, 44–45, 49, 228n19
Del Rio, Korra, 215
Delaney, Samuel, 210–11
Delgado, Anne, 166
Derrida, Jacques, 13
Desire and Domestic Fiction (Armstrong), 151–52
Destré, Sabine (Richard Seaver), 192
detachability of genital parts, 19, 33, 52, 53, 60, 71, 72, 235n100. *See also* dildos; prosthetics
The Dialectic of Sex (Firestone, 1970), 198
Dialogue Between a Married Lady and a Maid (1659, trans. 1740), 79
Dickie, Simon, 80, 239n42
Diderot, Denis, 238n31
digital media, pornography in, 214–19, 254n3

Dildoides (1706), 65, 88, 233n82
dildos: Dick (in *Woman of Pleasure*), as dildo, 64–67; in 18th-century pornography and culture, 63–72, 75, 85–88, 106, 121; ivory dildo with plunger (1700s), *85*; and gendered personhood, 63–72, 85–88; in print satires, 35–39, *37–39*, 65–66, *66*; in Victorian pornography and culture, 157–61, *159*, 247n62; women's and nonbinary people's use of, 69–72, 85–88, 157–61
Dines, Gail, 224n34
domestic abuse. *See* abuse of women
Domingo, Darryl, 94
dower, 52, 224n40
Drury, Joseph, 233n74
Dugdale, James, 155, 247n59
Dugdale, William: aliases, 244n26; Cleland and Rochester, editions of, 140–42, 144–47, 149, 155, 246n41, 246n50; *The Exquisite* (serial), 129, 133, 135, 177, 185; *Human Heart* and *Child of Nature*, republication of, 131–37, 174–75; misattributions and disregard of source texts, 200, 244–45n27, 244n25; modern edition (1968) of *Human Heart* compared, 174–75, 177, 181, 182, 183; as publisher, 129–31, 243nn14–15; sexual violence, eroticized by, 155
Dworkin, Andrea, 194, 200, 210, 211

Eger, Elizabeth, 242n77
ejaculation: of dildo, 85, 160; female, in *Human Heart*, 1–2, 16, 96–99, 105–6, 139–40, 144; male, 41, 84, 165; as response to pornography, 6, 77
enclosure, intercourse described as, 207–8
Enke, Finn, 196, 201
Epistle to a Lady (Pope, 1743), 110

An Essay on Woman, by the Author of the Essay on Man (print, 1742), 33, 34, 35, 53, 227n6
Excitable Imaginations (Lubey), 81
The Exquisite (Dugdale serial), 129, 133, 135, 177, 185

Fanny Hill. See *Memoirs of a Woman of Pleasure*
Fantomina (Haywood, 1725), 46, 56, 58
Farr, Jason, 69, 227n6
Female Husband (Fielding, 1746), 69–70, 234nn96–97
The Female Spectator, 82
feminism: affinity with pornography, 4–5, 20–23, 174–75, 203–12; antipornography, 4, 14, 21–22, 175, 194–97, 200–202, 204, 209, 210, 212, 218; in British versus French 18th-century works, 7–9, 79, 223n16; in *Child of Nature*, 112–13, 118, 121; counterculture pornography's disingenuous claim to, 174, 177–79, 182, 183–94; genital analysis by, 194–203; genital feminism, concept of, 73; heterosexuality, analysis of, 198–201; *History of the Human Heart* and, 96, 99–101; intersectionality and, 201–2; pornographic narrative as, xii, 2, 8–9, 15, 18, 75–78, 79, 82, 90, 112–13, 118, 121–22; racism and, 201–2, 208–9, 252n61, 252n63; rape, analysis of, 198–99, 203; second-wave, 174, 183, 184, 194–202, 205–7, 210–11; transfeminism, 18, 24, 82, 208; Victorian pornography and, 123, 124, 127, 128, 129, 132, 140, 141, 152
femme sole, 51, 53
Ferguson, Frances, 5, 9, 52, 79, 195, 199, 210, 211, 237n14, 242n72
Festa, Lynn, 53

Fielding, Henry: *Female Husband* (1746), 69–70, 234nn96–97; *Joseph Andrews* (1742), 58; *Tom Jones* (1749), 131
films, pornographic: *Deep Throat* (film), 196; portrayal of women in, 210–11
Firestone, Shulamith, 198, 242n74, 252n61
Fisher, Nicholas, 246n50
Fletcher, Anthony, 227n5
The Forbidden Books of the Victorians (Fryer, 1970), 185
Foucault, Michel, 9, 10–12, 77, 166
Frederick, Kitty, 108
Freeman, J. (publisher), 89, 238n37
French pornography, 18th-century, 7–9, 76, 78–79, 122, 223n16
Friedli, Lynne, 69, 240n52
Fryer, Peter: *The Birth Controllers* (1965), 186; and the Private Case, 237n27; *The Forbidden Books of the Victorians* (1970), 185; James Graham, pseudonym, 184, 249n9; on historical pornography and sexual liberation, 184–91, 193–94, 199, 200, 250n14; on *Human Heart*, 184–86, 188–89, 197, 245n36; *The Man of Pleasure's Companion* (1968), 185, 187–88; *Private Case—Public Scandal* (1966), 184–87; *Secrets of the British Museum* (1968), 184, 245n36; *Staying Power: The History of Black People in Britain* (1984), 186, 187; *Venus Unmasked* (1967), 185. See also Graham, James.
Fuentes, Marisa, 109

Ganz, Melissa, 50, 225n43, 229n29
Garrick, David, 138
Gatrell, Vic, 227n7
gender: binary, in counterculture pornography, 182–83; genitalia and identity, pornography contesting

link between, 28–29, 39; hierarchy, 18th-century, 30 77; men assumed producers/consumer of pornography, 10, 13, 21; nonbinary, in pornography, xii, 7, 9, 18, 23–25; transgender people and trans studies, 23–25, 28, 29, 168–70, 215, 248n79, 252n63, 254n6. *See also* nonbinary persons; women

Genet, Jean, 191

genital analysis, feminist, 194–203

genital anatomy, 18th-century theories of, 19, 40

genital parts, 28–73; in descriptions/analysis of heteropenetrative sex, 39–49, *47, 49*; detachability of, 19, 33, 52, 53, 60, 71, 72, 235n100; dildos as alternative to heteropenetrative sex, 35–39, *37–39*, 63–72, *66*; dispersed/distributed sexual conversation about, 30, 32–33, *34*; feminism, genital, 73; gender identity and genitalia, pornography contesting link between, 28–29, 39; men's efforts to claim women's genitals, 32–35, *34*, 50–51; in print satires, 32–39, *34*, *37–39*, 49; reduction of focus on, after 1750, 112; sapphic picaresques differentiated from heteropenetration, 60–63; social contestation, heteropenetrative sex as site of, 31–32, 35–39, *37–39*; women's control/ownership of, 28–30, 32, 49–60; women's genital lives, cultural focus on, 28–32. *See also specific parts*

Gentleman's Magazine, 237n25

Gentleman's Relish (1968 compendium, ed. Graham), 185, 187

Gladfelder, Hal, 31, 65, 71

Glass, Loren, 191

Gonda, Caroline, 77

Governing Pleasures (Sigel), 125

Graham, James: in British Library catalogue, 250n12; Peter Fryer, possible identity with, 184, 249n9; *Gentleman's Relish* (1968 compendium), 185, 187; *Memoirs of a Man of Pleasure* (1968 edition of *Human Heart*), 173–74, 175–83, *176*, 184, 185

Grebowicz, Margret, 79, 224n34

Gregg, Melissa, 216–19

Griffith, Ralph, 102

Grogan, Kristin, 23

Grove Press, 191–93

Gwyn, Nell, 147, 150

Hager, Lisa, 24, 167, 248n79

Hamilton, Mary, 69–70, 234nn96–97

Hard Core (Williams), 5, 14

Hardwicke, Lord, 49, 50, 51

Harris's List of Covent Garden Ladies (18th century), 187

Hartman, Saidiya, 4, 127–28

Harvey, Karen, 93, 239–40n52

Haslanger, Andrea, 60–61, 232n69

Hayward, Eva, 72

Haywood, Eliza, ix, 45–46, 66, 85, 231n54; *Anti-Pamela* (1741), 56–59, 62, 68, 86, 231n58; *Betsy Thoughtless* (1751), 51, 56, 58, 120; *Fantomina* (1725), 46, 56, 58; *The Injur'd Husband* (1722), 56

Heaney, Emma, 208, 248n81

Heath, Deana, 136

Helvétius, Claude Adrien, 112, 117–18, 119, 135, 137, 241n67

hermaphrodites, 41, 69, 72, 167, 168

Hershinow, Stephanie Insley, 223n19, 235n1, 251n52

heterosexuality/heteropenetrative sex: *Child of Nature*, absence of, 112; countercultural pornography,

heterosexuality/heteropenetrative sex (*continued*)
masculine dominance in, 174, 177–79, 182, 183–94; descriptions/analysis of, 39–49, *47, 49*; dildos as alternative to, 35–39, *37–39*; enclosure, intercourse described as, 207–8; feminist analysis of, 198–201; hierarchy entailed by, 5; queer alternatives to, xii, 7, 9, 18, 23–24, 60–63; normalization of/pornographic dissent from, 5–6, 15–16, 20, 77–78, 83, 90, 112; social contestation, as site of, 31–32, 35–39, *37–39*; in the Victorian novel, 152–55; Victorian pornography and, 125–27, 133, 137, 139–40, 141, 145–46, 150

The History of Sexuality (Foucault), 10

The History of the Human Heart (1749), ix–xi, 1–2, 74, 89–102; abridgement in successive editions, 105–6, 133, 173–74, 177–78, 193; at British Library, ix–xi, *x*; *Child of Nature* compared, 112–13, 118; Cleland's *Woman of Pleasure* compared, 89, 94, 249n3; as exemplum of pornography as narrative form, 2–3; footnotes: in original, 1–2, 75, 91–95, 92, 99–101, reduced, in Dugdale edition (1844), 133, reduced, in modern (1968) edition, 177, removed, in Rochester series (ca. 1885), 136, removed, in *Tracey* (1757), 105; Fryer on, 184–86, 188–89, 197; genital detail in, 97–99; humor in, 76, 89, 91–93, 95, 178, 239n43; *Memoirs of a Man of Pleasure* (1968 edition), 173–74, 175–83, *176*, 184, 185, 191, 249n3; *Memoirs of a Man of Pleasure* (1844 edition), 132–35, 142, 144, 173–74; *Memoirs of B—— Tracey* (1757 edition), 102–6, 112, 139, 240nn56–57; *Memoirs of the Celebrated Miss Fanny M——* compared, 107–8; modesty, feminist analysis of, 96, 99–101; posture girls in, 1–2, 96–99, 104–6, 121, 144, 139–40, 144, 175, 185; *Progress of Nature* bound with, ix, 82, 89; *Progress of Nature* compared, 90, 97; publication history of, 1–2, 4, 89–90, 123, 238n38; reading model suggested by, 93, 95–96, 101–2; Rochester Series edition (ca. 1885), 136–37, 139–40; Victorian editions of, 123, 124, 131–37, 139–140, 142, 144

Hitchcock, Tim, 20, 41, 95

homosexuality. *See* queer sexuality; same-sex relations between women

Human Heart (1749). *See History of the Human Heart*

humor in pornography, 15, 76, 80–81, 92–93, 95, 131, 132, 137, 182, 239n43

Hunt, Lynn, 7, 8, 79

Hunter, J. Paul, 80

hymen, 71, 72, 91, 93, 94, 102, 133

imperialism. *See* colonialism/imperialism

impotence trials, 18th century, 40

incest, 156, 166, 247n60

industrial capitalism, impact on pornography, 25–27

The Injur'd Husband (Haywood, 1722), 56

intersectionality, 201–2

The Inutility of Virtue (c. 1830), 156, 161–62

James I (king of England), 95

Jarvis, Claire, 153, 155

jointure, 52, 224n40

Jones, Angela, 254n6

Joseph Andrews (Fielding, 1742), 58

Joudrey, Simon, 242n4

Joyce, Simon, 190

Juengel, Scott, 65

Kaplan, Morris, 166
Kearney, Patrick, 187, 244n25, 245n36, 250n14
Kendrick, Walter, 12, 14
King, Thomas, 58
Kipnis, Laura, 14
Klein, Ula, 63, 87–88
Koch, Ed, 202
Koedt, Anne, 206–7
Kostos, Maia, 77
Koyama, Emi, 201
Kramnick, Jonathan, 52, 230n40

labia, 41, 42, 75
labor: pornography as critique of, 214–19; print satires of laboring women, 115, 115–16; sex work, 106–112, 167, 214–19
Lady Chatterley's Lover (Lawrence, 1928), 191
Lake, Crystal, 137
Lamb, Jonathan, 53, 230n43
Lanser, Susan, 7, 60, 61, 77, 80, 223–24n26
Laqueur, Thomas, 19, 30, 31, 77, 79, 93, 227n4
Lavery, Grace, 23
Lazenby, William, 155
Lee, Wendy Anne, 121, 231n52
lesbianism. *See* same-sex relations between women
Letters from Laura and Eveline (1883), 166–71, 248n79
Lewis, Sophie, 208
Locke, John, 135, 225n42
London, April, 50
The London Magazine, 82
Long Corks, or the Bottle Companions (Darly print, 1777), 35–36, 37
Lorde, Audre, 205, 206
Love, Heather, 25, 225n47
Lovelace, Linda, 196
Lowe, Lisa, 128

Lupton, Christina, 21, 80, 93
The Lustful Turk (1828), 162–63, 165, 166, 171, 247n70
Lynch, Deidre, 80

MacKinnon, Catharine, 15, 194, 211, 221–22n4
Macpherson, C. B., 18
Macpherson, Sandra, 52, 65, 230n30, 230n40, 233n77
male gaze, 246n43
The Man of Pleasure's Companion (Fryer, 1968), 185, 187–88
Mandeville, Bernard, 15, 41–44, 45, 49, 57, 85
Manion, Jen, 234n97, 248n80
Marcus, Sharon, 7, 95, 153
Marcus, Stephen, *The Other Victorians*, 9–10, 26, 87, 125–26, 154, 190–91, 192
marriage: abuse in, 108, 119–20; chastity of women and, 28; in *Child of Nature*, 114–21; in Cleland's *Woman of Pleasure*, 144; companionate marriage, 18, 154, 225n43; countercultural pornography's distancing from, 181–82, 189; 18th-century pornography's eschewal of, 75–78; feminine subjectivity and, 235n2; manuals and treatises on, 29, 40–45; personhood and property in, 30, 49–53, 229–30n33; Victorian pornographic parodies of, 154, 165–71; rape and, 144, 155, 157, 162, 164–66, 171; sex work compared, 106, 108–9, 241n63
Marriage Act of 1753 (Lorde Hardwicke's Act), 49, 50, 229n29
masturbation, 1, 12, 15, 16, 31, 38, 77, 79–80, 83–85, 93, 96, 98, 112, 140, 214
materialism, 7, 8, 78, 116–18, 135–37, 223n16, 233n74, 241n67, 242n72

McCalman, Iain, 243nn14–15
McClintock, Anne, 162
McKeon, Michael, 229n33
Meeker, Natania, 78
Mehrhof, Barbara, 253n78
Memoirs of a Coxcomb (Cleland, 1751), Victorian edition of, 137, 140, 147
Memoirs of a Man of Pleasure: Dugdale's 1844 edition of *Human Heart*, 132–35, 142, 144, 173–74; 1968 edition of *Human Heart*, 173–74, 175–83, *176*, 184, 185, 191, 249n3
Memoirs of a Woman of Pleasure (Cleland, 1749): Ashbee's entry on, 146–47; compared to British pornographic fiction, 76, 82, 84, 89, 94; copies of early editions of, 245–46n40; dildo in, 64–65, 66–67, 233nn73–74; French pornography compared, 8, 76; in history of pornography, 6, 8; sapphic sex in, 60–63, 144; title and editions of, 232n66; 20th-century editions of, 191; Victorian editions of, 129, 140, 142–47, *143*, 155
Memoirs of B—— Tracey (1757), 102–6, 112, 139, 240nn56–57
Memoirs of Miss Sidney Biddulph (Sheridan, 1761), 233n77
Memoirs of the Celebrated Miss Fanny M—— (1758), 106–8, 112
Mendes, Peter, 243n17
A Milk Sop (Rowlandson print, 1811), *115*, 115–16
Millenium Hall (Scott, 1762), 120
Miller, Henry, 193
Miller-Young, Mireille, 208–9, 215
Millett, Kate, 193, 198, 252n61
mindful pornography, 213–19
misogyny, 6, 20, 27, 102, 141, 204, 214, 225n47

A Modest Defence of Publick Stews (Mandeville, 1724), 15, 41–44, 45, 49, 57, 85
modesty of women: *Child of Nature* on, 118; *Human Heart* on, 96, 99–101, 133; parodied in Victorian pornography, 167–69
Mohanty, Chandra Talpade, 200
Monsieur Thing's Origin (1732), 65, 67, 69
Monthly Review, 102
Moore, Lisa, 61
Mulvey, Laura, 246n43
Murray, Fanny, 106–8
My Grandmother's Tale (1879–1881), 247n60
My Secret Life (1888), 190, 191
"Myth of the Vaginal Orgasm" (Koedt, 1970), 206–7

Naked Lunch (Burroughs, 1959), 191
narrative, as genre accommodating pornography, 74–82. *See also* pornographic narrative
Nash, Beau, 107
Nash, Jennifer, 5, 201, 208, 212, 214
Nead, Lynda, 243nn14–15
A New Cock Wanted (Rowlandson print, 1810), 65–66
New York Times, 184
Newman, Brooke, 109
Ngai, Sianne, 217–18
Nicolazzo, Sal, 234nn96–97
19th century pornography. *See* Victorian pornography
nonbinary genital sexuality, 203, 208
nonbinary persons: alternatives to binary gender in pornography, xii, 7, 9, 15, 18, 23–25; dildos, use of, 64, 69–72; feminist genital analysis and, 198; Mary Hamilton, 69–70, 234nn96–97; social vulnerability, pornography's awareness of, 82; in *Treatise on Hermaphrodites*, 72;

in Victorian pornography, 127, 161, 166–71; visibility in pornography, 254n6; Catherine Vizzani, 70–72
non-penetrative sexual activity in 18th century, 46, 228n20
novel genre versus pornography, 144, 152–55

objectification, 10, 198, 246n43
O'Brien, Karen, 121
Orenstein, Peggy, 222n4
orgasm, 14, 64, 76, 139, 158; clitoral 16, 97, 206, 240n52; as response to pornography, 6, 79, 152
orientalism, 127, 162–66
Ovid, 88–89

Paasonen, Susanna, 204
Paige, Morgan, 234n97
Pamela (Richardson, 1740), 46, 49–50, 54, 59, 139, 229n29
"Pamphlets and Poems Gallant" binding, British Library (Cup.702.t.14), ix–xi, *x*
Parisot, Mademoiselle, 33–35, *34*
Pateman, Carole, 200
Payne Knight, Richard, 36, *39*, *47*, 47–49, *49*, 229nn27–28
Peakman, Julie, 77, 79, 236nn5–6
A Peep at the Parisot! (Cruikshank print, 1796), 33–35, *34*
penis: as clitoris, 168, 248n83; dildos versus, and gender inequity, 63–69, 75, 85–88, 106, 121; in Payne Knight's *Worship of Priapus*, 36, *39*, *47*, 47–49, *49*, 229nn27–28; sex manuals on, 41, 42; in trans porn, 215; Victorian pornography and, 125–27, 133, 137, 139–40, 141, 145–46, 150. *See also* heterosexuality/heteropenetrative sex
Pepys, Samuel, 57, 231n57
Perry, Ruth, 51

personhood: defined in 18th-century pornography, 16–19, 25; non-persons and rape in Victorian pornography, 169–70; of women in 18th century, 16–19, 28
Petrarch, 57, 231n59
Pezzutto, Sophia, 215
Philips, Natalie, 96
Pitt, William, 33
pleasure, sexual, as pornographic response, 15, 30–31, 78, 79–80, 125, 127
pockets, 36, 84, 238n30
Pope, Alexander, 33, *34*, 35, 36, 53, 110, 227n6
porn studies, 6, 14–15, 171, 215, 224n30
porn versus pornography, 13
Porn Work (Berg), 214, 215
PornHub, 254n3
pornographic narrative, 74–122; adolescence of protagonists, 74–75, 83, 235n1; Cleland's *Woman of Pleasure* within, 76, 82, 84, 89, 94; defining pornography and, 81; discursive social consciousness of, 74–82, 122; feminist stance of, xii, 2, 8–9, 15, 18, 75–78, 79, 82, 90, 112–13, 118, 121–22; French versus British, 76, 78–79; heteropenetrative sex not central to, 77–78, 83, 90, 112; prostitution, 106–12, *111*; race and, 17, 106, 109–12, *111*, 224–25n41; reading practices of, 3, 79–81, 93, 95–96, 101–2. *See also* *Child of Nature*; *History of the Human Heart*; *Progress of Nature*
pornography, 1–27, 213–19; accuracy of critical insights of, 20–25; archive, lack of, ix–xi, 4, 221n2; archive of, xi, 4, 15, 127–28, 174, 177, 184, 188, 199, 221n2, 237n27; close reading of, 14, 25; defined, 2, 7–15, 25, 29–30, 81, 195; digital age and, 213–19; English translations of French, 8, 223n18;

pornography (*continued*)
French versus British, 7–9, 76, 78–79, 122, 223n16; as genre, ix–xii, 4, 11, 13–14; history of term, 7, 12–13; humor in, 15, 76, 80, 81, 89, 91–93, 95, 131, 132, 137, 181, 182, 239n43; industrial capitalism and, 25–27; male consumption assumed, 10, 13, 21, 223–24n26; mindful pornography, 213–19; pleasure and, 15, 30–31, 78, 79–80, 125, 127; porn versus, 13; power and, 10–12, 25; proliferation in mid-18th-century Britain, 15–20; publicizing sex, 10, 15, 23, 77; reprintings of, 1, 14, 25, 96, 101, 122, 123–24, 126, 128, 131, 133–35, 139–40, 142–45; researching, xii–xiii; scholarly approaches to, 4–7; social consciousness of, ix, xi, xii, 1–7, 9–10, 14, 21–22, 25, 74–82, 203–10. See also counterculture era, pornography in; genital parts; pornographic narrative; Victorian pornography

Pornography, The Theory (Ferguson), 9

posture girls: advertisements for, 239n51; in *Human Heart* and succeeding editions, 1–2, 96–99, 104–6, 121, 144, 139–40, 144, 175, 185

power: Foucauldian, relationship of pornography to, 10–12; intercourse and, 25, 210; phallic, 48, 84–88, 128, 145, 161, 200

Price, Leah, 26, 131, 141

print satires (18th-century): colonial-era sex work and, 109–10, *111*; genital parts in, 32–39, *34*, *37–39*, 49; of laboring women's bodies, *115*, 115–16; of women's fashion, 35–39, *37*, *38*. See also specific print authors and titles

The Private Case (Kearney), 187

Private Case, British Library, ix–xii, 82, 184–87

Private Case—Public Scandal (Fryer, 1966), 184–87

The Progress of Nature (1744), ix, 74, 82–89; *Child of Nature* compared, 121; child sexuality in, 83–84; classificatory history, ix, 82, 237n25; on dildos, penises, and gender inequity, 75, 85–88, 106, 121; feminist conversation in, 84–88; *Human Heart* bound with, ix, 82, 89; *Human Heart* compared, 90, 97; nonconsensual sex in, 83, 88–89; penetrative sex, absence of, 83

property: body, women's ownership/control of, 2, 16–17, 18–19, 24, 106–12; genitalia, control/ownership of, 28–30, 32, 49–60; marriage and, 30, 49–53, 229–30n33; personhood and, 16–19, 28, 50–51; women as, 18, 19, 50–51; women's ability to own, 17, 18, 50–53, 224n40

"prosthesis," 18th-century meaning of, 233n86

prosthetics, 30, 35, 47, 63, 67, 70, 217. See also detachability of genital parts; dildos

prostitution. See sex work/sex workers

public, sex as, 10, 15, 23, 77

pulp paperbacks, 1, 7, 90, 174–75, *176*, 181–86, 189, 191, 249n2, 249n6

Queensberry, Duke of, 33

queer sexuality: in Cleland's *Woman of Pleasure*, 60–63, 144; in counterculture pornography, 182; in Victorian pornography, 127, 162, 166–71, 190, 205, 248n79. See also same-sex relations between women; sodomy

Rabinowitz, Paula, 175–76

race: in 18th-century pornography, 17, 106, 109–12, *111*, 224–25n41;

interracial sex in pornography, 182; racialized women, 17, 109–12m201, 208–9, 224–25n41; whiteness, 16–18, 106, 112, 201

racism: feminism and, 201–2, 208–9, 252n61, 252n63; Fryer's *Staying Power: The History of Black People in Britain*, 186, 187; rape and, 201–2

rape: in *Child of Nature*, 114, 116, 117; in countercultural pornography, 179–81, 189, 194, 196; Defoe's *Conjugal Lewdness* on, 44; feminist analysis of, 198–99, 203; genitalia, control/ownership of, 52, 54, 55, 58, 59; male rape victims, 233n77; Mandeville's prostitution proposal and, 42, 43; marriage and, 144, 155, 157, 162, 164–66, 171; of non-persons in Victorian pornography, 169–70; in orientalist pornography, 162–66; pederastic rape, 169–70, 205; in *Progress of Nature*, 83, 88–89; in queer pornography, 162, 166–70; racism and, 201–2; in Richardson's *Clarissa*, 55–56, 230n48, 231n50, 231nn52–53; sapphic picaresques differentiated, 60–61; in pornographic film, 209–10; in Victorian pornography, 126, 150–52, 155, 157, 160–63, 165–71; as violation of woman rather than male kin, 232n63

Reader, Arthur, 130, 136, 147, 149, 155

reading, multifocal model of, 3, 79–81, 93, 95–96, 101–2

Réage, Pauline (Dominique Aury), *The Story of O* (1954/1966), 192–93

Reddie, James Campbell, 129–30, 132, 150, 155, 243n17, 244n25, 244–45n27, 246n44

reprinting of pornography, 1, 14, 25, 96, 101, 122, 123–24, 126, 128, 131, 133–35, 139–40, 142–45

Restoration era, Victorian associations of sexual license with, 133

Reynolds, Joshua, 57

Rich, Adrienne, 21, 22

Richardson, Samuel, 67; *Clarissa* (1748), 51, 54, 55–56, 59, 60, 68, 114, 121, 230n48, 231n50, 231nn52–53; *Pamela* (1740), 46, 49–50, 54, 59, 139, 229n29

Rizzio, David, 95

Rochester, John Wilmot, Earl of, 68, 140–41; Dugdale's biography of (1830/1860), 147–51, *149*, *150*, 167, 246n50; *Selected Poetical Works of the Earls of Rochester, Roscommon, and Dorset* (1757/1884), 147

Rochester Series of Reprints (ca. 1885), 130, 136–37, 139–40, 144, 146–47, 244n22, 245n36

Rose, Jonathan, 21, 130

Rosenthal, Laura, 43, 241n63

Rosset, Barney, 191, 192

The Rover (Behn, 1677), 181

Rowlandson, Thomas, 65–66, *66*, 109–10, *111*, *115*, 115–16

Rubin, Lillian B., 189

Rund, J. B., 245n36

Sade, Marquis de, 6, 8, 191, 205, 210, 242n72

same-sex relations between women: in Cleland's *Woman of Pleasure*, 60–63, 144; dildos, use of, 69–72; *Lady's Maid* (c. 1838), dildo episode in, 157–61, *159*; social consciousness of, in pornographic narrative, 77; Victorian excision from 18th-century texts, 144

Sartre, Jean-Paul, 191

Scott, Sarah, 120

Seaver, Richard (Sabine Destré), 192

second-wave feminism. *See* feminism

Secrets of the British Museum (Fryer, 1968), 184, 245n36
Sedgwick, Eve, 204
Sedley, Charles, 133, 233n82
Selected Poetical Works of the Earls of Rochester, Roscommon, and Dorset (1757/1884), 147
Sellon, Edward, 244–45n27
Seraglio Scenes (1830s), 162–65, 167, 247n71
Serano, Julia, 24
sex manuals, 18th-century, 39–45
sex work/sex workers: in *An Essay on Woman, by the Author of the Essay on Man* (print, 1742), 33, *34*, 35; feminist genital analysis and, 200; Mandeville's *A Modest Defence of Publick Stews* on, 15, 41–44; marriage compared, 106, 108–9, 241n63; narratives of, 106–12, *111*; social and sexed inequity of, 74–75; social consciousness of, 214–16; Times Square sex industry, 202
Sexual Politics (Millett), 193
sexual violence: feminist analysis of, 198–201; eroticism of, in Victorian pornography, 155–61; in orientalist pornography, 127, 162–66; in queer pornography, 166–71. *See also* abuse of women; rape
Sheridan, Richard Brinsley, 33
The Siege of Cork (Darly print, 1777), 36–38, *38*
Sigel, Lisa, 125, 133, 162, 200, 243n15, 244n21
Sins of the Cities of the Plain (1881), 166–67, 169–71, 248n79
Skinner, Gillian, 51
slavery: in 18th-century pornography, 17, 109–12, 224–25n41; in Fryer's *Staying Power*, 186, 187; in orientalist Victorian pornography, 162–66, 247n60

Smith, Chloe Wigston, 35–36
social consciousness: countercultural pornography and, 174, 186, 189, 191; feminist engagement with pornography's potential for, 203–12; heteropenetrative sex, as site of social contestation, 31–32, 35–39, *37–39*; labor in digital age, pornography as critique of, 214–19; mindful pornography, 213–19; in pornographic narrative, 74–82; of pornography generally, ix, xi, xii, 1–7, 9–10, 14, 21–22, 25, 74–82, 203–10; in *The Progress of Nature*, 75; rape in pornography and, 209–10; same-sex relations between women and, 77; sex workers, from perspective of, 214–16; users of pornography, from perspective of, 216–18; of Victorian pornography, 125, 127, 128, 140, 150–52, 161, 171–72. *See also* pornography
social/community environments, operation of pornography within, 210–12
sodomy: in Cleland's *Woman of Pleasure*, 8, 141, 146, 245–46n40; 18th-century stigmatization of, 20, 44–45, 228n19; hierarchy entailed by, 5, 222n6; in Victorian queer pornography 166–70
Sontag, Susan, 14, 22, 192
Spampinato, Erin, 210
A Spy on Mother Midnight (1748), 67
Squires, David, 221n2
Staves, Susan, 51–52
Staying Power: The History of Black People in Britain (Fryer, 1984), 186, 187
Steintrager, James, 78, 236n11, 241n67
Stephenson, Raymond, 65
Stewart, Potter, xi
Stone, Lawrence, 75, 76, 225n43, 235n2
Strub, Whitney, 183, 249n6, 251n44
Stryker, Susan, 24

Tallent, Allistaire, 223n16
Tandem Press, 175, 185
taverns, 56–57, 58, 59, 60, 231n57
Taylor, Keeanga-Yamahtta, 202
Tess of the D'Urbervilles (Hardy, 1891), 155
The Memoirs of B—— Tracey (1757), 102–6
thing theory, 53, 54, 230n45
Times Square sex industry, NYC, 202, 210–11, 218
Tom Jones (Fielding, 1749), 131
transgender people and trans studies, 23–25, 28, 29, 168–70, 215, 248n79, 252n63, 254n6. *See also* gender; nonbinary persons
transmisogyny, 254n6
A Treatise on Hermaphrodites (1718), 69, 72, 234n89
Tristram Shandy (Sterne, 1759), 131
Tropic of Cancer (Miller, 1934), 191
The True History and Adventures of Catharine Vizzani (Cleland, 1755), 70–72, 235n99
Trumbach, Randolph, 6, 20, 31, 222n6, 227n5, 240n53
20th-century pornography. *See* countercultural era, pornography in

Ups and Downs of Life (Sellon, 1867), 244–45n27

vagina: centrality to 18th-century culture, 15–16, 28, 57; in *Child of Nature*, 116; as "enclosure," 207–8; Koedt's "Myth of the Vaginal Orgasm" (1970), 206–7; in pornographic narrative, 15–16, 75–77, 84; as property, 53; in queer Victorian pornography, 168; sex manuals on, 42
Venus (publishing imprint), 191

Venus in the Cloister (1675, trans. 1725), 78–79
Venus Unmasked (Fryer, 1967), 185
Victorian pornography, 123–72; access to, 129, 130; ambiguous treatment of sexual injustice in, 124, 139–40, 141, 145–46, 152, 174; Cleland's works, editions of, 137, 140–47, *143*; feminism and, 123, 124, 127, 128, 129, 132, 140, 141, 152; *Human Heart* and *Child of Nature*, editions of, 123, 124, 131–40, *138*; market for, 124–29, 140–41; novel genre and, 144, 152–55; orientalist pornography, 127, 162–66; phallocentric masculinity supported by, 125–27, 133, 137, 139–40, 141, 145–46, 150; pleasure, association with, 125, 127; producers of, 129–31; queer pornography, 127, 162, 166–71; rape in, 126, 150–52, 155, 157, 160–63, 165–71; reading "against the grain," 127–28, 151; removal of eroticism excluding men, 140; reprinting of earlier works, 122, 123–24, 126, 128, 131, 133–35, 139–40, 142–45; Rochester, Earl of, 68, 140–41, 147–51, *148*, *149*, 167; sexual violence in, 155–61; social consciousness of, 125, 127, 128, 140, 150–52, 161, 171–72; streamlining of narrative in, 126–27, 140
violence, sexual. *See* abuse of women; rape; sexual violence
Vizzani, Catherine, 70–72

Wagner, Peter, 77, 79, 236n6, 239n43
Walker, Alice, 221n4
WAP (Women Against Pornography), 202, 210–11, 218
Warner, Michael, 23, 31, 253n90
Warren, Wendy, 109
Wilkes, John, *Essay on Woman*, 131

Williams, Linda, 5–6, 14, 214, 243n10
Wollstonecraft, Mary, 120
The Woman of Colour: A Tale (1808), 110–12
Woman of Pleasure. See Cleland, John, *Memoirs of a Woman of Pleasure*
women: and/as property, 17, 18, 19, 50–53, 224n40; gender identity and genitalia, 28–29, 39; genital lives of, 28–32; genitalia, control/ownership of, 28–30, 32, 49–60; independent financial life for, 51, 108, 112, 120, 139, 215; independent genital life for, 35, 38–40, 43, 120; male gaze, 246n43; ownership of own body, 2, 16–17, 18–19, 24, 106–12; personhood of, 16–19, 28, 50–51; in pornographic films, 210–11; social vulnerability, pornography's awareness of, 82; whiteness and, 16–18, 106, 112, 201. *See also* chastity, women's; clitoris; modesty of women; vagina
Women Against Pornography (WAP), 202, 210–11, 218
The Worship of Priapus (Payne Knight, 1786), 36, *39*, *47*, 47–49, *49*, 229nn27–28
Wyngaard, Amy, 191, 192

Young, Damon R., 23

Zebra (publishing imprint), 191
Zuroski, Eugenia, 70

The authorized representative in the EU for product safety and compliance is:
Mare Nostrum Group
B.V Doelen 72
4831 GR Breda
The Netherlands

www.ingramcontent.com/pod-product-compliance
Lightning Source LLC
Chambersburg PA
CBHW031759220426
43662CB00007B/460